HISTORY OF
OBION COUNTY

Towns and Communities
Churches, Schools, Farming, Factories
Social and Political

Assembled and Edited by
E. H. MARSHALL

Beginning with Goodspeed's published in 1887, proceeding
with Alexander's Reelfoot Lake in 1925.
Personal effort and interview.

Southern Historical Press, Inc.
Greenville, South Carolina

This volume was reproduced from
An 1941 edition located in the
Publisher's private Library

All rights reserved. No part of this publication may be reproduced,
stored in a retrieval system, transmitted in any form, posted
on to the web in any form or by any means without
the prior written permission of the publisher.

Please direct all correspondence and orders to:

www.southernhistoricalpress.com
or
SOUTHERN HISTORICAL PRESS, Inc.
PO Box 1267
375 West Broad Street
Greenville, SC   29601
southernhistoricalpress@gmail.com

Originally published: Union City, TN. 1941
ISBN #0-89308-934-6
All rights Reserved.
Printed in the United States of America

OBION COUNTY COURTHOUSE
UNION CITY, TENNESSEE

HISTORY
OBION COUNTY
TENNESSEE

County Organization — Colonel David Crockett — Bear Hunting — Reelfoot Lake—Internal Improvements — Houser Valley Farm Drainage and Extension — Civil, Spanish-American and World War Veterans — County Seat Removal — New Courthouse — Consolidation of County Schools — County Department Reports — State and County Highways — Centennial Celebration — Churches — Farm Bureau — Boy Scouts — Health Department — Red Cross — Parent-Teachers — TVA.

Troy, Obion, Kenton, Hornbeak, Reelfoot Lake, Elbridge, Glass, Woodland Mills, South Fulton, Rives, Clayton, Pierce, Harris, Caldwell, Crystal, Mason Hall.

FOREWORD

Historical and biographical material compiled for this work began with Goodspeed's History of Tennessee and Obion County, issued in 1887. It was taken and built up for a story in a special edition of The Commercial, Union City, Tenn., published in April, 1930. Material for Reelfoot Lake was written by T. H. Alexander, newspaper correspondent. Story of Davy Crockett was taken almost literally from his autobiography. Files of The Commercial, issued in Union City by Marshall & Baird, were used for many of the stories appearing since the beginning of its publication in 1901. Late county department reports are reproduced from contributions made to the Christmas Editions of The Union City Messenger.

A very large part of the work, however, has been gathered from time to time from interviews with old-time citizens, various sources and persons interested.

The work therefore may be preserved with some assurance of being as nearly accurate as possible.

On account of the volume of space necessary to complete this work there is no effort made to give a general outline of all the secret orders and lodges in the county. On the other hand record of the churches as near as possible is made to include organization and general outline.

—E. H. MARSHALL

Obion County History

Obion County is situated in the northwestern portion of West Tennessee, and is bounded on the north by Fulton County, Ky., east by Weakley County, south by Gibson and Dyer counties, and west by Lake County. It is one of the richest counties in Tennessee, and contains an area of 560 square miles, about 36 of which are covered by Reelfoot Lake. The surface of the county is varied, about one-third of it being hilly and broken, and two-thirds undulating and level. The soil is chiefly a black loam, more or less mixed with siliceous matter, and resting upon a subsoil of red or whitish clay. No building stone is found in the county, except a kind of sandstone found on the banks of Mill Creek, and perhaps in a few other localities. The county is well supplied with running water. The principal streams are Obion River, Davidson, Mill, Big and Little Clover, Harris, Deer, Cypress, Indian, Pawpaw, Grassy. Dillard, Lick, Big and Little Richland, Grove, Houser, Reelfoot and Cane Creeks. The most wonderful natural feature of the county is Reelfoot Lake, which previous to the earthquakes of 1811-12 had no existence. The following was related by Col. J. H. Tipton: "Colonel Walker, of Missouri, who, in company with an Indian, came over the Mississippi River into Tennessee for the purpose of hunting on what was then called Reelfoot Creek in December, 1811, stated that while there hunting the earth began to shake. Becoming very much alarmed he and the Indian started to return, but upon reaching the place on Reelfoot Creek where they had left their canoe they found that the earth had sunk, and that the waters from the Mississippi had rushed in and formed a great lake, which they afterwards found to be twenty-five or thirty miles in length."

Previous to the settlement of the county it was covered with a heavy growth of walnut, oak, poplar, cypress, hickory, maple, elm and other varieties of trees, many of them of immense size, and, after the lapse of years, much of this has been utilized for making furniture and shipped to the lumber markets. All farm products can be successfully grown in Obion County, but the leading staples are corn, soy beans, wheat, tobacco, cotton, oats, clover, etc. The following amounts of each were produced in 1880: Tobacco, 1,133,472 pounds; wheat, 230,243 bushels; corn, 1,501,881 bushels, and cotton, 4,225 bales.

The first white settlement within the present bounds of Obion County was made in 1819 by Elisha Parker in the northeast part of the county. In the fall of the following year Col. Wm.

OBION COUNTY HISTORY

M. Wilson, with his family, located about three miles southwest from Troy. He soon after removed to Jackson, but returned the next year, and his son, Thomas D. Wilson, is said to have been the first white child born in the county. During the next year or two the settlement went on quite rapidly. Rice Williams located near Troy, and after that place was laid out became the first resident. John Parr opened a farm five miles north of Troy; William Hutchinson nine miles west; George Davidson twelve miles west, on what was known as the Dyersburg road, and Joel S. Enloe about four miles east. Alexander Starrett settled about one mile south of the site of Glass, formerly Palestine, and John and William Carter in Civil District Number Seven. John Polk located at Polk Station, three miles southeast of Troy, in 1833. Among other early settlers were Obadiah Roberts, northwest of Union City; Benjamin Totten, at Totten's Wells, in the northeast part of the county; also in the same locality Jethro L. Byrd, John Harpole and Thomas Sayles; Willis and James Caldwell, west of Union City; John Killion, John Y. Brown and Henry Maupin, in the vicinity of Protemus. Indeed the settlements were made so rapidly after the opening of the territory that to give a list of all the early pioneers would be impossible.

During the first few years the settlers depended mainly upon wild game for their meat and Indian corn for their bread. Deer were very plentiful and bear were found in great numbers in the canebrakes, which were their usual resort. The county was a favorite hunting ground for Davy Crockett, who traversed it many times.

Indian corn before the erection of mills was ground, or rather crushed, into meal by means of a mortar and pestle, a pole beam being used to raise and lower the pestle into a bowl-shaped stump. Horse mills, however, were soon after erected. The first was probably built by Wyatt Bettis, who lived in what was to be the first civil district. Another was erected in 1823 by Colonel Wilson. The first water mill was built three years later by Thomas McDonald on Davidson Creek. It was afterwards run by James and John Blaine, and still later by Joel Enloe. The first cotton gin was built and owned by John Parr, four miles northwest of Troy.

INTERNAL IMPROVEMENTS

Soon after the organization of the county the question of internal improvements began to agitate the county, and as the rivers were then the main channel of transportation their improvement was of the greatest importance. In 1838 the State having appropriated $31,000 to be used in the improvement of Obion River, H. J. P. Westbrook, Jas. B. Harper and Jas. M.

OBION COUNTY HISTORY

Hunter were appointed commissioners on the part of Obion County to superintend the work. But little benefit, however, was derived from this project.

VIRGIN FORESTS AND FERTILE SOIL

Pioneers found themselves in the midst of a great forest of giant oak and poplar timber, with a variety of hickory, ash, gum, and walnut, and an abundance of wild game. Some of the poplar trees measured ten feet in diameter. So one can imagine why in the course of a number of years there were a hundred saw mills at one time located in the county and in operation cutting timber for the market and for the furniture factories of Union City.

In order to realize more fully the size of trees grown in Obion County before the saw mills in the sixties and seventies began cutting timber, it is related by the biographer of Judge W. H. Caldwell that from one of his farms he cut a poplar tree in 1879, and from four different forks cut 17 logs 12 and 14 feet long, averaging each 25 inches in diameter.

Another was a mammoth oak tree found on the farm of J. D. Caldwell, three miles northwest of Union City, which measured 9 feet in diameter at the stump. This farm was settled by David Hubert, father of Mrs. Addie Caldwell. Mr. Hubert was in the War of 1812 and the Battle of New Orleans under Jackson.

Surveys were made in 1850 and choice tracts of land were sold for four dollars an acre. John Maupin bought 1100 acres, now embracing the town of Rives, for fifty cents an acre. The farm owned by the celebrated oculist, Dr. T. J. Edwards, was at one time sold for three dollars an acre, and the land abandoned by the purchaser. Afterwards it was sold for eight dollars an acre.

Lands to the south of Union City were settled by Littleton and Monroe Ward, Arch White, John Thomas and John C. Grizzard. The Conrad land, lying in the Houser Creek bottom, afterwards one of the richest sections of farm land in the entire State, was bought by Uncle Billy Bell, Hugh A. Catron, Ira Bradford, Capt. Jas. Turner, Sam Wade, Sr., Rev. E. Osborne, Thomas Batte and others.

DAVY CROCKETT

In this particular instance it would no doubt be interesting to trace the colorful life and adventures of Colonel Davy Crockett, born and bred a Tennessee backwoodsman and raised with a roving spirit—soldier, statesman, rifle shot—whose life was concerned with patriotic service while his heart beat for the bugle horn and the romance of the wilds. It is therefore significant

OBION COUNTY HISTORY

that various claims were made about the Crockett homestead in West Tennessee. Fact is that Crockett spent very little time at home. He was either in public life and service or roaming the woods with his rifle and dogs. He was figuratively a "hound for the trail."

Therefore the very small importance that was really attached to the Crockett home. Truth is that the family resided in various places before coming to West Tennessee. In Middle Tennessee they lived in Lincoln, Franklin and Hickman counties. Coming to West Tennessee Colonel Crockett's autobiography states that with his eldest son and Adam Henry, another boy, he "cut for the Obion," "selected a spot . . . the home nearest being seven miles . . . on the different side of Obion River. It was a complete wilderness full of Indians."

Evidently the location was near a three-point intersection of Weakley, Gibson and Obion counties, a few miles probably southeast of Crockett Station, later a stop on the M. & O. R. R. between Rives and Kenton.

From his home in Weakley County in 1823 Colonel Crockett was elected to the Legislature, then in 1825 as a candidate defeated for Congress. He took his defeat bravely and started to the Obion bottoms to engage in stave making, for many years a very active pursuit among early settlers. He took some hired hands and was proceeding to make staves and boats for the river traffic. He hadn't suspected it probably but he was right in the immediate region of wild life, a country full of bears and other game. His intentions were good, but "as soon as the bears got fat" he turned to hunting and soon killed and salted down his meat. And then he and a neighbor went down toward the Mississippi (River) and killed 15 bears in two weeks. With the sport in his blood Colonel Crockett then took his boy and crossed over the lake (Obion), killing bears on the way, mentioning particulars of the hunt. Proceeding farther they "cut out again for a creek called Big Clover". Here in no time, two weeks probably, 20 bears were killed and another thousand pounds for a poor man out of meat.

Next morning Colonel Crockett and the boy "started to take a hunt between the Obion Lake and 'Red Foot' (Reelfoot) Lake". Here it is probable that they left Big Clover to the south and trailed up the lake under the bluffs. At the time neither Samburg nor Walnut Log was known, but Crockett spoke of places too steep to climb. At one place they found a bear "which got down into one of the cracks that the earthquake had made in the ground." It was dark and there was a general melee between the dogs and the bear. Finally with the dogs at the bear's head, Colonel Crockett got down into the ditch, four feet deep, and lunged his knife into the bear's heart. It was in the early winter and Crockett began to get cold and thought he was about to freeze. Failing in his attempts to get warm he tried the very heroic alternative of climbing up a tree two feet thick, going up thirty feet to the limbs, then with his arms tightly clasped around the tree sliding to the bottom. This was repeated probably a hundred times before daylight.

Here we take a whole paragraph from Colonel Crockett's book: "We prepared for resting and laid down by the fire, and about ten o'clock there came a terrible earthquake, which shook the earth so that we were rocked about like we had been in a cradle. We were very much alarmed, for though we were accustomed to feel earthquakes we were right now in the region which had been torn to pieces by them in 1812, and we thought it might take a notion to swallow us up, like the big fish did to Jonah."

Another paragraph closing the fall and winter hunt: "The morning came and we packed our horses with the meat, and had about as much as they could possibly carry, and reached home the second day. I had now accommodated my neighbor with meat enough to do him and had killed, in all, up to that time, 58 bears during the fall and winter."

Another paragraph: "As soon as the time came for them (the bears) to quit their homes and come out again in the spring, I took a notion to hunt a little more, and in about one month I killed 47 more, which made 105 bears I had killed in less than one year."

So we take it that a history of Obion County without the exploits of Colonel Crockett would indeed be leaving out the "meat" of the story.

And then again Colonel Crockett was present and invited to help lay out the town of Troy. This suited Colonel, and he indicated how much he would like it, but inquired of W. M. Wilson, in whose home the county was organized "What is a man to do away from home without money." To which Mr. Wilson replied: "Go to Rice William's hotel, stay as long as you please and I will pay the bill." This favor was afterwards rewarded by Colonel Crockett, who mailed from Washington City to Mr. Wilson at Troy, a fine Bible, now in the possession of the Morris family at Obion.

Settlements: Some years later the pivotal points of population in Obion County, beginning with the county seat at Troy, were the settlements of Totten's Wells and Jacksonville, a few miles northeast of the town of Union City; Fairfield, half way between Union City and Troy on the public highway; Wolverine, south of Troy; Palestine (Glass), ten miles southwest of Troy;

OBION COUNTY HISTORY

Wilsonville (Hornbeak), between Troy and Reelfoot Lake on the highway; Troy Station (Rives), south, and Paducah Junction (Gibbs), east of Union City on the I. C. R. R.; East Troy (Polk), southeast of Troy.

ONE HUNDRED TWENTY YEARS
(By R. T. CURLIN)

A few years before my father, Thomas R. Curlin, died I asked him to tell me about Obion County when his father came here, and the conditions in his boyhood. As this is centennial year, I thought a copy of some of these notes would be interesting reading to descendants of old settlers.

One among the first pioneers of Obion County was my grandfather, Samuel P. Curlin, who came from Halifax County, North Carolina, to Lebanon, Tenn., in 1822, where he married Charlotte Edwards, whom he had known in their former home in the old North State. They came to Obion County in the fall of 1827. With him came John Harpole and family, ancestor of Mr. Andrew Harpole. The names of some of the old settlers who came near that time were Reuben Jackson, Isham Conner, Jones, Hill, Thornton and Bettis. Bettis put up the first home mill in the county. You took a sack of corn and furnishing the horse, ground your corn, then paid toll for the use of mill.

Elisha Parker was the first settler of upper part of county.

As in all pioneer settlements the schools were very poor. The closest school was a log cabin schoolhouse five miles from my father's home. When he was six years old he walked this distance with his sister who was two years older. His father plowed a furrow thru the forest so the children would not lose their way. As yet there were few roads. The first good road was the Hickman & Dresden road.

Ben Totten came to Obion County in 1824, put up the first store and kept the postoffice. This place was called Totten's Wells. It was not very far from Harris Station. Ben Totten was ancestor of Mrs. J. F. Gregory and L. D. Allen, Sr., grandfather of Miss Marene Allen (city schools), When father was about ten years old he went to a barbecue and heard David Crockett speak and saw him play his famous joke of buying drinks for the crowd three times with the same coon skin.

The first wheat was planted by Lemuel Curlin and John Harpole. They cleared the land together. The forest was so very heavy, clearing land was no easy task. The people subsisted chiefly on bread made of corn and wild meat, such as deer, elk, bear and smaller game was plentiful. My father had hunted elk and deer where Union City now stands, finding his way thru heavy canebrakes, sometimes fifteen feet high. West Tennessee was the last hunting ground of the Indians east of the great river. On the land, known as the Pleasant Farm, Calhoun built a race track and a cotton gin. They called it Fairfield. It was the gathering place for pioneers when they had barbecue.

TOTTEN'S WELLS

One of the most interesting points of settlement in the county was Totten's Wells. It was here that Benjamin Totten settled in 1824, from which stemmed a community of people who had much to do with the formation and development of that particular section, which after the advent of railroads centered at Harris Station.

Here was the midway point on the stagecoach line, combined with U. S. Mail Service, from Dresden to Hickman, operated for some time by Jeremiah Swiggart, father of Judge W. H. Swiggart, Sr., and on this line it was that Wm. Ford, from his high top seat, drove the coach and blew his powder horn for the signal of approaching stops. The distance from Dresden to Hickman was 36 miles.

Totten's Wells became a trading point with the opening of a general store, cotton gins, blacksmith shop, Odd Fellows Hall, church and school.

Benjamin Totten settled on a tract of land comprising 3500 acres, made as a grant to Mr. Totten by the State under the administration of Governor William Carroll. Mr. Totten was head of a large family. A son, Judge A. O. W. Totten, locating in Gibson County and following the practice of law, was elected to the State Supreme Court as associate justice serving from 1850 to 1855. A daughter, Polly Totten, married James N. Cullom, a brother of Senator Shelby Cullom, of Illinois, many years a member of the United States Senate. Elizabeth, daughter of James and Polly Cullom, married Jeremiah Swiggart, father of William Harris Swiggart, Sr., who for many years practiced law in Union City and West Tennessee, and served the Twelfth Judicial Circuit, first as Attorney General (six years) to succeed R. A. Pierce, and then as Judge, completing two terms of sixteen years altogether.

Judge Swiggart was also honored with two very important commissions. One was issued by Governor Bate in 1885 to Mr. Swiggart to sit as special judge of the State Supreme Court to try the case of the Bank of Tennessee against the State, serving in the place of Judge Thomas J. Freeman, who signified relations in the suit which rendered him incompetent to act. Another was by members of the State Supreme Court, by appointment choosing Judge Swiggart as special Judge to act for Chief Justice M. M. Neil in the impeachment trial of Judge Edgerton and Judge

OBION COUNTY HISTORY

Estes of Memphis—sitting with the court in Nashville.

In the course of a few years Totten's Wells seems to have been superseded as a location by a new settlement known as Old Jacksonville, which appeared to be developing along the same road slightly to the south by a new colony of pioneers seeking the benefit of desirable natural surroundings.

Judge W. H. Swiggart, Sr., was born near Old Jacksonville in 1849 and was married to Miss Mary Fields in 1876.

COUNTY OFFICERS

Clerks of the County Court (1825 to 1940): Samuel D. Wilson, William S. S. Harris, George Sheeks, A. S. Hord, Samuel C. Henry, E. D. Farris, G. F. Isbell, W. S. Scott, A. J. Stanfield, John Bell, S. F. Howard, C. S Talley, R. H. Bond, N. L. Williams, John F. Semones.

Clerks of the Circuit Court (1824 to 1940): Jonas Bedford James L. Totten, A. O. W. Totten, John R. Hubbard, Daniel St. John, H. J. S. Westbrook, Samuel C. Henry, James M. Meacham, W. H. Caldwell, John Crockett, Lysander Adams, C. Goad, W. S. Harris, W. G. Huey, J. H. Bittick, J. B. Meacham, J. J. Lancaster, W. D. Jones, J. W. McCorkle, J. M. Hickman, H. M. Golden, Alva Reeves (appointed), J. N. Ruddle, Jas. L. Mott, R. A. Everett.

Trustees (1824 to 1940): Obadiah Roberts, William Hutchinson, John C. Wilson, J. M. Bedford, Samuel Hutchinson, John C. Reid, James H. Guy, John T. Abington, B. L. Stovall, Archibald Crockett, Benjamin Evans, George A. Herald ————; W. R. Hogan, J. L. Moultrie, W. H. Hollomon, George P. Hurt, J. W. Bransford, Elisha Askew, Alva Reeves, J. H. Whipple, S. T. Haydon, H. Parks (appointed), G. W. Worley, J. A. Hefley, J. H. Sanders, T. J. Easterwood, W. E. Jackson, D. E. Tucker, C. G. Moore, Garrett Pruett, S. W. Easterwood.

Registers (1824 to 1940): Asa P. Hurt, Moses Parr, W. S. S. Harris, ————, John Parr, S. S. Calhoun, W. P. Hill, George P. Summers, R. A. Hewatt, R. H. Marshall, D. Hubbert, John E. Evans, A. C. Lancaster, John Eastwood, C. M. Sanders, J. M. Chapel, R. B. Milner, W. J. Edwards, W. A. Jackson.

Sheriffs (1824 to 1940): Fletcher G. Edwards, Joel S. Enloe, Thomas A. Polk, William Hutchison, Archibald Crockett, John B. Hogue, John Crockett, James W. Bransford, William S. Scott, William H. White, Jas. B. Walker, Joseph R. Brown, Pleasant W. Duncan, H. W. Hickman, D. H. Dalby, G. F. Thomasson, F. B. Taylor, W. S. Jackson, Frank Pardue, John Finch, J. T. Chiles W. T. Mathes, J. M. Hickman, J. W. Cherry, J. R. McCain, J. D. Hubbs, Chas. Brush, J. S. Burcham

Clerks Law Court—Union City: Dr. Turner, W. W. Hall, J. H. Edmonston ————Edwards.

OBION COUNTY HISTORY

Tax Assessors: I. J. Howard, G. W. Robey, Scott Easley, Mrs. Scott Easley, Clint Adams.

County Judges: W. H. Caldwell, A. J. Lawson, G. R. Kenney, J. B. Waddell, H. C. Stanfield, J. W. Buchanan, J. A. Hefley.

MEMBERS OF THE LEGISLATURE

Representatives to General Assembly: Joel R. Smith (Carroll, Gibson, Obion and Dyer), 1833; William M. Wilson, 1835, John B. Fizer (Obion and Dyer), 1837; Osborne Purcell, 1839; Thomas A. Polk, 1841; Dr. Purcell, 1843; G. W. L. Marr, 1845; R. P. Caldwell, 1847; Samuel C. Henry, 1849; E. A. Ferguson, 1851; B. L. Stovall, 1853-57; R. C. Nall (Obion and Lake County), 1859; James R. Gardner, 1861; Frank Smith, 1865; R. A. Hewatt, 1868; B. Boyett, 1870; J. A. McCall, 1872; J. A. Board, 1873; Henry Adams, 1874; A. B. Enloe, 1876; William Jones, 1878; S. W. Cochran, 1880; J. H. McDowell, 1882; T. J. Bonner, 1884; T. P. Callicott, 1887; F. M. McRee, 1889-91; T. J. Bonner, 1893; Seid Waddell, 1895-7; Geo. P. Hurt, 1899; H. C. Alexander, 1901; R. W. Oglesby, 1903; F. M. McRee (Floater for Obion, Dyer, and Lake), 1903; J. H. McDowell, 1905; Geo. R. Kenney, 1907; E. N. Moore, 1909-11; G. R. McDade (Floater), 1909; S. F. Howard (Floater) 1911; G. R. McDade, 1913-15; J. L. Cochran (Floater), 1913-15; S. R. Bratton, 1917; J. A. Howard, 1919; S. R. Bratton, 1921-23; J. A. Howard, 1925; S. R. Bratton, (Floater) 1925; Jesse Finch, 1927; H. P. Naylor, 1927-31; Perry Browder, 1933-35; Dave H. Burnett, (Floater) 1935-37; Fred Latimer, 1937-39; Basil Maxwell, 1941-43.

State Senators from Obion, Weakley and Lake Counties to the General Assembly: T. R. Shearon, 1879; J. H. McDowell, 1887; W. W. McDowell, 1889; John E. Wells, 1893; Seid Waddell, 1899; F. M. McRee, 1907-09; D. P. Caldwell, 1917-19; S. R. Bratton, 1927-29; C. G. Moore, 1937-39.

CIRCUIT COURT

The first Circuit Court in the county was held at the house of W. M. Wilson, on May 10, 1824, with John C. Hamilton, judge of the Ninth Judicial Circuit, presiding. Jones Bedford was appointed clerk, and James R. Chalmers produced his commission as solicitor-general. The grand jury consisted of Evan Crawford, William Cunningham, Joseph Taylor, John Parr, John McKee, Charles Owen, Jonathan Finley, Nathan G. Pinson, Thomas Hewlett, N. Lindsay, Rice Williams, W. M. Wilson and Seth Bedford, who, after due inquiry, failed to make any presentments. The first case to come before the court was that of Nathan G. Pinson against the magistrates of Obion County, contesting the election of Samuel D. Wilson, Sr., to the office of clerk of the county court. It was affirmed by Pinson that two of the magistrates voting for Wilson were not residents of the county when commissioned, and that Wilson himself was holding the office of trustee of Madison County when elected clerk of Obion County. The case went to the circuit court of Henry County on a change of venue, but Pinson lost his case, and Wilson continued to hold the office for several years.

The judges who have occupied seats upon the bench in this judicial circuit since John C. Hamilton, have been John W. Cooke, William R. Harris, afterward a judge of the supreme court, mention of whom is made in another chapter; William Fitzgerald; Samuel Williams, who was on the bench at the beginning of the war; Isaac Sampson, appointed by Gov. Brownlow; John A. Rogers; James D. Porter, resigned to accept the office of governor in 1874; S. W. Cochran, appointed to fill out the unexpired term; Joseph R. Hawkins, Clinton Aden, W. H. Swiggart, John B. Bond, R. E. Maiden, J. E. Jones and R. A. Elkins. In 1869 special courts of chancery and law were established at Union City, having jurisdiction over Civil Districts One, Two, Three, Thirteen, Seven and Eight. The law court was organized on April 19 of that year, by John A. Rogers. The clerk of the circuit court at Troy served as the clerk of this court by deputy, until 1874, when N. K. Moore was elected clerk of the special court. Since that time the office was filled by S. O. Higgason, T. H. Turner and J. H. Edmonston.

CHANCERY COURT

The chancery court at Troy was organized in 185—, with John W. Harris, of Paris, Tenn., as chancellor, and P. H. Marbury, clerk and master. At the next election William M. Smith was chosen chancellor, and so continued until the suspension of the court during the war. Upon its reorganization, John W. Harris presided at the first session, and since that time the office has been filled by John Somers, Judge Livingston, Judge Cooper, Judge Hal Holmes, Judge W. W. Herron.

The chancery court was organized on April 26, 1869, by John Somers, who appointed David D. Bell, as clerk and master. He continued in that office until 1873, when he was succeeded by his son, John Bell, who continued as clerk and master, with the exception of six years from 1877, during which time George G. Bell filled the position.

BAR OF TROY

The first resident attorneys of the county were Charles McAlister and ———— Davis, who located at Troy, a short time after the organization of the county. McAlister was then quite a young man, of moderate ability and a fair knowledge of the law. He continued for several years and for a time did a considerable business. At the February term, 1842, Alfred M. Bedford and Richard B. Brown, both young men of ability, were admitted to the bar. They opened an office in Troy, but remained there only three or four years when the former removed to Missouri and the latter to Mississippi. At about the same time Samuel Williams, afterward judge of the circuit court, located in Troy, but in a short time removed to Trenton. He was a man of limited education, but possessed a great ability, and although not an eloquent speaker, was a close reasoner. He was industrious and energetic, and upon the bench was generally popular. During the year 1842 S. W. Cochran also became a resident of the town and opened an office. He had formerly practiced his profession at Kent, Ohio, and he at once assumed a prominent place among the members of the profession in West Tennessee, a position he sustained for forty years. For many years land suits were very numerous, and in this branch of the profession he was especially skilled. Another attorney, who obtained some reputation as a land lawyer, was James Davis. He had been a cabinet maker by trade, and for some time chairman of the county court. Soon after opening an office he took into partnership John Somers, once chancellor of the Tenth Chancery Division. In 1853, A. B. Enloe was admitted to the bar. He had been a student under Maj. Cochran, and he formed a partnership with his preceptor, which continued until the latter's retirement, a period of thirty years. A clear thinker, a thorough student and an eloquent speaker, he made an enduring reputation as one of the leading advocates of this portion of the State. In 1857 Thos. R. Shearon opened an office in Troy. He was thoroughly educated, both in general literature as well as the law, having attended both Yale and Harvard Colleges. At about the breaking out of the Civil War James G. Smith and William Smith, then young men, formed a partnership for the practice of law at Troy. The latter died soon after. The former continued and ranked as one of the best advocates in the county, possessing great energy and a thorough knowledge of the law. Other members of the Troy bar previous to the war were J. W. Buford, T. C. Swanson, S. M. Howard, William Caldwell, John C. Hawkins, and Attorney Atkins. In addition to those already mentioned the bar consisted of John E. Wells, a partner of Maj. A. B. Enloe, Charles Wright and W. W. Cochran, son of S. W. Cochran.

BAR OF UNION CITY

The bar of Union City, in point of character and ability, compared favorably with that of any other town in West Tennessee. The first attorneys to locate in the town were Charles N.

and William B. Gibbs, sons of Gen. Geo. W. Gibbs, a Nashville lawyer and surveyor, who located and established the town of Union City. C. N. Gibbs in 1874 was elected Secretary of State of Tennessee, under Governor Porter, and at the expiration of his term of office in 1881 moved to Chattanooga. At the close of the Civil War Col. David D. Bell, who had previously located in Union City, resumed the practice of law which he had begun in Nashville. He was a scholar, a man of fine intellect and an eloquent speaker. Colonel Bell was the son of John Bell of Tennessee, candidate for President in 1860.

Andrew J. Lawson, partner of Colonel Bell for a short time, attained high rank in practice. W. P. Caldwell, native of Weakley County, a man of fine native ability and legal training, served one term in Congress and settled in Union City with a fine law practice, remaining only during the latter part of the last century. Rice A. Pierce, native of the Pierce community in Obion County, Confederate veteran, life-time member of the Union City bar, silver-tongued orator, earned high reputation as a criminal lawyer. Mr. Pierce as a young man was elected Attorney General of the Twelfth Circuit. Afterwards he was elected and served his district in Congress 14 years.

W. H. Swiggart, native of Obion County and graduate of Cumberland University, ranked high in county and State as one of the foremost lawyers of his day. He was elected and served two terms as Circuit Judge of the Twelfth Judicial Circuit and was commissioned as special judge in important litigation on the State Supreme bench. F. W. Moore, member of the Union City bar commanding prominence in his profession, began the practice of law in Union City in 1874. He and J. G. Smith at Troy afterwards formed a partnership which resulted in important legal assignments. Upon removal of the county seat from Troy to Union City in 1889, J. E. Wells, of Troy, located in Union City and entered into partnership with Judge Moore. This partnership was dissolved upon Mr. Wells' death. W. E. Hudgins, beginning the practice of law, was accepted as the junior partner of Judge Moore. In 1910 Judge Moore was appointed as associate justice to succeed Judge Lamb as a member of the Tennessee Court of Appeals, the latter retiring on account of illness. Judge Moore served seven years, and as a candidate aligned with the faction favoring Prohibition, was defeated for re-election. He retired again to his legal practice in Union City and the partnership of Moore & Hudgins was renewed. Others of local bar distinction were C. N. Lannom, J. L. Fry, W. M. Miles.

Attorneys General of the Twelfth Judicial Circuit from Obion County included R. A. Pierce, D. J. Caldwell, Union City, Thos. O. Morris and E. A. Morris, of Obion.

CHAS. N. GIBBS

Very active in private and public affairs in the early days of Union City—a lawyer, scholar, politician, sportsman—serving Tennessee as Secretary of State from 1873 to 1881. Mr. Gibbs was the son of Gen. Geo. W. Gibbs, pioneer locating and establishing the town of Union City. C. N. Gibbs was born March 29, 1828, and died at the home of his daughter in Chattanooga January 12, 1920, nearly 92 years of age.

OBION COUNTY HISTORY

Members and well known practitioners of the Union City bar included, first and last, Seid Waddell, A. J. Harpole, J. A. Caldwell, John Bell, J. B. Waddell, A. N. Moore, O. Spradlin, H. C. Stanfield, F. J. Smith, J. A. Whipple, E. H. and W. D, Lannom T. F. Heathcock, Robt. Bell, David G. Caldwell, J. T. Gwaltney, Paul Hudgins, John Hart, C. W. Miles, III, J. R. Glover, George Dahnke, T. F. Elam, Sam C. Nailling, C. H. Cobb, E. F. McClure.

CIVIL WAR

As a portion of the "Volunteer State" Obion County well supported that title, Upon the declaration of war with Mexico a company was promptly organized by Maj. S. W. Cochran and Wm. Motheral, and tendered to the Governor, but the quota had already been filled by the more populous counties, and it was never called out. The first company recruited for service in the civil war was company —— of the Fourth Tennessee Regiment, which was organized at Union City May 1, 1861, with J. H. Dean as captain. At the reorganization which took place at Corinth, the following year, an entire change of officers was made. S. F. Maxey was chosen captain.

One of the best known and most gallant companies organized for service in the Confederate cause was Company H. of the Ninth Tennessee Infantry, better known as the "Obion Avalanche". It was recruited in the vicinity of Troy, and was organized at Jackson, Tenn. The commissioned officers at that time were Capt. J. W. Buford, afterward colonel of the regiment; first lieutenant, S. T. Swanson; second lieutenant, S. M. Howard; third lieutenant, Warren McDonald; orderly sergeant, Thomas S. Williams. A year later the company was reorganized at Corinth, when Warren McDonald was elected captain; Daniel Bell, first lieutenant; William Latimer, second lieutenant; "Pink" Buchanan, third lieutenant; and H. W. Head, orderly sergeant. The last named was soon after promoted to third lieutenant, and finally became captain. At Murfreesboro the company was consolidated with Company G, known as the "Hickory Blues," and June Hall was placed in command.

OBION AVALANCHE

Roll of the famous Company H, Ninth Infantry, United Confederate Veterans, the Obion Avalanche:

Officers of the company are found as above Privates: Tom Buford, Jas. and Spencer Buford, John M. Bell, Jas. Beauchamp, Hugh Bell, Holland Bittick, Jabez Brown, Jas. Buchanan, Thos. Burnett, R. P. Catron, Ira P. Clark, S. H. Calhoun, A. W. Dock Crockett, Rolla P. Crockett, Robt. Cunningham, Ed Carroll, John Cunningham, Wm. Corum, John Cavanaugh, G. W. Carmack, W. H. Dillard, Wm. Chanley, John Dooley, Charlie

Davis, R. Edwards, John Foster, Larkin Foster, Jim Fields, T. J. Godsey, Wm. Fields, F. M. Gardner, W. J. Guy, R. Grooms, Josh Glover, Jesse Glover, John Garrett, Noah Glynn, John Gallop, T. Gynn, B. Gowan, J. Grogan, B. T. Garrison, Joe Harper, John W. Head, W. S. S. Harris, Wm. Hamilton, F. Holloway, Polk Holloway, Ben Herold, Hugh Hamner, Ben Hays, Tom Henry, Robt. Joyner, J. A. Kirkpatrick, C. L. Keaton, Geo. King, Polk Kersey, T. J. Latimer, Pony King, Sam Lyons, Eli Lorance, Bill Lawson, J. K. Morris, Bailey Milner, Marion Gardner, F. M. McRee, Sim McDonald, Wm. McGaw, Sylvester McDonald, Rufus McGaugh, Bill Myers, Jim McWherter, John Nipp, John Nix "Hop" Nix, H. E. Oglesby, Jas. M. Payne, Warren Moody, W. A. Page, Green and John Pruett, M. E. Prather, Wm. Pride, Robt. Patterson, Henry Pryor, Jas. Rumage, Dr. E. C. Richardson, John Ramsey, Joe and Frank Robinson, Bob Scearce, C. M. G. Ray, John Thriff, C. C. Sinclair, Harvey Sinclair, Tom Turner, F. B. Taylor, Josh and E. S. Walton, J. Thompson, D. W. Wicker, P. M. Wright, Tom Williams, Jas. H. Whipple, Jack Williams, Allen Wright, Geo. B. Wilson, Tip White, Seay Williams, Charlie White, Robert Whitaker, Wilford Wright.

Company B of the Twenty-seventh Tennessee Infantry was organized at Troy on August 20, 1861, with A. W. Caldwell as captain; J. W. Wright, first lieutenant; Oliver Farris, second lieutenant; John Starrett, third lieutenant. At the battle of Shiloh the colonel of the regiment was killed, succeeded by H. Campbell, and James Harper, Cahal Peery and Israel Moffatt were elected lieutenants with Thos. Sowell as orderly sergeant. C. Peery was placed in command of the company consolidated with another company at Corinth.

Company A of the Forty-seventh Regiment was organized at Troy December 1, 1861, with J. R. White as captain; William Stacey, first lieutenant; Gibson Dickey, second lieutenant; John McDonald, third lieutenant, and Joel Faulk, orderly sergeant. At the reorganization of the company William Stacey became captain. T. R. Shearon, a private in the company, was promoted to the rank of major.

Company I of the Forty-seventh Regiment was organized at Troy with William S. Moore as captain; Ayers, Butler and Gleason, lieutenants; J. R. Oliver, orderly sergeant. The last named officer was placed in command at Corinth as captain.

Company H of the Forty-seventh Regiment was raised in the vicinity of Kenton with B. E. Holmes as captain; S. H. Reeves, first lieutenant; W. H. Hollomon, second lieutenant, M. S. Wilkes, third lieutenant; and Robert T. Jones, orderly sergeant. At Trenton Holmes was made lieutenant colonel, succeeded by John Duncan, killed, and then by W. H. Hollomon, as captain.

Company A was organized with Ellison Howard as captain, Henry Hickman, first lieutenant; William Fleming, second lieutenant; Benjamin Gray, third lieutenant, and Jas Hickman, orderly sergeant. The company was reorganized with Henry Hickman as captain; T. H. Hickman, third lieutenant; and F. M. Johnson, orderly sergeant.

Company C was commanded at first by John Bedford, but at the battle of Murfreesboro, it was consolidated with Company D.

Company I was organized at Union City about September 1, 1861, with J. M. Wilson, captain; Wiliam Caldwell, first lieutenant; William Jackson, second lieutenant, and Thomas Stovall third lieutenant. The company was reorganized with William Caldwell as captain; William Jackson, first lieutenant, and Thos. Barham, second lieutenant.

Company E was organized at Union City about September 1, 1861, with T. R. Hutchinson as captain; D. Pearce, first lieutenant; A. J. Milner, second lieutenant; Frank Brooks, third lieutenant, and W. P. Hutchinson, orderly sergeant. The company at that time numbered about 110 men. It was reorganized on May 8, 1862, with J. R. Walker as captain; W. P. Hutchinson, first lieutenant; L. Oliver, second lieutenant; J. C. Riley, third lieutenant, and Joel Hatchett, orderly sergeant. W. P. Hutchinson was killed at Murfreesboro, and was succeeded by O. D. Brown. The company was afterward consolidated with Company A, and Capt. B. Jones was placed in command. Later he was succeeded by H. Adams.

Company K, of the Second Tennessee Cavalry (Bartow's regiment), was organized at Oxford, Miss., in the fall of 1863. It was made up of men from Gibson and Obion counties, who had stolen away after these counties had fallen into the hands of the Federals. A part of the company had been partially organized at South Gibson, and had gone out with Russell's cavalry. The officers chosen were S. H. Reeves, captain; William Latimer, first lieutenant; J. H. Bittick, second lieutenant; William Roberts, third lieutenant, and J. W. Howell, orderly sergeant. The regiment was composed of good material and it saw much arduous service in Mississippi, Alabama and West Tennessee.

In the early part of 1864 a company of about forty members known as King's Scouts, was organized in the vicinity of Kenton, for the purpose of maintaining order and punishing lawlessness. It acted under orders from Gen. Forrest. The officers were George King, captain; J. W. Norton, first lieutenant; Samuel A. Thomas, second lieutenant, and John E. Thomas, orderly sergeant.

A cavalry company was also recruited in the western portion of the county, and with Oliver Farris as captain, served in Russell's Twentieth Regiment.

OBION COUNTY HISTORY

COLORS PRESENTED BY MISS ELLEN ISBELL

The Forest Rovers, or Company D. had their first meeting at Beulah Church August 14, 1861. The company completed its organization by September 5, 1861. The roll of the officers and entire company taken from the original roll that A. E. Ratliff had and carried throughout the war, it being the only thing the enemy would allow him to keep, and he has not got in a good humor yet with the Yank that struck him with his bayonet after he was wounded and a prisoner at Chickamauga. The roll is as follows:

Captain, W. H. Frost; First lieutenant, J. R. Scott; second lieutenant, P. J. Cummings; third lieutenant, N. Payen; orderly seargeant, D. W. Caldwell; third sergeant, Paul Isbell; fourth sergeant, A. E. Ratliff; first corporal, S. W. McDaniel; second corporal, J. I. Emmons; third corporal, John Thomas; fourth corporal R. B. Ward.

I. N. Bramham, W. H. Cummings, M. M. Caruthers, M. A. Calhoun, T. W. Crenshaw, G. C. Cox, I. N. Duncan, A. Duncan, W. S. Douglass, C. Fisher, G. Phelps, J. W. Gills, J. A. Hook, G. M. D. Haislip, W. E. Isbell, J. Jackson, W. H. Johnson, J. T. Soundon, J. W. Laster, Wet Lawson, J. W. McGinnis, L. Mahan, G. W. Norrid, E. M. Oliver, J. M. Page, T. H. Park, R. M. Park, T. M. Park, J. W. Phillips, D. W. Pursley, W. B. Reed, B. Scott, W. Stone, W. J. Lemmon, J. W. Wyatt, J. A. Walton, W. S. Walton, H. S. Wilson, H. C. Williamson, J. M. Williams, W. F. Whot, G. W. Williams, W. C. Yates, R. H. Cloys, G. W. Bonahan, M. Creed, Wilson Cunningham, M. P. Chambers, J. E. Caldwell, W. Duncan, J. H. Douglas, J. A. Douglas, F. Fourtman, A. C. Garrison, G. B. Godsy, W. F. Henderson, T. B. Henshaw, G. C. Isbell, T. B. Jackson, W. T. Joyner, A. S. Soundon, J. S. Lynch, W. C. McDaniel, R. H. Miller, J. M. Naylor, J. F. Osborne, C. B. Page, J. S. Park, M. M. Park, R. C. Park, J. M. Park, T. J. Pursley, G. W. Pursley, T. J. Roberts, A. Stone, M. Blackley, Van Williams, O. M. Whitely, W. P. Walton, S. M. Wilson, N. B. Wilson, W. W. Whipple, P. T. Williams, R. D. Wilson, W. F. Williams, D. C. Cannon, R. H. Sanders.

There were in all 102 men that started to follow the fortunes of Company D. Our colors, beautifully wrought, were presented to us at Lawson's Academy Sept. 6, 1861, by Miss Ellen Isbell and received on behalf of the company by the second lieutenant, P. J. Cummings.

SEMINOLE WAR

Hugh Alexander Catron, who located in Obion County, immediately west of Union City in 1840, served both in the Seminole War in Florida and in the Civil War. He was mustered in 1836 for a six months tour in the Seminole campaign under Brig-Gen. R. Armstrong and enlisted from Drake's Creek in Sumner County, Tenn., in mounted infantry. He was honorably discharged in 1837.

H. A. Catron entered the Civil War from Middle Tennessee and was commissioned as a colonel, engaged principally in drilling troops around Nashville.

SPANISH-AMERICAN WAR

Below is a roster of Company I, Fourth Regiment, Tennessee Volunteer Infantry, War with Spain, which was taken from the muster out rolls of this company. A number of other boys from this vicinity enlisted in this company, and went to mobilization camp at Knoxville, Tennessee, but failed to pass physical examinations. The company was organized by Captain Harvey C. Alexander, assisted by Lieut. John Bell.

The men of this company were enrolled and organized at Union City and Knoxville, Tennessee, during the month of June, 1898. They were mustered into U. S. Service at Knoxville, Tennessee, July 5, 1898. While in camp there the regiment passed through a military review before Secretary of War Alger. They broke camp November 28, 1898 for Savannah, Georgia, and, on December 1st embarked for Cuba, passed on the way San Salvador and Crooked Island. The vessel ran aground December 6, 1898, just off the coast of Cuba, and then the regiment disembarked and was divided into two detachments, one staying at Casilda and the other, including this company, under Lieut. Col. Harvey H. Hannah, proceeded to Sancti Spiritus, Cuba, thirty miles from the southern coast of the Island. This company took an important part in assisting in the rehabilitation of the town and country around Sancti Spiritus and of the reorganization of civil authority there, and also in distributing rations to the destitute Cubans, during its stay on the island. The company sailed for Savannah, Georgia, on March 29, 1899 and encamped at Savannah until May 6, 1899, on which date it was mustered out of service.

Officers: Captain, Harvey C. Alexander; first lieutenant, John Bell; second lieutenant, Samuel D. McAlister; sergeants: James A. Alexander, Charles W. Moss, Frank F. Engle, Charles Fulton, Warner Brevard, Joseph N. Ray; Corporals: John C. Evans, Otho Midyet, Walter J. McMurry, Deck Porter, Wesley I. Bolin, William A. Stephenson, Eugene Williams, John Q. Provow, John L. Ricketts, William S. Stanley, Thomas N. Ferguson, William I. Rogers; Musicians: Otis Brock, Edwin C. Gray; Artificer: Charles M. Edwards; Wagoner: William Alexander.

Privates: M. Frederick Burdick, Richard M. Butler, Eugene

OBION COUNTY HISTORY

Bolin, William Boucher, George F. Baird, Calvin Byrge, Jackson Byrge, Dorser Burleson, Hays Brown, Peter Brown, J. Van Bryson, John C. Blain, George Carter, James Caldwell, William Caldwell, Henry Carroll, Eulas Cox, Arthur W. Douglas, J. David Edmondson, Jr., Charles Fisher, Benjamin Grindell, Columbus Green, Alphred S. Gilbert, John Haltman, Frank Harris, Albert Hart, Julian Hogan, Lee Jones, Thomas F. Jordan, Caut Jackson, Louis F. King, George W. Lowe, Robert P. Lester, Michael Long, Guy McConnell, James McConnell, Menry Moss (Cook), L. Nevins McClerkin, William Mauk, William McFetridge, Lauman R. Moore, Felix O. Meredith, Martin Moody, J. Baxter Mitchell, Harvey Porter, James Posey, John B. Preuth, John A. Phelps, Benjamin Phillips, John Patton, Robert A. Phillips, Dude Riggs, Robert M. Rogers, William Raymer, Marion Roberson, Archie Lee Shuck (Co. clerk), John Stacy, Oscar Slate, David Spurgeon, Joseph Simpson, Issac Shelton, Henry W. Stephenson, John V. Shephard, Russell V. Scruggs, James Tudor, Carson Taylor, D. Luther Vaden, James E. Wright, Elijah B. Wilson, William Witt, John Williams, James A. Young. Transferred: Private William E. Holcomb to Regimental Band.

AMERICAN LEGION

From farms, from schools, out of banks, stores and from all walks of life almost 1,000 young men, the pick of the man power of Obion County responded to the call for service in the World War, giving added prestige to Obion County and Tennessee in its reputation as the Volunteer State.

Few of these men had any training other than Boy Scout, and the National Guard under the command of Capt. Claude Andrews. Yet these men, both colored and white, served with credit, securing recognition both as commissioned and non-commissioned officers.

A large portion of these men came back with different visions of life. Ideals of loyalty and patriotism were more impressive and service to the community, state and nation an obligation of honor.

In the fall of 1929 a number of the returning ex-service men made application for a charter and organized Post No. 20 of the American Legion.

Since its organization Milton Talley Post No. 20 of the American Legion has been a militant outfit, always on the alert to serve needy ex-service men and to render community service when opportunity presented itself.

The activities of the post in part are as follows: On nation wide endowment drive for children of disabled vets — in this was first post in state to raise quota; won state cup for largest increase of membership over previous years in 1924; sponsored 4th of July celebration; sponsored first Cotton-Day celebration, which was the forerunner of county fair; maintained club rooms; presented nationally known Royal Scotch Highlander Band at a great cost; conducted two Red Cross county-wide drives; co-operated with city wide crime clean-up drive in 1925; contributed handsomely to High School Band and to gymnasium; helped entertain confederate veterans in state convention held here in 1929; secured number of tombstones for our dead veterans; make annual pilgrimage to graves of departed ex-service men on Memorial day of each year, decorating each grave with handsome floral offering at a great expense; maintain firing squad for funerals of veterans. Milton Talley was the twentieth post in the State to be organized.

Officers for Milton Talley Post for the year 1940 are as follows: Joe H. White, commander; R. E. Rankin, adjutant; G. M. Woosley, finance officer; J. A. Caraway, service officer. Vice commanders: H. M. Harper, Union City; R. M. Pruett, Woodland Mills; Bond Fox, Obion; Clay Jackson, Kenton; Dewey Darnell, Hornbeak; W. B. Forrester, Troy. C. B. Dement, historian; Rev. L. R. Niell, chaplain; A. V. Johns, sergeant-at-arms. Executive committee: F. A. Nailling, Dixon Williams, Joe H. White, Cecil Moss, R. E. Rankin.

Anxious to preserve and care for the graves of its departed comrades the post has attempted to locate the graves of all ex-service men. The following list includes those now known.

Union City cemeteries: Geo. Jackson, L. H. Provow, Homer Reeves, W. D. Walker, Clarence Jenkins, Roberts R. Grooms, John Mitchell, Roy Mitchell, Joe J. Sherrill, Marvin Thornton, Robert E. Knox, W. B. Inman, Luther Morris, Pettus Ruffin, Clifford McClanahan, Clyde Joyner, John Barry, and Ferd Kirby.

McAlister cemetery: Herring; Sanders Chapel: Arthur Frazier (colored) J. L. Meals, Albert McCampbell, Ed Ridgeway, Wm. H. Hess; Chapel Hill: Elbert Nanny; Shady Grove: Paul Payne, Earl Stennett, Hugh Cloys; Johnson Grove: Alfred Owen; Beu'ah: Milton Talley, Dixie Corum; Mt. Zion: Richard McConnell, C. B. Hale; Antioch: Robert H. Hicks, Carey Goff, Griffin Goff, Pleasant M. Williams, Herman Edwards; Troy: Howard Stonewall Maxwell, Emmett Rogers, Harold Neal Smith; Ebenezer: Fred Reeves; Stanley Chapel: John R. James; Hornbeak: Newland Burnett, Wm. J. Matling; Cobb's Chapel: Gus Calhoun; Camp Ground: Dewitt Huey, John R. Tune; Somme cemetery: Geo. W. Hamilton, Pless F. Reese; St. Mihiel cemetery: Charles Allen; Argonne Meuse cemetery: Marion H. Marlin, Walter Eads, and Marshall Wright, somewhere in France.

OBION COUNTY HISTORY

AMERICAN LEGION AUXILIARY

During his term as State Commander, Hon. Jere Cooper was instrumental in forwarding the organization of the American Legion Auxiliary.

While the boys braved the perils of the camp, the submarine infested seas and the conflict on the different battle fronts, their wives, mothers, sisters and sweethearts knitted sweaters, prayed and worked at home. As in all wars they bore their suffering as the spartan mothers of old, many sacrificing all that they had for their country. With the ending of hostilities they were anxious to perpetuate the ideals of the war, as were those who participated, and as a result the Auxiliary came into being to serve the Legion as a support both in rehabilitation work and in the care of orphans of veterans.

In 1921 the local Auxiliary was organized, with Mrs. R. A. Napier as the first president. The Auxiliary has shared the triumphs and tasks of the Legion. always ready to serve in making club rooms attractive or in any of the enterprises fostered by the legion.

MILTON TALLEY

According to the custom followed in the naming of Veterans' organizations, the local post was named after a comrade, Milton Talley. Being the first of the local boys to make the supreme sacrifice he was given this honor.

Milton Talley, oldest son of Mr. and Mrs. C. S. Talley was born on July 28, 1891, in District Two, three miles north of Union City. He was a member of Beulah Baptist church of that locality. He graduated from the Union City Training School in 1911, when it was under the leadership of Mr. "B" Moore, one of Tennessee's best known educators.

The family moved to Union City and Milton began work with the Union City Lumber Company in 1912, where he remained until 1917. He then went to New Orleans, engaging with the Krauss Brothers Lumber Company. He was in line for promotion, but patriotism stirred his heart, and during the latter part of the year 1917 he enlisted as a volunteer with Twentieth Engineers of Forestry Company F, 6th Battalion—the largest regiment of lumbermen soldiers in the United States Army. After a few days' visit at home he started for encampment at Washington, D. C. He sailed on the 24th of January 1918, on the ill-fated British Tuscania, which was sunk off the Irish coast by a German submarine on February 5, 1918.

Two years later, October 16, 1920, the body of Milton Talley arrived in Union City from overseas, under military escort and was turned over to the family.

OBION COUNTY HISTORY

The casket, draped with the American flag, was taken to the Talley home and on October 17 the Milton Talley Post, No. 20 American Legion, escorted the body to Beulah church near the family home, with a large funeral train, where services were held with a tribute by Rev. H. E. Waters, a former pastor.

TENNESSEE NATIONAL GUARD

Company K, 117th Infantry, assigned to Union City Department, Tennessee National Guard, headquarters Union City Armory, including regulars and recruits enlisted for training service, entrained September 23, 1940, and stationed at Camp Jackson, S. C., comprises the following organization:

Captain, Thos F. Elam.

First Lieutenant, Thos. W. Lee.

Second Lieutenants: James S. Corbitt, Opie Chick, J. T. Weatherspoon.

Sergeants: Ted H. Clymer, Thea J. Easterwood, Richard O. Ferguson, Wilburn E. Grant, James A. Owen.

Corporals: Jas. M. McNiell, Jas. W. Campbell, Julian D. Hall, William D. Hendricks, Geo. H. Niles, Theron E. Townsley.

Privates, first class: Albert M. Cunningham, Leon Faulkner, Joseph H. Frankum, Clay B. Grant, Whitesell H. Harpole, Robert A. Harry, Jr., Marshall A. Hogan, Marshall B. McCormack, Earl M. Overton, Otis L. Pannell, Milton E. Ratliff, Ernest F. Ring, Kenneth M. Vick, Frederick B. Williams.

Privates: James L. Argo, Marion L. Barton, William G. Boston, George C. Britton, William J. Cook, Jr., Robert E. Combs, William T. Copeland, Billie P. Corbitt, John W. Cockran, Charles T. Corum, Homer A. Cruce, Marion P. Crutchfield, Robert L. Crutchfield, Jas. W. Dollar, Claud R. Dunn, James P. Dunn, James W. Dyer, George H. Freeman, Coble R. Garrett, Buford M. Gill, Charles E. Green, Robert L. Harrison, Jr., Jas. R. Hatchett, Jessie L. Henderson, Ervin B. Hickman, James M. Jackson.

Clavin C. Jimerson, David H. Jones, Claud T. Lovelace, Chester M. Luker, J. C. Mann, William E. Maupin, Spencer E. Millard, Robert C. Moore, James M. Myrick, James R. Morgan, Turner D. McFarland, Royal C. O'Daniel, John D. Palmer, Sam Palmer, William E. Priest, Lee T. Primrose, Benjamin P. Rawdon, James E. Reeder, Arnold D. Roberson, Harold D. Roberts, James N. Sinkler, Billie C. Snyder, David M. Synder, Thurman L. Snyder, Henry T. Waddell, William O. Walker, Jr., Hubert H. Walker, John H. Webb.

Recruits: Maurice Alexander, William F. Burnes, Willie M. Burnes, Jess W. Childress, Rollie W. Condra, Jr., George L. Corum, Robert S. Davis, Thomas W. Forbis, James L. Fowler, Robert W. Gaddis, Clearon Gardner, James H. Green, Harry O. Guy,

OBION COUNTY HISTORY

William T. Hall, Horace T. Huey, Leland C. Hamilton, Jr., Robert D. Hastings, Patrick L. Hogan, Joe C. Hughey, Leonard D. King, Walter R. Lewis, Gayle I. Malone, Martin T. Mayhall, Raymond C. Morgan, Robert W. Nagle, Paul Nelms, Ernest P. Norred, Herman E. Parson, Warren H. Payne, Thomas R. Phelps Milton E. Pierce, Guy W. Powell, Charles R. Priest, Bernie G. Roberson, George E. Sergerson, Marion J. Sharp, Johnnie F. Smith, James R. Tanner, Henry W. Whipple, Jr., Charles A. Williams, Lloyd H. Williamson, William A. Williamson, James W. Yoes.

With reference to field practice on company rifle range at Fort Jackson, S. C., prior to Christmas holidays, 1940, Lieut. Thomas V. Lee won title to high-score honors, while Sgt. Robert A. Harry scored high record with light machine gun.

It is worthy of mention that Lieutenant Lee is a direct descendant of Thomas Lee, founder of the Stratford estate, Virginia (1725-30), and father of the five "Revolutionary Lees". His sons, Richard Henry and Francis Lightfoot, were chief among the leaders of the cause of American Independence and signers of the Declaration. The Stratford Mansion was afterwards occupied by the great Revolutionary General, Lighthorse Harry Lee, and his son, the beloved Confederate General, Robert E. Lee, was born at Stratford.

OBION COUNTY COURTHOUSE

Some very interesting facts in regard to the building of court houses in Obion County from the fall of 1825 down to the present handsome structure are related herewith:

The original Act establishing Obion County itself was passed October 24, 1823, and was entitled "An Act for the establishment of a new County in the northwest part of the State." It was given the name "Obion" from the Obion River which had received its name many years previously, and up until the year 1870 it included what is now Lake County. It was organized on January 19, 1824, at the house of William M. Wilson, three miles southwest of Troy. The first County Court was composed of the following Justices: John McKee, Seth Bedford, Joseph Taylor, George C. Davidson, Rice Williams, William M. Wilson, William Reynolds, William Wilkinson, Samuel D. Wilson, Jr., John Parr, and Stephen Mitchell, of whom Seth Bedford was elected chairman. After this organization meeting, an election of officers for the county took place, in which the following officers were selected: Clerk of the County Court, Samuel D. Wilson, Sr.; Sheriff, Fletcher G. Edwards; Register, Asa P. Hurt; Trustee, Obadiah Roberts; Ranger, James Bedford; Surveyor, Robert B. Harper; Coroner, Jno. T. Abington; and Josiah G. Clark, Wyatt Bettis and

William McKinney were constables. It is of interest to note that at that time there were only three constables selected for the entire county, and that they had the office of Ranger. At this same time Stephen Mitchell, Rice Williams, and John McKee were appointed to make out the tax list for their respective neighborhoods. Provision was also made for the laying out of various roads in the county, as at that time there were very few roads in this section of the country, and those that we had were almost impassable during certain seasons of the year.

The Court continued to meet at the house of Colonel Wilson until the following January, when it met for the first time at the Courthouse in Troy. During the previous meetings, as stated above, Court had been held in the home of Colonel Wilson.

The first courthouse ever erected in Obion County was a structure almost round in it construction, eighteen by twenty feet, with only one window and one door, and it stood on the public square in Troy. It seems almost incredible now that Court at any period during the history of Obion County could have been held in a courthouse of this size. Certainly this small log house is a far cry from the beautiful building which is now completed here in Union City. The log courthouse referred to above was erected in 1825 by William B. Hutchinson. It is interesting to note that the public square in Troy had been cleared by James Harper, and that he received all of the sum of $23 therefor. Mr. Harper was also the builder of the first jail ever to be erected in Obion County, the same being a log building for which he received $270.42. The second jail was built of hewn logs about the year 1844. Necessity demanded that this be replaced by a brick jail, and this was done several years later. This, however, was for some reason replaced by a frame structure which only stood for a few years before it was destroyed by fire, and another of a similar style was erected. This, too, was destroyed by fire, and about 1881 a brick jail was erected at a cost of $9,000. It is said that at that time this jail was one of the finest in West Tennessee with the exception of the one in Memphis.

We now find that in 1831 a brick courthouse was erected in Troy which was fifty feet square and two stories high. This building was really a very good one for that period of time, but unfortunately it was badly damaged by an earthquake shock in the spring of 1842. It was so badly damaged in fact that it had to be taken down and a one story building was constructed in its place with the same material. This building proved to be inadequate as litigation began to increase with the growth in population in the county, and it again became necessary, as it had in the past, to move to better and roomier quarters.

With this in view, on January 28, 1848, an Act was passed by the Legislature loaning to Obion County the State taxes for the years 1848, 1849 and 1850, for the purpose of building a courthouse. It was further provided, however, that the revenues thus loaned to the county by the State should be repaid in three annual installments, the first to be made on October 1, 1852. Thus we see that State aid for local projects had a rather early beginning. Accordingly this plan was carried out and a new courthouse was erected in Troy in 1852. It was a two-story frame building which was somewhat larger than the two-story brick structure which had been erected earlier.

In pursuance of an act of the Tennessee General Assembly, passed in 1858, the Obion County Court in 1860 appointed three commissioners to draft plans for a courthouse and jail building for that part of Obion County west of Reelfoot Lake. The act also provided for the appointment of a Deputy County Court Clerk for that part of the county, his duties being defined to probate deeds, issue merchants and marriage licenses, and to collect taxes from boats engaged in river traffic and trade.

An additional act of the General Assembly was passed June 9, 1870, to establish a new county on the west side of Reelfoot Lake, establishing the calls and boundaries, to be known as Lake County. Thus the county of Lake was formed.

COUNTY SEAT REMOVAL

By a special act of the General Assembly of the State of Tennessee, amending the constitution, the counties of Obion and Cocke were excepted from the general provisions of the law requiring two-thirds of the qualified voters to cast their ballots for removal in the event an election is held for the purpose of ascertaining the will of the people in regard to removal or changing the site of county government. As amended the constitution substituted no provision as to the number of votes necessary, whether by simple majority or otherwise as a legal return of votes required for removal.

Thereupon in compliance with the petition, generally circulated and signed, the County Court of Obion County ordered an election to be held May 18, 1889, for submission to a vote of the people the question of removal of the county seat from Troy to Union City—whether for or against removal as expressed by the voters at the polls on the day of election in the various civil districts of Obion County.

Said election resulted in a vote of 3455 in favor of removal and 1906 against removal.

Not being satisfied with the returns under the law as it applied to the voters of Obion County, an injunction was filed in Chancery Court, to be heard before Chancellor H. J. Livingston, by a number of citizens, seeking first to prevent the canvass of returns by the County Court; second, enjoining and restraining meetings of the court for the transaction of business at any other except the regular meeting place at Troy; third, enjoining removal by officers of the law of the county records from the courthouse at Troy.

Injunction proceedings were heard by Chancellor Livingston in 1890 and suits in all cases were dismissed and injunctions annulled.

Court met for the last time in Troy on the first Monday in July, 1890, with adjournment on Tuesday sine die. The county records were soon after removed at the direction of a committee appointed by the court, as follows: W. J. Phillips, S. F. Howard, F. B. Taylor, J. M. Ownby and Officer W. A. Page. Records were loaded in a wagon and moved to Union City, accompanied by a number of citizens.

The first session held in Union City of the Obion County Court was on the 11th day of August, 1890. Chairman of the court at the time was S. F. Howard, A. J. Stanfield, Clerk.

The courthouse building in Union City was constructed at the expense of the citizens of the town of Union City and presented to the county. T. L. Bransford was awarded contract of construction.

The old building at Troy was finally removed to be used as an annex to the Troy school buildings.

Something like twenty years afterward another election was called and held to determine action upon a petition for a branch court at Obion. A very large majority voted against the petition and petition was lost.

NEW COUNTY COURTHOUSE

The building of a courthouse in Obion County, a WPA project located on the sight of the old building in Union City, under construction for more than a year, was completed and the furniture and fixtures installed, some time after the first of January, 1940. It remained then for acceptance by Federal authorities, who had charge of the contract, and this followed without objection in a short time.

Early in the year the records and all the fixtures in the old building, which had been used in temporary quarters, were moved to the new courthouse.

Total cost of the new building and equipment was a little more than $200,000. The lot or square around the building was graded to a level surface, concrete curbing and steps finished, and the work complete met approval of the committee, named by Obion County Court as follows:

OBION COUNTY HISTORY

J. A. Hefley, County Judge; J. L. Fry, chairman; T. F. Heathcock, T. R. Meadow, J. W. Kerr, L. E. Maloney, N. L. Williams, Walter Howell. The contractors: F. C. Correll & Sons; architects: Marr & Holman.

Outside measurement of the courthouse building is 75 by 100 feet. There are three floors, including basement, utilized for court rooms and the different county offices and departments.

The jail constitutes another story of much smaller dimension at the top of the building, provided with the finest processed steel cells of new and approved design.

The courthouse, in a limited way, is modeled something similar to the Capitol at Washington, with a corridor opening straight through from one end, north and south, to the other, with rotunda in the center. In the rotunda is a metal cast, embedded in the floor, an engraved design outlining the county of Obion, the civil districts, townsites and main highways, rivers and streams. This plate was made from actual survey and blue prints, and is indeed a fine index for students and others seeking correct points of location in the county.

The building comprises probably one-third additional or double the floor space of the old courthouse and a greater number of office rooms. The Circuit Court room, occupying the southeast quarter and most of the south end of the second floor is slightly smaller, but much more audible and comfortable than the court room in the old building. The Judge's stand reflects a greater impression of majesty, the jury and witness boxes of conventional type.

The County Court room is comparatively smaller, but for all practical purposes more suitable for the transaction of business. After all, if there are necessarily any speeches to be made, the county owns the building and there would be no valid excuse or reasonable objection in moving the meeting to the Circuit Court room.

Composition and general construction of the building are all definitely more substantial and complete than any other building project ever attempted in the county. Frame work is of steel and concrete, basement solid concrete, walls, capstones and mountings of gray stone, window frames and doors of steel, locks and hardware all of modern type and processed steel and copper. The floors are all of terrazo composition, excepting the office of the County Judge and the trial and judge's stand in the Circuit Court room, made of rubber tile.

As we view the new county courthouse building there appears no greater symmetry and harmony in general outline and contour to be found in any other of the new county building projects.

OBION COUNTY HISTORY

ACKNOWLEDGMENT

It was not without patient and persistent effort and appeal in the name of the county and the condition of the old building, the utter lack of office room, heating and plumbing facilities, etc., that the facts were understood and allotment from the WPA finally made. It took more than two years, the combined efforts of the County Court, the Chamber of Commerce and other local organizations, committee meetings, appointments with Senators and Representatives, volumes of letters and telegrams, editorial appeal, all for the proper presentation of facts and the exigencies of the case, together with the addition of personal and private effort and expense to pursue the work. And through it all, attended with disappointment and discouraging delay, it is no more than proper and just that public acknowledgment be made of the fact that the Secretary of the Union City Chamber of Commerce, Harry M. Harper, continued with singularly disinterested and unceasing confidence and effort in the justice of the claim for a new courthouse in Obion County, and that he never failed or faltered until the project was approved by the President and allotment finally made from the headquarters of the WPA.

In lieu of this a vote of thanks was tendered to Mr. Harper by the Chamber of Commerce.

JUSTICES AND MEMBERS OF OBION COUNTY COURT

Justices of the Peace and members of the County Court of Obion County for the various Civil Districts and municipalities are at present now serving as follows:

Civil District No. 1: A. E. Luten, T. W. Jernigan; No. 2: W. T. Garrigan, T. M. Flack; No. 3: Marvin Harper, J. E. Hicks; No. 4: W. A. McNeill, E. T. Jones, J. S. Garrett; No. 5: Will Burton, Charlie Summers, Newt Williams; No. 6 D. H. Burnett, John Buchanan, Wm. Sanders; No. 7: B. V. Jernigan, Raymond Caudle; No. 8: Jesse Finch, Harry Smith, H. A. Moore; No. 9: Guy Upton, Ernest Maloney; No. 10: Luke Latimer, Fate Maupin; No. 11: Harmon Caudle, J. B. Skinner; No. 12: Guy Calhoun, Fred Kinsey; No. 13: J. P. Cloar, T. R. Meadow, W. F. Tate, G. A. Houser; No. 14: J. T. Foster, P. A. Wall; No. 15: Woody Cunningham, A. Wilson, R. H. Beaird; No. 16: Will Robey, S. A. McDade, Heywood Jonakin.

OBION COUNTY HISTORY

OBION COUNTY FINANCES

Statement of Real Estate and Personalty Assessment and Revenues—Totals sixteen districts (as of September 30, 1939):

Number of lots, 5468, value	$ 3,443,690
Number of acres, 334,112, value	7,367,360
Personalty value	518,280
Public Utilities, value	2,893,138
N. C. & St. L. R. R. (1937)	302,331
TOTAL	$14,524,799

TAX RATE 1940

The tax rate for Obion County is $1.88 divided as follows:

General fund	$0.28
Bond and interest	.35
Elementary schools	.50
High schools	.26
Highways and bridges	.43
Workhouse and county farm	.02
Armory building	.01
Social Security	.03
	1.88
State tax	.08
TOTAL	$1.96

COUNTY OBLIGATIONS

Bonded Debt (as of April, 1940):

Purpose	Amount
Schools	$351,000.00
Highways	183,000.00
Courthouse	107,000.00
Refunding	28,000.00
Funding	38,000.00
Total County Obligations	$707,000.00

STATE ASSUMED BONDS

Highways	733,000.00
Total Obion County Bonds	$1,440,000.00
Total Floating Debt (April, 1940)	1,200.00

OBION COUNTY HISTORY

OBION COUNTY SCHOOLS

Schools were established in Obion County soon after its organization. They were taught in private houses and numbered but few pupils. The teachers, as a rule, were qualified with only limited preparation. One of the first schools of which there is any reference was taught in a house on the farm of Col. W. M. Wilson, three miles southwest of Troy, by William Rochford. He was succeeded by Thomas Macon, who taught at the same place as early as 1832. At about the same time Rev. Eleazar Harris had a school about two miles north of Troy, and an old man by the name of Hargis taught at what is known as Beulah Church. The latter was succeeded in 1839 by Nathaniel Macon, a man of no ordinary ability but possessing a strong penchant for "the flowing bowl."

According to record in the office of the County Superintendent, the first "Common School Commissioners" of Obion County were elected in 1838, pursuant to Act of the Legislature. The school districts "corroberated" with the civil districts, and were as follows: No. 1—James Matthews, justice of the peace; John Manier, John Harpole, Ezekiel Heraldson, Nathaniel Murphy. No. 2—A. K. Mills, George White, Alexander Marshall, John Cloar, John Pulliam. No. 3—Seth Bedford, justice of the peace; Jonas Dancer, Alfred McDaniel, William Pankey, A. R. Cunningham. No. 4—Thomas A. Fowlkes, F. D. Pinon, Reuben Anderson. No. 5—Edmond Carroll, Samuel M. Simpson, William Edmonds, David D. Pollock, William Evans. No. 6—R. B. Brown, Jubilee M. Bedford, Chas. McAlister, L. Norrid, R. H. Crockett. No. 7—Moses D. Harper, Jonathan Whiteside, William Carter, John Hall, George W. Bright. No. 8—John Hollomon, J. M. Hunter, H. W. Wright, W. C. Miles, Norton Oakes.

The scholastic population for the year was:

District No. One, 152; No. Two, 128; No. Three, 107; No. Four, 158; No. Five, 256; No. Six, 222; No. Seven, 112; No. Eight, 121. Total, 1256.

The annual statistical report of District No. Three, which was typical of the reports of the period, when any were given, is as follows:

Number of scholars in district, ages 6 to 16, 121; Number enrolled in school, 20. Amount of public funds received from County Trustee, $75.25. Amount of public funds paid to teacher, $36.54. Balance in public fund, $38.71. Amount paid teacher from Rate Bill (tuition), $23.46. Amount paid teacher from voluntary contribution—nothing reported and nothing paid for furniture, wood, etc. Number of times commissioners inspected schools 3. Length of school term, 3 months. Number of schools: finished, 1; unfinished, 3. Cost of schoolhouses — voluntary employment. General remarks: Schoolhouses should be built on a cheaper plan than any laid down by the "Superintendent."

The above report did not give the average daily attendance. A later report included the following: Of a total enrollment of 148 pupils, an average of eleven and two-thirds attended regularly for three months.

Early in the years beginning in 1840 John Crockett taught a school in what was then known as the Wolverine neighborhood. The first school in Troy is said to have been taught by S. N. Martin, in a house standing on the site of the old Presbyterian Church. About 1845 an academy was established one and one-half miles northwest of Troy. It was built by Waller Caldwell and known as Westbrook Academy. This continued to be a school at which the youth of Troy were educated for many years.

During the period of 1850-60 the two most important schools in the county were Bell Forest Academy, situated three miles north of Union City, and the academy of Pleasant Hill, four miles south of Union City. At Bell Forest Academy Professor and Mrs. Brannock and daughter, Miss Eva, constituted the faculty. Among the pupils were Andrew J. Lawson, Sam Scott (former County Court Clerk), James and Jack Scott, Don Corum, Jane Warren, Henry Thomas (uncle of Rev. J. H. Thomas), the Hendersons, Talleys, Pursleys, Turners. The schoolhouse was located on the Bell farm. For two or three years of that decade Pleasant Hill Academy was under the management of George B. Wilson, and attained a high reputation. In 1860 Mr. Wilson took charge of Westbrook Academy with Ira P. Clark as assistant. Both were excellent teachers. At the beginning of the war between the States, the school was suspended and the teachers both entered the Confederate ranks, but at the close of hostilities resumed work and continued for another year, after which Mr. Wilson resigned his position and Mr. Clark continued for another year, succeeded by Professors Sample and Underwood, the latter being the father of Miss Dora Underwood and R. H. Bond (Mrs.)

There were no graded schools in Tennessee until 1855 and then only in Nashville. In 1858 Memphis had adopted a system of graded schools. As before, experiments and failures followed. There was lack of coordination and the system of taxation was imperfect.

In 1867-9 the George Peabody Fund was made available to the Southern States to assist normal school instruction and to encourage cooperation in school organization. Thus graded schools were opened in Knoxville, Cleveland and Clarksville and other places.

There still remained a prejudice against the public school system. It was especially trying after the Civil War to reconcile

OBION COUNTY HISTORY

the South to common schools. There was no effort to mix the races, but universal education encountered hurdles of select schools and privately conducted preparatory schools.

But the State Teachers Association, organized many years before, never gave up the fight until every county in the State subscribed to the law enacted by the General Assembly in March, 1873, providing for normal instruction, a State Superintendent, County Superintendents and Boards of Education and a complete system of graded schools, finally an eight-months school term in every county in the State.

This was a long stride from primeval conditions when New England was adopting a system of public education, the Atlantic and Middle States following the example, and the South lagging, with Tennessee lowest in rank of literacy of all but a single State.

The reorganization of the public school system followed with the election of County Superintendents in Obion County, to wit:

SUPERINTENDENTS

W. F. Shropshire, 1873; W. A. Harrison, 1880; W. B. Stovall, 1886: J. H. Jackson, 1891-95; R. E. L. Bynum, 1895-1901; J. M. Moore, 1901-1906. Geo. R. Kenney was appointed by the County Court to fill the vacancy caused by the death of Mr. Moore. W. H. Cook, 1906-1909; C. L. Ridings, 1909-14; B. A. Vaughn, 1914-18; C. L. Ridings, 1918-19; B. A. Vaughn, 1919-23; C. F. Fowler, 1923-29; J. M. DeBow, 1929-35; C. F. Fowler, 1935-39; Milton Hamilton, 1939.

The Obion County Court, at its April term in 1875, appointed commissioners to lay out the county of Obion into school districts, who after being duly sworn proceeded to the task, as follows: J. S. Watson, J. C. Harris and J. H. Thomas. The report is on file in the County Superintendent's office, in which the county was divided into 64 school districts, giving the exact boundaries of each. These were subdivided by the County Court on petition of citizens, until in 1907 there were a total of 92 white schools.

COUNTY SCHOOL STATISTICS

The total school population of Obion County in 1838 was 1256. Average enrollment was not given, nor report made of total annual expenditures.

In 1875 the scholastic population was 6248; enrollment, 4900; number of teachers, 75; total expenditures, $14,273.36. In 1885 the scholastic population was 8237; enrollment 6894; number of teachers, 102; total expenditures, $18,235.

In 1939 the scholastic population was 6681 (6 to 17 years of age). Enrollment for 1939 was 7288. Total expenditures for the operation of Obion County schools in 1939 were as follows: From state revenues, $94,789.63; from county revenues, $116,697.95. Grand total, $211,487.58. Number of teachers, 222.

In 1921 Obion County was organized as a unit under a County Board of Education. The original board members were D. H. Burnett, chairman; A. W. Harpole, Dr. C. C. Marshall, T. C. Callicott, S. A. McDade, Dr. Ilar Glover and J. C. (Neal) Thompson. Seven high schools were established as follows:

Hornbeak, Kenton, Mason Hall, Rives, Troy, South Fulton and Obion.

The first report under the County Board, made June 30, 1922, shows there were 33 white schools and 15 colored schools, including Union City. Special Districts were Hornbeak, Kenton, Mason Hall, Rives, Troy and South Fulton; with Obion and Union City as municipal districts.

There were 32 white schools and 6 colored schools under the direct supervision of the County Board of Education. The elementary schools are inspected by a State Supervisor, and in 1939 nine were graded, which was a high average compared with the schools of the State. All except two in the county were approved.

Pupils may not be accepted in high school who come from an unapproved elementary school. This is a step forward. All schools are working toward the end of being graded. The high schools are graded, their graduates being accepted in the colleges without examination and making honor rolls.

The schools of the county and those from which they are consolidated are as follows: (Names in parentheses are original).

CONSOLIDATED SCHOOLS

Central—Consolidation of the following schools: Hazlewood, Crittendon Grove (Grove), Cane Creek, 1925; Penn's (Nelms), 1937; Stovall, 1937; Alamo (Hollis), 1939.

Cloverdale—Consolidation of the following schools: Cloverdale, Elbridge (Hailey), 1925; Union (Zion), 193—.

Community Pride—Consolidation of the following schools: Beech, Maple Grove (Saterford Springs), 1920; Old Republic, 193—; Housey Valley Academy, 192—.

Crystal—Consolidation of the following schools: Antioch, Mount Olive, 1922; Shapard.

Cunningham—(Cunningham), 1873; Lansdown (Push), 1937.

Dixie—Old Fremont (Caldwell's); Kedron, Pea Patch, 1920; Reelfoot; Clayton (Cloar), Rogers, 1938.

Ebenezer—Cunningham, Jones, Mineral Spring, 1928.

Glass—(Palestine), 1873.

Harris—Harris, Jacksonville, 1927.

OBION COUNTY HISTORY

Hiland—Gibbs, Pleasant Valley, 1927; Shady Grove, 1937.

Hillcrest—Chapel Hill (Love), Weaver, Shady Grove, 1925; Holman, 192—.

Hornbeak—(Center), Bethel, 1937; Fowlerdale, Turnage, Jackson Hill.

Kenton—(Kenton Academy), Oak Grove (Midyett), 1935.

Lindenwood—Oakdale (Tow Spring), Lucknow, Corum, 1920.

Lonoke—Cobb's Chapel, Owens (Possom Trot), 1936.

McConnell—McConnell, Rawles, 1926.

Macedonia—(Keathley), 1873.

Mason Hall—(Salem), 1873; Liberty, Bingham, Beech Valley (Bradford).

Midway—Crescent (Mosier), Spout Spring, 1925.

Minnick—Minnick, Long (Stover), Lakeview, 1925.

Oak Ridge—(Oak Ridge), 1873.

Obion—(Included in Beech Grove until 1887).

Old Maupin—Bethel (Kirk), 1925; Wells, 193—.

Parkview—Lee's (Chigger Ridge), 1923; Glady (Glady Hollow), 1927.

Protemus—(Dickey), 1873.

Rives—(Troy Station), 1873; Pleasant Hill (Shores), 1935; Callicott, Holloway, Harper's Valley, 1925.

South Fulton—Hampton, Weaver, Pierce (Winstead), Bowers, Walnut Grove (Prospect), Oak Glade, Barnhart, Fairview.

Sunnyside—(Brand), 1873.

Troy—(Troy Academy), 1873; New Hope (Finch's); Baker, (Horseshoe), 1924; Polk, Mount Moriah and Campground, Whiteside.

Walnut Log—Established in 1930.

Wayside—McAnna (Obion Chapel), Curry (Widow Phillips), 1925.

Woodland—Greenwood (Salem), Garrigan (Cole), Hale, (Oak Grove, Sanders).

Woods—1873.

Schools mentioned in the scrap book, location not reported, are Hughlett, Gilhams, Forest Hill, Reed and Comma.

School buses, 17 of which are standard and new, are far above the average, and drivers are subject to the rules and regulations provided by the school laws, sober, attentive and accommodating, transporting children with safety and comfort.

Every county high school has a well equipped home economics department. Eight have vocational agriculture departments; three have commercial departments. All courses are designed to give students a working knowledge of mechanical tools to be used later in life. All teachers are college graduates.

Today the schools of Obion County are second to none in

the State of Tennessee. The buildings are modern, commodious, well lighted and well equipped. The grounds are well planned and well kept.

SCHOOL RECORDS

In addition to the foregoing outline of county schools a partial list of the principals engaged in school work beginning 1921 and the directory of principals and teachers of the last report for the county, excepting those which are enumerated at Union City, Troy, Obion, Kenton, Rives, Mason Hall, Hornbeak, Cloverdale, are given below:

Principals at Central High, beginning in 1925: W. H. Hodges, L. A. Oliver, T. H. Kennedy, R. W. Nichols, R. J. Glover. School faculty for 1940-41: H. W. Moss, principal, Martha F. Logan, Frankie C. Farmer, Jeanette Pruitt.

Principals at Community Pride, beginning in 1923: C. F. Fowler, J. B. Barr, Robert Hicks, M. Hamilton. School faculty for 1940-41: R. D. Latimer, principal; Gertrude Bond, Erdice Latimer.

Principals at Cunningham, beginning in 1921: Herbert Miller, J. H. Stover, J. E. Summitt, R. H. Ray, A. G. Haworth, J. V. Lewis, F. H. Snow. School faculty for 1940-41: Melvin Sturgis, principal; Jimmie Finch, Alberta Hoover, Lucile B. Hurt, Lucile Sturgis.

Principals at Dixie High, beginning in 1923: L. D. Williams, F. S. Stokes, V. E. Boyett, E. L. Russell, C. D. Parr. School faculty for 1940-41: C. D. Parr, principal; Mary E. Adams, Bonnie Cleek, Camelia Cunningham, Guy Finch, Elizabeth Graham, B. N. Houston, Evelyn Nichols, Pearl Patton, Louise Tilson, Henry Wise.

Ebenezer for 1940-41: Wilton Wade, principal.

Principals at Harris, beginning in 1925: H. B. Donnell, J. V. Lewis. School faculty for 1940-41: A. B. Cooper, principal; Mayme Cooper, Mary W. Gore.

Hiland for 1940-41: Marie Caldwell, principal; Maggie Holland.

Principals at Hillcrest, beginning in 1927: A. G. Haworth, S. H. Snow. School faculty for 1940-41: Roy Green, principal; Jeannette Williams.

Principals at Lindenwood, beginning in 1925: R. J. Glover. School faculty for 1940-41; Jessie Pruett, principal; Manie B. Garth.

Principals at Lonoke, beginning in 1927: A. B. Cooper, J. D. Gore. School faculty for 1940-41: Jas. T. Kendall, Monette Wallace.

McConnell for 1940-41: Mrs. S. C. Atkinson, principal.

Macedonia for 1940-41: W. C. Stewart, principal, Myla Smith, Allie Keathley.

Midway for 1940-41: C. C. Thomas, principal, Maudie Pepper.

Minnick for 1940-41: Pauline T. Bradshaw, principal.

Oak Ridge for 1940-41: Summers Neely.

Old Maupin for 1940-41: Cecil Caldwell, principal; Lois Mitchell.

Parkview for 1940-41: Spencer Cunningham, principal, Hattie M. Cunningham, Rebecca Lowery, Eleanor Williams.

Protemus for 1940-41: J. L. Key, principal, Ruby E. Touchstone.

Sunnyside for 1940-41: Browning Ball, principal, Lara C. Bruer.

Walnut Log for 1940-41: Icie B. Pepper.

Wayside for 1940-41: Earline C. Stricklin.

COLORED SCHOOLS—1940-41

Kenton: E. W. Casey; Obion: Henrietta B. Foster; Rives: Dora Williams; South Fulton: J. J. Bills, principal, Bulah Dumas, George Newbern, Viossa Calloway, J. L. N. Calvert; Troy: W. C. Casey; Woodland Mills: Dorothy Casey, Tommie Currin, principal.

(Other schools and teachers in the county are named under the different "Community" headings)

COUNTY CHURCHES

The establishment of schools and churches began almost with the organization of the county, and even before that time settlers had occasionally met for divine worship under the protecting boughs of some large tree. The first sermon preached in the county, it is said, was by Reverend Scott, a licentiate in the Cumberland Presbyterian Church, but the first organization was probably made by the Associate Reformed Presbyterians, better known as "Seceders." who had established a church as early as 1830. Many of the first settlers of the county were natives of South Carolina, and had been members of the denomination in that State. So it was here in 1827 that the venerable Rev. William Blackstock, a native of Ballynahinch, Ireland, appeared as a visiting minister, who gathered them together and held service under a spreading beech tree, standing on the site of the church later to be used as a location by the congregation for the first church building. The church in 1832 was organized with 17 members, of whom Samuel Hutchinson and James Harper were elders. The minister in charge was Rev. Eleazar Harris, who came to this field from Chester, S. C., and remained until 1838, succeeded by Rev. Robert Galloway.

OBION COUNTY HISTORY

The Cumberland Presbyterians were also pioneers in church organization and missionary work. At the organization of Obion Presbytery in March, 1833, two church societies were established in the county—Troy and Mount Comfort. Jas. McCullom represented the Troy church in the Presbytery. The minister assigned to the Troy circuit was Chas. E. Hay, who continued for many years as a very active and devoted member of Obion Presbytery. Other pioneers in that body were Benjamin Lockhart, Samuel M. Johnson, Eli S. Jones, John B. Hubbard, Jethro L. Byrd, Levi Calvert, John W. Ward, F. E. Roberts, David Morrow and Charles McBride. The first session of the presbytery after it was organized was held at Mount Comfort in September, 1835, the second one year later at the residence of Jas. J. McCullom, at which time W. S. S. Harris, of Troy, was chosen its stated clerk. The third society organized in the county was that of Bethlehem, admitted into the presbytery in March 1839. At the same time F. D. Piner was assigned to preach at Rives schoolhouse. From this time growth of the church was very slow, so much so that in 1842 a day was set apart for fasting and prayer for the welfare of the denomination. In 1849 New Ebenezer and Pleasant Hill societies were admitted into the presbytery, and J. W. Ward and F. E. Roberts were assigned, respectively, as pastors. Other societies were admitted as follows: New Prospect, in 1853; Antioch, 1856; Beech, 1860; Camp Ground, 1862; Union City, 1867; Crittendon Grove, 1867; Star of Bethlehem and Mount Ararat 1880. Some of the above churches were organized several years previous to their admission into the presbytery, notably Antioch, Camp Ground and Union City. Prior to 1881 that portion of Obion County south of the river belonged to Hopewell Presbytery, but in that year this territory was constituted a part of Obion Presbytery. It then included three churches: North Union, organized about 1845; Beech Valley, about 1857; and Kenton in August, 1867.

So nearly contemporaneous were the Presbyterians, Methodists and Baptists, in beginning the work of preaching the gospel and establishing churches in Obion County, that the honor of priority cannot, perhaps, be ascribed to any one of them.

Of the Methodist Episcopal Church, South, the first congregation organized in the county was probably at Troy, not far from 1830. Another was formed at W. M. Wilson's, at a date almost as early, and during the decade, New Chapel, Salem and Mount Zion were established. Among the first circuit riders were Wm. P. Ratcliffe, Robert Tarrant, Arthur Davis (a man of remarkable talent but limited education) and Reverend Ramsey, one of the most wonderful exhorters. Among the presiding elders were Dr. Geo. W. Harris (eldest brother of Senator Isham G.

Harris and father of the former presiding elder of the Union City district), Robert Payne, John M. Holland, Thomas Joiner and Finley Bynum, all heroic and self-sacrificing men.

The first organization of the Missionary Baptists in the county was at Beulah, formed some time in the thirties. Another society at an early date was organized at Mount Olive, a new house having been erected. At the same time, or nearly so, a church known as Rehoboth was established about three miles northwest of site later known as Kenton. A short time after the Civil War, a new house was erected about three-fourths of a mile southeast of the old building and the name changed to New Concord. Macedonia, about two miles northeast of Kenton, was also an old organization. Among the early ministers of this church in Obion County were David Halliburton, James Hall, Samuel Cryder and David Wagster.

Of the Presbyterians there were but two congregations, one at Union City and the other at Pierce Station. The organization at Union City is set forth in that section of this history under the head of Union City.

The Church of Christ was organized October 29, 1848, at Old Republican Meeting-house, four miles west of Union City, constituted with the following members: Willis Caldwell, James Caldwell, Ezekiel Harelson, Isaac W. Caldwell, William M. Craig, Sarah Caldwell, Harriet E. White, Robert T. Caldwell, John C. Harris, David P. Caldwell, Martha C. Harelson, John K. Skinner, Sophronia Skinner, Geo. W. Whipple, Harriet Polsgrove, Emaline Polsgrove, George Polsgrove, Logan Kindell, Mary M. Caldwell. Services for a few years were held at Old Republican, after which they were transferred to a schoolhouse three miles northwest of Union, City, and there the church increased in membership. A chapter on this church appears under the Union City section. Prior to the Civil War two other churches, Palestine and Pleasant Hill—were organized, and after the war the Wilsonville and Caldwell organizations.

One of the oldest churches in the vicinity appears to have been an Interdenominational Church known as the "Solitude Church" which was used by Methodists, Baptists and Cumberland Presbyterians who lived north of Union City in the Beulah and Mount Zion neighborhood. This church was erected in the year 1830 and continued as an Interdenominational Church until about the year 1838 when it was destroyed by fire. Another early church was the Macedonia Baptist Church near Kenton, which dates from 1832. It has been impossible to obtain the history of all of Obion County's pioneer churches, but there follows hereafter a partial history of some of the churches.

BEULAH BAPTIST CHURCH

Over a century ago, before the organization of the present Beulah church, the Methodists, Presbyterians and Baptists worshiped in the same building. This church was located about four and one-half miles north of Union City, and was called Solitude. In 1838 this church was destroyed by fire.

In 1841 the pioneer Baptists of this locality organized and built Beulah church, situating it about two miles north of Union City, on land given by Mr. John White.

There is no record for the next twelve years. In 1853 an association, including some churches in Western Kentucky, was organized. The association was named "Beulah" in honor of the old Mother Church. The first recorded session of the association, it being its fourth annual meeting, indicates that it met with Madrid Bend church on October 10, 1857, in Fulton County, Ky. At that meeting it was resolved to meet with Beulah church in 1858. W. H. McGowan was pastor at Beulah at this time. There were seventy-two members who received their mail through the postoffice at Beulah, Tennessee.

There were only fourteen churches in the association then, namely: Beulah, Mount Olive, New Concord, Walnut Grove, Pleasant Hill, Sycamore Chapel, Hickman, Reelfoot, Macedonia, Republican, Madrid Bend, China Grove, Shady Grove and Poplar Grove.

At some later date the old church building went down, the members scattered, and no accurate record was kept for several years. In 1883, the church, six members in number, but strong in faith, reorganized. Members at that time were: Messrs. John Corum, Ben Pulliam, Mesdames Mark Corum, John Hale, Alfred Naylor and Teresa Talley.

In 1884 or 1885 a new building was erected. Records show that in 1886 Rev. R. A. Beauchamp had been called to pastor the church. During his pastorate the church in October, 1891, entertained the association.

On Sunday morning, March 10, 1922, a violent windstorm demolished the old building. No time was lost in erecting a new one, which was dedicated October 29, 1922. The dedication sermon was delivered by Rev. G. L. Ellis who used the subject, "My Father's House."

Those who have pastored the church since 1886 are Revs. R. A. Beauchamp, F. F. Moore, G. L. Ellis, C. H. Bell, H. E. Watters, Rev. Wilbanks, Earl Gooch, W. A. Butler, Rev. Padfield, Charles Felts, G. T. Mayo, E. L. Carr, W. A. Gardner, Earl Ferrell, O. L. Reeves, H. D. Hagar, V. L. Richardson and J. B. Andrews.

Historians for church: Mrs. J. L. Holt, Sr., and Mrs. Sam Corum.

OBION COUNTY HISTORY

MACEDONIA BAPTIST CHURCH

One of Obion County's oldest Baptist church organizations is that of the Macedonia Baptist Church near Kenton. It was on July 18, 1832, that the church was first constituted by Baptist pioneers living in that community. A church house was built but as was the case in many communities the church building became inadequate and was torn down. Thereafter Sunday school and church was held in a neighboring schoolhouse. Soon this proved too small in size and the official board of the church authorized the erection of a new church house. Such a building was erected in 1899 and has served the people of this community for many years. However, due to the continued growth of the church and Sunday school, it was necessary to add three new Sunday school rooms. While this work was being done the entire building was renovated by painting inside and out, putting in new windows and doors, and generally remodeling the building.

In July, 1932, the church celebrated with appropriate services the One-Hundredth Anniversary of its founding.

The present pastor is Rev. J. L. Robertson, of Jackson, Tenn. Among the church officers are Oran Warix of Kenton, treasurer; Harbard Patterson of Kenton superintendent of the Sunday School; Mrs. Harbard Patterson, Kenton, president of the W. M. S., and Mrs. C. F. Flowers, Kenton, who for the past twenty years has served as clerk of the church. Church membership totals 174 with 149 enrolled in the Sunday School in 1939.

MOUNT MORIAH BAPTIST CHURCH

According to available records the Mount Moriah Baptist church, located west of Obion, Tenn., was constituted in 1893. In this same year, or possibly some earlier, the present church building was erected. It is said that Mr. Jack Beard hauled the sills and planed the lumber by hand that was used in the construction of this church. Still evidence are the old fashioned square nails that were used in its construction. After the fashion of the day the one large room, seating 300, was built with an eighteen-foot ceiling. The church is situated upon a white oak tract containing nearly two acres.

In connection with the church property there is a five-acre cemetery that is well cared for by the cemetery association of the church. An interesting story in connection with this cemetery is told about Tom Russell, a settler in this neighborhood and a pioneer churchman. Prior to the constituting of the present church there was an old neighborhood log church used by the community. This church stood near the present church grounds and the present cemetery. Mr. Russell requested that he be the first person to be buried on the grounds of the old log church.

OBION COUNTY HISTORY

Upon his death in 1849 his wish was carried out and thus began the large five-acre cemetery which now serves this community. The old log church is still standing across the road from the present church.

The present membership at large consists of about 228, with an active membership of about 71. There is no record of the church having ever been without a pastor. The pastor, Rev. A. B. Harrison of Obion, conducts services on each fourth Sunday. The present clerk is Mr. Dave Miller of near Obion, Tenn.

MOUNT OLIVE BAPTIST CHURCH

Constituted at Old Shiloh, afterwards known as Old Republican Meeting-house, Mount Olive Baptist Church, now located near Crystal, was organized July 22, 1844, Elder H. Halliburton and Jefferson Taylor officiating as ministers in charge. The following names were recorded as charter members: Jessie Glover, Polly Glover, Jobe Fare, John H. Fare, James H. Fare, Calvin Cloar, Elder George White, Julius Davis, John C. Misdom, Ann Good, E. D. Hickman, Julius A. Iler. M. L. Glover, Obdieme Glover, John Y. Brown, Berry Hickman.

Some time after the organization the church was moved to its location on the old Hickman and Troy road,

Ministers called to serve the congregation, recalled as near as possible, were as follows:

George White, Jefferson Taylor, R. A. Beauchamp, Dr. C. P. Glover, Tom Moore, J. H. Milburn, O. D. Watson, O. W. Taylor, L. P. Flemming, Lum Hall, Roger L. Clark, R. J. Williams, C. V. Prince, O. T. Phillips, David H. Halliburton, James Ware, R. A. Coleman, Rev. Williams, Tom Petty, W. B. Clifton, L. W. Russell, H. E. Watters, N. M. Stigler, W. A. Butler, Joe Clapp, W. H. Kuykendall, Rev. Andrews, Teddy Evans, W. H. Hargrove.

Members of the church called on to furnish the records, Frank Scott, M. L. Glover, W. E. Gray, S. D. Grooms, are descendants of the charter members, the grandparents, great grand parents and great-great grandparents of some of the younger generations connected with the church.

NEW EBENEZER C. P. CHURCH

Located about four or five miles west of Troy one finds the New Ebenezer Cumberland Presbyterian Church, a church that for over ninety years has been serving the citizens of this farming community. This church was organized following and as a result of a revival of religion at Ebenezer "meeting house" in the month of October, 1848. About thirty souls were converted during this service. The officiating ministers were Rev. John Ward and F. E. Roberts. The organization was perfected on December 3, 1848, with forty-six charter members, including most of the new converts and others coming by transfer from other congregations.

Early records indicate that Benjamin Garrison and David Hubbard were ordained to the office of ruling elders, as were also G. W. L. Marr and William Reeves, and following their ordination were elected to that office in the new congregation.

Among the ministers who have served this congragation were John W. Ward, 1849; E. D. Farris, 1863; A. I. Owen, 1876; J. B. Calhoun and others, these being only a few of the early ministers.

From available records it is found that at least 726 names have been enrolled upon the church roll, of whom about 75 joined upon profession of faith, the remainder by transfer from other congregations.

New Ebenezer has fostered an evergreen Sunday School for more than half a century, which has more than 100 enrolled and an average attendance of about 80. The school and church are now in new class rooms built for the Sunday school. The present pastor is A. D. Salisbury of Halls, and the clerk of the session, Mr. John G. Cunningham.

BAPTIST CHURCH AT GIBBS

Election of officers and teachers for the Gibbs Baptist Church in 1940 resulted as follows: Woodrow W. Emery, superintendent; Alvin Eddington, assistant superintendent; Westell Easley, secretary and treasurer.

Teachers elected were: R. E. Goulder, Woodrow W. Emery, Lynn Evanson, Mrs. Rebecca Ray, Mrs. Helen Bruer, Mary Woodfin, Mrs. Birdie King. Mrs. Lucile Pruett, pianist and Alvin Eddington, choir leader for the Sunday school and church.

Rev. Wm. R. Shelby, of Martin, in 1940 was elected to serve the church for half time, beginning his first year in October. Mrs. Rebecca Ray was elected church clerk and Alvin Eddington, treasurer.

CUMBERLANDS AT CAMPGROUND

The Cumberland Presbyterian Church at Campground, southwest of Troy a few miles, celebrated its centennial anniversary on the fifth Sunday in June, 1930, with sermon by Rev. Hamp McLeskey and other appropriate exercises. The church was organized in 1830, with the following charter members: Wm. McCullom and wife, Wilford Farris, Sr., Wm. Pickard and wife, Sam Sampson and wife, Mr. and Mrs. Wm. Walls, Mr. Farris and others.

During the life of the church old ministers serving the congregation were Rev. Jack Ward, 1830-60; Rev. Joe B. Calhoun, 1860-81; Revs. John A. Dunlap, J. N. Bryson, J. G. Braley, Geo. McIlwaine, John A. McIlwaine.

In the records of the church the professions of religion include the names of James Harper, E. D. Farris, R. H. Marshall and the elder Garrison.

POLK A. R. P. CHURCH

The first preaching services to be recorded were held by Rev. J. P. Weed at Old Horseshoe. He preached Sabbath afternoon once a month until Rev. T. P. Pressly came to Troy in 1875 and took charge of the work. These services were continued until the fall of 1886 when they were changed to Baker's schoolhouse later to the schoolhouse at Polk, more central location. A Sabbath school was organized at Baker's. Mr. Lee S. Lancaster was the first superintendent, Mr. R. C. Moss, assistant.

A congregation was organized March 31, 1900, and in the same year a church building was erected. Mr. J. W. Scearce gave the lot where the building now stands. Cost of the building was $1300. On September 29, 1900, the building was dedicated. The sermon was preached by Rev. T. G. Boyce, with Rev. T. P. Pressly in charge. The first elders were W. J. Erwin and J. B. Buchanan. Deacons: Samuel G. Erwin and W. J. Caskey.

Rev. T. P. Pressly supplied as pastor until 1902, when Rev. E. P. Lindsay was sent as supply and the church continued with supply pastors.

In the year 1904 Ross Brown and Wm. R. Lancaster were ordained elders, David Guy and W. S. Smith deacons. Rev. Lindsay remained as pastor until November, 1906. After his resignation arrangements were made for him to continue as supply, which he did until February 26, 1911. Mr. Lindsay then gave his full time to Rives and Union City. Without a pastor for some time, the congregation was supplied from the different ministers of the Presbytery. Rev. M. R. Gibson served as supply for two months in 1912. Rev. W. O. Wier supplied until September 5, 1915, when he accepted a call and was installed as pastor December 12, 1915.

On January 9, 1916, J. L. Peery and James Cunningham were elected as elders, B. W. Buchanan, Robert Cunningham and Paul Erwin as deacons. These officers were installed March 12, 1916.

Upon the death of Rev. Wier in 1916 the congregation was again without a pastor. Rev. T. P. Pressly then supplied until January 14, 1917, when Rev. J. L. Boyd took charge of the work. The relation was continued until June 1, 1920, when Rev. Boyd accepted a call to Brighton, Tenn.

Rev. J. A. Baird supplied the congregation during the summer of 1921. Rev. B. Dale White supplied the congregation during the summer of 1922.

Rev. L. R. Niell preached his first sermon as pastor the second Sabbath of November, 1922, and is still on the field.

BEECH C. P. CHURCH

About three miles southwest of Union City there is located one of Obion County's pioneer churches. The Beech C. P. Church was organized in 1857 with 14 members. Through the influence of Thomas Latimer, Sr., Jack Latimer, Sr., and Rev. Wm. Guthrie, the first church was organized and the first building erected.

"Beech" was not named as some might suppose from having been built in the midst of a beech forest, but from "Old Beech Church" in Sumner County, Tennessee, which had been the church home of a number of the county's early settlers.

Beech deserves the distinction of being a pioneer church, its first building having been erected soon after the first settlement of farmers in this particular section of Obion County.

Rev. Guthrie presided at the organization of the church, ordained the elders, preached the dedication sermon, and served as the first pastor. Among the first church officials were Messrs. Thomas Latimer, Sr., Jack Latimer, Jr., and Caldwell Pleasant. There were forty accessions to the church during the first year as a result of a revival.

Succeeding Rev. Guthrie as pastor was Rev. Charles McBride, who served from 1858 to 1866. During his pastorate Messrs. T. B. Joyner, D. A. Latimer, Joe and Samuel Calhoun and P. G. Hamilton were ordained as elders. Succeeding ministers up to 1874 were Revs. Weir, Webb, Farris, and McCutcheon.

A new church building house of worship was erected under the influence of the church's pastor. Rev. W. B. Cunningham. The church was dedicated in May, 1912.

An active Sunday school and young people's department, in connection with church aid, give to this church and community a spiritual blessing. Pastor is Rev. Russell Tatum.

MOUNT ZION METHODIST CHURCH

Mount Zion Methodist Church, first located at a school called Greenbrier, where it was organized in 1845, was provided with a house of worship built of logs in 1847 on a site selected by Gideon Bransford, father of the late Rev. E. K. Bransford, the vicinity afterwards the home place of J. A. McGaugh. W. B. McConnell and J. G. McMurry were associated with Mr. Bransford in locating the church. A delegation of volunteers met on the ground with axes to cut and hew the logs for the building.

The land was donated by S. C. DeBow. Rev. Bob Gregory was presiding elder and Rev. E. L. Ragland was pastor. Bennet Marshall and James W. Bransford were class leaders.

This log building was completely wrecked in 1856 by a falling tree. In the fall of that year negro slaves cut and hauled the logs to be sawed for a new building. It was erected in 1857 and stood until 1906, when it was replaced by the brick building, a substantial and comfortable home for the congregation and its church work. It is significant that the brick work was contracted to T. L. Bransford, son of the man first to engage in the work done on the old building, and T. H. McMurry, son of J. G. McMurry who was also a workman hewing logs.

The new church was dedicated May 2, 1909, Rev. S. F. Wynn preaching the sermon. Ministers present for the dedication were: Revs. Simpson, Weaver, J. H. Witt, T. J. McGill, C. D. Hilliard, R. E. Brassfield, W. C. Waters, A. C. Moore, former pastors, and the late pastor, Rev. C. C. Newbill. The trustees were: M. P. McMurry, A. K. McConnell, J. M. Glenn. Among the Sunday School Superintendents serving the church were: W. L. Alexander, A. E. Brevard, D. D. DeBow, J. H. Carter, S. S. Alexander, T. H. McMurry, Marshall DeBow, Samuel DeBow, Robert L. Cloys, S. C. DeBow, C. W. Brevard, Jr., and R. J. Glover.

Miss Queenie Majors organized a Missionary Society in 1890. A Junior Missionary Society was organized in 1900 by Mrs. Kate Reeves of Cayce. Miss Nellie Bowen, elected Lady Manager of Missions, volunteered and went to China as Missionary, and after several years in service died on the Mission Field.

An Epworth League was organized in 1897 by Rev. and Mrs. Albert C. Moore. A second organization was led by Miss Annie Murphy. Another was formed under the leadership of Rev. J. T. Walker in 1931.

Revival meetings beginning with the work of Rev. James G. Purtle in 1871, were continued by Rev. Pewitt, resulting in the salvation of sinners and revival of the church, in great numbers. The second revival was held in 1914, under the preaching of Rev. H. A. Butts. In one class there were 38 additions to the church.

The records show a membership of 155, with the following officers in charge: C. G. McMurry, C. W. Brevard, J. B. McGehee, H. D. Roberts, R. J. Glover, T. H. McMurry, P. G. Browder, Mrs. P. G. Browder, Mrs. J. A. McGaugh, Miss Mary Crabtree and Mrs. I. W. Crabtree.

PLEASANT VALLEY CHURCH

Pleasant Valley Church was organized in 1875. A school building and a brush arbor were used and the schoolhouse as a place of worship for a period of approximately ten years. This was the locality of the late W. M. Stone residence. The organization resulted from the labors of Rev. T. L. Wood, of Ralston, and Rev. J. H. Roberts of the Union City station.

In 1884 a lot just north of the school building was deeded by J. W. Ward and wife to James Luton, E. T. Jernigan, J. R. Oliver, A. T. White, W. L. White, J. B. Ward and S M. Stone, trustees, and a frame building erected as a house of worship. This house was used until 1914 when it was replaced by a suitable and comfortable brick building during the pastorate of Rev. Albert C. Moore.

During this period of more than sixty years only four Sunday School Superintendents have served—J. R. Oliver, J. B. Akin, F. S. White and G. B. White, Sr., the last named from 1889. Blessed with health and missing only those Sundays when called to his duty as undertaker, Mr. White's administration has continued for almost half a century. During that time fifty-four teachers have taught in the Sunday School and eighteen entered the public schools as teachers.

Members of the church in 1940 enrolled 88, with officers as follows: G. B. White, Sr., W. M. Stone, Cecil Stone, Billy Moss, V. D. McCord, Lloyd Riley, E. M. Stone, A. Harris, David Byrn, Sally Byrn.

This church is located in a fine community and the people have been very liberal and loyal to church work.

ANTIOCH UNION CHURCH

A country church of brick veneer, very inviting and comfortable, the Antioch church is located one mile west of Crystal and eleven miles west of Union City. This for more than three-quarters of a century has been a church union of Cumberland and Methodist congregations. The first building was a log house, and the date of church organization is not available. Land for the present building was deeded by J. B. Hudson to J. E. Park, D. W. Owen, W. F. Gray, trustees of the Cumberland Church and A. Cloar, A. B. Williams and John K. Williams, trustees of the Methodist Church. Deed was made in 1875. A frame church built in 1874 was replaced by the new church in 1926.

Among the pastors serving from the Methodist organization appeared the names of W. C. Sellars, J. H. Collins, R. M. King, J. A. Russell, J. R. Bell, J. V. Fly, J. E. Jones, C. D. Evans, T. G. Lowery, E. E. Spears, W. A. Lambkin, E. W. Maxedon, W. A. Banks, Humbert Weir, Sam McLaughlin, Walter Jones, P. D. T. Roberts, Sam Martin, and R. A. Stanfill. On the part of the Cumberlands the following are recalled: Jo McLeskey, C. H. Cobb, Abe Owens, Joe B. Calhoun, W. M. Robinson, E. D. Farris, B. L. Holder, W. B. Cunningham, R. E. White, G. P. McIlwaine, E. M. Jennings, O. A. Gardner and Rev. Leonard.

OBION COUNTY HISTORY

Many citizens making worthy contributions to the church include: J B. Hudson, Dr. F. M. McRee, W. F. Gray, W. I. McDaniel, W. O. Jordan, D. E. Park, J. E. and Leon Park, Jake Caldwell, T. B. Underwood, Gus Lancaster, H. G. Reeves, R. L. Cummings, Alex Hudson, Dr. E. L. Williams, Tom Council, Jerry Cloar, A. Cloar, A. B. Williams, John K. Williams, Dee Cole, W. J. Johnson, Mrs. Sarah Council, Mrs. Lee Williams, Mrs. Mattie White, Bee and John Covington, H. D. Park, and many others.

Eldership of the Cumberland church include: A. O. McDaniel, J. F. Powell, Marvin Vaught, J. Malone, John Hudson, Jas Threlkeld, J. A. Bumpious, W. A. Cravens. The present official roll of the Methodist church include: W. A. Council, W. P. Vaught, Mrs. Kate Hudson, Mrs. Dick Barksdale, R. L. Kersey, J. B. Wheeler, Mrs. Vern Brewer, Rev. M. Youree Rev. J. M. Kendall.

SALEM CHURCH

This church is located five miles northwest of Union City on a beautiful five-acre plot of land well shaded. The land was deeded by Jas. R. Powell in 1851 to Bob Marshall, Ben Marshall, Louis Patton, Samuel McDaniel and Jas Powell, trustees. The first house was built of logs, replaced after twenty-five years with frame building, which during the present century was wrecked by a storm, and another frame building of more suitable construction took its place.

The congregation of Salem is small, a total of thirty-two members, but for most part they are loyal and active. Preaching services are held once a month on the first Sunday morning at 10 o'clock. Officers of the church are: J. M. Marshall, J. C. Pruett, Porter Harris, L. K. Marshall, Mrs. E. A. Ratcliff, Mrs. J. C. Pruett.

SHADY GROVE CHURCH

This church is located four and one-half miles northeast of Union City. New building, erected in 1911, takes the place of three others, which have served the congregation for a long existence. The church was built on a lot given by O. H. Anderson and wife and deeded to G. H. Bynum, J. R. Edwards, B. E. P. Mathews, Wm. S. Hubbs, E. H. Verhine, W. G. Bynum, and Robt. Mathews, trustees of the Methodist church.

Former officers of the church include: J. S. Cloys, M. R. Box, W. S. Hubbs, J. F. Bloodworth, S. L. Sherrell, G. W. Mitchell, E. D. Mansfield, R. H. Hubbs, J. C. McClard, Officers: H. H. Council, Herman Keene, C. D. Williams, Lewis McClard, Marshall Mitchell, Mrs. H. H. Council, Mrs. Nell Gordon, Mrs. Vivian Coates, J. B. Woodfin, Warren Mitchell, Membership is small and not close by.

OBION COUNTY HISTORY

COUNTY HIGHWAYS

It is very probable that the citizens of Obion county, not being thoroughly familiar with the Obion County Highway System, do not appreciate what a wonderful asset this is to our community. It is, therefore, the purpose of this article to set forth a few interesting facts on this system.

The system in operation is under the able supervision of Mr. A. L. Burrus, Supervisor, and the commission composed of the following:

Charles Everett, chairman, zone 1, districts 1 and 16; Russell Meek, zone 2, districts 4 and 7; Russell Henderson, zone 3, districts 8 and 11; Waller Whipple, zone 4, districts 3 and 12; J. C. McRee, zone 5, districts 3 and 12; H. D. Smith, zone 6, districts 5 and 9; W. P. Beard, zone 7, districts 6, 14 and 15. T. M. Flack, bookkeeper.

It is a well known fact that our county rates among the first four of the ninety-five counties in Tennessee for operating efficiency, and it is without question the leading county among all other counties of its size in the State.

We can fully appreciate the value of the system to us when we stop to consider the following facts:

"There are, at present, sixty men employed on a full time basis". "The average pay roll amounts approximately to $1,057.00 per week." "The system operates sixteen gravel trucks, which are consistently in operation, supplying material for the construction of new roads or the repairing of bad roads."

"The trucks are operated with the utmost economy, due to the fact that they are kept in perfect mechanical condition by the system's own mechanics, and in their own garage; and also due to the fact that one-half of them are traded each year. This procedure eliminates any large depreciation and prevents any unnecessary loss of time due to any worn-out equipment."

"Along this same line all purchasing is done on a basis of competitive bids, and these purchases must meet all required specifications. In order to get the best possible prices on commodities which are used extensively the system purchases in large quantities gasoline, oils and greases in tank, car and carload lots. This affords a considerable saving on these items. The gravel for the construction and mantenance of the roads is purchased from individuals on whose farms it is available. A fair price is paid for this gravel and it is hauled by the county's own trucks."

In order to appreciate and fully understand the efficiency with which this system is operated, let us look into their means of getting money for these purchases. The tax rate for Obion county is $1.88 and the State tax is 8 cents, making a total of

OBION COUNTY HISTORY

$1.96. Of this amount the Highway Commission is allotted 43 cents. It also has a further allotment of 2 cents per gallon out of the local State tax on gasoline of 7 cents. Bringing these allotments down we see that our county receives approximately $55,000 annually out of the gas tax and receives from the county approximately $65,000. This is the total amount allotted for the highway system operation annually.

The latest figures available reveal that under our present system Obion county has the following: "110.5 miles of State roads, 600 miles of county gravel roads and 125 miles of county dirt roads." This makes a total of 835½ road miles in Obion county.

It is interesting to note the rapidity with which the dirt roads are being converted into gravel roads, and we are further told that within a short time the remaining 125 miles of dirt roads will be converted into gravel. This rapid conversion has been made possible by a special allotment of 43 cents. This was granted for a four-year period for the purpose of buying new equipment to thus enable them to gravel the 450 miles of dirt roads in existence at the time. It is interesting to note that this program is almost two-thirds completed in about one-half the time designated. This is, indeed a fine tribute to the Supervisor and the personnel of our county highway system.

Of interest to the people of Obion County is the fact that the Obion County Highway Commission has purchased equipment enabling them to construct concrete tile from 15 to 42 inches in diameter. These tiles are being used extensively for the construction of culverts and for replacement of obsolete and worn out wooden culverts. In order to make this program effective it was necessary to purchase $4500 worth of equipment. This equipment is now in operation pouring cement concrete into the forms, of sizes mentioned, and in one year from April, 1939, when the outfit was installed, about thirteen thousand feet, lineal measure, of culverts were made.

It may be mentioned at this time that these culverts formerly had to be purchased at a much higher cost then that of 68 cents per foot, at which the county now constructs them. Another interesting fact is that these culverts are permanent fixtures and will not soon decay like the old wooden culverts with an average life of three years.

The old district commissioner system, which was operative in the county until 1923, was changed by the County Court, under an enabling act of the Legislature, to that of a County Supervisor and a Department of County Highways. J. W. Buchanan was elected and served six years until 1929, the department constructing 125 miles of improved highways. County Road Bonds in a

OBION COUNTY HISTORY

total of $200,000 were issued in 1927, and short-term notes, at different times, issued for road and county purposes.

Since A. L. Burrus was inducted into the office of Supervisor in 1929, at his own suggestion, the county has provided for highway construction without a single issue of county bonds for road purposes. The highway tax has been fixed at a rate very little in excess of the former tax, which has been ample to serve the purpose.

It is also a creditable record for the County Highway Department that since the administration of Mr. Burrus 600 miles of improved gravel county highways have been constructed, with the prospect of soon completing the work of the remaining county road system of approximately 125 miles.

Through the efficency of Mr. Tom Flack, the Department bookkeeper, a complete and thorough record of operation is maintained. With this record the Supervisor is able at all times to proceed with a full knowledge of the work at hand and of the various cost and expense items attached to the operations of the Department.

LOCAL HIGHWAYS

1. Troy to Mount Pelia—Rives, Central Hi-School — 15.5
2. Troy to Mason Hall—Turnpike Levee — 10.5
3. Trimble to Kenton—Mason Hall, Beech Valley — 17.5
4. Central High—Hinson, Shipp Levee, Alamo church — 16.5
5. Burnt Mill Hollow—Hornbeak, Glass, Sharps Ferry — 9.5
6. Obion—Minnick, Elbridge, Lake Co. Line — 15.5
7. Jackson Hill—Hornbeak, Elbridge, Cloverdale — 11.6
8. Foothill—Push, Gratio, Dyer County Line — 14.0
9. Shawtown—Protemus, Cobb's Chapel — 12.5
10. Hickman To Troy—Crystal, Jim Gray's, Ky. Line — 11.0
11. Union City to Mount Zion—Beulah, Ky. Line — 7.3
12. Burrus—A. L. Brevard, Crystal, Gus Lancaster — 11.0
13. Section Line—Across St. Hi. 3.22 and Henry Moss — 10.6
14. Union City to Fulton—Bob Holman, Chapel Hill — 16.0
15. Woodland to Harris—Lindenwood, Hastings Cor. — 15.5
16. Frank Sellars—Johnson Grove, Bud Gossum — 5.0
17. Troy to Protemus—Mineral Springs, Jim Hickman — 12.5
18. Walnut Log—McQueen's Store, Ky. State Line — 7.3
19. Bruer and Wheeler—Antioch church, Ky. State Line — 7.2
20. Campground—Troy, Mount Moriah — 7.5
21. Bennett and Darnell—Troy, Co. Road at Mount Moriah — 7.5
22. Polk Station—Albert Cross, Polk, Bill Erwin — 7.2
23. Mason Hall-Trimble—Gaulden Farm, Co. Hi. 3 — 5.0
24. Tom Finch—Mason Hall, Union Grove Church — 6.0
25. Sam Finch—Christian Chapel, Concord church — 4.5

OBION COUNTY HISTORY

26 Will Dickenson—Co. Highway, No. 1, Weakley Co. _____ 4.5
27 Old Martin Highway—Sunnyside School, Weakley _____ 3.5
28 Will Parish—Co. Hiway 27, Jodie Jacob _____ 8.5
29 Herman Carter—Meeks, Ellis Wagster, Hiway 4 _____ 5.5
30 Oscar Nanny—Rucker's Cor. McConnell, J. Parrish _____ 5.5
31 Bob Rowland—Co. Hiway 30, Weakley Co. Line _____ 2.0
32 Walnut Grove—Church, Speights, Killebrew _____ 6.1
33 Rufus Sellars—Finch, Houston, Stubblefield _____ 5.0
34 Horace Reams—Ky. State Line, Lee Reeves, Jolly _____ 4.5
35 Barnhart—Ky. St. Line, Gibbs, McDade, Peeples _____ 6.4
36 Pleasant Hill School—Rives, Phebus, St. Hi. 3 _____ 6.5
37 Miles—Miles Farm, Reece Alexander, Joyners _____ 5.0
38 Let Houser—Campbell, Houser, Moffatt _____ 8.5
39 Oats Hill—Minnick, Co. Hiway No. 8 _____ 5.0
40 Sharps Ferry and Cloverdale—No. 5, Bud Phillips _____ 7.5
41 Will Short—Hornbeak, Webb's Store, Lake Co. Line _____ 6.6
42 Lum Smith—Fowlerdale, Bud Barker, Zion School _____ 10.0
43 Ernest Wisner—Zion School, Co. Hiway 39 _____ 3.5
44 Putnam Hill—Co. Hiway 42, 8 _____ 3.5
45 Ebenezer and Liberty—Ebenezer church, Boston Store _____ 2.5
46 Mill Creek—Boston Store, Eve Williams, Willett _____ 7.3
47 Bogus Hollow—Joe McBride, Chas Cloar _____ 5.0
48 Mt. Manuel Church—Co. Hiway 18, Thelbert Rogers _____ 5.7
49 Buck Escue—Robertson, Wilson, McCain, Frazier _____ 6.5
50 Maupin and Hayes—County Hiway 10, Owen Bridge _____ 8.0
51 Bethel Hollow—Beech church, Old Maupin, Protemus _____ 7.0
52 Samburg and Odd Treece—Shaw's Store, B. Fraley _____ 5.7
53 Ira Wright—O. Sturgis, Wright's, Oak Ridge _____ 9.5
54 Clint Word—St. Hiway 29, Hank Miller, Co. Hiways 5 _____ 4.9
55 Key Road—Dee Haislip, John Culberson, Hiway 45, 46 _____ 6.5
56 State Line—Dresden Road, Thedron Wheeler, Gray _____ 10.2
57 Walter Whipple—Antioch church, C. Edwards, Duncan _____ 6.2
58 Dan Marshall—Whipple, Cloar, Marshall, Graham _____ 5.7
59 Salem church—Hiway 5, M. Flippin, Co., St. Hiway 3 _____ 7.5
60 County Farm—B. Latimer, B. Rone, Rock Springs _____ 5.2
61 Sanders Chapel—Dallas Hill, Hugh Catron, Hiway 51 _____ 4.6
62 Marshall Kirk—Jackson, Clayton, Reelfoot church _____ 6.6
63 Arch Thompson—Ky. St. Line, Thompson and Brevard _____ 4.0
64 Walter Morris—Harris Sta., Albert Owens, Ky. St. Line _____ 4.8
65 Pierce Sta.—Hutchison Cor., Pierce, Browder _____ 4.2
66 Black Lane—Co. Hiway 2, McDonald, Co. Hiway 22 _____ 5.9
67 Bates Anderson—L. Maxwell, Andrews, Sardis church _____ 5.9
68 Macedonia church—Co. Hiway 3, Flowers, W. Co. Line _____ 7.0
69 Larry Finch—Hiway 24, Georgetown, Hiway 23 _____ 4.5
70 Harman Caudle—Co. Hiway 24, Co. Hiway 2 _____ 2.6
71 Mayme Stovall—Co. Hiway 1, Gardner Farm, Hiway 27 _____ 4.0

OBION COUNTY HISTORY

72 Bob Hamilton—Stovall's Cemetery, Owens Farm 5.0
73 Ben Taylor—St. Hiway 22, George Janes, Hiway 4, 27,.. 3.2
74 Beaver Arm—Cashtown, Ernest Murrell, St. Hiway 78 ___ 3.0
75 Beeler—Hiway 8, Beeler Farm, Lake Co. Line _____ 4.2
76 Ivy Lippard—Elbridge, Lippard Farm, Hiway 42 _____ 1.6
77 Robert Woods—Co. Hiway 53 and 7 ____ ___ 5.0
78 Joe Kendall—Cobb's Chapel, C. Davis, Antioch church _ 3.6
79 Earl Jones and Ligon—Co. Hiway 37 and 1 _____ 5.8
80 Walker Tanner—Hiway 3, Wade Wiley, Hiway 37, Mott _ 3.0
81 Bud Phebus—Higay 22, Thos. Clark, Hiway 38, 80 ____ 2.6
82 Wilson and Ernest Maloney—Hiway 6, Elbridge, Dyer ___ 4.6
83 Clarence Fox and Frank Lawson—Woods School ____ 8.5
84 McSpedden—Hiway 4, Gene McSpedden, Hiway 28 ___ 2.4
85 Dolphus Leigh—Hiway 26, Leighs, Hiway 1 _____ 1.4
86 Briston Hall and Griffin, Hiway 27, Hiway 1 _____ 3.0
87 J. C. Walker—Hiway 4, Cully McRee Crockett Sta. _____ 3.0
88 Raymond Caudle—Hiway 4, Cane Creek, Hiway 72 _____ 1.0
89 Taylor Moore—Hiway 4, Dennis Crockett ___ _____ 2.4
90 Oak Grove and Bruce Switch—Hiway 24, 25, No. 5 _____ 5.0
91 Hurt—Hiway 24, Hiway 3, Concord Church Road ___ 6.0
92 Concord Church—Hiway 3, C. Chapel, Oak Grove. H. 24 2.8
93 Jim Midyett—Hiway 92, Farm, Hiway 25, St. Hiway 5 ___ 2.0
94 Cody Lane—Hiway 24, 90 ___ _____ 0.5
95 Dan Pierce—Hiway 69, Hiway 2 _____ 1.5
96 Old Fulton and Martin Road—Horace Reams, Fry ___ 3.0
97 Ed Mansfield—Hiway 14, Mansfield, Fowlkes, Owens ___ 5.3
98 David Crockett—Hiway 97, Crockett and Love _____ 3.0
99 Cheatham—Hiway 30, Cheatham's ___ _____ 2.0
100 Cravens—Hastings Corner, Bess Morris _____ 2.0
101 Jack Douglas—Ky. State Line, Hiway 15 _____ 4.1
102 Davidson and Taylor Bros.—Ky. State Line, Cardwell _ 5.0
103 Nash—Hiway 101, Nash Place, Hiway 13 _____ 3.3
104 John Robertson—Hiway 65, 64 _____ 2.0
105 Claud Tucker—Jordan Road, Buck Hubbs, D. Ragsdale _ 5.5
106 Gibbs and Shady Grove—Hiway 22, Church, Hiway 105 _ 3.0
107 Ed Reese—Hiway 106, 13 __ _____ 1.3
108 Bethlehem Church—Hiway 15, Church, Hiway 3 _____ 1.5
109 Clifford Reeves—Hiway 11, P. Browder, H. Woods ___ 3.5
110 Hubert Harris—Hiway 109, H. Harris, Hiway 105____ 1.1
111 Dock Reeves—Jordan Road _____ 2.1
112 Puss Erwin—Hiway 22, D. Roney, I. C. Railroad ____ 1.5
113 Carter Road—Hiway 14, Carter's, Hiway 22 _____ 1.0
114 Andrew Wheeler—Hiway 12, Wheeler, Hiway 22 _____ 1.0
115 Knox Glover—Woodland, Bess Glover, Hiway 15 _____ 3.0
116 Wiley Neeley—Hiway 1, Neeley, Hiway 36 _____ 1.5
117 Tobe Hampton—Hiway 2, Brown Sanders _____ 1.6

118 Garrett Williams—Hiway 22, Joe B. Vaught   2.7
119 Hubert Bruer—Ky. State Line, Bruer, Hiway 19   2.2
120 Rives Road—Wade Moss, Don Simpson, Hiway 36   1.7
121 Warren and Petty—Hiway 120, 37   2.7
122 Clint Callicott—Hiway 5, Latimer, Hiway 22   2.0
123 Cleveland Brown—Hiway 51, Frank Brown, Hiway 17   1.5
124 Blackley Road—Hiway 52, Blackley Place, Hiway 78   3.0
125 Arch Corum—Hiway 9, Corum, Hiway 9   1.3
126 Luther Davis and Lyons—Sam Davis, Glady H. Church 5.0
127 Little Obion Church—Hiway 7, Zion School, Dyer   3.5
128 Simrell—Hiway 7, Dyer County Line   1.5
129 Long Lane—Lawson's Store, Field Place, Hiway 82   3.4
130 Henry Evans—Hiway 43, Evans, Hiway 8   2.1
131 Inman Hollow—Hiway 39, Hollow, Hiway 6   2.1
132 Jack Long and Sharp—Hiway 21, Hiway 3   2.6
133 Bob Rowland, Hale School—Hiway 11, Lon Corum   2.5
134 Norman—Weakley Co. Line, Mrs. Roach, Hiway 34   1.8
135 Jim Morgan—Hiway 22, Etheridge, Hiway 13   0.7
136 Harrison—Renfro, Wess Davis, Hiway 3, Ky. State L 1.8
137 Sudie DeBow—Hiway 15, DeBow, Ky. State Line   1.0
138 Geo. Kendall—Ira Wright, Kendall, Mt. Moriah   1.5
139 Bob Slough—Hiway 22, Samburg, Hiway 21   3.5

        Total   716.7

STATE HIGHWAYS — OBION COUNTY PROJECTS — 1938

	Miles		Cost	Complete
Union City to Troy	9.470	Cement - Concrete	$302,331.09	11-16-24
Bridges to span	0.034		30,615.28	12- 1-23
Union City to Ky. State line	10.038	G. and D.	48,689.41	7- 8-27
Bridges to span	0.035		40,863.09	12- 3-26
Pave surface	10.029	Cement - Concrete	232,148.35	9-22-28
Tiptonville toward Union City	8.010	S. Tr. Cement - Concrete	106,265.55	7-31-24
Spillway-Reelfoot Lake	0.044		51,838.71	7-21-31
Obion to Troy	5.774	G. and D.	33,119.84	10- 3-27
Bridge to span	0.012		19,549.78	10- 3-27
Paving surface	5.799	Cement - Concrete	129,175.94	12-26-28
Weakley County Line to Kentucky State Line	6.570	G. and D.	59,536.18	4-22-29
Bridge to span	0.175		69,665.40	5-10-29
Paving surface	6.470	Cement - Concrete	111,821.63	12-24-30
Draining			997.43	3-14-30
Kenton to Pt. 4.5 miles— North Pt. 8 Mi. to Union City	13.267	Cement - Concrete	226,813.53	11-13-30
Appr. Bridges K.-Rives	1.784	Concrete Pave	49,055.58	6- 3-37
Street paving Union City	0.520	Cement - Concrete	40,970.37	7-19-34
Union City, No. to Ky. St. Line	6.681	G. and D. Gr.	46,672.23	7-19-34
Bridges to span	0.047		12,814.79	7-19-34
Union City to Ky. State Line	4.800	G. D. and Chert	41,248.51	10-20-36
Bridges to span	0.025		12,596.32	10-20-36
Hornbeak to Troy	8.021	G. and D.	76,214.08	10- 5-25
Bridges to span	0.009		15,305.31	10- 5-25
Hornbeak Project 71B to Reelfoot Lake	4.590	G. and D	40,623.91	8-20-25
Troy to Lake Co. Line	14.600	Surf Tr.	106,765.50	9-16-29
Obion to Lane Ferry	14.750	Gravel	39,555.06	11-12-26

Description	Miles	Type	Cost	Date
Union City to Weakley Co. Line	6.284	G. and D.	48,195.39	9- 5-27
Bridges to span	0.012		77,473.40	9-17-27
Pave surface	5.851	Cement - Concrete	116,538.21	1-15-29
Overhead I. C. at Gibbs	0.288		32,455.19	8-10-27
Approach I. C. R.R.			174.02	
Dyer Co. line to Lake Co. line	1.044	G. and D.	23,299.22	9- 6-29
Bridges to span	0.060		14,032.38	10- 8-28
Surf. Br.			922.46	3-28-32
Kenton to Union City	13.442	G. and D.	111,280.82	6- 6-29
Pt. 5 Mi. No. of Kenton to 8 Mi. So. of Union City	1.676	Grading	44,151.67	10-30-29
Obion R. Bridges	0.807	Bridges	273,986.29	12-13-29
Overhead I. C. Rives	0.432		35,831.55	3-14-30
M. Glady Hollow to Troy	13.000	Gravel	17,163.37	6-21-26
Troy to Obion	6.000	Gravel	6,498.45	3-16-26
Union City to Reelfoot Lake	22.000	Gravel	12,585.82	12- 5-27
Weakley Co. Line to Union City	7.700	Drainage	1,463.09	8- 7-30
So. End Obion River Bottom to North End	1.700	Gravel	14,561.46	3-31-33
Guard Rail			6,300.15	12- 3-30
Union City to Reelfoot Lake	23.500	Gravel	28,187.89	7- 7-31
Union City, Clayton, Samburg Road to Walnut Log	3.600	Gravel	1,000.00	2-27-31
Junction R.3, Union City to End Concrete R. 22	1.000	Gravel	7,964.44	10- 4-31
Union City to Woodland Rd	3.900	Gr. and Dr.	6,214.13	12- 1-35
Union City Resurf. and Seal	0.400		586.81	12- 1-34
Gibson Co. Line to Junction R. No. 3, 22, Union City	0.900	Tr. Br. Floors	3,538.19	11-15-37
Glady Hollows S. E. to North End	2.000	Heavy Mtce	4,028.21	11-15-37
Elbridge to Obion	8.000	Stone and Oil	6,790.00	4-21-38
Union City Municipal Project		Cement - Concrete	28,708.29	7-22-32

OBION COUNTY HISTORY

OBION BRIDGE PROJECTS

Between Dyer County Line and Obion:

	Miles	Cost	Complete
G. and D.	3.242	$ 52,644.35	4-19-28
Bridge	3.203	116,189.29	4-14-28
Cement - Concrete	0.212	9,656.14	12-26-28
Gravel	0.212	21,373.30	7-18-29
Surf. Tr.	0.476	12,000.58	9-30-36
Guard Rail		13,578.50	7-31-31

Between Obion and Trimble:

	Miles	Cost	Complete
Bridge	0.567	227,050.04	3-16-29

TOTAL MILEAGE 1940

State No.		Miles
3	Jeff Davis—Fulton to Dyer County Line	31.0
5	Union City-Kenton—Ky. State Line to Kenton	22.5
22	Union City-Martin—Weakley Co. Line to No. 22	29.0
21	Reelfoot Lake—Troy to Lake County Line	15.0
43	Fulton-Martin—Fulton to Weakley Co. Line	7.0
78	Dyersburg-Tiptonville—Lake Co. to Dyer Line	1.0
	Jordan Road—Union City to Jordan, Ky.	5.0

Total Mileage State Highways in Obion Co. _____110.5

COUNTY POLITICS

In the early years of Obion County no party nominations were made for candidates for county office. Conventions were held to nominate candidates for Congress and the General Assembly. The primary system was not instituted until late in the nineties, and they began with the nomination of candidates for county office. They were afterwards to include candidates for Congress, for Governor and for the General Assembly. The General Assembly was still authorized to name candidates for the United States Senate, and it was not until a general campaign was made by William Jennings Bryan to elect United States Senators by primary nomination that the election of Senators was changed to the primary system.

After that the convention system had no function except to name delegates to special conventions for the adoption of platforms and policies and for making constitutional changes.

There have been only two active political parties in Obion County and only one with the ruling majority. The Democratic party in the county has a record poll of more than eight out of ten votes cast in county elections.

Each party has its organization, the county executive committee, the primary commissioners, and the regularly constituted

OBION COUNTY HISTORY

Board of Election Commissioners. The last named is constituted with representatives of both political parties, organized as follows: C. L. Dismukes, chairman; Joe Gwaltney, secretary and J. C. Burdick.

The county Democratic Executive Committee is as follows: No. 1, R. J. Glover; 2, C. W. Brevard, Jr., 3, A. O. McDaniel; 4, Archie Cultra (chairman); 5 Claude C. Summers; 6 Mrs. B. B. Maxwell; 7, J. C. Walker; 8, W. M. Tankersley; 9, Dr. J. H. Dorgan; 10, Denzil Maupin; 11, R. O. Green; 12, Guy Calhoun; 13, David Walker Harris; 14, Lennie McCorkle; 15, Horace Yates; 16, Will Robey.

The Obion County Democratic Primary Board is as follows: Archie Cultra, C. C. Summers, R. O. Green, Horace Yates, Will Robey.

HEALTH DEPARTMENT

Broadly speaking, health agencies in Obion County may be divided into two groups: Those which are official in nature, and those which are unofficial. To the former belongs the Obion County Health Department. To this may be added such organizations as the Red Cross, the Tuberculosis Association, the Parent-Teacher Association and other civic bodies, which while not official in the sense that they are supported by public funds, do function in a public manner. The Central Planning Committee has as an objective the improvement of health in the county. Also a number of governmental agencies that have shown themselves to be thoroughly co-operative in their endeavors to improve the health of the people. In this group will be found the offices of the Board of Education, the County Farm Agent, the County Home Demonstration Agent, the Works Progress Administration, the Farm Security Administration and others. Included in the unofficial group are the doctors, the dentists, trained nurses, and the various hospitals. These may be considered the strong arm of the health department. The group in Obion County has been most co-operative in assisting in the work by the giving of time for the correction of physical defects in children as well as in teaching the fundamental principles of health to the citizens of the county. Likewise the various groups mentioned above have been of inestimable value in sponsoring various health activities.

Following its organization about 1922, the Obion County Health Department was quartered in various offices about town until five years ago when it was moved to the courthouse where offices were maintained until the old building was abandoned. At the present time, adequate offices are in a special building constructed for this purpose from funds provided from county and govermental sources. The building, constructed for a sum somewhat under $10,000, was paid for as follows:

OBION COUNTY HISTORY

PWA Grant, 45 per cent, Obion County 55 per cent.

One-half of the money advanced by the county is being repaid by the state in the form of a "monthly rental", so when the transaction is completed, this building, including a considerable new equipment, will have cost the county some $2,700.00. This, as will be seen, is an excellent investment.

At the present time, the staff consists of:

Health Officer, Dr. E. W. Barkdull; two nurses, Miss Violet Crook, Miss Margaret Mahoney; one sanitarian, Dr. John A. Caraway; one clerk, Miss Mildred Howard.

The department is supported cooperatively by the State Health Department, Obion County and the city of Union City. A further breakdown of funds shows that money coming from the State Health Department is derived from State funds proper, from the United States Public Health Service and from the Children's Bureau.

During the year 1938 there was one death from typhoid fever, one from whooping cough, none from diphtheria or scarlet fever. There were reported to the department two cases of typhoid fever and two of diphtheria. In the years that are past, before the people availed themselves of protective inoculations against these two diseases, they ranked high as a cause of death. There has not been a case of smallpox in the county in almost seven years.

Communicable disease control is one of the major activities of the department. During 1938 vaccinations were administered by health department personnel as follows:

Smallpox, 2454; diphtheria, under 1 year, 147; diphtheria, 1 to 5 years, 462; diphtheria, 5 years and over, 719; typhoid fever, 5169.

Records would indicate that 54 percent of the pre-school population of the county is immunized against diphtheria. Parents are urged to have given to their babies this protection at 6 months of age. A child is not considered to be immune until he is later tested for immunity and found to be negative.

In an effort to control the spread of syphilis and gonorrhea there is conducted a weekly clinic where treatment is given to indigent cases, stress being laid on early infective cases. During 1938 there were 4540 visits made to this clinic for diagnosis or treatment. Recently two branch clinics have been opened in the county, one in Obion and one in Samburg.

At intervals of about one month case-finding clinics for the diagnosis of tuberculosis are held. By means of these examinations numerous undiagnosed cases have been uncovered, with resultant benefit to the patient himself and the protection of those with whom he comes in contact. During 1938 examinations of 297 were made. Under the direction of the attending physician, nursing visits are made to known cases of tuberculosis, when instruction is given as to the proper mode of life for such persons.

Nursing visits are also made to prospective mothers, to infants, pre-school and school children, in each case the mother being taught approved methods of care.

During the summer pre-school conferences are held, where infants and pre-school children are given physical examinations, and mothers instructed. During 1938 there were made 727 such examinations. At these conferences no attempt is made to treat the sick. On the contrary, mothers are taught the normal upbringing of the child. Pre-school children are encouraged to participate in the Blue Ribbon Program held in the schools. In connection with this program, there were 2369 examinations of school children and 1755 inspections. Almost 2700 children qualified for blue ribbons.

A co-operative dental program has been carried on in the county for the past two years. Funds are obtained from the State Health Department, the Obion County Department of Education, the Obion County Health Department and from the individual communities with which corrective work on the teeth of indigent children is done. The dentists of the county co-operate fully in making this possible at low cost.

By means of the Crippled Children's Service, funds supplied jointly by the State Health Department and Obion County are used for corrective work, mostly of an orthopedic nature, all done for underprivileged children. Such children are admitted to a Memphis hospital where treatment is given by physicians of national reputation. None of the funds are used to pay for medical services, all of which is donated, but are used to defray actual necessary expense incidental to the treatment.

The sanitation program has for its object the improvement of the surroundings of the home, school or public building. By means of a Works Progress Administration grant, there is conducted a privy building program. It is necessary under this program for the property owner to pay for material in a sanitary privy only, the labor being given free. During 1938 there were a total of 363 such privies installed, an average of about one a day. The sanitarian made inspection of 2958 private premises and also made 81 school inspections.

In malaria control there were completed about 70,000 feet of minor drainage ditches. Local ordinances relating to the production of milk are enforced.

The laboratory service is conducted co-operatively with the State Health Department. By it there are made sanitary analyses of water and milk. Patients are examined for such diseases as tuberculosis, typhoid fever, diphtheria, syphilis, undulant fever, tularemia, malaria, and others.

During the year there were reported to the department a total of 308 deaths from all causes and a total of 548 live births. Do you have your birth certificate?

In 1939 a Blue Ribbon Health parade was sponsored by the County Health Bureau under the supervision of Miss Violet Crook, with a formation of approximately 3000 (2607) children, a very fine commentary upon the work of the department in the county. The following schools, uniform rank and file, appeared in line on the streets of Union City:

Central No. 7, Crystal, Ebenezer, Old Maupin, Walnut Log, Glass, Woods, Sunnyside, Macedonia, Community Pride, Wayside, Protemus, Alamo, London, Midway, Cunningham, Reelfoot, Hiland, Minnick, Oak Ridge, Harris, Lindenwood, McConnell, Parkview, Hillcrest, Westover, Central (Union City), Dixie, Obion, Woodland, Cloverdale, Rives, Mason Hall, South Fulton, Troy, Hornbeak and Kenton.

AMERICAN RED CROSS

It was in 1917 after the boys and young men of Obion County had been called to take up arms and follow the colors into the battlefields over there, that the Obion County Chapter, American Red Cross was organized. Mrs. J. F. Howard, Mrs. W. H. Swiggart, Mrs. Robert Whipple, Mrs. R. A. Napier and Dr. W. M. Turner were members of the official board who made the application for the Charter. From that day to this one, with a short holiday in 1933 and 1934, the American Red Cross has stood ready to assist in any emergency that might arise.

Twice in the history of the Chapter we have met the High Waters, once in a small way and then again in 1937 when the entire county was affected and we realized the true need of experienced leadership. This came through the National Red Cross.

During 1939, in all 2191 families applied to the local office for aid of one kind or another, 475 of these given material aid, 385 families of the boys and young men who went out as Obion County's quota to the World War in 1917 had assistance with their claims for Government help, hospitalization, markers, etc.

A first aid class was given in the spring by Ellis D. Fysol of the National Headquarters, and as a result of this class Obion County now has 16 instructors in First Aid. Six classes have been conducted by these instructors, with three other classes in sight at this time.

Junior Red Cross has been enrolled in 7 schools and with their slogan of service for others.

Fitness for service—we hope to enlist many other schools

in this work. One highway First Aid Station has been established at Hornbeak. This station has already served a number of injured people.

The local chairman is Carl J. Timm; B. C. Cox is the treasurer; Mrs. W. F. Thweatt, executive secretary; Dave Shatz, Cecil Moss, Chas. Dietzel, Mrs. W. W. Heathcock, Mrs. W. J. Jones, Mrs. Ruth Forcum Lannom, R. J. Hubbs, Rev. L. R. Niell are members of the Executive Board.

AGRICULTURAL EXTENSION

The Agricultural Extension Service of Obion County is a cooperative agency of the University of Tennessee, financed also partly by the United States Department of Agriculture (through the Land Grant Colleges) and partly by the Obion County Quarterly Court.

The local Extension Service consists of the County Agricultural Agent, the Home Demonstration Agent, and the Extension Office Secretary. Each is considered an employee of the University of Tennessee, receiving all state and federal salary funds from the University.

The University of Tennessee consists of three distinct branches: (1) Resident teaching staff for students enrolled at Knoxville, Martin, or Memphis; (2) Experiment Station, with branches at Jackson, Columbia, Knoxville, Greeneville, Crossville, Murfreesboro, and Clarksville, all existing to develop new information for agriculture; and (3) Extension Service, with Agricultural Agents, Home Demonstration Agents, and Subject Specialists to carry information from the Experiment Stations and the United States Department of Agriculture to the farms and the homes of the state.

Federal legislation made the Extension Service possible.

The first Morrill Act became a law in 1862 with the signature of President Lincoln, establishing an agricultural and mechanical college in each state.

The Hatch Act, providing Federal aid for the support of agricultural experiment stations in each state, was passed by Congress in 1887.

The Smith-Lever Act, creating the Extension Service was passed and signed by President Wilson in 1914, 27 years, after having been requested in 1908 by a committee of the Association of American Agricultural Colleges and Experiment Stations.

The Smith-Lever Act was intended to foster agricultural extension in the states and to co-ordinate the extension work of land-grant colleges and the U. S. Department of Agriculture, both of which had been active in certain parts of the country. The Act provided:

OBION COUNTY HISTORY

(1) That extension work in agriculture and home economics should be carried on by the land grant colleges in co-operation with the U. S. Department of Agriculture.

(2) That extension work should consist of giving instruction and practical demonstrations to persons not attending a land-grant college.

(3) That each state was to receive certain funds from the Federal Government, to be matched by state or local funds.

It should be made clear that the Extension Service (County and Home Agents) is a co-ordinating and educational agency, and is not directly responsible for the agricultural adjustment administration (farm program)—the Farm Bureau, the Co-operative Supply Associations, the Farm Security Administration, the Co-operative Rural Electric Association, Etc. The Extension Service works in an advisory or educational capacity with each.

4-H CLUB NOTES

The major project of the Extension work since passage of the Smith-Lever Act has been the 4-H Club. These clubs began as corn and potato growing projects for the boy and tomato growing and canning project for the girl. And have grown until there are now approximately one and a quarter million rural boys and girls in the United States and outlying possessions enrolled in one or more projects each year.

The 4-H emblem is the 4-leaf clover, each bearing an "H". The "H's" stand for training of the head, heart, hand and health.

The 4-H Club Pledge is:

My Head to clearer thinking,
My Heart to greater loyalty,
My Hands to larger service, and
My Health to better living for my Club, my Community, and my Country.

The 4-H Club Motto is: "To Make The Best Better."

4-H clubbers learn by doing; they profit as they learn; they play in meetings, encampments, conventions, and the National 4-H Club Congress in Chicago, as well as working at home and preparing themselves for future careers in college, in business and on the farm.

The 1939 organized 4-H Clubs are at: Central (No. 7), Crystal, Cunningham, Dixie, Elbridge-Cloverdale, Hornbeak, Lonoke, Mason Hall, Parkview, Rives, Midway, South Fulton, Troy, Union City, Wolverine and Woodland Mills.

The 1939 enrollment for Obion County was approximately 750 boys and girls (ages 10 to 20 years). Members do not have to be enrolled in school, or they may have graduated from school. There are approximately 6000 boys and girls of 4-H Club age in the county.

OBION COUNTY HISTORY

COMMUNITY CLUBS

The organized basis of the Home Demonstration Agent's work in each county is the Home Demonstration Clubs for women. In Obion County, however, men and women jointly compose what is called locally the "Community Club", in which both men and women attend, hold office, stage programs, with one or more hostesses in each home, National recognition was obtained in February, 1939, when eight representatives of Obion County clubs staged a 30-minute extemporaneous discussion of community organization in a nation-wide radio hookup on the National Farm and Home Hour.

Community clubs active during 1939 are:

Bethel (inactive now), Bowers, Central (No. 7), Cloverdale-Elbridge, Community Pride, Crystal, Glass-Mt Moriah, Mason Hall, Pierce, Oak Grove, Midway-Clayton, Pleasant Hill, Pleasant Valley, Polk-Obion, Protemus-Dixie, Salem, Shady Grove, Sunnyside, Troy-Ebenezer, Union Grove and Wolverine.

That activities of all agricultural interests of the county might be coordinated, the Secretary of Agriculture named the following farmers and home-makers about a year ago to a long-time planning committee, said committee not to change with each calendar year, or otherwise:

Richard B. Andrews, chairman; Mrs. Mamie Wood, vice-chairman; B. V. Jernigan, J. M. Marshall, Trent Johnston, Mrs. O. T. Sanders, Mrs. D. C. Maddox, Mrs. Milton Hamilton.

COUNTY FARM LOAN ASSOCIATIONS

Obion County National Farm Loan Association was organized at Rives in May, 1917, with J. H. Shore as Secretary-Treasurer and Directors as follows: G. W. Phebus, W. A. McNeill, E. T. Mitchell, T. F. Shipp, T. M. Flack.

Now the Directors are as follows: J. C. McRee, Alwyn Brevard, E. L. Houser. I. H. Etheridge, P. G. Browder, with A. C. Fields as Secretary-Treasurer.

Loans, 466. Total amount, $1,293,600.

Kenton National Farm Loan Association was organized at Kenton in November, 1917, with R. B. Gray as Secretary-Treasurer and Directors as follows: W. L. Fowler, J. R. Orr, J. H. McAfee, W. P. Wade, H. K. Dodson.

Now the Directors are: H. K. Dodson, J. N. Midyett, A. J. Harris, C. C. Needham, Clarence Bogle, with A. C. Fields as Secretary-Treasurer.

Loans, 322. Total amount, $545,300.

Hornbeak National Farm Loan Association was organized at Hornbeak in August, 1917, with L. H. Moultrie as Secretary-Treasurer and Directors as follows: R. Barnett, R. P. Moultrie, C. C.

Summers, W. E. Stover, R. L. Cunningham.

Now the Directors are: Dr. C. C. Marshall, W. S. Cranford, C. H. Neely, W. E. Stover, J. H. Moultrie, with A. C. Fields as Secretary-Treasurer.

Loans, 105. Total amount, $251,400.
Grand total of loans, 893.
Grand total amount, $2,090,300.

These three Associations were moved to Union City in October, 1935, and M. H. Underwood was elected Secretary-Treasurer of all three.

In October, 1937, after the death of Mr. Underwood, A. C. Fields was elected Secretary-Treasurer.

PARENT-TEACHERS

Cloverdale has the distinction of being the first organized Parent-Teacher Local in the county. It was organized in 1935 by Mrs. H. T. Williamson, of Trezevant, who was district president and Mrs. L. W. Hughes, Arlington State President. Cloverdale affiliated with the State and National Congress with 20 members. Mrs. Avery Roddy was local president. For two years this was the only affiliated unit in the county.

In the fall of 1937, under the leadership of Mrs. E. A. Peacock, district president, the following units were organized:

Mason Hall, Rives, Westover, Central in Union City, South Fulton, Woodland and Troy.

March 17, 1938, a meeting was called by these eight affiliated units with the purpose of organizing a County Council. Mrs. E. A. Peacock was in charge of the meeting. Miss Cara Harris, Field Secretary, and Mrs. L. W. Hughes, State President, assisting her. Mrs. Hughes, in an impressive ceremony, installed the following officers of the County Council:

Mrs. Glennie Jones, Rives, President; Mrs. Knox Glover, Woodland, Vice President; Mrs. John Miller, Mason Hall, Secretary; Mrs. Noel Glover, Union City, Treasurer.

The Charter Associations, number of members, and names of Local Presidents follow:

Cloverdale—33 members, Mrs. Herbert Via, president.
Central (U. C.)—20 members, Mrs. LaNelle Brouse, president.
Mason Hall—25 members, Mrs. John Miller, president.
Troy— 20 members, Mrs. W. B. Forrester, president.
Rives—30 members, Mrs. M. H. Underwood, president.
South Fulton—30 members, Mrs. I. M. Jones, president.
Westover—20 members, Mrs. Robert Wade, president.
Woodland—20 members, Mrs. Rose Alexander, president.
This made a total of 198 charter members in the council.

OBION COUNTY HISTORY

The next month thirteen new associations affiliated and came into the Council:

Macedonia—28 members, Roy Perryman, president.
Dixie—20 members, Holland Robert, president.
Cunningham—20 members, Mrs. Roxie Cunningham, president.
Central (No. 7)—20 members, Mrs. Kate Davis, president.
Obion—20 members, Mrs. Arch Shires, president.
Lonoke—20 members, Guy Calhoun, president.
Crystal—21 members, Mrs. Ed Taylor, president.
Hornbeak—21 members, Miss Retta Moultrie, president
Kenton—35 members, Mrs. Price B. King, president.
Harris—20 members, Mrs. O. W. Williams, president.
Parkview—20 members, Mrs. D. Shaw, president.
Hillcrest—20 members, Mrs. W. D. Owens, president.
Midway—20 members, Rice Wilson, president.

This brought the total membership in the twenty-one units to 483 members, making it at this time the largest council in the 13th district.

Later in the year of 1938 five other Locals had come into the council. These were:

Oak Ridge—20 members, Mrs. Ella Gwaltney, president.
Walnut Log—23 members, Mrs. Pearl McQueen, president.
Community Pride—20 members, Mrs. Hugh Catron, president.
Ebenezer—20 members, Mrs. R. A. Kendall, president.
Sunnyside—26 members, J. R. Hinson, president.

This year Hiland has affiliated with 20 members; president, Mrs. Frank Jimerson. The council now consists of twenty-seven local units with a total membership of over one thousand members.

Parents-Teachers council works with the schools in the standardization program, also assisting in libraries, beautification, and other projects. The council works in close cooperation with the health department, assisting in summer round-up, correction of defects, etc.

The Parent-Teachers cooperate with the relief agency in the serving of free lunches, furnishing books and clothing to the under-privileged.

RURAL ELECTRIC T. V. A.

Approximately 1550 families in Obion County are enjoying "yard-stick" rates for electric service.

Of these, nearly 900 never used electricity in their home until the organization of the Gibson County Electric Membership Corporation about three years ago. The remaining almost 700 families were paying the old Kentucky-Tennessee Power Company $1.00

OBION COUNTY HISTORY

for the first 11 KWH of electric energy each month, before the local rural electric cooperative organization purchased the power company properties and resumed their rates the first of this year.

Approximately 235 miles of rural line serve Obion County members of the electric association. The entire corporation has approximately 540 miles of line in Obion, Gibson, Dyer, Lake and Crockett counties, by which some 5000 electric consumers cooperatively purchase electric energy from the Tennessee Valley Authority and serve themselves.

The cost to users for household (town or farm) electric service is based on the following rates:

First 50 KWH per month at 3c; next 150 KWH at 2c; next 200 KWH at 1c; next 1000 KWH at 4 mills.

Until the lines are paid for, one cent per KWH is added each month, up to the first 100 KWH (not over $1.00 per month) for amortization of the lines.

At the above rates, the associations are rapidly paying their loans borrowed from the Rural Electrification Administration, which is a division of the United States Department of Agriculture. Several cities, towns, and rural cooperatives have already reduced their rates even below the rate above. (TVA sells the electric energy wholesale to these retailing groups at a very few mills per KWH.)

Rural distribution lines touch each of the 16 civil districts within Obion County.

Residents of Troy, Obion, Hornbeak, Rives, Kenton, Mason Hall, Woodland Mills, Elbridge, Clayton, Glass, Cloverdale, Polk, Mount Pelia, McConnell, Harris, Pierce, Samburg, and Gratio also receive electric service at these low rates.

(Note: Practically all of middle and West Tennessee, including all the large cities of Memphis, Jackson, Nashville, Chattanooga, and Knoxville, enjoy these same low rates.

According to Supt. Floyd Jones, of the local cooperative, the average customer in the entire project pays approximately $2.97 per month. The average meter shows 86 KWH per month per family.

Farmers use more electricity than do city customers, however, Mr. Jones pointed out. The average farm bill is $3.10 per month with 111 KWH being average meter reading for the farm customers only.

These statistics prove, as extension workers have long contended, that farm people need electricity even more than do city residents.

With Obion County, Mr. Jones reports an estimate of 250 electric cooking ranges, 650 electric refrigerators, 600 automatic or electric water pumps, 60 completely automatic electric hot water heaters, 75 automatic electric baby chick brooders, and a radio and electric iron in the homes of 90 per cent of the members.

Many small appliances are enjoyed by rural people for the first time, including sweepers, cleaners, perculators, toasters, waffle irons, electric washing machines, fans, heating pads, churns, separators, sausage grinders, motors and tool grinders.

Several large motors operate hammer-mill feed grinders.

One purebred hog breeder has an electric brooder for baby pigs farrowed during cold weather, reporting that the pigs leave this warm place only for nursing.

BOY SCOUTS OF OBION COUNTY

Scouting was organized twice in Union City before it "caught hold." Vague tales are told of the original organization here, a troop started in 1912, with Rev. C. M. Zwingle as scoutmaster, and of the period of scouting which started in 1916, with Rev. R. W. Walker at its head.

The present organization, before it came under jurisdiction of the chief Paducah Area Council, had birth September 8, 1922, with R. V. French as its scoutmaster. It was Troop One of Union City and the Troop committee was composed of Rev. E. S. Baker, A. E. Kirkland and Tommy White. Mr. French served as scoutmaster until December, 1923, when he was made commissioner and Ernest Wuench, his assistant scoutmaster, became scoutmaster, to serve the troop in that capacity for over ten years.

It was during this arrangement that Troop One was made Troop 16 by national headquarters, and Troop Two, started in 1924 with H. F. Jones as scoutmaster, became Troop 17. Mr. Jones was scoutmaster of Troop 17 for several years until he left for Panama, when H. C. Marsh took over the troop.

Scouting here was at its highest point since its birth, when H. F. Jones organized Troop 18 in 1933. It was in 1933 that the American Legion Drum and Bugle Corps began its career, as a boy scout organization, inspired by the Paducah Corps.

In February, 1936, Union City became the center of the Reelfoot district of the council. Tom Lee was made district commissioner and served as such until Charles Herman Scates, then scoutmaster of Troop 51, was given this job.

Shortly after Mr. Scates had been made district commissioner intensive training and organization work took effect and scouting in Union City started on its upward trek. The troops began to expand. A colored troop was formed, and scouting was organized outside Union City proper. In 1940, scouting in Union City began its fourth year of existence under the council, and at a report by the district commissioner and the scout executive, it was shown that the district has already passed the goal that was allotted to it by the council to reach in 1940, in numbers of scouts and cubs, based on population and the availability of boys of scouting age.

DISTRICT COMMITTEE

For the Reelfoot district committee to serve for the year 1940: Fenner Heathcock heads this committee as chairman and C. J. Timm and C. D. Hilliard as vice-chairmen.

The executive organization is headed by Chas. Herman Scates as district commissioner, John Earl Hurt, assistant district commissioner; Donald Duke, neighborhood commissioner. Chief scout executive, Roy C. Manchester, of Paducah, supervises the work of these men.

The district committee chairmen are: Field and Senior scouting, Dave Shatz; organization and extension, Dr. M. T. Tipton; leadership training, Dr. H. F. Bower; camping, Cecil Moss; activities, G. B. White, Jr.; health and safety, Dr. Frank Kimzey; finance, James L. Rippy; cubbing, Robert M. McAnulty; negro scouting, Francis Young; publicity, Chas. Fontenay; senior scouting, David McAnulty.

Members at large are C. B. Dement, Walker Kerr, Walker Tanner, Thad Lee, W. M. Warterfield, Claude Botts, Father Dolan and Rev. O. A. Marrs.

Cubs are composed of boys of pre-scouting age. The age limit is from 9 to 12 years.

Cubbing is rapidly finding its way into the scouting program. Cubbing leads to scouting and might be said to serve as a gateway to scouting. Through cubbing it is possible to get scouting into certain communities which for some reason or other have not been able to get started with a scout troop.

Parents are usually so anxious to have this program for their boys that they are willing to serve as den mothers and pack committeemen.

This great parental interest also assures local councils of more substantial support. At the present time the ratio is one cub to every six scouts.

The pack committee is composed of H. P. Moss, Jr., Roy C. Wehman, Ray Merrick and F. R. Freid.

The total number of Scouts, cubs and scouters in the Reelfor district are 277, nine troops, one cub pack and 58 scouters as follows:

BOY SCOUT TROOP

Troop 51, oldest troop in Reelfoot district organized in 1926, is sponsored by the WDW class of the Cumberland Presbyterian Church. Scoutmaster, Jimmie Bramham; assistant, Ted Clymer;

R. J. Hubbs, troop chairman. Committeemen: J. L. Rippy, Paul Hudgins, E. C. Crenshaw, P. M. Pitzer.

Troop 52 is sponsored by the Character Builders Class of the First Methodist Church. Scoutmaster, R. N. Vincent; assistants, Edwin Rinehart, Bill Roper. Troop chairman, Dr. Homer E. Gibbs. Committeemen: C. R. Grigsby, H. F. Bower, T. H. Cowden, Louis Wrather.

Troop 53, colored, is sponsored by the African Methodist Episcopal Church. Scoutmaster, Francis Young. Chairman, Dola Board; committeemen: Haywood Davis, M. F. Faulks, E. D. Walker.

Troop 54, organized under sponsorship of A. R. P. Church. Scoutmaster, Rev. L. R. Niell. Scoutmaster, Fred Clark; assistant, J. H. Jonakin. Troop committeemen: W. B. Forrester, R. L. Jones, L. R. Niell.

Troop 55, largest troop in Reelfoot district, is sponsored by the First Presbyterian Church. Scoutmaster, A. L. Garth; assistant, Bob Nethery. Troop chairman, R. C. Garth; committeemen, J. C. Greer, J. Walker Kerr, A. R. Treadway, C. M. Mathis.

Troop 56, sponsored by the Comrades Sunday School Class of the Union Church, Scoutmaster, Wm. Algea, assistant, Joe D. McClure. Troop committeemen: Leonard Stovall, E. T. Jones, Leonard Shore.

Troop 57, sponsored by the Chamber of Commerce of Obion. Meets in High School Gym. Scoutmaster, Snead Clift; assistant, Robt. Harrison, Troop committeemen: C. D. Hilliard, M. E. Whitson, Dale Glover.

Troop 58, sponsored by the Loyal Sons Class of the First Christian Church. Scoutmaster, Donald Duke; assistant, Lewis C. Bramham. Troop chairman, C. W. Miles, III, committeemen: Milton Andrews, Dr. N. E. Wentworth, Paul Jones, Jack Burdick.

Troop 59, youngest troop in Reelfoot district. Meets in Samburg school. Scoutmaster, Spencer Cunningham. Troop representative, S. T. Denton. Outdoor scouting is a major feature of this troop. At Camp Pakentuck the boys of this troop won honors in swimming and nature study.

The new Boy Scout Cabin is a realization of a long desired dream. Much credit for this is given the District Chairman, Fenner Heathcock, whose efforts made the cabin possible. The cabin is located on the Claude Botts farm, three miles south of Union City.

All of the district meetings will be held at the Scout Cabin, as well as all the joint meetings and jamborees.

Each year Reelfoot Scouts have a one-week period of camping at Camp Pakentuck, four miles from Ozark, Ill., a great place to get next to nature.

OBION COUNTY HISTORY

COUNTY FORMATION
(By Franklin Yates)

Date of formation: 1823—from State lands ceded by Chickasaw Indians.

First settlement: 1819 in northeastern part of county; 1820 in southwestern part of county.

First settlers: In 1880 the birthplace of 22,793 people in Obion County were: Tennessee, 19,893; Kentucky, 1263; North Carolina, 513; Virginia, 438; Mississippi, 337; Alabama, 239; Ireland, 39; Germany, 28; England and Wales, 17; British America, 12; France, 8; Scotland 6. Other countries, 990.

Size of county: 552 square miles (353,280 acres). Tennessee counties average 442 square miles. Shelby is largest county in Tennessee with 801 square miles. Trousdale is smallest Tennessee county with 106 square miles.

Number of farms: 3404, according to 1930 census, in Obion County; in Tennessee, 273,783.

Average size of farms: 91.2 acres in Obion County; 67.7 acres in Tennessee.

Tenure—1935: Full owners, 1379; part owners, 322; managers, 22; all-tenants, 1681; share croppers, 519.

Assessed value taxable property: (see page 33)

Number of livestock—January 1, 1935: 2795 horses and horse colts; 6642 mules and mule colts; 24,427 all cattle; 44,871 all hogs; 12,004 all sheep; 110,672 all poultry. (Poultry record April 1, 1930).

Crops planted in 1939: (Acreages do not include hay and pastures already seeded)—311,108 acres total farm land; 216,188 acres total crop land (so classified by AAA); 82,000 acres corn; 30,000 acres lespedeza estimated (incorrectly called Japan clover); 16,125 acres cotton; 7042 acres wheat; 5013 acres crimson clover; 4810 acres red top; 4075 acres red clover; 2000 acres oats, rye and barley; 1209 acres white clover; 860 acres timothy; 615 acres alsike clover; 480 acres tobacco (mostly dark fired—4 burley growers); 223 acres blue grass; 90 acres sweet clover; 84 acres sericea lespedeza; 53 acres alfalfa; 47 acres vetch; one acre bur clover.

A few other crops are grown commercially, including sweet potatoes, tomatoes, strawberries, sorghum, kudzi vine, cabbage, etc., but no figures are available as to exact acreage.

Soils: Uplands are known as "loess," having been deposited here by winds ages ago; highly productive silt loams, usually easily tilled, but generally in need of nitrogen, lime and phosphate. Bottoms are mostly alluvial soils, having been deposited by water, highly productive but often hard to cultivate. Little sand in most of our soils distinguish them from many other West Tennessee

OBION COUNTY HISTORY

counties where sand from hills has covered productive bottoms, ruining same.

Obion ranks with other Tennessee counties—First in acres of corn; first in number of hogs; fifth in value of all farm products per farm; twelfth in value of farm products for entire county; seventh in acres sweet potatoes; eleventh in number of cattle, all types and ages; eleventh in number of sheep all ages; seventeenth in bales of cotton produced, 1934; seventeenth in number of colts all ages, 1934; eighteenth in wheat threshed, 1934; eighteenth in dairy products sold, 1939; twentieth in number of milk cows over two years of age, 1920; twenty-eighth in tobacco produced, 1934; twenty-ninth in number of chickens, 1939; thirty-fourth in number of chickens and eggs sold; forty-eighth in value forest products sold.

Type of farms: 819 farms classified as general farms; 1148 farms classified as cotton farms; 385 farms classified as livestock farms.

Average value of farm products used per family in Tennessee, $253; average value of farm products used per family in Obion County, $218.

Only 68.6 per cent of all farm families in Obion County reported having a milk cow in 1930.

Only 90.4 per cent of all farm families in Obion County reported having poultry in 1930.

Obion County crop acreage varies considerably: Cotton, per farm, 2.9 acres in 1879; six-tenth of an acre in 1909; 9.2 acres in 1924; 5.9 acres in 1934.

Obion County wheat, per farm: 10.1 acres in 1879; 22.2 acres in 1899; 7.1 acres in 1909; 1.4 acres in 1924; 2 acres in 1934.

Obion County sheep, per farm: 2.8 head in 1879; 4.7 head in 1919; 1.8 head in 1924; 3.5 head in 1935.

FARM CREDIT ORGANIZATION

The Dyersburg Production Credit Association (PCA) serves six counties, including Obion, being a part of the Louisville branch of the Farm Credit Administration. Local representatives include: Clarence Fox, county representative and appraiser; Richard B. Andrews, county director in the six-county organization; Fred Moore, Dyersburg, executive secretary.

The Federal Land Bank is the long-term agency paralleling the Production Credit Association, which makes short-term loans for production. The Federal Land Bank lends money for the purchase of land, buildings, long-term improvements, etc., for paying debts against the farm.

Land bank loans are made in the county through the National Farm Loan Association, composed of a board of directors elected by the borrowing stockholders.

OBION COUNTY HISTORY

Land bank money is also secured from the investing public through the Intermediate Credit Bank of Louisville, under the farm credit act.

The Federal land banks, however, are older than the 1933 farm credit act. They were created in 1917.

The Federal Government guarantees the bonds of the Federal land banks, but does not supply the money for any of the farm credit administration agencies.

Obion County is served by three boards of directors, viz: Obion County NFLA, Alwyn Brevard, president; J. C. McRee, vice president.

Hornbeak NFLA: Dr. C. C. Marshall, president; C. H. Neely, vice president.

Kenton NFLA: Harry Dodson, president; Clarence Bogle, vice president.

A. C. Fields is secretary of all three national farm loan associations, having headquarters in Union City.

All funds secured and loaned locally, either by the Production Credit Association or the National Farm Loan Association, is first borrowed by the Intermediate Credit Bank.

COUNTY FARM

The new Obion County Farm was moved to its present location, about four miles west of Union City, in 1930. It was purchased by the late County Judge J. W. Buchanan, assisted by three commissioners. A. C. Houser, Charles E. Keiser and J. M. Smith from an insurance company. This farm is known as being formerly owned by the late George W. Moody. The 295 acres was purchased for approximately $11,250.

The old County Farm, near Polk, was sold for $5,800, which was used as a down payment on the present farm. They made improvements consisting of a home for the inmates and a residence for the overseer of the farm. The two buildings are equipped with all the modern conveniences..

The inmates help in every way that they are able to do, such as laundering and cleaning up the buildings.

The farm is cultivated by the prisoners that receive work sentences through the court. They raise many kinds of vegetables, which are used for feeding inmates and prisoners. The surplus is canned and dried for winter use.

They also raise hogs and cattle, some of which are killed for the use of the farm and others are sold and applied on buying other necessities such as clothes and staple groceries.

There were in 1939 twenty-seven inmates being cared for at the home. The average cost of feeding these is about 28 cents per person per day.

TROY COMMUNITY

According to the records Troy was located on March 16, 1825, by Rice Williams, John Parr, William Terrell, G. W. Adams and Joseph Taylor, commissioners appointed to fix the seat of justice for Obion County. Fifty acres of land were donated as a site by William Polk, of North Carolina, who afterwards added fifteen acres to be used forever as a public commons. The site, which was then covered by a heavy growth of timber, was laid off in lots, streets and a public square. The sale of lots at once began, the prices paid ranging from $5 to $158. Lot No. 4 sold for the latter amount. In 1831 ninety-six lots had been sold for an aggregate of $3,936.50. The first house, a double log house, was erected by Rice Williams, and there he kept a tavern until his death in 1829. The first store was opened by Col. Lysander Adams, who for more than half a century continued a prominent and honored citizen of the town. Adams did an extensive business for a number of years, and it was he who shipped the first bale of cotton and the first hogshead of tobacco from the county. The next merchant of note, locating in 1827, was W. S. S. Harris, father of the druggist, who was afterwards in business at Troy. A little later Porter & Partee did a large and profitable business for a number of years. J. H. Moran, of Dresden, also did an extensive business in a branch house in Troy, for two or three years. D. Glass was another prominent merchant. The firm of Polk, Crockett & Co., composed of Thomas A. George, Alexander Polk and John M. Crockett, at a little later date controlled a large share of the business. They were succeeded by J. S. Moffatt, who was for many years one of the leading business men of Obion County.

The first physician to locate in the town was Samuel Teator, who practiced his profession for several years. The next was Dr. Wilkerson, a brother-in-law of William M. Wilson. Among the other early physicians were William K. Waddy, W. H. D. Covington, Wood & McBane, Cutler, Burroughs, Horace Head, and his son, Henry Head, and David Bright, who for nearly fifty years sustained a high reputation in his profession.

The first newspaper established was the Western Advertiser, in 1858. The type, press and other material were purchased by a joint stock company composed of many of the leading citizens of the town. The first publishers were Cowan & Parsons, the former of whom withdrew in a short time. In about a year Parsons was succeeded by D. A. Chambers, who continued the publication under the name of the Troy Times until the beginning of the Civil

War. After the war it was revived by S. M. Howard and J. B. Maxwell, who were succeeded by Sumpter Baker. Baker published the Signal of the South for a short time, after which the office material was sold to a firm in Fulton, Ky. The next journalistic enterprise in Troy was the Obion News, established by Thomas A. Batte, who was succeeded by Sherrill & Doughty. They continued until January, 1879, when they sold the office to Dr. W. Bricè and T. P. Walker. In June, 1881, the News was consolidated with the Troy Banner, a paper published a short time by the Banner Publishing Co., Dr. Brice afterwards becoming sole proprietor of the News-Banner. The New Era, established in May, 1885, by the New Era Publishing Co., edited by W. B. Stovall, J. W. Bransford and H. C. Stanfield, was suspended about September 1, 1886, the subscription list having been transferred to the Obion Democrat, of Union City. In 1888 Dr. Brice, who was by the way one of the ripest scholars in the county, sold the News-Banner to his nephew, Jas. M. Brice, whose journalistic career in Troy for a period of twenty years was notable in many respects for a degree of dash and brilliancy. Mr. Brice moved to Union City and merged with absorbing the Obion Democrat by the News-Banner.

It was in 1889 perhaps that Lowe Shearon and Andrew Scott established a new paper. It tarried for a short time, but served as a stimulus for Mr. Shearon's training in journalism. He located in Texas and then entered the field of newspapering as a Chicago and New York reporter. He was in New York for many years.

In Dr. Brice's office, the News-Banner, came a Baltimore printer, G. W. Matchett, a very interesting character, whose work as a typesetter had taken him to every State in the Union—to Canada, Central and South America, and as a sailor shipped to Europe. He was an interesting story teller, and in his travels enjoyed the acquaintance of newspaper writers of special note who made such papers as the Detroit Free Press, the Peoria Transcript and the Burlington Hawkeye famous for their humorous stories. One of these, Robert J. Burdett, with others, published the romance of Mr. Matchett's wandering life, a column story of the sudden death of his bride upon the wedding altar, and then the adventures of an American printer.

At another time there was a Belgian portrait painter in Troy, Mr. Mathis. He was also a photographer, and remaining in Troy for a few years was called upon to paint the portraits of a number of leading citizens. There really was a gallery of fine prints made, and some of these remain in a fine state of preservation.

It is presumed that few people remember that there was at one time a telegraph line in Troy. It was probably strung on poles and trees, and extended from Trenton to Hickman. The Morse telegraph service in the United States was instituted with the

JAMES S. MOFFATT

Born in South Carolina 1808
Pioneer engaged in general
merchandising at Troy 50 years
    1840 to 1890
Interested in Southern Confederacy
contributing equipment and supplies
    Business Destroyed by War
After the War occupied with
general merchandising with business
increased extensively in sales
and volume over the county
Member A. R. P. Church at Troy
Married a cousin in South Carolina
One son, Israel P., Confederate soldier
A daughter married Dr. Walter Brice
Another daughter, Mrs. Elizabeth Brice
First wife died, married Mrs. Williamson
A. P., another son
and a daughter, Mary.

OBION COUNTY HISTORY

first line of 45 miles from Washington to Baltimore. This was in 1844, and the Trenton-Hickman line was put into service in 1856, with R. H. Marshall, operator at Troy.

During a score of years from 1870 to 1890, with the county seat still at Troy, there was a very notable coterie of lawyers, including the name of Jas. G. Smith, nestor of the bar of lawyers, a genuine Chesterfield and a man of fine distinction as a scholar and counsellor. He began in the schoolroom as a teacher and lived a very long and useful life, practicing in the courts of this part of the State. His son, F. J. Smith, afterwards became one of the well known attorneys of the Union City bar. Thos. R. Shearon, another attorney at Troy, was a graduate of Yale and Harvard Universities. A. B. Enloe (cousin of the late B. A. Enloe, late Chairman of the State Public Utilities Commission) was a man of rugged exterior, but remarkable for a combination great ability and gentle character. John E. Wells, a native of the county, was a brilliant young lawyer at Troy, practicing with distinction and moving with the location of the county seat at Union City. Here the attorney assumed the role of leadership in law and private citizenship. Chas. J. Wright, son of the schoolmaster, Charles Wright, began his practice in Troy, where he appeared some years afterwards as orator of the day in a centennial celebration of the organization of Obion County. Making a career of his profession Mr. Wright moved to the capital of Missouri. Here he was employed by a client to gather evidence in a case which took him to London and the native associations of his father. W. A. Bonner, a Troy lawyer, a rising young citizen, moved to Texas, and became one of the leading citizens of Dallas.

The first secret society organized in Troy was the Western Sun Lodge, No. 88, A. F. and A. M., which has ever been an active organization. The charter was granted October 16, 1839, to A. M. Chamberlin, W. M.; H. W. Wright, S. W.; Jethro L. Byrd, J. W.

The town was incorporated in 1852. The officers elected were Alfred M. Bedford, mayor; J. S. Moffatt, Dr. David Bright, Allen Hord, Dr. Horace Head and S. W. Cochran, aldermen.

The business of Troy, in 1885, was represented as follows: J. S. Moffatt & Co., Geo. B. Wilson and Cave J. Crockett, general merchandise; E. S. Walton, dry goods; J. A. Rochell, John Bennett and Jerry Stephens, groceries; W. S. S. Harris, drugs; S. E. Lyons, blacksmith shop and grist mill; J. B. Faulk and Jas. Everett, steam flour mill; Harris & Murphy, wagon makers and blacksmith shop; D. H. Dalby, livery stable; Dr. W. Brice, News-Banner; J. W. Hildebrant, Bright House; Chas. Inman, Inman House. The physicians were W. M. Bright, W. Brice, A. W. Caldwell, A. B. Weddington and W. H. Coover.

ADDENDUM

Under the head of Troy Community reference to the lawyers of Troy should include the name of Solomon W. Cochran. "Major Cochran," as he was well known, was a native of Portage County, Ohio. Attending school there, he continued in the schoolroom as teacher, and then began the study of law at Cleveland, Ohio. Licensed by the Ohio Supreme Court, he entered the practice of his profession at Kent, Ohio.

In 1840 Major Cochran moved to Henry County, Tenn., and taught school, in 1842 locating at Troy, Tenn. Here he practiced law for 40 years, with many honors conferred upon him as a citizen and in his profession. A notable instance was his appointment as special judge sitting with the Tennessee Supreme Court. In 1874 he was appointed Circuit Judge of the Twelfth Judicial Circuit, filling an unexpired term. He was twice appointed by the State Department with other able jurists as Commissioner of Arbitration. In 1880, when the State needed its best men in the Legislature, Major Cochran was honored by his fellow-citizens without opposition as a member of the General Assembly.

Nobleman by nature, the elements of character were so commingled as to combine the making of a man of great mind and gentle manner. Major Cochran was a son-in-law of the pioneer citizen, Col. William M. Wilson.

Sam D. Cochran, of the lumber manufacturing and exporting firm of Wilson & Cochran, operating in Louisiana for a number of years, and Mrs. Laura Cochran Wells, formerly residing in Union City, son and daughter of Major Cochran at Troy, later became residents respectively of Union City, Tenn., and Bedford, Va.

TROY COMMUNITY

CONFEDERATE SERVICE

Roster of Company B, 27th Tennessee Volunteers, appears detached from the county records of the Confederate soldiers. It came to our hands too late, so it is used in the next section of the book, that of the Troy community. Company under Capt. A. W. Caldwell left Troy August 16, 1861. Other officers are named in the county record. Following is the roll.

Returned from war: F. M. Boon, John Barrum, Will Bettis, John Burnett, Jess Campbell, Henry Chiles, Dick Cashon, Shalby Carmack, Obadiah Davidson, Harris Fox, L. A. Ford, Oliver Farris, Peter Frield, Jimmie Hart, Jack Harris, Dan Hopper, Tom Inman, George Lee, Sam Miller, John Morgan, Tom Marshall, Israel Moffatt, Will Morris, Cahill Peery, Sam Rines, John Sterrett, Tom Sowell, John Watson, George Wright, J. M. Wright, John Tucker, Will Boon, Yance Brannon, Tom Barrum, John Bettis, Monroe Buchanan, Helms Campbell, John Calhoun, George Cashon, John Dickey, Henry Darnell, Dan Fouse, Peter Foulks, Jim Huey, Jim Harper, John Hood, John Haley, Ki Inman, Dick Miller, Bob Moultrie, Tom Mullins, Fayette Morgan, John McAlister, Will Pankey, Tom Pruitt, Rufus Rines, Dud Sinclair, John Sandling, Buck Wilson, Wilford Wright, Dick Tucker, Will Valiant.

Following are named who failed to return: W. A. Alexander, Noah Barnett, Bunk Board, John Cooper, Will Chiles, Charlie Dudley, John Denny, Will Davis, Jim Darnell, John Fox, Will Garner, Dock Huey, John Hayes, Peter Hayes, Sid Hill, Perry Huffstutter, Sid Ingram, Steve Jenny, Sam Jenny, Will Jamison, Rome Jackson, Bob Kirby, Bob Miller, Morris Miller, Coleman Moultrie, Spencer Mathis, Culp Marbray, Joe Pankey, Bob Pankey, Will Pruitt Tinie Shepard, Lum Simmons, Steve Sanford, Rice Williams, Jim Ware, John Wilson, Jack Weeks, Will Weeks, John Rittenbery, Dick Wright, Will Walls, George Pickard.

TROY SCHOOLS

The town of Troy has always been interested in schools from every standpoint. From its organization, the itinerant teacher, teaching in private homes, and later the pioneer log schoolhouse, and as early as 1845 Waller Caldwell built what was known as Westbrook Academy about one and one-half miles west of Troy. This continued to be the school where the youth of Troy were educated for many years. It was really the first school of higher education established in Obion County. In 1860 Geo. B. Wilson and Ira P. Clark, both natives of Geneseo, New York, one a graduate of Temple Hill Academy, the other a graduate of Princeton University, assumed charge of the institution. Both were very excellent teachers. At the beginning of the Civil War they suspended school and entered the Confederate service, but at the close of hostilities resumed school work and continued for one year, when Wilson resigned his position and Clark continued for another year. They were followed by Professors Sample and Underwood. The late Jas. G. Smith and Chas. Wright, later referred to were also teachers of this institution. In 1874 Obion College was chartered, the original incorporators being Solomon W. Cochran, Lysander Adams, Walter Brice, Stephen M. Howard, Joe T. Brown, Geo. B. Wilson, and Wm. H. Jackson, and in 1875 a handsome building was erected by the cooperation of the citizens, aided by a munificent gift of land from the late James S. Moffatt, and the first semester began Sept. 6, 1875, under the administration of Prof. B. Moore, assisted by Profs. Underwood and Shaw. Miss Jennie Smith was teacher of the primary department and Mrs. Frank Hornbeak was instructor in music. They were succeeded by Profs. T. P. Walker and Chas. A. Brown, later by Rev. R. W. Erwin, J. E. and Robert Harrison, the last three being graduates of the famous Sawney Webb School at Culleoka, Tenn., and of Vanderbilt University. Other principals have been A. B. Cummings, Fred J. Page, A. B. Collom, J. C. Reid, Furman J. Smith, C. F. Fowler, A. H. Grantham, C. E. and C. A. Davis, R. C. Murray, A. M. Witherington. The incumbent, W. B. Forrester, in 1940 had held with fine ability and able administration the position for a period of ten years. Some years ago the trustees deeded the property to the High School Board of the county in perpetuity, as State high schools were attaining very high rank, and Troy still has one of the outstanding schools of the county, an institution proud of its sixty-five years of continuous service. In 1890 the original building was burned, but was immediately replaced by a substantial brick structure, and on the campus there are three well equipped and commodious buildings.

Prior to the erection of Obion College private schools in Troy were conducted after the Civil War by Miss Cora Dickey and Rev. H. C. Wheeler. Chas. Wright, a native of London, England, built his own schoolhouse and operated a private school not far from Westbrook Academy. Mr. Wright came to this country and served the Confederacy during the Civil War. In London he was a court reporter and probably one of the pioneers in this country to teach stenography and reporting in shorthand. He taught the youth of Troy and vicinity from the years immediately after the War until 1890 and his school was patronized by students from nearby States. Mr. Wright was very thorough, and in the higher branches, in literature, English, and mathematics, he was very proficient. Leaving Troy he came to Union City and taught for some time, and then located in Chicago, where his daughter, Miss Fannie, was employed in stenographic work in the City Hall for many years.

TROY COMMUNITY

TROY SCHOOLS—1940-41

W. B. Forrester, principal. High School: Janie Moffatt, Mrs. Sarah Moss, Mrs. Frances Carmack McNeill, Miss Noami Taylor, J. H. Jonakin, M. M. McBurrough.

Grammar School: Mr. Fay Schnider, Mrs. Bertha Polk, Mrs. Bessie Curry, Mrs. Herbert Hooper, Miss Hill Moffatt, Miss Mary Myers.

TROY CLUBS

Troy Book Club (organized September, 1939): Mrs. L. R. Niell, president; Mrs. James Jonakin, vice-president; Mrs. J. C. Moss, secretary.

Fin de Seicle: Mrs. J. O. Bennett, president; Mrs. W. B. Anderson, vice-president; Mrs. B. B. Maxwell, secretary-treasurer. This club was organized on the 4th of March, 1890.

TROY DIRECTORY

Troy business directory for 1940-41 was as follows:

Hall Mercantile Company; Walter Forrester heirs, managed by Robt. Jones; Groceries—Stanley Roberts, A. H. Overall, Spurlin Griffith.

E. A. McAdoo Drug Store.

R. W. Harrigan's Restaurant, Troy Cafe.

Barbers: Jimerson & Paschall.

Filling Stations: Troy Service, Paul Thorn; City Service, Charley Bailey; Pan-Am; Paul Thorn and Reynolds Bros.; Standard Oil, Austin Dickey; Pure Oil, Obe Kincaid.

TVA Substation.

Postmaster, Jno O. Bennett.

H. M. Sharp Lumber Yard.

Kelly White Cotton Gin.

White-Mahon Furniture Company.

Physicians: Dr. E. A. Boswell, Dr. W. F. Roberts.

Dentist, Dr. J. H. Meeks.

Mike Bright Produce Co.

1940 Census Enumeration: Population, 513.

Board of Mayor and Aldermen: Mayor, B. B. Maxwell; aldermen: D. H. Burnett, A. H. Overall, Wilford Morris, Paul Thorn, Dodds Griggs. Marshal, Oscar Wilkerson.

BANK OF TROY

The Bank of Troy, Tenn., is one of the oldest in the county, but one of the strongest, having survived some heavy drafts upon its resources, and recouping becomes stronger as the years increase.

The first cashier was Thomas Shearon, his successor Paul Ingram for a period of thirty years, and then Mr. Ingram's successor, R. W. Mahon, who was born and reared in Martin.

O. C. Berry succeeded Mr. Mahon as cashier some years past and has been directing the operations of the Bank of Troy in a very satisfactory and efficient manner. His assistant, Mrs. J. E. Moffatt, has served also for a term of years as a very accomplished and popular officer of the bank.

Troy is a busy center for bus and truck traffic, located at the junction of two main highways. Greyhound buses reach all points and local buses ply between Union City, Troy, Reelfoot Lake, Hornbeak, Tiptonville, Hickman, Bruce, Woodland Mills. Through bus tickets are on sale for all points.

Troy and its rural areas are all practically supplied with electric power for lighting and utility purposes. Current comes from the TVA with its schedule of low rates.

On October 22, 1929, was a day set apart to celebrate the paving of the entire public square with concrete surface. Some time before that date contract was made for this work, including the work of curbing and grading of the lot in the center of the public square, which is used for open-air assembly and for tent meetings.

All of these improvements, including municipal waterworks, greatly enhance the value and desirability of residence property in Troy.

CUMBERLAND PRESBYTERIAN CHURCH

The Cumberland Presbyterian Church at Troy began with an organization in 1833, as stated in early history, but made slow progress before the Civil War. As the congregation is remembered after the War, Rev. Webb was pastor for some time, then E. D. Farris, with occasional appointments by Rev. Jo McLeskey and J. B. Calhoun.

At one time a great revival was held by Reuben Burrow in the locust yard of the R. H. Marshall home, nearby the church. A bell used for church purposes, there being no belfry on the church building, was swung in one of the locust trees. It was not very large, but of such rare metal, brass in composition, that it was sometimes heard for a distance of five miles. The Burrow meeting, a great event, created general and profound interest and the church grew in numbers and in all the branches of the work. A cabinet organ was installed and the music was led by a choir.

Some years followed and D. T. Waynick came to the church as minister. He was married in Troy to Miss Ella Bright, daughter of Dr. David Bright, and his ministry in Troy continued for a longer time probably than most of those who held the pulpit of that church. It was 1878 when he was called and then for two

TROY COMMUNITY

or three years, from 1887, he preached in the Cumberland Church in Chelsea, Memphis, after which he returned to Troy and remained until 1902, and then located at Harrison, Ark.

Rev. Buchanan came while Rev. Waynick was in Memphis. Then in 1900-01 Rev. W. H. McLeskey occupied the pulpit. Jas. D. White came to the church in 1903 for a few years. Other ministers came according to time as follows: R. L. Keathley, 1908; G. W. Burroughs, 1912; J. A. McIlwain, 1918-19; E. Rueb, 1921; G. P. McIlwain, 1922; H. J. Burroughs, 1926; J. K. Patterson, 1931; R. E. White, 1916-17; 1928; 1934-5-6-7-8-9.

HISTORICAL REVIEW A. R. P. CHURCH

People of Troy on Saturday and Sunday, September 5th and 6th, 1925—the congregation and the friends of the Associate Reformed Presbyterian Church—held a two-day meeting observing the history of the local church and the foundation of the church in Scotland, in a series of services, a church pageant and a visit to Reelfoot Lake.

An address of welcome by Mrs. W. S. Crockett was delivered at a gathering on the public square, followed by a fish-fry dinner at Reelfoot Lake, and then assembly was held on the woodslot of the former well-known church leader and citizen, J. S. Moffatt. An improvised stage of rustic construction was the scene of the afternoon and evening pageant and historical review of the church.

Here took place, something after the fashion of the Passion Play, the action of the forefathers in seceding from the Presbyterian Church of Scotland, emigration to the Carolinas and the setting up of the church in America, finally the founding of the church in Obion County.

The Associate Reformed Presbyterian Church was formed two hundred years ago at Gairny Bridge, near Kinroth in Scotland. Secession was not the result of a doctrinal dispute, as has been the popularly accepted theory, but a culmination of church delinquency in the flagrant violation of the Westminster Confession of Faith and the rules of the church.

The forming then of the church in 1733 was commemorated in the pageant at Troy. The founders, Ebenezer Erskine, William Wilson, Alex Moncrieff and James Fisher were represented in the pageant by Jas. R. Moffatt, W. J. Erwin, Lon King and Wm. Curry.

From this part of the entertainment the scene changed to the Carolinas. There the Associate and Reformed, heretofore two bodies, are united in one body, the Associate Reformed Presbyterian Church. Then came the forefathers in ox carts or wagons moving to West Tennessee. The wagon and oxen were driven upon the stage with the pioneers in primeval attire. The forefathers were represented by Jas. W. Pressly, Jno. O. Bennett, L. A. Smith and Lon King, and the families of the caravan were as follows: Mrs. Jas. W. Pressly, Mrs. Jno. O. Bennett, Mrs. L. A. Smith, Mrs. Lon King, Mrs. P. W. Moffatt, Miss Mary Pressly, Mrs. W. A. Smith, Mrs. Kate Holloman, Mrs. Lizzie Stephens Pressly, Miss Sancy Bennett, Miss Edith Maxey, Miss Ruth Maxey, Miss Frances Carmack, Jack Tate, Robert Brice Moffatt, Calvin Smith, David Moss, Finis Turnage. The ox team was driven by Harry Ellison and the two colored servants were Aunt Martha Young and Alfred Young.

The recital of history and the announcing of events in the pageant was done by Father Time in the person of Rev. R. D. Strong.

The next event in the moving of the caravan from the Carolinas and Virginia, was the meeting of the Indians, subduing of the savages and making peace with the tribes, then hardships and exposure, sickness and death, all depicted in the pageant. The Indians were represented by Paul Erwin, Sport Weatherspoon, Andrew Scott, Wm. J. Turner, Coachman Cloar, Davy Crockett Burnett, Tom Berry, Jas Pryor, Paul Neely, Robert Tate, Samuel Curry, Herbert Andrews, Clea Reamsnyder, Jack Moffatt, Lynn Jackson, John Bennett, Jr.

After many long weeks and months the objective was reached and won. The forefathers settled on the hills west of the Obion River and around a center which afterwards became the town of Troy. Here under a large oak tree the A. R. P. Church was organized by Eleazar Harris, who was impersonated by J. R. Moffatt in 1832. Here they felled the trees, hewed and built a log church. The second and third houses of worship were frame buildings on the site of the present Troy Cemetery. The fourth was the present brick building located on the northeast side of the public square. The story of the church at length is related in the following—

HISTORICAL SKETCH ASSOCIATE REFORMED PRESBYTERIAN CHURCH
(By L. R. NIELL)

May we, the members of the Associate Reformed Presbyterian Church of Obion County, Tennessee, turn back the pages of history and read again the thrilling experiences of the forefathers in this country, which was then known as "the Far West".

On the banks of the Catawba river, in York County, South Carolina, near what is now known as Riddles Mill, in the year 1824, possibly during Christmas week, a pioneer wagon train was formed. It was customary for these wagon trains to appoint a

TROY COMMUNITY

leader, and James Harper was probably the leader of this train. The only names mentioned are: James Harper with his son-in-law, Samuel Hutchison, Mrs. Rosanna Harper, with her son-in-law, William Hutchison, with their families, consisting in the aggregate of forty-three souls, white and black. The objective of this train was some place in what was then known as Forked Deer County, in West Tennessee.

When the train reached Nashville, the leader was advised to go to a new county in extreme northwest Tennessee, Obion. After a tedious journey of nine weeks they came to the banks of Obion River, one mile east of Rives. Their baggage was taken across in canoes and then the empty wagons were pulled across with bed cords. As there were no roads on the west side of the river, it was necessary for them to cut their way through the undergrowth. They reached their destination on February 17, 1825, and settled about four miles west of where they had crossed Obion River.

In quick succession other trains were formed in the Carolinas and Virginia, bringing many families whose names are prominent in our early Church history. Among these we find the names of James Hogue and John Hutchinson. Later we find the names of Reeves, Garrison, Polk, Wade, Mills, Moffatt, Wilson, Lathan, Erwin, and others.

Obion County was organized January, 1824. The inhabitants were few. The surface of the country was covered with a dense forest of gigantic trees and luxuriant undergrowth; the deer, wolf, bear and panther abounded.

Not only were our forefathers progressive in material things but they were progressive in spiritual affairs. Although they did not hear a sermon for two years, these devout Christians held their religious services in their homes. In 1825, Rev. William Blackstock came to minister to them. His first service was held somewhere near a spring, west of the home of Calvin Pleasant, on the Troy and Union City road. He was possibly the first Presbyterian minister to preach in Obion County. He also preached at Troy and on a second visit in 1827 while on a missionary tour from South Carolina through Alabama and Tennessee. At this time he preached at least once under an old beech tree, near where the old church stood, now Troy cemetery.

Rev. Robert Galloway next visited this field. His first visit was in 1831, and the other was the following year.

In the fall of 1832, Rev. Eleazar Harris came to this field from Chester, S. C., and organized a church.

Rev. John Wilson and Rev. Ralston supplied the church until the arrival of Rev. Robert McCoy, in 1838. Arrangements were made for him as full time supply, and he accepted. Soon after this James Harper died. He was one of the faithful and active members of the church.

The first church building was erected in 1831 cr 1832, about four miles east of Troy, near the Moses Harper home, immediately north of the J. H. Guy home near the Troy and Rives highway. This was a log house. Another church building at the same time was erected two miles northwest of Troy, near the Hogue home and cemetery.

A church nearer the center of the congregation was needed, and in 1839 a design was made and approved. The site selected was the spot where the church was organized. The land was the property of James Polk, and he very graciously and gladly donated two acres for a church site and cemetery.

Building a church at this time was a serious undertaking, as membership was only 16 and their means very small. However, Col. Robert Crockett, a friend of the church, gave $25, William Hutchinson $18 and Benjamin Garrison $15, a total of $58. The rest was accomplished with the help of hands and donations of timber. The building was not completed until 1847. The pulpit was donated by Mr. and Mrs. Wm. Moffatt of Chester, S. C. Since the church was now located at Troy Rev. McCoy and family settled there. Records during the ensuing year show additions of three by certificate and twelve by examination, making a total membership of thirty-one. The church prospered and Rev. McCoy served this field from Jan. 8, 1839, to September, 1845.

Without a minister the church petitioned for supply. In response Rev. J. P. Weed was sent to Troy. He arrived in February, 1846. He preached for a few months and his services proved acceptable. Call was made and accepted. He was ordained and installed in April, 1847, by Revs. Bryson and Wilson. The salary of Rev. Weed was to be $300. Of this $80 came from the Tipton County congregation of Salem. Conditions were that Mr. Weed spend seven Sabbaths each year with Salem and seven as missionary in destitute places nearby his church in Obion. At this time the elders were Robt. Harper, Benjamin Garrison, Hiram Reeves, Benj K. Harper and J. S. Moffatt. The membership was 64 but during the war was increased to 78.

In 1858 Mr. Weed resigned on account of ill health. He asked to be retired, and sought rest upon his farm west of Polk, afterwards the home of W. J. Erwin. A lasting service was rendered the church after his retirement.

Rev. Jas. Penny Weed was the son of Nathaniel Weed and Polly Wiseman, born in South Carolina April 6, 1820. Resulting from sickness in early life he became an invalid. Graduated from Erskine College in 1843. Studied theology in Erskine and licensed to preach the Gospel in 1845. After a year or two in missionary

TROY COMMUNITY

work Rev. Weed was called to the pastorate of the church at Troy, Tenn. He was ordained and installed April 17, 1847. He was married to Mary Moffatt, daughter of James Moffatt at Troy. Of this union there were three children. Widowed by the loss of his wife, Rev. Weed married again to Eliza Terrell.

Though physically afflicted, and suffering intensely during the time. Rev. Weed was always a student and of deep mental qualities, with retentive memory and the virtues of a chaste imagination.

The congregation again without a pastor, Rev. R. L. Grier was called to the field. He was ordained and installed November 19, 1860.

Possibly the greatest revival in the church was in 1861. Rev. John G. Miller, pastor of Mount Zion, Mo., was the preacher, assisted by Rev. J. P. Weed. The first services were held at Pleasant Hill, five miles east of Troy.

There were twenty-eight professions of faith in Christ, and about twenty accessions to our church.

During the ministry of Rev. Grier the church prospered. The membership was now one hundred and twenty-five, the largest in the history of the church up to that time.

Soon the war came on with its blighting influences. Members of the church and the young men of the congregation enlisted in the service. It was not long before Troy was within the Federal lines, yet the pastor continued his work.

After the War, the house of the Lord was remodeled in 1868 and worship established regularly on the Sabbaths.

After serving the congregation for about ten years, Rev. Grier resigned, and took charge of the Mount Carman congregation in Mississippi.

In 1872 Rev. J. P. Weed quite feebly again assumed the pastoral relation at Troy, and served the people to the best of his ability for three years, after which he resigned. On September 4, 1875, he requested Presbytery to dissolve the pastoral relation between the Troy congregation and himself. This Presbytery granted.

About this time the revised edition of the Psalms was introduced, and the Troy congregation dedicated a new church building, June 13, 1874.

Rev. T. P. Pressly having completed his theological training was licensed to preach by the Memphis Presbytery, and was directed to supply the church at Troy until the following May. His services were acceptable to the congregation, and a petition to send him back was presented to Presbytery in May, 1876. This was done and Rev. Pressly received a call from the Troy congregation at the next meeting of Presbytery, September, 1876. The call was accepted. Presbytery ordained him at this meeting, and on October 14, 1876, was installed pastor.

The congregation under its new pastor moved forward in membership and all the activities of the church.

The congregation, under his leadership, erected a most attractive and modern church building in 1909. The location of the church was changed from the present Troy Cemetery to the east side of the square. The building of this handsome structure was a worthy undertaking. The people of the community had been richly blessed in material things and were well able to build. The building was dedicated on March 27, 1910. The dedicatory sermon was preached by Rev. W. B. Lindsay.

It was the ambition of Dr. Pressly to serve this congregation for a half a century, the Lord willing. However, on May 10, 1924, God saw fit to reward him for his services already rendered. Only a few hours before his death, knowing that the end was near, he conducted family worship and led in the singing of the 124th Psalm. Among his last words were: "I have spent all my life preparing for this day, and it is the happiest day of my life." Thus a triumphant Christian came to a victorious end. The good influence of this Godly man upon the church and community cannot be overestimated.

Thomas Peden Pressly was the son of Rev. David Pressly, D. D., and Sarah Brown Peden, and was born near Starkville, Miss., January 15, 1853, graduated from Erskine College, Due West, S. C., in 1872, and the Theological Seminary at Due West, in 1874.

He was married at Troy, Tenn., December 25, 1877, to Miss Dora Augusta Smith. She died April 15, 1890. He was married the second time to Mrs. Elizabeth (Stephens) Bittick, December 22, 1892.

The congregation was then without a pastor. Rev. L. R. Niell of Rives supplied occasionally and assisted them in securing supplies. Among these were Rev. E. E. Strong, Rev. R. M. Bell and Rev. Roy Dale Strong, who supplied during the summers of 1924 and 1925. On account of finances, the congregation was unable to secure a full time pastor, and a meeting of the sessions of the three churches resulted in the call of Rev. L. R. Niell for one-third time. He has served this congregation since that time.

This backward glance through more than one hundred years of our history reveals to us a rich inheritance, for few, if any, have a history so rich in faith and so rare in Providence.

U. C. V. RECORD

In publishing the roster of Confederate companies under the head of the Civil War in this work, the names of two well

TROY COMMUNITY

known members of Obion Avalanche failed to be mentioned, in some way overlooked. One was Dr. Walter Brice, army surgeon, and the other was lieutenant W. M. Cunningham, both distinguished in service for the war period and honored citizens of Troy and vicinity in a long and useful life.

OBION COUNTY CENTENNIAL CELEBRATION

A gathering of patriotic citizens and numbers of natives returning home assembled at Troy August 1st and 2nd, 1924, to observe and celebrate with appropriate ceremonies the organization of the county of Obion, which was held three miles southwest of Troy at the home of W. M. Wilson January 19, 1824, following an act of the Legislature of Tennessee in 1823 establishing the county, at that time including all of Lake County.

In charge of arrangements were the chairman, C. P. Wilson, G. R. McDade, Mayor Mike Bright and others. Welcome address was delivered by Mr. Wilson, and speakers following with review of citizens and communities connected with early history included Judge Joel B. Waddell of Union City, John White of Hornbeak, Col. L. D. Tyson, of Knoxville (incidentally a candidate for the U. S. Senate), and Congressman Finis J. Garrett. Mr. Garrett spoke with reference to the Representatives in Congress from West Tennessee and of that particular district now including the counties of Weakley, Gibson and Obion.

Two days were devoted to the celebration, with open homes and hospitality, music and barbecue dinner on the grounds. A few of the former citizens returning for the occasion were Chas. L. Moffatt of Tullahoma, Tenn., Henry Canaday of Mayfield, Ky., Mrs. Lizzie Farris of Caruthersville, Mo., Sam Parker of Hickman, Ky., Mr. and Mrs. W. N. Calhoun of Lake County.

Speaking on the second day was the orator of the occasion, Hon Chas. J. Wright, of Springfield, Mo., a native of Troy and son of another old-time citizen, a noted educator, Charles Wright, an English-born soldier and patriot of the South. The speaker's remarks in part were as follows:

"With the pleasurable experience of my visit to Obion County years ago, and with the memories of childhood and the friends of my youth and young manhood. I never think of returning to Obion County but that I feel that I am coming back home."

In the opening remarks of address the foregoing were in substance the words used by Hon. Chas. J. Wright, attorney, of Springfield, Mo., on the occasion of the centennial celebration at Troy. Mr. Wright's address was delivered on the afternoon of the second day of the centennial. He was introduced by Mr. Carroll P. Wilson, who is also a native of Troy and one of its foremost public citizens and business men.

Mr. Wright remarked that in leaving he told his family that

he was going back home, not that he is any less a loyal citizen of Missouri, sensible and grateful for the things that have surrounded him with a happy home and family and hosts of good friends, but that the call of youthful associations is taking him back.

It is indeed then on this occasion a pleasure to meet those of another generation, some in the audience whose faces are familiar, some again who have come on since and fill the positions of responsibility in life, and again the younger generation in whose faces we trace the kinship of the old-time citizens of Troy and other sections of the county. It makes me feel that it is good to live and that I have not lived in vain. There are no better people on earth than those in Obion County and I feel that I am fortunate to be one of them.

I have returned to speak on the ground where the old courthouse stood within a few feet of where I stood to plead my first law suit.

It was a speech of fourteen minutes duration, but I felt that it was much longer.

I am standing today before those who have known me since I have known anything. This is a great occasion in Obion County. Yesterday and today the gathering fills me with a feeling of solemnity as it carries us back to the days before any of us were born. It is a time to pause and think of how we have lived and for what we have lived, and to recall and pay honor to the memory of those who have made life what it is. But when we stop to consider these things our minds revert to the place of abode and the burial place of that man or woman, whose character and influence have made its impress upon our lives. We do not forget them but fail to preserve the things they have done and said that became a part of our lives and thought. 'As a man thinks, so he is' As the currents of life are controlled so are we influenced by men. And so should men and women guard their thoughts.

I have been in many places. I had the pleasure of traveling in Europe. There the monuments and tablets made an impression upon me. The custom of marking the places where this or that man lived was interesting. It revived historical characters and subjects. I saw the Tower of London, four stores high, built of stone between 1066 and 1083 by William the Conqueror. I saw a dungeon where traitors of the crown were executed. The tower was used as a prison during the late war. I saw in Paris where Marie Antoinette was imprisoned.

There is just as fine scenery in the Ozarks where I live as there is in Scotland. It is just as beautiful, but in Scotland the knights and chiefs and all her great names have been made famous in history, and in literature. Sir Walter Scott has added lustre and renown to his country and its people. You see therefore the things invisible, a panorama with eyes closed and it becomes more interesting.

America also has its beautiful summits, lakes and vales, its interesting men and periods, but there are very few tablets and the resting places of its famous men and women are not all where

TROY COMMUNITY

they may be known. I think of England's shrines and they are mine because England's history is my history.

Think of what this country was in 1824. This square was covered with virgin timber. The county was dense in primeval forests of oak, poplar, hickory, beech, gum, and the streams were then the Obion and Reelfoot rivers, Davidson and Mill creeks and dozens of others. Going farther back you have the wonderful history of Reefoot Lake,, about which I am often asked. Your imagination takes you back to all these things. You look at the people and wonder what it was that brought them here. It was the restless spirit of the pioneers seeking the open country and larger dominion. They came to Tennessee from North and South Carolina in wagon trains. They came to Frankland, afterwards Franklin and then the State became known as Tennessee. They were not imbued with community life as we are now, but they were a sturdy race of people, the best that ever walked the earth. They pursued their way, many of them, into West Tennessee and among others the county of Obion was settled.

Civilization has always traveled westward. Our ancestors came from the mother country, which had its origin in Roman civilization. Northern Europe was half civilized when Rome sent her scouts there to find new territory. They took charge and established a new civilization which gave us our ancestors. Here again the spirit of the race sought freedom in America. They came here that they might not be circumscribed. They came to escape the fate of the martyrs who were circumscribed. They chose to worship God according to the dictates of their own consciences.

And so were our pioneers seeking independence and freedom.

Judge Waddell told you that the first road laid out in Obion County ran from the Obion River at the Weakley County line to the residence of William Wilson, three miles west of Troy, whose home was built in 1820.

(Here follows a history of the county and its organization, heretofore related in another chapter of the book.)

I am proud of my adopted city, Springfield, and I take pleasure in the fact that, due to the University Club, and other clubs, of which I am a member, a number of markers have been erected, singling out the first schoolhouses and county buildings.

The first court held in Troy was in a little brick office, afterwards occupied by Mr. LaMotte, as a tailor shop.

It was again used as a law office by Messrs. Howard, Clark, Shearon and others. A log house was erected in the center of the square, which was the first courthouse in Troy. The public square was cleared off by James Harper, afterwards a merchant of Troy. The courthouse was erected in two days, so the story goes. Two men and a negro cut the logs one day and the house was built the next. So there is a tradition about the old house which should be carved into a tablet marking the place.

(When Mr. Wright took up the organization of the county, Mr. Robert Bond, County Court Clerk, passed into the tent and handed to Mr. Wright a bound volume, the original minutes of the organization of the county, from which several quotations were made. The book is well preserved and in a legible handwriting. It is kept in the vaults of the courthouse, with the other county records.)

Troy dates its existence from March 16, 1825. Fifty acres were donated as a site by William Polk, of North Carolina, who afterwards added fifteen acres to be used forever as a public commons, afterwards known as the "boneyard."

It is not necessary here to repeat those names that follow the organization, but to pass over the early history until the period of Civil War, when the Obion Avalanche was formed. I see one of those here today who was one of that immortal band of volunteers. These men should have a monument. They were a part of the Southern hosts which fought for State rights and political freedom, a vested right of constitutional government, and tho they lost it was not in vain. These men, if they were here today, could tell us of the struggle and the reconstruction. I would like to shake their hands because my father, tho a British subject, was willing to lay down his life for that cause. These veterans are passing along. In my own home town a beautiful Confederate monument stands in Springfield. Some of the men for whom this monument was erected were Tennesseans.

In the wake of civilization came the men who developed the country, its farms, schools, churches. The farmer came first, then the ministers, the teachers, the lawyers. There is no civilization like Christian civilization and citizenship. The Man of Galilee must be the inspiration of every State and county, of every true home. So the minister had his mission. The teacher came next then the business man. They all had their part in the making of Obion County. Those are the men you should honor. One of the first schoolhouses here was Westbrook Academy, northwest of Troy. The teachers were Smith, Sample and Underwood. The academy was north of town. Over towards the northeast another schoolhouse was built by Chas. Wright, my father. (Here we will say for him that his father was one of the most important factors in the educational history of the county. He was a man of fine intellect and polished manner, a Chesterfield, a scholar, and an accomplished instructor).

I want to close with the statement that I am overwhelmed with the pleasure of this occasion. I can never forget this as my home. I was born on the banks of the Mississippi River on the soil of Lake County, at that time a part of Obion, and so I say I am proud of my native land and of whatever share I may have had in its history. I realize that life has not been a failure if, in the discharge of duty, here in Obion or Greene County, Mo., I have in any way contributed to the cause of my people and their welfare and happiness.

I thank you for your courtesies and kind attention. I thank you in the name of my father who passed away twenty years ago. I am deeply sensible for all these kindnesses. I thank Mr. Carroll P. Wilson for his assistance and for the minutes of the County Court, I thank Mr. Bond, your County Court Clerk.

May kind Providence be with you ever.

TROY COMMUNITY

ONLY ONE LEGAL EXECUTION IN THE COUNTY

Joe H. Robey, assigned to the Obion County branch of W. P. A. in the department providing for the "Copying of Historical Records," reveals the fact that only one death sentence, through the legal process of trial by judge and jury, was rendered with final execution of defendant by hanging—only one in the history of Obion County.

This was the case of the State versus Tom Conder, who was brought for the last time to trial at the March term of the Circuit Court in the year 1889, and found guilty as charged of murder in the first degree.

The circumstances were involved in the charge that Conder had formed illicit relations with M. J. Riley, wife of the murdered man, Jack Riley, and that Conder on the day of the murder found them at home together, and proceeded with the help of Mrs. Riley to remove the husband from his wife and property by death.

The killing of Riley occurred some time in the afternoon, probably soon after dinner when the murdered man was in his chair taking a nap. It was evidently a conspiracy, for the reason that Conder was seen leaving the Riley home soon after the gun was fired. The shot was heard some distance away, and Riley had been shot from behind, it is supposed from evidence, the circumstances of which were that one of the conspirators held the gun and the other operated the trigger to fire it pointed at Riley.

Evidence was circumstantial but sufficient for the verdict of death. Mrs. Riley was arraigned for separate trial immediately and found guilty as an accomplice, and sentence of life imprisonment imposed.

Conder was hung at Troy on the 10th day of May, 1889, in an inclosure of frame work provided for that purpose, on what was known as the "Public Commons," that being at the time suited for the occasion.

The Rileys lived in the county about four or five miles west of Troy. Conder was also a resident of that part of the county.

POLK STATION

Polk Station is on the Illinois Central Railroad three and one-half miles southeast of Troy. It was begun in 1872, and was named for James Polk, whose father, John Polk, settled there and opened a farm in 1833. It was known on the railroad as East Troy.

Some of the family names of Polk community include Polk, McDonald, Cunningham, Brown, Anderson, Neel, Baker, Buchanan, Wilson, Moffatt, Bennett, Peery, Hamilton, Stewart, Pryor.

OBION COUNTY HISTORY

RIVES COMMUNITY

Rives, a small town five miles south of Union City, at the crossing of the G. M. & O. and I. C. railroads, in the middle of the nineteenth century (1859 to be exact) had a small beginning not unlike an uneven cowpath meandering over a green sward or a bridle path among some half dozen neighbors. Much of the early settlement came as a result of the establishment of convenient shipping by the railroads. Through the course of the past sixty years livestock, grain, hogs, lumber, poultry and other commodities were shipped north to Chicago and St. Louis or south to Mobile and New Orleans.

Among the early settlers in the immediate locality of Rives, first probably was Waller Caldwell, who had much to do with the establishment of schools, churches and business affairs. Mr. Caldwell operated a hotel in Rives, probably the first building in the business section along the railroad. He was a citizen when Rives was called Troy Station and Peter West operated a "hack line" and a mail route west to Troy. It was before the I. C. Railroad ran a spur to Troy.

Going back to the earliest settlements in the vicinity of Rives it is found that William Nelms, father of A. J. Nelms, located in the undeveloped farming country two miles west of Rives in 1821. Joel S. Enloe, miller and farmer, located three miles west of Rives in 1824. James Harper, with a caravan of pioneers from South Carolina, traveled overland to Obion County in 1824, and in 1825 located on the road leading westward four miles from Obion River—later known as the Rives-Troy road. His son, Ben K. Harper, then 13 years of age, fifteen years later married Margaret Smith and cleared a farm in the rich valley section south of the road mentioned, not far from Rives. On the same road just north of the Harper settlement was the home of I. N. Farris, son of Wilford Farris, Sr., who located in Obion County in 1828. Here also in the same community was the home of H. I. (Ki) Wade, who married Jane Harper, eldest daughter of Ben K. Harper. The Wade home was settled in the fifties. Two sons, B. J. and Ike, and two daughters, Martha and Mrs. Lindsay, of the family remained in 1940. Joe Harper, son of Ben K. Harper, married Dell Farris, and a son, Knox Harper, lives at Rives. Wilford Farris, grandson of the pioneer Wilford, married Laura Harper, daughter of Ben K. Harper. All this neighborhood centered around Pleasant Hill church and school.

Not far west of Pleasant Hill was the Cal Pleasant home and a little farther westward Fairfield, one of the oldest settle-

THOMAS B. MOFFAT

Born in South Carolina 1835
Located at Troy 1858
Entered Southern Confederacy
Volunteered in Co. A, 47th Tenn.
First Lieut. 1863, Captain 1864
While in front lost right arm in
Battle of Franklin Nov. 3, 1864
Merchant at Rives 1866 to 1898
Married Nannie Hamilton
Member A. R. P. Church

ments in the county, now to be located on the highway half way between Union City and Troy. It is said, but hard to establish as a fact, that after the county was organized at the home of Colonel Wilson southwest of Troy, the first session of the County Court was held at Fairfield. It is, however, a fact that Fairfield was a considerable settlement, affording a general store, cotton gin, blacksmith shop, school, church, and the sporting blood of a race track. On the Pleasant farm in the eighties, something very rare in the county, was a fine peach orchard of many acres, cultivated in the same manner of the Georgia peach orchards.

Returning to the immediate locality of Rives, in the early days of settlement Isham Wallace operated a flour mill by water power and Calvin McCaw a steam saw mill.

John F. Clemmons bought and settled on the Horace Head farm west of Rives, later the Claude Botts home. To Mr. Clemmons and his wife, Martha, the following children were born: Porter, John, Polk, Andrew, Oscar, Hattie, William, Mollie, Maggie and Bettie, all well known in the various activities of business and social life.

Other well known families included John and Jane Faulks Dickey and the children—John, Lee, Frank, Laura, Alice, and Lizzie; Mr. and Mrs. J. B. Caudle and the children— Dee, Ernest, Dell, Alvia, Minnie, Willie and Ammie; T. B. Moffat, wife Nan and the children—Luther, William, Robert, Walter, Greer, Jennie and Anna; Dr. P. A. Wright, wife and sons, Lon and James.

Thos. J. Bonner, merchant, druggist, and at a period in the Prohibition movement in Tennessee, was elected to represent Obion County in the Legislature. Mr. Bonner entered the T. B. Moffat store as salesman and finally became a partner. He was married to Miss Perkins. A son, Cothon Bonner, succeeded his father in the drug business. A daughter, Miss Aletha Bonner has achieved distinction in national music councils. She is a member of the National Federation of Music Clubs, chairman of Music Research, also a writer and contributor to well known music publications.

Clinton C. Callicott, a man of fine church and school connections, was for years chairman of the County Board of Education. His brother-in-law, J. T. Mitchell, a citizen of Union City, is well known for his church and business interests.

A railroad hotel, located at the Rives crossing, an institution established by the M. & O. R. R. as an accommodation to the traveling public and the benefit of the road as an aid to publicity, was forty or fifty years ago conducted under the management of Bumpass and Dismukes. W. M. Dismukes was later connected with the Palace Hotel in Union City. About that time or earlier Robert

RIVES COMMUNITY

Hamilton was express agent at Rives and later his son, Bob, express messenger on the M. & O.

Geo. F. Botts and T. A. Cummings were merchants and well known citizens of Rives.

One of the large and influential families of Rives community was that of Joel Shore, Sr., whose sons have been for many years identified with business affairs and public interests. One of these, J. H. Shore, has served for a number of terms in succession as County Deputy Trustee.

There were others, including Williamson Morris, Jas. C. McCaw, Dr. T. P. Palmer, Dr. E. H. White, Dr. T. P. Callicott, Dr. W. C. Pressly, Drs. J. B. and Snead Adkerson, Drs. Bean, Friedman, Watson and the ministers, Revs. J. H. Thomas and P. F. Johnson.

In the county east of Rives, comprising the community of Number Seven District, the families of old settlers and others were the Stovalls, Crittendons, Dickensens, Walker, Shipp, Olive, Bryan, Davis, Wagster, Stanley, Bowers, Cheatham, Askins, Howard Phebus, Reynolds, Carter, Jackson. E. F. McSpedden, newspaper contributor, is also a farmer of this locality.

A farmer and a citizen of the Rives community was Anselmo Harris, particularly interested in soil conservation and intensive farming. Mr. Harris had a great deal to do with agricultural display at the State and county fairs, installing and supervising ornamental farm-booth exhibits, which attracted general attention. In spare time he was also occupied with hand carving in wood, a hobby in which he became skillful, making some very interesting specimens for exhibits.

RIVES SCHOOLS

Progress has been made from the one-room, one-teacher school of the early eighties of the last century to the present main high-school building and annex, which houses the first through to the sixth grades, the gym and the agriculture building. The annex was completed in 1939.

Principals of the Rives High School have included well known teachers as follows: First, W. H. Cook, who held the position for nearly fifteen years, with increased building additions and the number of teachers. Successors to Professor Cook—Professor Watson, one term; Professor Atkins, two terms; Professor Johnson, two terms. Professor Hays, very efficient in organization and leadership, followed, assisted by Miss Sadie Fry, of Fulton, Miss Winnie Woody, of Obion and Miss Florence Botts, of Rives.

In 1921-22, under the management of W. H. Cravens, the school grew very rapidly in rank and number. In 1939 Professor Cravens was succeeded by C. A. Palmer and in 1940-41 Prof. Wm.

OBION COUNTY HISTORY

Algea became principal, with the following faculty of teachers: Science, Tom Stevenson; home economics, Mrs. Joe McClure; agriculture, Joe McClure; assistants for the twelve grades, Mrs. Wm. Algea, Walter Wilson, Mrs. Nell Foresee, Mrs. Leslie Shore, Mrs. Louise Marshall, Miss Edith Bond, Mrs. Wm. Jennings; Mrs. Bud Mosier, piano.

BUSINESS DIRECTORY

The Farmers and Merchants Bank of Rives was organized in 1903, with a capital stock of $15,000. The first president was Thos. J. Bonner; vice-president, J. B. Caudle; cashier, Dave Clemmons. Mr. Bonner was succeeded by B. J. Wade as president and Preston Shore as cashier. J. H. Shore was vice-president. J. M. Fisher followed Preston Shore as cashier and H. P. Reeves as assistant. Banking in Rives has been very successful under safe and capable management. Rives mayor, J. A. Hight; recorder, O. A. Brown; aldermen, C. D. Reeder, Monroe McCowan, Leslie Shore, Press Callicott; marshal, Polk Houser.

Business set-up: Arthur Johnson, grocer; Leslie Shore, grocer and service station; O. A. Brown, grocery and general merchandise; Willie Griffith, grocery and creamery; Bonner & Sons, drug store; Morris Callicott, service station, Farmers and Merchants Bank corner. Claude Woody, grocery and food specialist. Morning Star Nursery, Cultra Bros. Saw mills, J. S. Garrett, Lee Tull: Stock buyers: B. J. Wade and Monroe McCowan—first-class mules a specialty. Agent at I. C. and G. M. & O. R. R. depot, Sam Jones. 1940 census enumeration, 481.

MORNING STAR NURSERY

The Morning Star Nursery near Rives is owned by E. S. Cultra and A. J. Cultra. The latter lives in Onargo, Illinois.

Including a lease of some fifty acres, the total acreage embraces a tract of more than three hundred acres in plants, shrubs and innumerable variety of flower growth. An average of twenty men working six days a week are employed. George and Sayre Cultra are the local managers in charge of the farms, while landscape department is managed by Archie and Robert Cultra. These four young men are the sons of E. S. Cultra. In the main the business consists of shipping shrubbery and plants in car load lots.

NAVAL OFFICERS

Among others who have very kindly assisted in collecting material for this work is Mrs. T. P. Palmer, of Rives, for many years a valued correspondent of the county press. Mrs. Palmer is generally interested in community affairs and particularly active in cultural and educational movements. She has two sons in the

RIVES COMMUNITY

U. S. Navy, connected with the Pacific Fleet. One is Khem Wade Palmer, Commander of the U. S. S. Whitney, the other, Mars Watkins Palmer, Chief Wireless Operator (C. R. E.) on the U. S. S. Louisville. He is due for retirement in September, 1941. Both have had service in China and other foreign countries. The U. S. S. Whitney base is at San Diego.

RIVES C. P. CHURCH

The Cumberland Presbyterian Church at Rives was organized in 1878 by Rev. J. B. Calhoun, with 12 members. It was then admitted as a part of Obion Presbytery. Cumberland Presbyterians in this vicinity had worshiped with other denominations in a school building. Isham Wallace gave the lot on which the first church building was erected. Among the first elders of this church were the following: J. B. Caudle, Baxter Cummings, Isham G. Wallace and G. W. Stovall. The Rev. J. B. Calhoun was the first pastor, serving a growing congregation of forty faithful members. Following him Rev. Jo McLeskey served as pastor for seven years.

Mrs. J. B. Faulks, of Troy, in 1895 organized a Woman's Missionary Society.

About the year 1900 it was decided to move into a house of worship farther removed from the railroad. The old building was then dismantled and the material used for a new building in a more convenient location. The late G. W. Stovall figured largely in financing the rebuilding of the church and in the purchase of new pews.

In the year 1915 the Pleasant Hill congregation united with the Rives church, thus adding strength to the organization. At this time the eldership was increased to include T. C. Callicott, L. A. Callicott, R. L. Harper, T. A. Cummings, Hubert Shore, W. W. Agnew and W. J. Caldwell. The Sunday School, with T. C. Callicott as superintendent, and the Christian Endeavor, with R. L. Harper as leader, made splendid contributions to the growth and increasing interest of the church.

In 1930 it was deemed best for the Cumberland Presbyterian, Methodist and Associate Reformed Presbyterian churches to occupy t he same building. Satisfactory plans were made and this union was perfected in January, 1931. This union has been altogether satisfactory. The names of E. E. Shore, E. T. Jones, H. P. Callicott, Leonard Stovall and C. A. Palmer were added to the roll of elders. L. A. Callicott and W. W. Agnew are the oldest in the service. Rev. Ernest Cross, of McKenzie, served the church as pastor for some time.

The church conducts an active Sunday School with Leonard Stovall as superintendent and Cothon Bonner as secretary and treasurer; Young People's Work under the leadership of Mrs.

E. E. Shore. For a number of years the church has had an active Woman's Missionary Society. The late Mrs. T. C. Callicott was president for ten years. She is succeeded by Mrs. W. C. Stovall as president, with Mrs. Ed Houser as secretary and treasurer.

Through this triple capacity as a union church the church is contributing largely to the spiritual and moral growth of the community.

RIVES M. E. CHURCH

The Methodist Episcopal Church in Rives was organized in the Associate Reformed Presbyterian building on October 12, 1890, by the Rev. W. C. Waters, pastor, with twenty-nine members, fourteen of whom were transferred from the Pleasant Hill congregation, three from Obion Chapel, nine by letter and three by confession of faith.

In the year 1894, under the administration of Rev. J. H. Witt, the place of worship was changed from the A. R. P. church to the Cumberland Presbyterian church, remaining at that place until the erection of a new church under the pastorate of Rev. W. M. Midyett in 1897, the same being dedicated in September of the same year by the late Rev. Ashley Wilson, presiding elder.

Beginning with Rev. W. C. Waters in 1890 following is a list of pastors serving the church since that time: Rev. W. O. Lanier, J. A. Vaughn, J. H. Witt, S. Weaver, D. C. Johnson, W. M. Midyett, W. W. Armstrong, J. M. Hamil, J. A. Moody, R. M. Walker, C. D. Hilliard, J. W. Joyner, W. F. Barrier, R. R. Hart, R. C. Whitnell, E. H. Stewart, J. T. Bagby.

RIVES CHURCH OF CHRIST

The Church of Christ of Rives was established about 1890 with 35 members, among whom were E. Laster, and wife, M. T. Warren and wife, Mrs. Hanna Farris, H. Botts and wife, W. S. Long and wife, Geo. F. Botts, and others whose names are lost to the records. Since that time the following brethren have labored regularly for this congregation: Elihu Scott, J. S. Haskins, John R. Williams, Elder Wright, A. G. Freed, N. B. Hardeman, W. C. Hall, and others have preached there in series of meetings as follows: J. C. McQuiddy, F. W. Smith, F. B. Soygley, J. W. Dunn and others.

RIVES A. R. P. CHURCH

The Rives congregation was organized at Pleasant Hill November 18, 1882, with thirteen members. Mr. T. B. Moffat made the promise to the Lord that he would give all the money he made buying cotton in the fall of 1887 for a new church in Rives. God greatly blessed him and that year he purchased a lot and gave most of the money needed to build a church. This building was dedicated January 8, 1888. Rev. J. P. Weed preached the sermon, with Rev. T. P. Pressly in charge.

Rev. T. P. Pressly supplied the congregation, preaching once each month until 1902. In this year Rives and Polk united in one pastoral charge, and Rev. E. P. Lindsay of the Tennessee and Alabama Presbytery was sent by Synod as stated supply. He began his labors January 1, 1902, and was returned the following year as supply. He accepted a call to the charge June 30, 1903. Rev. Lindsay continued in this field for about ten years.

He married a daughter of the congregation, Miss Sallie Wade, who was a helpful and efficient helpmeet.

In the year 1912 he accepted the work at Memphis. Possibly no better work has ever been done in Synod than Dr. Lindsay and Mrs. Lindsay did in Memphis.

The congregation was without a pastor for some time. Rev. T. P. Pressly and others supplied until 1915 when Rev. W. O. Wier accepted the work. This was his first charge.

Mr. Wier also married a daughter of the congregation, Miss Bess Harper. Mr. Wier was an excellent worker.

Mr. Wier died in 1916 and was buried in the cemetery at Union City, Tenn. He came from Kings Mountain, N. C.

Again the congregation was without a pastor, and again Rev. T. P. Pressly and others supplied until January 14, 1917, when Rev. J. L. Boyd accepted the work. Rev. Boyd remained as pastor three and one-half years.

In the summer of 1921, Rev. J. A. Baird supplied the congregation, and in the summer of 1922 Rev. B. Dale White supplied until he accepted the work in India as a missionary.

In the year 1922, the first Sabbath of November, Rev. L. R. Niell took charge of the work, and is still on the field.

Possibly in all the state of Tennessee you could not find so fine a spirit of co-operation among denominations as prevails in Rives. So complete is that spirit that the Cumberland Presbyterians, Methodist and the Associate Reformed Presbyterians have united in one building.

OBION RIVER IMPROVEMENTS

Probably the Obion river drainage district, authorized under a special act of the Tennessee general assembly in 1913, will be recalled and the failure of the project as a result of its promotion, which was to serve as a means of drainage and the reclamation of Obion river bottom lands in Obion county, for which it was intended.

Reviewing the subject some years after the unfortunate undertaking, it is of no particular interest or importance, except as to the fact that a portion of the work in the particular section affected was brought into requisition, under the recent act providing for flood control and channel clearance in Obion and Dyer counties, and made to serve as a nucleus for a new channel tapping the Rutherford fork of Obion river at a point two miles south of the main body of the river, extending southwest 28 miles, almost parallel with the main river channel, to a point on the river near Sharp's Ferry. This work has been done to provide a double outlet for the overflow waters from Rutherford fork branch of Obion river, with the object of maintaining both channels instead of one to protect the low lands from high water.

All this is included in the work embraced in the Federal project authorized by a special act of Congress, providing relief for Dyer and Obion counties for flood control and channel clearance on Obion river.

The work was handled by the engineers of the war department, under the sponsorship of the U. S. Geodetic and Coast survey, for the counties of Dyer and Obion in the State of Tennessee, and under the personal supervision of C. G. Little, associate superintendent U. S. Engineers, Memphis, Tenn.

The entire project embraces work on the Obion river and tributaries from a point two miles eastof the line in Carroll county, extending west through Weakley county 25 miles to Terrell in Obion county; thence with the main channel of Obion river three miles to the G. M. & O. R. R.; thence southwest six miles to Federal Highway 45; thence nine miles to Obion; thence seven miles to Sharp's Ferry, and then into Dyer county, and following the river to its mouth, entering the Mississippi river at Hale's Point, a total of 110 miles of river improvements, 50 miles of which are included in the Obion county project.

The work of flood control and channel clearance in this project comprises the cutting out of channel, dynamiting and dragging logs from the channel, removing drift, overhanging trees and limbs, excavation, etc.

Five miles of excavation work was done from the G. M. & O. R. R. to Federal Highway 45, cutting out channel all the way from five to fifteen feet with drag line, clearing the old river bed, leaving for maintenance a 25-foot channel from the G. M. & O. R. R. at Rives to the deep waters of Obion River in the vicinity of highway 45. Drag lines have been in general use from time to time in bringing the bed of the river to a uniform level.

The work complete was accomplished by the collaboration of the U. S. Engineers and Ralph G. Hornbeak, representing the W. P. A. in Obion County, as sponsors of the project. Labor was furnished by the W. P. A.

The entire project has been pursued with systematic effort

RIVES COMMUNITY

for the purpose of increasing the depth of fall and flow of water from the river channels without obstruction and with sufficient velocity to prevent overflow in the farming country adjacent to the river, and these objects have no doubt been effectively achieved. The fall of water has been accelerated to a total drop of three times the descent heretofore made.

Elevation around the river bottom in the vicinity of Rives is 293.0 feet above sea level. The natural ground around highway 45 is 287.0 feet above; the 25-foot channel at highway 45 is 269.0 feet above, and the bottom channel at Rives is 280.0 feet above sea level.

A very satisfactory report is made of labor conditions in connection with the project. Work was pursued under ordinary hardships with the highest degree of coordination and success and the results accomplished were highly satisfactory.

Returning to the disasters of the old drainage district, no doubt there have been many misfortunes which may be restored and farm lands reclaimed, under the new system of improved flood control. It is confidently expected that this Federally-controlled project will be worth millions of dollars to the low-land farmers, increased resources and generally improved conditions among all our people in the county.

MURDER OF REV. HOLDER

One of the most inhuman acts in the annals of crime was the murder of Rev. B. L. Holder, a Cumberland Presbyterian minister, on the night of December 27, 1906, at his farm home on the road between Troy and Rives, out in the field near what was known at the time as the "twin bridges." Rev. Holder was shot while riding in his buggy. It was related that he jumped out of buggy to get away from pursuit, but was followed into the field and there he was bludgeoned and beat to death with the gun, found with a broken stock near his body after the crime.

Evidence produced at the examination by Sheriff Finch showed that the minister was killed with his own gun and that the shoes worn by the murderer were found next morning at the home of the family. The gun was bloody.

Lee Holder, the minister's son, was afterwards tried and convicted, and sentenced to be hanged at the courthouse yard in Union City. Execution was postponed by suspension of judgment, through the efforts of defense attorney, R. A. Pierce, on account of the effects of a public hanging in the immediate vicinity of the homes nearby. The boy was returned by order of the court to prison and there some time afterwards died of lingering illness.

KENTON COMMUNITY

(By WALTER HOWELL)

This is an early history of that portion of Obion County lying south of the Obion river in which is located Civil Districts seven, eight, and eleven. This statement is compiled from information furnished by various residents who were among the early settlers of this district. Names and events mentioned are prior to 1880. With our limited information we will no doubt fail to mention the names of many of the early settlers of Kenton.

Kenton is the only town located in this part of Obion County and is partially in Gibson County. The entire business section of Kenton, its schools, and churches are located in Obion County. A large portion of the residential section is in Gibson County.

The original town site of Kenton was surveyed about the time the Mobile & Ohio Railroad was being constructed through this section. On the west boundary line of the depot grounds in the center of Main street there is buried an iron car coupling pin which was used as one of the starting points of this survey. This was prior to 1858. It was laid out on forty acres of land belonging to J. R. Moore. The Mobile & Ohio Railroad received as a gift a strip of land 150 feet wide on each side of the railroad through the center of this tract and was referred to as depot grounds. For this and other concessions it was agreed that the depot and other buildings necessary for the railroad at this point would be located on this particular property.

A post office was established on May 27, 1852 in Gibson County, Tennessee in the vicinity of the present location of Kenton. This post office was called Andalusia and the first postmaster was Harvey Eckley. This post office was moved to Kenton in Obion County on March 18, 1859. Village free mail delivery for the residents of Kenton was established on March 1, 1912. This is a privilege enjoyed by only about ninety-six of the small towns in the United States.

It was not until 1874 that Kenton was incorporated giving it local town government with a mayor, aldermen, and other officials. W. C. Pharr was the first mayor.

During the early history of Kenton a number of saloons were open which furnished intoxicating liquor to those desiring it. This gave an opportunity to the more or less bad element in the community to become intoxicated, especially on Saturdays and cause considerable distress to the better law abiding people of the community. Many fights and numerous feuds of the opposing lawless factions marked the early settlement of this community.

KENTON COMMUNITY

WALTER HOWELL Sr.

Native of Kenton, Tenn., with early training in local schools and general store, advanced with marked ability as bank cashier at Kenton, Obion and Union City, then to the presidency of the Old National Bank of Union City, succeeding L. S. Parks.

Recognized for his banking ability and general qualifications, Mr. Howell was selected by the Federal Government to supervise the organization of the Federal Land Bank of Louisville, one of the twelve regional land loan banks of the United States. Having to do with the lending of millions of dollars, Mr. Howell, in 1922 resigned to accept presidency and organize the Louisville and the Union Joint Stock land banks, operated by private capital under the Federal Farm Loan Act. In 1928 he was Chairman of the Board of the two banking institutions named.

Failing eyesight and indications of blindness caused Mr. Howell's resignation to return to his home in Union City. Here he established the Fidelity Finance Company, with Walter Reynolds Howell and Marjorie Howell, son and daughter, as associate operators and managers of the company.

Elected as director and member of the Finance Committee of the Third National Bank of Union City, Mr. Howell is regular in attendance and active at meetings.

Mr. Howell is the son of Jethro Howell, Jr., and Annie Ware Howell and was married to Joliet Reynolds in October, 1903.

OBION COUNTY HISTORY

Like all newly settled communities this section was covered with virgin forests, and the principal occupation of the citizens was the clearing of these forests and building houses for their homes, principally of logs. Not much progress was made until after the Civil War. The early citizens of Kenton were for a large part the sons and daughters of the first settlers in this vicinity. From 1865 to 1875 Kenton became a thriving small town due to the fact that it offered good facilities for the shipping by railroad of the corn, cotton, cattle, and hogs, and other farm commodities produced by the farmers in this vicinity. It soon had many general stores where these farmers could purchase the supplies they needed.

Some of the families living in this vicinity may be mentioned as follows: the McCrory family living south of Kenton; the Rosson family, southeast of Kenton; another Rosson family, west of Kenton; J. R. Carrol who married Susanne Needham and after her death married Mary Elizabeth Norton lived just west of Kenton; a brother, Jim Carrol, lived north of Kenton, later moved to Kenton with his family and was for many years mayor; the Perkins family, west of Kenton; the Thomas Ware family, just west of Kenton; the Tisdale family west of Kenton; the Simmons family, north of Kenton; the McNeely family, north of Kenton; the Wade family, east of Kenton; the Taylor family, northeast of Kenton; the Clement family, west of Kenton; the Mathes family, north of Kenton; the Potter family who moved in from Middle Tennessee; Aunt Polly West and her husband "Parson" West who operated a boarding house and hotel in the central part of Kenton; her daughter, Mattie, married Sam Turner, a railroad locomotive engineer, who had become partially paralyzed and operated the pumping station at Kenton for the railroad; the Mitchell family who operated a hotel and boarding house in east Kenton; the Harris family who moved to Texas; the Boone family who moved to Oklahoma; the Enoch Needham family that moved to Van Buren, Arkansas; and many other families which were the early settlers in this vicinity. Each of these families had numerous sons and daughters who married sons and daughters from other communities and moved to Kenton to engage in the mercantile business or professions which caused it to become a thriving community and trade center. During this period mention might be made of Tom Hollomon, who lived in the Boyett store community, who married Miss Zaricor, and moved to Kenton. John Hollomon, a brother, married Miss Garrison and moved to Kenton. They opened a general store to the firm name of Hollomon Brothers. Dr. Powell moved into Kenton and established the first drug store in partnership with Mattie Tilghman. Jethro Howell married Annie Ware and moved to Kenton and formed a

KENTON COMMUNITY

partnership with Jim Taylor in the grocery business. Henry Flowers married Miss Howell from North Union community, moved to Kenton and formed a partnership with W. H. Wilson and opened a general store under the name of Wilson & Flowers which was operated there for many years. Nathan Garrison, one of the earliest settlers of Kenton, opened a harness and saddle shop which continued in business for a number of years. Sam Rosson married Roberta Tisdale, and his brother, Mike Rosson, married Miss Perkins. They moved into Kenton and established a blacksmith and wagon shop. Another drug store was established by Garrison brothers. Another store was established by W. F. Jones who was one of the early postmasters of Kenton. He married Sue Potter. W. C. Pharr moved into Kenton as the railroad agent and married Belle Wade. Dr. Ramsey, one of the first doctors in Kenton, married Kate Potter. Squire Bob Foster married Sally Potter. Dr. E. A. Taylor, from district number seven, married Miss Crittendon and moved into Kenton. His brother, Dr. Z. F. Taylor, a dentist, married Callie Holland and moved into Kenton. Another brother, Dr. A. J. Taylor, married and moved into Kenton. T. L. Moseley, a young lawyer, married Ella Tilghman from the North Union community and became Kenton's first attorney. W. A. White, who lived west of Kenton, moved into Kenton. He had a large family of boys and girls. Dr. Northern was one of Kenton's first doctors. J. W. Howell married Miss Dozier and moved into Kenton. W. H. Wade married Ellen Powell, daughter of Dr. Powell. W. A. Montgomery, who lived west of Kenton, married Lou Wade and came to Kenton. Another old time resident of Kenton was Seid Porter, who with his wife and daughter, Molly, lived in east Kenton. Dr. H. T. Fullerton married Miss Black, moved into Kenton and was a well known physician there for many years. J. W. Clayton married a Miss McCrory and opened a drug store. J. A. Killingworth was for many years the section foreman of the railroad for Kenton. R. F. Tisdale married Mary Simmons and later moved with his family to Union City. There was the Kerr family who had a large number of boys living west of Kenton. W. F. Collins, who married Octie Fisher and was at one time postmaster of Kenton. W. W. Casey, who married Miss Westmoreland and lived in west Kenton. These are only a few of the pioneers

The railroad locomotives burned wood as fuel. The railroad company established a large wood yard on the depot grounds just south of Main street. The farmers of the community in clearing their lands cut the timber into proper lengths for this fuel and brought it to this wood yard and sold it to the railroad. Almost every train passing through town would stop at this wood yard where the train men would load this wood into the tender of the locomotive.

OBION COUNTY HISTORY

BUSINESS OF KENTON

The first store buildings in Kenton were built south of Main street and faced the railroad depot grounds. About five of these buildings were built on the south side of Main street and only one of these buildings was two stories. This building was occupied by Dr. Powell as a drug store. Between Main street and College street facing the depot grounds, about seven buildings were erected for mercantile establishments. One was erected on the south side of College street, which was two stories and the upstairs was used as a Masonic Hall, and the lower floor used as a drug store. The first brick store house, to be built in Kenton, was erected on the north side of College street facing the depot grounds. It was a two story building about 80 feet long and 50 feet wide. This was made into two store rooms and was occupied by Wilson & Flowers as a general store. There were many other people who established various enterprises in Kenton. Rev. Jo McLeskey, with a large family of boys and girls, moved into Kenton and in addition to preaching on Sunday he operated a sawmill during the week. W. J. Mathes moved into Kenton and erected the first flour mill, which ground the wheat and corn on mill stones. This furnished the flour and meal for all the people in this vicinity. It was operated by steam power. Later he built a gin across the road which was operated by a wire cable from the flour mill. It is not possible to name the various mercantile and other establishments that were brought into Kenton during this period.

At the close of the Civil War Gray & West and Howell, Carroll & Hollomon constituted the business firms of the town. The former firm soon closed out and others succeeded, the most important of which was Wilson & Flowers, Willingham & Milner, and W. W. Cacey. Business men in 1885 were White & Bogle, Turner & Robinson, J. L. Smith, Kerr & Co., general merchandise; Wade Bros., groceries; W. A. Montgomery, J. T. Senter, drugs. Physicians: Dr. Henry Fullerton, Drs. Raymer, J. M. Capps, and A. J. Skiles. A blacksmith for 50 years was Tom Wall.

A steam flouring mill was operated in Kenton by White & Bogle in 1882, later improving output to 60 barrels a day. J. D. Graham was appointed postmaster at Kenton in 1886.

Before and after the Civil War period cotton, grain and other products were taken to Hickman (first known Mills Point) and sold to commission merchants. People living as far south as Trenton and as far east as McKenzie, practically all between traded at Hickman. Products were hauled to Hickman in farm wagons and returning loaded with dry goods, provisions and farm supplies. The trip from Gibson and Weakley counties was made in two days, camping the first night near Hickman. It is said that

KENTON COMMUNITY

early settlers in Obion and Gibson counties bought salt in barrels at Hickman and returning came by Reelfoot Lake for a supply of fish, which was salted down for winter use.

KENTON SCHOOLS

In 1878 a school was established in Kenton known as the Kenton Academy. In connection with the Masonic Lodge and the I. O. O. F., a two-story brick building was erected on the present site of the Kenton school buildings. Among the first teachers were Prof. Hayes, Prof. Decker, Prof. Hodges, Miss Donna Brooks, Prof. Roberts and others. In 1880 Miss Ida Flynn came to Kenton as an assistant teacher to Prof. Roberts. Later she established "Miss Flynn's Select School" whose enrollment was limited to twenty-five. This school was operated as a private school for a number of years.

For reasons involved in the suspension of school funds in 1883 public schools did not open again until the fall of 1886. Prof. Throop took charge, and in succession J. M. DeBow was elected superintendent of the Kenton schools. In the election of Mr. DeBow as County Superintendent of Public Instruction, Robert C. Mayo succeeded Mr. DeBow as superintendent of the Kenton schools. Principals of the Kenton High School from 1921-22 ranged as follows: E. L. Hall, J. M. DeBow, R. C. Mayo, A. E. Caldwell, Jr., J. M. DeBow, G. S. Moffat.

Latest directory of the Kenton Public Schools is as follows: G. S. Moffat, principal; Marguerite Adams, Mary B. Brewer, Ruby B. Crowe, Joe Fields, Marie Hollomon, Zelma Johnson, Frances Montgomery, Margie Robinson, Jane Sue Scott, Jas. E. Tice, Wilmac Walker, Cordia Zaricor.

The newspapers of Kenton were as follows: Capt. J. H. Dean, in 1878, published the Kentuckian. Next was the Kenton Recorder, established by Colonel Long. Some years later J. C. Potter and Joe. J. Kirby conducted a local paper. Afterwards Editor Grimes published the Kenton Argus. Then the Rooks Bros. published the Herald. Chas. Smith was the next publisher with the Kenton News. The latest is the Tri-City Reporter, published by Luther L. Robinson, Jr.

This portion of the county is one of the best sections of Obion. The town of Kenton, although yet small, has for its citizens some of the best people of the county. Its boys and girls have gone forth from this community and have made for themselves names in their chosen professions. They will be found as teachers in the schools and universities of the country, executives in banks, railroads and other important professions throughout the country. The virgin forests have been transformed into fertile fields and splendid highways, good homes, well kept farms, and every evidence of thrift and prosperity of its citizens.

The Shatz mercantile interests had an interesting connection with the history of Kenton for a portion of time, beginning in the early part of the present century, when Mr. Sol Shatz, a native of Lithuania, adjoining Poland, settled in the United States and came to Kenton. Mr. Shatz was a man of fine vision, business integrity and ability, and beginning as a merchant at Kenton branched out into other lines of industry, establishing a cotton gin and engaging as a commission and wholesale dealer, buying and shipping from the local market. His interests included livestock, cotton, grain, lumber, etc. Mr. Shatz is head of the Shatz system of stores, with headquarters at Kenton, his sons, Abe and Sam Shatz in charge, three stores at Union City, with Dave Shatz and Shatz and Byer in charge, one at Hickman, with Gaither Jones in charge, one at Mayfield, with Louie Shatz in charge, one at Martin, with Joe Shatz in charge, and one at Dyer, with Eulus Beasley in charge.

The Shatz Gin Co., Abe and Sam in charge, is remodeled and enlarged with four new Continental stands and a heavy hydraulic press for baling.

KENTON BUSINESS DIRECTORY

Dry Goods Stores: Shatz General Store, Draper's Store, Jitney Jungle Store operated by McMakin & King, F. & H. Variety Store operated by Geo. and Wm. Freeman.

Grocery Stores: Our Cash Grocery, Freeman & Hamilton Grocery, W. M. Hollomon Grocery Store.

Doherty Second-hand Furniture Store.

McKee Feed Store.

T. M. King & Son, lumber yard.

Restaurants: Ann's Cafe, Newbill's Restaurant, Caldwell's Tourist Home.

Drug Store: T. M. Bogle.

Insurance: Howell Insurance Agency, Brush Insurance Agency.

Service Stations: Cities Service, Jamie Allen Service, Jenkins Service.

Motor and Oil companies: Aycock & Hollomon Motor Co. Tilghman Motor Co., Mid-South Oil Co.

Beauty Shops: Roberta's Beauty Shop, Evelyn's Beauty Shop.

Barbers: Rochell & O'Daniel, Keathley Barber Shop.

Kentucky Ice & Coal Co.

Physicians: Dr. J. M. Capps and Dr. J. H. Gray.

Dentists: Dr. R. B. Baucom.

Bryant's Shoe Shop.

G. M. & O. R. R. Agent, Gray Moseley.

KENTON COMMUNITY

BOARD OF MAYOR AND ALDERMEN

Mayor of Kenton, John R. McKee; recorder, Price King. Aldermen: I. W. Freeman, Tom Wade, R. C. Tilghman, J. Frank Johnson, Sam Shatz, R. W. Walker.

Marshal, Corbett Barner. Night police officer, A. J. Flowers.

Postmaster of Kenton, Joe F. Penn.

Kenton attorney, Joe Gordon.

Lions Club: President, R. C. Tilghman; secretary, Gordon Moffat; Tail twister, Geo. W. Freeman.

Mason Hall Bank of Kenton: I. W. Freeman, president; J. W. Newman, cashier; J. H. Herndon, assistant cashier. This bank was organized in 1910 and moved from Mason Hall to Kenton in April, 1933. Presidents who have managed the bank are as follows: A. T. Thompson and J. H. Smith. Former cashiers: W. A. Thompson and J. J. Thompson.

1940 census enumeration, 809.

KENTON CUMBERLANDS

The Cumberland Presbyterian Church at Kenton was, according to Goodspeed's History, organized in August, 1867, a part of Hopewell Presbytery. In a few years it, with North Union and several other congregations, made a part of Obion Presbytery.

The early records of this congregation, prior to 1893, have been lost. At that time the list included Rev. S. H. Braley, pastor; H. T. Fullerton, clerk of the session, and the following board of ruling elders: W. F. Collins, A. A. Fleming, H. T. Fullerton, Jas. W. Howell, W. F. Jones, W. C. Pharr, R. A. Turner, C. C. Tilghman, W. A. White and C. R. Wade.

The small frame building, used by the congregation of the Church of Christ, was constructed soon after the organization of the Cumberland Presbyterians, and after the merger became by decree of the State Supreme Court the property of those remaining Cumberland Presbyterians. In 1910 this building was sold to Rev. Gentry Reynolds for the use of the "Christian Church," and later sold by him to the Church of Christ. Then a new brick building on College Street was erected by the Cumberland Presbyterians under the administration of Rev. R. L. Keathley.

The Board of Ruling Elders was then constituted as follows: W. R. Holmes, clerk; W. A. Montgomery, C. R. Wade, C. C. Tilghman, A. A. Fleming, J. A. Reeves. Since then a new board was constituted as follows: W. R. Holmes, clerk; A. M. Howell, assistant clerk: C. M. Montgomery, Cleve Hollomon, Edd Arnold, Inman Freeman, Ray Craft. The Board of Deacons was as follows: Tom Wade, Geo. W. Freeman, Carthel W. Elder. Pastor, B. J. Reagan.

The congregation is grouped with North Union and Cool Springs and has services two Sundays in each month. It is an organization of fine spirit and loyal service.

KENTON PRESBYTERIANS

The Presbyterian congregation was organized at Kenton in 1906, meeting in the school building. Some of the ruling elders appeared as follows: Dr. C. A. Hudson, W. D. Kerr, Buck Collins, Henry Flowers, Sr., T. M. Bogle; deacon, Jesse Carroll. Pastor in 1907, R. R. Brown; pianist, Mrs. T. M. Bogle; later Miss Florence Sinclair.

In 1909 the U. S. A. Church was built west of the school building. Pastors included Revs. Lewis, A. B. Pritchard, W. G. Stockton, W. J. Shelton, W. M. Gilliam, G. F. Burns, W. D. Parish, R. A. Cody, Revs. Eaves, Whitfield, J. B. Oakley. Pastors serving in 1940; Rev. J. Bonkemeyer of Dyer; with ruling elders, R. D. Walker, E. E. Smith, J. M. Howell and Cecil King; deacons, Jesse Carroll and Clarence Bogle. Sunday School officers: Cecil King, superintendent; Clarence Bogle, assistant; Albert King, secretary; Miss Wilmac Walker, pianist; treasurer, Mrs. Cecil King. Sunday school teachers: Mrs. Latine Bogle, Mrs. Jesse Carroll, Mrs. Cecil King, Mrs. Kathleen Bogle.

Officers of the Presbyterian Woman's Missionary Society: Mrs. Cecil King, president; Mrs. Latine Bogle, vice-president; Mrs. Jesse Carroll, secretary; Mrs. W. D. Kerr, secretary of stewardship ;Mrs. Henry Flowers, treasurer. Mrs. Clarence Bogle, corresponding secretary.

KENTON CHURCH OF CHRIST

The Church of Christ congregation was organized in Kenton about 1908. The church was established some years later. The following elders have preached for the congregation in Kenton: G. Dallas Smith, A. G. Freed, J. L. Holland, R. C. White, J. W. Dunn, J. D. Tant, L. L. Briggance, A. D. Foster, F. O. Howell, S. B. Pitman, D. D. Woody, Paul Slayden, Adrain Doran and W. D. Parker.

Elders of the board in 1940: John R. McKee and Roy Carroll; treasurer, Dr. J. M. Capps. Teachers in Sunday School: J. R. McKee, Arthur Spencer, Mrs. Horace Scott, Mrs. Roy Carroll, Mrs. Price King, Miss Annie May Connell and Miss Jane Sue Scott.

KENTON METHODIST CHURCH

The Methodist Church, the first church established in Kenton, was formed in 1850, and a building was erected on the site of the Kenton school buildings, on a grant of land made to the Mobile & Ohio R. R. by J. R. Moore for church purposes. Here for a number of years a union Sunday School was conducted.

KENTON COMMUNITY

Organization of the church in 1940 stood as follows: Board of Christian Education for 1940-41, assuming duty in 1940: Mr. J. Frank Johnson, superintendent church school; Miss Myra Taylor, superintendent children's division; Mrs. R. A. Freeman, superintendent of young people's division; Mr. Travis Bryant, superintendent of adult division.

On the Board of Christian Education, Miss Earline McFarland represents the young people; Mrs. Jas. Thomas represents the Woman's Society of Christian Service, and Miss Beulah Watts represents the Board of Stewards.

Board of Stewards: A. H. Gardner, chairman; Travis Bryant, Mrs. R. C. Pullen, Miss Beulah Watts, B. A. Caldwell, B. L. McCullough, honorary steward.

Board of Trustees: J. Frank Johnson, J. E. Garrett, L. N. Garrett, P. L. Draper.

KENTON BAPTIST CHURCH

The Kenton Baptist Church was organized around 1888-89 and met in the Methodist Church house near the old music room. Charter members were: Mr. Nick McNeely, Mrs. Jane McNeely, Alice and Margaret McNeely, Mrs. Belle Ates, Mrs. Lelia Taylor (only one living)—address: Halls, Tenn.—Mr. and Mrs. West McNeely.

First Baptist Church was dedicated June 9, 1895, by Rev. J. N. Hall. Among the pastors serving the church were: J. T. Early, Rev. Hill, J. R. Taylor, J. E. Bell, I. N. Penick, R. J. Williams, W. R. Puckett, R. K. Bennett, W. M. Pratt, Simpson Daniel, Ernest Blackford, V A. Rose, Pastor in 1940 was W. C. Agnew.

The deacons in 1940 were: T. M. King, J. C. Derryberry, John Arnold, L. E. Keathley, Price King, Herbert Taylor, Alvin Glisson.

Pastor in 1940: Rev. W. C. Agnew; church clerk, Mrs. B. M. O'Daniel; church treasurer, Herbert Taylor; church pianist, Mrs. Carn Tilghman; chorus leaders, Elihu Keathley and Price King; Sunday School Superintendent, James E. Tice; secretary, Mrs. B. M. O'Daniel; pianist, Miss Marie Hollomon.

Baptist W. M. U. officers for 1940-41 are: Mrs. J. C. Derryberry, president; Mrs. B. M. O'Daniel, first vice-president; Miss Lena Brush, second vice-president; Mrs. R. T. Aycock, third vice-president; Mrs. J. W. Newman, treasurer; Mrs. A. J. McNeely, secretary; Mrs. Gerald Ridgeway, corresponding secretary; Mrs. Cleve Hollomon, Y. W. A. leader; Mrs. Will Fowler, Intermediate G. A. Leader; Miss Mollie B. Smith, Junior Leader; Mrs. J. B. Barner, Sunbeam Leader; Mrs. W. C. Agnew, Prayer Leader.

The Baptist Training Union, which includes the Junior, Intermediate, Senior and Adult departments, has for its general officers for 1940-41: Mrs. Molly B. Smith, director; Miss Hildreth

Smith, associate director; Price King, chorister; Miss Shirley Brewer, pianist; Miss Emma Noel Freeman, secretary.

The first Superintendent of the Baptist Sunday School was Prof. Maury, the second A. L. Hurt.

PARENT-TEACHER

Parent-Teachers Association was organized at Kenton when Mr. Clayborn Finch was principal of the school, though it was not known at the time by that name. They did much work for the school, raising about three or four hundred dollars. Mrs. J. Frank Johnson was the first president.

Later the association was reorganized with Mrs. C. M. Montgomery as its first president, serving for a number of years. Among other presidents who served were: Mesdames A. M. Howell, L. C. Abbott, Sam Shatz, Carmen Tilghman and Price King.

Three years ago the Parent-Teachers Association at Kenton entered the Federation, and since that time has been in active work in Obion County. Presidents serving so faithfully during that time were Mrs. Price King and Mrs. Carmen Tilghman.

This organization has been actively engaged in creating funds to buy library books, stage curtains, home equipment, providing for unfortunate children, etc.

Officers serving during 1939-40 were: Mrs. Carmen Tilghman, president; Mrs. Ray Craft, vice-president; Mrs. Roy Carroll, secretary; Mrs. H. D. Howell, treasurer; Miss Janie Sue Scott, Mrs. Harry Dodson, Mrs. Roy Green, program committee. Among the former members of the Parent-Teachers Association were: Mesdames C. M. Montgomery, J. Frank Johnson, A. M. Howell, B. R. Baucom, Pratt Ramsey, Carrie Elder, Homer Scott, Miss Mary Ramsey.

A Shakespeare Club was organized in 1936, chairman in charge, Mrs. J. Frank Johnson.

KENTON MASONS

Masonic Lodge No. 392, charter granted in 1860. Officers are: Bud Zaricor, W. M.; Walter Barner, S. W.; Cecil Stewart, J. W.; Edward Arnold, treasurer; A. M. Howell, secretary.

BOY SCOUTS OF KENTON

Boy Scouts of Kenton had their first meeting at the Methodist Church June 17, 1940; charter granted August 25, 1940. Charter members are: Eugene Witherspoon, James Hamilton, Jr., Albert King, Joe Perris Penn, Charles Inman Freeman, Malcolm Cowsert, Harry Thetford, Billy Skiles, Robert Whitworth, William Ross Horner, James David Long, Mark Shatz, Edgar Jones.

KENTON COMMUNITY

There are 17 members now attending this Boy Scout Troop No. 71 of the Reelfoot District, Chief Paducah Area Council.

The Kenton Lions Club sponsored the organization, with Jimmy Herndon, Scoutmaster, and Rev. J. R. Crowe, Assistant Scoutmaster. Other officers elected include: Mark Shatz, bugler; Lamar King, quartermaster; Billy Skiles, scribe; James Hamilton, Jr., patrol leader for Flying Eagle Patrol; Charles Inman Freeman, patrol leader for Lion Patrol; Joe Ferris Penn, patrol leader for Rattle Snake Patrol; Billy Skiles, patrol leader for Crow Patrol.

Meeting nights are weekly—on Friday nights. Colors: Purple and Gold; Motto: "Be Prepared."

GARDEN CLUB AT KENTON

The Kenton Garden Club was first organized in the spring of 1934 at the school building by Mrs. Carrie Elder, member of the Woman's Club, sponsor. It proves an advantage to the township in civic beauty.

Reorganized in 1936, with Mrs. Carrie Elder as the first president, meeting at the home of Mrs. Sam Shatz and sponsored by every club in town. Each club was represented by at least one member voicing approval of a Garden Club organization. Mrs. J. M. DeBow was the leader or chairman. Dozens of shrubs, roses and evergreens have been put out and ugly spots in Kenton made beautiful.

Last election of officers are as follows: Mrs. Carrie Elder, president; Mrs. R. T. Aycock, vice-president; Mrs. C. H. Rochelle, secretary and treasurer.

Objective of the president is to have every home owner in Kenton a member of the Garden Club.

REVIEW CLUB OF KENTON

The Review Club of Kenton was organized by Mrs. Cecil King in November, 1925, at the home of Mrs. W. D. Kerr, on Vine Street. Charter members were: Mesdames Cecil King, Emerson Smith, Roy Carroll, Alta Fullerton, Leonard Kerr, Rob Gray and Mrs. Elmer J. Connell. Mrs. King was the first president. Club colors are yellow and white. Club flower is yellow chrysanthemum. The club met weekly for years, now every two weeks. The programs are miscellaneous, considered preferable to those which are prepared for sale. Membership has increased greatly and gradually from the first meeting when each charter member was authorized to invite a visitor. This privilege has been increased. Motto is "Jog On," taken from Shakespeare (?). Present officers for 1940 are: Mrs. R. C. Tilghman, president; Mrs. Harry Dodson, vice-president; Mrs. Cecil King, secretary; Mrs. Alta Fullerton, treasurer; Alta Fullerton, corresponding secretary. Mrs. Elmer J. Connell, Ray Craft, Roy Carroll and Cecil King, program committee.

WOMAN'S CLUB OF KENTON

Woman's Club of Kenton was organized by Mrs. Eugene Elder in 1917 or 1918 for the purpose of providing for Belgian orphans. Mrs. Eugene Elder was first president. After the World War it became a literary club, named as before indicated. First meeting was held in Mrs. Elder's home and among the first members were: Mesdames Eugene Elder, Clarence Bogle, B. R. Baucom, Jessie Elder, C. M. Montgomery, Will Wade, Eugene Wade, Elmo Odom, Will Rob Holmes and Miss Kate Moseley.

Members of the Woman's Club are studious, avidly delving into many subjects. It was federated after twelve or fifteen years. Officers for 1940-41 were elected as follows: Mrs. Sam Shatz, president; Mrs. Jessie Elder, vice-president; Mrs. John L. Bingham, secretary-treasurer. The organization meets weekly on Wednesday from fall to spring.

OBLIGATIONS

(This work is made possible by the help of kind friends in different parts of the county, but none more than Miss Harriet King, of Kenton, who has gone to great trouble and given much of her time to make a complete and accurate outline of the churches, woman's clubs and business organizations of the town of Kenton.)

JUNIOR WOMAN'S CLUB

Organization of the Junior Woman's Club in November, 1936, was in the home of Mrs. B. R. Baucom, member of the Woman's Club and sponsor of the junior club. Among the charter members were: Mrs. Raymond Sharp, Mrs. Jimmy Herndon, Mrs. Geo. Wm. Freeman, Miss Beulah Montgomery, Miss Frances Montgomery, Mrs. Gilbert Combs, Mrs. Ralph Tilghman, Mrs. Howard Mackin, Mrs. Carthal Wilton Elder, Miss Wilmac Walker.

Newly elected officers: Miss Frances Montgomery, president; Miss Janie Sue Scott, vice-president; Mrs. Howard Mackin, secretary-treasurer.

SEWING CLUB OF KENTON

The Sewing Club at Kenton was first organized by Mrs. Alex Montgomery in the fall of 1932. Charter members meeting with Mrs. Montgomery were: Miss Beulah Montgomery, Miss Rachel Raines, Miss Frances Montgomery, Mrs. Alex Montgomery, Miss Imogene Garrett, Miss Helen Gardner, Miss Ella Blanche Glisson, Miss Eulene Walker, Miss Elizabeth Alston, Miss Mozelle

KENTON COMMUNITY

Dodds, Miss Wilmac Walker. Officers for 1939-40 were: Mrs. Jimmy Herndon, president; Miss Roberta Bussert, secretary.

SEW AND SO CLUB

Six years existence in 1940, first meeting was in the home of Miss Helen Fullerton by a group of girls deciding to form a sewing club. Charter members were: Misses Mary Nell Raines, Amanda Howell, Helen Fullerton, Margaret Flowers, Lucile Gordon, Virginia Abbott, Virginia Frances Finch. Others have been added. Officers elected were Miss Sue Helen Henderson, president; Miss Lucile Gordon, treasurer.

EASTERN STAR

Kenton Chapter No. 366, Order of the Eastern Star, instituted and constituted in 1935. Officers are: Mrs. Gray Moseley, Worthy Matron; Walter Barner, Worthy Patron; Mrs. Alpha Price Becton, Associate Worthy Matron; A. M. Howell, Associate Worthy Patron; Mrs. Melba Brush, Conductress; Mrs. Mary Barner Brewer, Associate Conductress; Mrs. Florence Craft, secretary; Miss Lena Hurt, treasurer; Mrs. Ella Howell, marshal; Mrs. Maggie Barner, chaplain; Mrs. Tillie Pullen, pianist; Mrs. Vera Brown Alston, Ada; Miss Maud Nowlin, Ruth; Miss Margaret King, Esther; Mrs. Andrew Bryant, Martha; Mrs. Velma Harmon, Electra; Mrs. Christine Spikes, Warder; Mrs. Jessie Elder, Sentinel.

MASON HALL COMMUNITY

One of the oldest settlements in the county, Mason Hall has furnished her quota of thrifty farmers, merchants, millers, ginners and contributed to the schools and churches of her material and spiritual support.

Before the Civil War there were the families of Capt. John Hollomon, Jimerson Garrison, W. B. (Bab) Boyett, W. M. Midyett, Dr. P. N. Matlock, and after the War those active in the various relations of business and social life were the families of William, Nat and Jeff Hollomon, John A. Hargett, Wm. Hargett, David King, John E. Finch, J. B. Skinner, W. H. Caudle, Elzie West, Curg Boyett, Wm. Henry Nichols, Dr. Bart Boyett, Jas Nichols, Cas Corum, Henry Smith, Sid Clark.

One of the first stores was operated by Bab Boyett, a dealer in general merchandise. Mr. Boyett was also elected and served as a Representative in the Tennessee Legislature. Capt. John Hollomon was a member of the Obion County Court before the War. David King was for some time a member of the County Court. After the War Nat Hollomon operated a cotton gin. John A. Hargett served as deputy sheriff under Sheriff F. B. Taylor, J. B. Skinner has been a magistrate and member of the Obion County Court for many years. His wife, Mrs. Skinner, who was a Hollomon, has a sugar bowl brought with the Hollomon ancestors from Scotland. John E. Finch was elected, re-elected and served as Sheriff of Obion County for two terms. George P. Hurt, who owned a fine farm near Mason Hall, was deputy Trustee under Capt. Hollomon and then elected and served as Trustee for two terms. Afterwards Mr. Hurt was elected to the Legislature. He was the son of a pioneer citizen, John A. Hurt. Dr. Bart Boyett is a practicing physician at Mason Hall. Larry Finch, a former member of the Tennessee Legislature, is a member of the Obion County Court. Some of the forementioned were farmers, including Elzie West, Curg Boyett, Wm. Henry Nichols, Jas Nichols, Bud Zaricor.

NEW SALEM BAPTIST CHURCH

The New Salem Baptist Church of Mason Hall is distinctive in several respects. With a history dating back to its organization in December 1848, it can truthfully call itself a "revival" church, for it holds an enviable record of having held a summer revival since the summer of 1849, including the years of the Civil War. The ninetieth consecutive revival was held in 1939.

The first pastor to serve the church was the Rev. David Halli-

MASON HALL COMMUNITY

burton whose faithful service continued for a period of 19 years. For many years church services were conducted in the neighborhood school building. In the year 1896 the church membership totaled 102. Under the direction of the pastor a new church building was erected. The first musical instrument for the use of the church was purchased in 1903 when an organ was installed at a cost of $63.00. This early church building was located some distance back of the old location, it being moved up near the road in 1910. In 1928 the building was remodeled and eight Sunday School rooms added with a large auditorium. Continuing its policy of modernizing the church edifice, T. V. A. power was added and in 1937 a basement was constructed with a kitchen and four additional Sunday School rooms. The 211 members of this active County Church can be justly proud of their valuable church building with its seating capacity of nearly 500 and its adequate Sunday School department.

The pastor of the church is Rev. W. A. Farmer, and he has the distinction of being the first pastor in the history of the church to "live on the field." The church clerk is Mrs. Ira West of Kenton, Tenn.

Among the charter members of the Cumberland Presbyterian Church were Dr. P. N. Matlock, Jas Nichols, Cas Corum, Henry Smith, Sid Clark. Those of the Methodist Church included Bab Boyett, Jimerson Garrison, Elzie West.

MASON HALL SCHOOLS

Principals of Mason Hall high schools since 1921-22 were as follows: W. O. Hornaday, G. T. Holland, C. C. Barron, A. M. Taylor, C. J. Huckaba, R. M. Grills, A. E. Caldwell, J. W. Roberts. Before these men served the Mason Hall schools, other principals were A. J. F. Day, John C. Wright, Tyson Holland, Mr. Gooch. Principal elected for the term of 1940-41, J. W. Roberts. The faculty of teachers is as follows: Bonnie Alexander, Katherine Bradshaw, Thelma C. Buchanan, Eula C. Collins, C. C. Gorman, W. B. Hargett, A. C. Jones, Anabel W. Jones, Wray Newman, Mrs. J. W. Roberts, Annie Taylor, Virginia G. Ward.

A business directory of Mason Hall is as follows: Thornton three-stand cotton gin, others at Yorkville and Dyer; E. F. Thompson, general store; Emmett Thompson, groceries; Mason Hall Garage and Service Station operated by Albert Crain; 66 Service Station and lunch stand operated by L. E. Allen; Giles Keathley Barber Shop; I. F. West Shoe Shop; F. E. Brown Funeral Home.

GLASS COMMUNITY

Originally Glass was known as Palestine. Even in the early days the community was referred to as "Soonsupper," but it is to be presumed that this was merely a good natured jest. However it was a community of fine people, for a schoolhouse was built as early as 1857, and soon the churches were organized. The first dwelling house was erected by David Miller and the first store opened by W. R. Hardison, who afterwards was a Nashville wholesale merchant. Other merchants were A. B. Woody & Co., S. W. Tate & Co., and Geo. P. Wright. The physicians were Samuel Hornbeak, John Peacock, J. J. Wells and J. L. Ivey. John Hopple had a blacksmith and wagon shop and Quincy Taylor a grist mill.

Palestine Lodge No. 296, F. & A. M., was organized about 1860 and Brown Lodge I. O. O. F. about ten years later. The Masonic lodge was consolidated in 1929 with Obion and moved to the latter place, retaining its original title.

One of the finest preparatory schools in the county or in the State, was taught at Glass by W. R. (B.) Moore, who was a graduate of Vanderbilt and the University at Leipzig, Germany. Mr. Moore taught in periods, five years each time, at Glass, and among his students were such men as Lexie Parks, Calvin and Robert Brown. Altogether Mr. Moore taught for a quarter of a century in Obion County —at Glass, Cloverdale, Troy and Union City. He was principal of Obion College at Troy and of Union City Training School. Thence to Texas Mr. Moore taught again and retired from the school room.

Some of the Glass citizens of earlier days included John Miller, Paul Chiles, Philip Wright, E. N. Moore, J. C. Revell, F. M. Woody, Calvin Brown, Sr., Jesse Wells, Rufus Woody, Alex Smith. One of the pioneer settlers south of Glass was Alexander Starrett.

Alex Smith was the depot agent at Obion when the Paducah & Memphis Railroad was completed, and claims to have been a passenger on the first train passing Obion. He served six years as Postmaster at Obion. Many years ago Mr. Smith bought a fine farm near Glass and built one of the most attractive homes of that community. He was a leader in forward looking movements— in schools, churches and general welfare.

The Church of Christ at Glass was established in an old schoolhouse by the first settlers. H. D. Bantau, a well known pioneer in the church, was the first minister of the Glass church, and others followed including: T. B. Osborne, Homer T. Wilson, W. T. Officer, F. B. Shrigley, J. T. Slayden, A. G. Freed, John R.

GLASS COMMUNITY

Williams, A. D. Foster, Phillip Wall. Early members were P. A. Wright, T. H. Mills, Jesse Wells, Rufus Woody, A. K. Wells. The first church house built was blown down and the next destroyed by fire. Another was a building which now remains as a house of worship for this congregation. Originally the Church of Christ was the meeting place for the Sunday Schools of three denominations—the Baptist, Presbyterian and Methodist besides the Church of Christ.

The school at Glass is now conducted by Miss Rachel Smith as principal. The High School at Cloverdale provides facilities for students in high school work. The faculty is named under the report from Elbridge. The business directory of Glass is as follows:

Gantlett Variety Store; general stores, A. B. Church and M. C. Corkran. Postmaster for a period of six years, A. B. Corkran. Preceding Mr. Corkran as postmaster were J. Foster, Alex and Louis Mitchell, J. E. Byrd. Blacksmith, Alvy Grisham; saw mill, Fox & Watson.

ELBRIDGE COMMUNITY

The community of Elbridge was settled some time before the Civil War. Among the pioneers were George Davidson, Theo. Lippard, George King. Among others arriving at different times were Peter Bradshaw, J. T. Call, Esq. Barker, Charley Strain, Ed Carroll, J. A. Jackson, C. N. Shires and J. A. Buchanan, father of Wilkes Buchanan.

Beech Point was the first name given to the settlement. Some of the first business institutions which engaged the interest of those forming the settlement were located as follows: Walter Via, son of William Via, operated a general store at Elbridge for many years. Wm. Via resided in the vicinity later designated as Minnick. Ed Carroll operated a tan yard. John Hailey was a shoemaker. Jack Wortham probably operated the first general store. The stock of merchandise was later sold to H. C. Davidson, one of the active citizens of that community afterwards more generally known as the proprietor of the Cloverdale Stock Farm. Talmus King was another extensive farm and livestock operator.

Here it was that Tom W. Cunningham engaged in the newspaper business for a term of years, publishing the Elbridge Pioneer. He was the brother of Rev. W. B. Cunningham of Union City.

The country around Elbridge has some picturesque farm homes. On an eminence overlooking and almost entirely surrounded by an expanse of valley farms is the home of Mr. and Mrs. Ivie Lippard, comprising a modern dwelling inclosed in a cluster of beautiful shade trees and sloping gardens. The home of William Morris nearby is another attractive site and surroundings on the highway west of Elbridge.

Here again W. R. (B.) Moore, one of Obion County's educational leaders, conducted for a number of years the Cloverdale School as principal. Following Mr. Moore came a number of school principals as follows: R. J. Glover, S. H. Snow, F. S. Stokes, J. W. Roberts, A. E. Caldwell. The school faculty for 1940-41, inclusive, is as follows: A. E. Caldwell, principal; Mrs. A. E. Caldwell, A. S. Thomas, Miss M. Margaret Ramsey, Harold Polsgrove, G. W. Moore, Mrs. Ione Jackson, Miss Elva Hicks, Miss Ruth Corum, Irene Alexander, Wyatt Cunningham, Edith Fleming.

The business directory includes, first, the Bank of Elbridge, organized in 1910. The first president was W. T. Call, the first cashier, N. I. Manly, succeeded by L. E. Maloney, who continued as cashier, with the exception of the years 1927-8-9, when the cashier was E. A. Watson.

ELBRIDGE COMMUNITY

Business houses are conducted as follows: General store, H. T. King; grocery store and notions, V. G. Hailey; grocery store, J. P. Wells; grocery, H. P. Roddy; restaurant, H. P. Hailey; garage and service station, W. T. Shires. Postmistress, Mrs. Euna Fleming. Lane Cotton House. Cloverdale: Robt. Fleming Grocery Co.; Dr. J. P. Cunningham, physician. R. C. Sanford, rural route grocery.

ELBRIDGE METHODIST CHURCH

More than one hundred years ago early settlers at Elbridge, those who were members of the society of the M. E. Church, saw the need of a suitable place where they could assemble together for worship. They therefore banded together and constructed a building of logs, as was the custom in those days. Split logs were used as benches and the ground as a floor. This log church was located very near the site afterwards used for the building of a new church. No names of the original organization can be located, due probably to the fact that the old building in a dense forest was consumed by forest fires.

In the year 1852 a parcel of land containing about five acres was deeded to the Methodist Church of Elbridge by one J. C. Davidson as a donation coming from the late Dr. Carroll. On this land a new church of frame construction was in process of building when again fate intercepted and the building was demolished by storm. But, courageous and faithful, members again rebuilt and dedicated the house of worship as New Chapel.

This building withstood the storms and elements for forty-five years, and then was torn down and replaced by a new building in the year 1897. Rev. R. L. Norman was pastor in charge at the time.

As recorded in the church register of 1885-86 (the oldest to be found), New Chapel was then in the Dyersburg district, later placed on the Obion Circuit.

About the year 1900 the Elbridge Circuit was formed, comprising four churches as follows: New Chapel, Minnick, Zion, and Cunningham, and this new circuit was placed in the Union City District. At the same time a district parsonage was acquired and provided by subscription from members of the four churches in the charge. In 1914 this parsonage was replaced by a new and comfortable home for the minister.

The 1885-86 record shows that New Chapel had an enrollment of 70 members, which by the year 1902 was increased to 277. Pastors in charge and presiding elders, beginning with this record, are as follows:

S. L. Jewell, P. C., 1885; W. T. Harris, P. E., 1885-86; H. B. Owens, P. C., 1886; A. J. Wheeler, P. C., 1887; J. H. Evans, P. E.,

1887-88; R. Y. Blackwell, P. C., 1888; G. W. Evans, P. C., 1889-90; B. Medlin, P. C., 1891; H. W. Brooks, P. E. 1889-92; B. F. Peeples, P. C., 1892; J. S. Renshaw, P. C. 1893; followed by other pastors as listed: S. B. Love, D. M. Evans, R. L. Norman, J. B Winsett, R. S. Harrison, J. T. Alexander, C. E. Norman, W. H. Collins, E. J. W. Peters, W. A. Banks, C. A. Riggs, J. T. Banks, B. D. Cavin, T. N. Wilkes, B. A. Walker, W. A. Lampkin, W. S. Lockman, R. E. Hickman, W. K. Lovett, O. H. Boatwright, H. D. Hurley, J. E. Hopper, W. A. Baker. Other presiding elders as follows were listed: G. W. Wilson, H. B. Johnston, W. C. Waters, J. M. Pickens, R. A. Clark, R. L. Norman, J. M. Jenkins, F. B. Jones, W. C. Barham.

To mention some of the good work accomplished by these men, outstanding is that four Methodist preachers were ordained and sent out from this charge, and now are prominent ministers of the Methodist Conference. They are as follows:

C. E. Norman, superannuated, Jackson, Tenn.; A. E. Holt, pastor of Milan Circuit, Milan, Tenn.; M. S. Sanford, pastor of Arlington Circuit, Arlington, Tenn.; J. E. Hopper, pastor of Cayce Circuit, Cayce, Ky.

Others who have served officially in the New Chapel Methodist Church are as follows:

Sunday School Superintendents (as of record): W. T. Call, deceased, has the honor of serving this church as Sunday School Superintendent for more than forty years; others in the same service: W. E. Wray, W. S. Sorrell, J. H. Lippard, V. G. Hailey, J. W. Cunningham and J. H. King.

Church stewards (on record): outstanding in their work as pillars of the church are mentioned here: C. T. (Uncle Thea) Lippard, C. N. Shires, Esq. E. C. Carroll, W. J. Call, H. B. Fleming, B. W. (Uncle White) Fleming, P. A. Lippard, F. H. Lippard. All these have passed on while others in their places have carried on.

Officials of the church in 1940 are enumerated as follows: W. A. Barker, pastor in charge; W. C. Barham, presiding elder of the district; J. H. King, Sunday School Superintendent. Stewards: Ivie Lippard, J. H. King, E. W. Hughes, V. G. Hailey. Trustees: Ivie Lippard, V. G. Hailey, J. W. Cunningham. Present enrollment of members, 140.

HORNBEAK COMMUNITY

Hornbeak, known for a period of years as Wilsonville, was settled soon after the Civil War by James Wilson, of Middle Tennessee, Eli Hornbeak, Billy Barnett, James Ellington, John White, W. B. Ashley and others.

The first general store was operated by Lishnet, with Jas. Ellington as clerk. Logan Moultrie opened another store, operating for some years, and then again James Wilson entered the mercantile business, afterwards the H. M. Wilson & Co. store. There were other merchants, including John Barnett, Peery & Hornbeak.

One of the first schools was taught by Dr. John Hornbeak and daughter, Miss Lillie. James Wilson donated one acre of ground for the school building.

W. B. Ashley operated a wood shop where the Methodist Church is now located. Mr. Ashley built the Peery & Hornbeak store. Eli Hornbeak built another store, the Moultrie stand, where the Bank of Hornbeak is now located.

Logan Moultrie operated the first cotton gin, with mule power operating the drive wheel. After this Albert Maloney started a new gin with steam-drive stands.

There were two saloons in town when business was off to a good start.

A small hotel was operated by Henry Wilson, Mr. and Mrs. Wilson afterwards moving to Obion and continuing there in the hotel business.

Dr. C. C. Marshall, resident physician, operating a drug store was in 1940 a citizen of Hornbeak for 43 years.

One of the first school teachers in Hornbeak was John R. Williams, who was also a leader in church and in the ministry of the Church of Christ.

A spoke factory was operated at Hornbeak on the Methodist Church property by Henry Wilson, Will and Dan Jackson in 1881-83.

Jas. Rumage and John Barnett operated a flour mill at Hornbeak for a period of forty years, and for more than sixty years a saw mill has been almost continuously in operation west of town.

In 1887 Frank Hornbeak, operating store and serving as postmaster at Wilsonville, declined to continue handling the work of the postoffice and submitted his resignation to the Postmaster-General. The work, he insisted, became onerous without salary. Mr. Hornbeak was notified by agent in person that if he would consent to continue as postmaster the office might be placed in the salary class and changed to Hornbeak. All of which was agreed to, and the name of the town thereafter was Hornbeak.

The Bank of Hornbeak was organized in 1904, with James Rumage as president, J. W. Darnell vice-president and R. Lilly cashier. Mr. Rumage served very successfully and acceptably until his death in 1917, and H. D. Smith, the president now serving the bank, became successor to Mr. Rumage, with the present cashier, Paschal Ellington, and Laura Rumage assistant, now in charge of banking operations by the Bank of Hornbeak.

Hornbeak was incorporated in 1916. The first mayor was John Hodge. Succeeding him were G. S. Kendall and Ralph G. Hornbeak, C. M. Ashley was the first marshal. Elected 1941 the Board of Mayor and Aldermen: Mayor, W. P. Ellington; aldermen, D. I. Blackley, T. J. Rogers, Frank Short, H. D. Smith, E. S. Williams, E. O. Wilson.

The 1940 census gave Hornbeak a population of 387. Esq. J. H. Tate was for some time magistrate from Hornbeak.

One of the older citizens of Hornbeak resides in the first home built there during the Civil War. This is Sion Williams, cabinet maker and inventor of many patent utilities and devices. He served his people as undertaker and made coffins for general use. He made hundreds of boats for use on Reelfoot Lake. Among his patents are a combination ironing board and stepladder, a window sash stop, very simple and ingenious, a small piece of wood with spring and button sunk in one side and fastened to the side of the window frame.

Mr. Williams also has a large center table made of walnut taken from the waters of Reelfoot Lake, 120 years of age, upon which is a revolving wheel about four feet in diameter and eight inches deep, swinging upon a center shaft after the manner of a carousal, and all around the beveled rim little pieces of wood, two by eight inches, 55 altogether, are arranged in order as specimens of the various and different varieties of trees or timber grown in Obion County.

Mr. Williams also improvised a large moving platform 30 by 40 feet, mounted on solid wooden wheels, upon which the original Methodist Church building at Center in 1885 was loaded and, with yokes of oxen hitched to tongue, pulled over rough roads to town. The building was sold and used by the Presbyterian denomination.

Mr. Williams has a certificate of membership in the Institute of American Inventors as a reward for a number of useful inventions. All of these, since his retirement, he greatly prizes. Like Noah Vale, the inventor in "Poor Relation," or more specific, like the schemer's man of prey, he has the memory of a valuable life's work and the other a misspent life.

HORNBEAK COMMUNITY

HORNBEAK DIRECTORY

The present business setup or directory of Hornbeak is as follows:

Dry goods: Wigdor & Son; dry goods and furniture, King & Williams. Druggist: Marshall Drug Co. Groceries: Fields Grocery Co., Dewey Darnell, grocery and restaurant. Funeral Home: King & Williams, Blackley Chevrolet Co. salesroom and garage; O. C. Williams, garage; Cities Service Station, Frank's Tavern Station; Lennie Blackley, restaurant, Hamilton Barber Shop, Cunningham Shoe Shop. Beauty Shops: Mrs. Flossie Cooper, Mrs. Hazel Harris; Resident physician, Dr. C. C. Marshall. Postmaster, Dewey Darnell.

HORNBEAK M. E. CHURCH

A pioneer and a leader in the religious life of the Hornbeak community, John F. Williams was one of the citizens responsible for the organization of the Methodist Church, which came into existence at Center a few miles from the present township of Hornbeak. Mr. Williams was a speaker and singer and during the organization of the church led in building a church house and in the services that were held in the church.

Charter members of the church, including the first few years of its organization from 1860, included the following: J. F. Williams, M. E. Williams, Rutha C. Barnett, Elisha C. Ephlin, Judy L. Ephlin, John Tomlinson, Mary Tomlinson, Jonathan King, Rebecca A. Miller, Samuel M. McElzea, John M. King, Nancy F. King, Samuel Davis, Wincy Davis, Mary Tucker, John W. Mays, Mary E. Mays, Larrah Mays, William Tucker, Rebecca A. Moultrie, Mary Barnett, L. A. Barnett, Wm. Barnett, B. F. Gates, Wm. Maloney, A. Fields, Sarah Ezell, M. J. Alison, G. W. Blankenship, E. A. Barnett, L. J. Wilson, A. W. Jackson, V. Tucker, M. E. Williams, Sarah E. Scaggs, Martha A. Chadwell, Robert Barnett.

The first presiding elder mentioned was F. Bynum, the first pastor in charge, J. H. Cooper—the organization March 6, 1860. Presiding elders and pastors came in the following order: F. Bynum, P. E., M. D. Robinson, P. C., 1861; F. Bynum, P. E. J. E. Beck, P. C., 1862; E. C. Slater, P. E. M. D. Robinson, P. E., 1863; G. W. Harris, P. E., B. F. Avery, P. C., 1864; F. Bynum, P. E., J. M. Flatt, P C., 1866; F. Bynum, P. E., J. E. Beck, A. P., 1868-69; F. Bynum, P. E., E. D. Baker, P. C., 1870; J. H. Witt, P. E., J. H. Frost, P. C., 1872.

At this point the church records were not available. But beginning in 1900, when the present church building in Hornbeak was erected, Rev. Sam Wynn, who was active in the work, was pastor in charge. He was succeeded by Rev. W. F. Barrier in charge for two years. Then the Hornbeak church and the church at Obion were served by the same pastor, Rev. W. A. Cook, who was succeeded upon the death of Rev. Cook by Rev. S. R. Hart. About the year 1906 the Protestant church joined the Southern Methodist denomination and Rev. J. G. Jones became the first pastor of the Hornbeak circuit, with Rev. G. W. Wilson presiding elder. The pastor following in succession was Rev. B. T. Fuzzell, who served the church four years. Rev. S. A. Martin followed, and others in succession, viz: Rev. Calhoun, Revs. W. A. Banks, A. N. Walker, Revs. Stubblefield, W. A. Lambkin, Rev. Simmons, Revs. Paul McClaren, S. A. Parham, John M. Jenkins, Stacy Riddick, Revs. Harris, Gault, Stedman, Hopper, J. T. Banks, McMims.

Our presiding elders have been Revs. G. W. Wilson, J. G. Clark, W. C. Waters, W. W. Armstrong, Robert A. Clark, C. E. Norman, Revs. Jones, J. Mack Jenkins and Barham.

Our Sunday School Superintendents have been Sion Williams, B. W. Flemming, W. F. Reeves, Frank Short, Sr., and at present Frank Short, Jr.

Chairman of the board of stewards at the present time is W. F. Reeves.

HORNBEAK CHURCH OF CHRIST

Organization of the Church of Christ at Hornbeak began with a membership including Mr. Britton, Jas. Wilson, T. H. C. Peery and others.

Ministers engaged in the work were Elders H. D. Bantau, Tommy Osborne, C. R. Hays, Isaac Sewell and John R. Williams.

For many years John R. Williams labored with the Hornbeak congregation and for evangelism in the churches of this particular section of the State with great devotion and success, and the power and influence of his work is left with the people as abiding evidence of his efforts.

HORNBEAK SCHOOLS

Beginning in 1921-22 principals of the Hornbeak High School were as follows: P. Y. Isbell, S. C. Finch, H. E. Smith, T. H. Kennedy, H. E. Smith, M. E. Whitson, Milton Hamilton, L. C. Bowers. Faculty for the school year 1940-41: L. C. Bowers, principal, Ernest Greer, W. J. Moore, Mrs. F. S. Hamilton, Mrs. Lillie S. Cunningham, Miss Madge Short, Frank Short, Miss Mary Lynn Shore, Miss Margaret Dowdy, Mrs. Bruce Wisener, Miss Agnes Garrigan, Mike Orlich, Miss Katherine Jones, Eulah Head.

HORNBEAK BAPTIST CHURCH

The Baptist Church of Hornbeak, Tennessee (which was then known as Wilsonville) and community was organized on November 29, 1891.

Elder W. B. Clifton of Martin preached a sermon and gave opportunity for membership, with intention of organizing a Bap-

HORNBEAK COMMUNITY

tist Church. The Declaration of Faith was, on that day, adopted with John White acting as Clerk protem and Mr. Clifton, Moderator. When a hymn was sung and the following presented themselves on forth-coming letters: Mr. John White, Mr. James Rummage, Mrs. Mary Cockran, Mrs. Sallie Moultrie, Mrs. Tinnie Edwards and Mrs. Fannie Watson. Mr. Walter Roberts was approved for baptism and is the only living charter member of the church today.

On December 5, 1891, Reverend J. W. Mount was elected pastor for the church for one year with Rev. E. L. Watson serving as Church Clerk. Rev. Mount was succeeded by Rev. D. A. Ellis with the assistance of Mr. W. L. Willingham as Church Clerk. Then Rev. Terry Martin was called as third pastor, and so the Baptist Church of Hornbeak grew.

In 1896 G. L. Trosper, W. Hewitt, Mr. and Mrs. Edward Usher and others were added to the church.

Other pastors were I. L. Barker, R. J. Williams, W. H. Stigler, W. R. Puckett, V. E. Boston, B. F. Smith, S. P. Andrews, A. A. Jones, Melvin Woods, G. H. Craddock, W. C. Nevill.

In 1938 the old building was replaced with a new, modern building.

Rev. L. C. Bowers is the present pastor.

(Very interesting sketch contributed by Mrs. A. C. Fields)

CLAYTON COMMUNITY

Here is where we find among the early settlements the names of James Caldwell, M. S. Marshall, Dave and Cal Cloar, Dick Mosier, Alfred Howard, Esq. Dick Cole, Lee Gray, and as time passes others, including M. L. Frazier, Scott Green, Green Cloar, W. S. Green, Jas. Wheeler, Gus Lancaster, John Bruer, Jack Mosier, John Cloar.

Here is the location of a general store operated for a period of 56 years, with a partnership between Albert Caldwell and John Reeves. Quite a long span of years a cotton gin was also operated in connection with the store. At times this store did an extensive business in wholesale quantities, with sugar and flour in barrels, coffee in original sack lots and other articles in proportion.

In the early days H. H. Green operated a tread-wheel wheat thresher and Mrs. Lou Wheeler a horse-power cotton gin. Billy Owen was a blacksmith. Joe Cole operated a grist mill, saw mill and wheat thresher. Another blacksmith was George Barnes. Henry Lightfoot ran the first steam cotton gin.

The Cloar and Reelfoot schoolhouses were consolidated at Dixie.

The business directory at Clayton includes the Frank Ray general store and gas station, the W. R. Underwood store, and E. L. King store and gas station, Cleve Williams, blacksmithing; also the Barger Gin Co.

Clayton is situated on the Reelfoot Lake highway and Reelfoot Church is one and a half miles north of Clayton.

The Reelfoot Baptist Church was organized in 1845 by Rev. David Halliburton, whose work among the early Baptist churches of the county was very fruitful. There were eleven charter members of the first church, eight of whom were as follows: Mrs. Mary Cloar Marshall, Tommie Sanders, Jack Mosier, Elisha Cloar, Fred Carpenter, George Puckett, Lee Gray, and Jas. W. Caldwell.

The first church building was located about one mile west of the new church built in 1911. A church built in 1878 took the place of the first church occupied by this congregation. This was during the yellow fever epidemic at Hickman, and George Puckett, one of the charter members of the church, succumbed to this disease.

The church erected in 1878 was burned and the new house of worship, built in 1911, had a seating capacity of 500 persons, with a total membership of 136 on the church records.

Rev. Roy Keathley, of Trenton, is the last of a line of well known ministers to serve the church, with Marvin Harper, of Troy, as clerk.

CALDWELL COMMUNITY

A very interesting community of people whose point of contact was formerly old Fremont and then Fremont in a new location—on the Reelfoot Lake highway.

This particular locality embraced in the Tenth Civil District was largely settled by the families of James and Willis Caldwell, descendants of Irish stock. They came from the Atlantic coast to Obion County and both branches of the family had much to do with daily pursuits and the development of community interests and general welfare.

Wm. H. Caldwell, a son of James, was engaged in farming, merchandising and a diversity of interests; in later years served for a considerable period as Chairman of the Obion County Court. Robert Caldwell was a farmer who made agriculture a medium of improvement and profit. Houston Caldwell, before the Civil War, operated a grist mill and cotton gin. He was also postmaster, and upon his death Oscar, his brother, became postmaster. Oscar later moved to Missouri.

Judge Waller C. Caldwell, Associate Justice of the Tennessee State Supreme Court, was a son of Willis Caldwell. Judge Caldwell entered school in Obion County and completed his education in Cumberland University, where he took a course in law. He was married in Lebanon to a daughter of Judge Nathan Green and located in Trenton in the practice of law. From Trenton Judge Caldwell was elected as a member of the State Supreme Court and served on the bench from 1886 to 1902. He left a family of five children, two of them surviving in 1940. J. H. Whipple and Mrs. Dicie Barksdale, of this county, were double first cousins of Judge Caldwell.

Returning to the James Caldwell branch of the family, D. J. Caldwell, son of W. H., for a term of years served the Twelfth Judicial Circuit of Tennessee as Attorney General. Albert Caldwell operated a general store at Clayton for about fifty-six years. J. I. (Bud) became a resident of Union City, for years a magistrate, juror, judge and clerk of elections, etc.

Elva Caldwell, son of Houston, has had practically a life interest in the mercantile business of Union City, operating a grocery store.

John W. (Jockey) Caldwell, was the son of John Caldwell, who did not come with his son, Jockey, and family to Obion County. The sons of Jockey were John Matt, William and Butler Caldwell.

F. B. Caldwell has been located in Union City for some years engaged in livestock and grain business.

Another Caldwell, Joe, operated the first blacksmith shop at Fremont. S. K. Barnes and H. C. Clack operated general stores.

Jack Freeman opened a blacksmith shop at Crystal in 1909, operated a grist mill beginning in 1914 and a grocery store at Fremont in 1922.

Abner Cloar, father of Jerry Cloar, was a resident of old Fremont and sold goods there. Billy Childers was one of the first settlers of Fremont.

R. A. Bumpious, Esq. Theo Ferrell, Wm. Cook, Austin Maupin, and Bowlen Glover were well known citizens of the Caldwell community.

In the Protemus community John Killion, John Y. Brown and Henry Maupin were first settlers. A grandson of the first named is John D. Killion of Union City, a Protemus farmer, who received his education at Cumberland University.

The old homestead of Dr. C. P. Wiley was formerly in the Caldwell neighborhood. Later the family residence was with Mr. Wade Wiley, a few miles southwest of Union City.

The Church of Christ at Old Fremont was first known as Mount Gilead. There it was organized. Among the ministers were John R. Williams, W. S. Long, Tom Carney, Dorence Woody, E. P. Smith, J. Claude Hall, W. A. Foster, H. H. Royster.

At a meeting conducted by Gardner Hall the church was generally revived and interest greatly increased.

CRYSTAL COMMUNITY

This point located on the old public road half way between Troy and Hickman was one of the early settlements of Obion County.

Here the Kersey brothers (Ed and John) were born and reared and operated a general store for forty-six years. They were sons of H. T. Kersey, who settled and married in the Third Civil District. E. B. Kersey died in 1934.

In this particular locality Dr. F. M. McRee, who was a Civil War veteran, at one time under the command of General Forrest, began the practice of medicine and operated largely in general merchandise and the various community interests, including a saw mill and cotton gin. Here the rearing of the family and the birthplace of his son, J. C. (Cully) McRee, well known citizen of Union City.

Here is where Dr. (Ras) Williams, well known citizen, practiced medicine for a lifetime.

Jerry Cloar sold goods at Crystal, and for some time George Cross and Dr. McRee operated in partnership a general store.

Jack Freeman was located four or five years at Crystal, after the Civil War, with a wagon and blacksmith shop. Other smiths were Thos. H. Park and J. N. Huff.

H. B. Stiles was engaged in saw mill operations for some time in the Crystal vicinity. N. B. Fluty was a well known farmer.

Here Capt. T. B. Underwood taught school and reared his family. Like others, his school was finally merged in county school consolidation.

Near Crystal were the Mount Olive and Antioch churches. The Cumberland Presbyterians organized a church at Crystal, with D. E. Park an elder for fifty years. Dr. McRee was one of the members, and the following ministers served there from the beginning as pastors: E. D. Farris, Jo McLeskey, Geo. McIlwain, Rev. Dunnigan.

The stores in later years were operated by E. L. King and B. E. Brown.

The Crystal school teachers for 1940-41: Mrs. LaNele Chadwell; O. W. Fowler, principal.

OBION COUNTY'S SLEEPING BEAUTY

Well known by the older generation of Obion County and often repeated in earlier times is the story of the county's "sleeping beauty," the beautiful girl who slept for twenty-four years at her home near Woodland Mills. Widely known because of the unusual character of her disease. Miss Susan Godsey lay in a coma that differed in many respects from that about which one occasionally reads, caused by encephalitis or sleeping sickness, and the best scientists and doctors of the time were apparently unable to successfully diagnose her trouble.

Following is an authentic story written by "Jonas Jutton," newspaper correspondent, and published in the state and county papers early in the nineties of the last century:

Within twelve miles of Union City there died on October 27, 1873, at the age of 37 years, a lady, who for twenty-four years was a puzzle and wonder to the scientific and medical world. Her name was Susan Carolyn Godsey, known throughout the United States as the sleeping beauty, and she deserved that appellation, for rarely have eyes of man rested upon more beautiful features than those of Miss Godsey.

Before her death, many articles were written about her, some of which were true in part while others were base fabrications almost in toto. To acquaint myself with the facts, I drove out to the home of Mrs. Mary E. Jurney, Miss Godsey's sister, with whom lives her brother, B. W. Godsey, Mrs. Jurney has reached the alloted span of life, while her brother has passed the meridian.

They are all that remain of the family. Mrs. Jurney is a widow, whose children are all married, and she and her bachelor brother live alone upon a little farm of twenty-four acres, which they own.

Susan Caroline Godsey was born in 1836, in Gibson County, Tenn. When seven years of age she moved to Obion County with her parents, who settled twelve miles northwest of Union City, near the Kentucky line.

Susie, as her family and acquaintances called her, was as healthy as most children up to her eighth year, when she took the chills. The usual chill remedies would stop them for a while, but they invariably returned. When ten years of age she made a visit to her sister, Mrs. Jurney, several miles away, and while there had a chill. A quack, named Wasson, who had lately moved into the neighborhood from Middle Tennessee, was called in. He gave her medicines and left others, which were administered according to his directions, but the next day Susie had a chill as usual. The day following she missed her chill, but had a convulsion resembling a fit. From that day she began having cramping spells, the peculiarity of which was that in a second her heels would strike the back of her head, and before one could snap his finger her knees and chin would come together.

Other physicians were called in, who declared that the medicines Wasson had given her were the cause of her peculiar malady. But two of the remedies were known, delphinin and sulphuric ether. Of the former he gave her a spoonful, enough to kill any three men. But Susie's system was such that it did not kill her, but in conjunction with the other drugs threw her into a condition to which death would have been preferable. Susie's father was going to prosecute Wasson for malpractice, but he fled to Middle Tennessee, where he soon died.

Daily, for three years, Susie had these twisting, cramping spells, and every night, exactly at twelve o'clock, she would vomit blood after suffering terrible tortures. In three years, her peculiar afflictions left her, and she went into a sleep which, with frequent awakenings, kept her in bed twenty-four years until death relieved her.

When her sleep was prolonged past the usual time, physicians were called in, but none of them could arouse her from her death-like slumber.

Her condition soon became widely known, and physicians from abroad came to see her and study her case, which proved beyond all their skill. A physician came from Paris, France, to see her, and procuring an interpreter at Hickman, Ky., visited the sleeping beauty at her humble home, but the satisfying of his curiosity as to the truth of what he had heard was all that was accomplished by his visit.

In 1867, her brother, B. W. Godsey; her brother-in-law, James Jurney; her niece, Zenoba Jurney; and Mr. Jonah Montgomery, a friend, carried her to Nashville, where for several days under the care of the celebrated Dr. Robert Eve, she was exhibited to the students of a medical college of which Dr. Eve was president.

In 1870, her physician, Dr. C. P. Glover, and Dr. John Ray, accompanied by Susie's mother, her brother, B. W. Godsey; and Zenoba Jurney, niece, carried her to a medical college in St. Louis. While in that city celebrated physicians from all parts of the country came to see her but her case baffled the skill of them all.

During the twenty-four years of her sleep she would awake every morning at six o'clock, then every hour until noon. In the afternoon she would wake at three o'clock and then at sunset, and night at nine and eleven o'clock. These hours were never varied, except every Wednesday, when she would wake at ten a. m. She would have cramping spells in the chest and hiccoughs, followed between ten and eleven o'clock by a vomiting of blood sometimes as much as a pint.

She generally remained awake but five minutes, never over seven. Doctors present when she awoke would endeavor to keep her awake by animated conversation and by telling her of the pretty things they were going to bring her, but no diversion could prevent her falling asleep at the expiration of five minutes.

The house was visited daily by sightseers, and all were welcome to see the sleeping beauty, and no charge was made, though some left small presents of money. When feeling that she was going to sleep, she would invariably bid them good-bye, ask them to call again, then fall into her death-like slumber.

Her sleep was more the appearance of death than a peaceful slumber. There was no sign of life. A mirror held to her nose and mouth exhibited not the slightest blur of moisture upon it, the lightest filmiest down laid upon her nostrils would not be agitated.

She was a small eater, though she enjoyed three regular meals a day and was fond of sweets and knicknacks.

Though Mr. and Mrs. Godsey were poor and had to battle for a living, they were too proud to gain wealth by their daughter's misfortune, notwithstanding they had excellent opportunities to do so. Many showmen and museum managers offered them princely sums for the privilege of exhibiting their daughter. Among them was P. T. Barnum, who made them several propositions, the last being $1000 a week and the expenses of the family. To all these tempting offers the parents turned a deaf ear, and when they died left their children but a few acres of land.

Though but thirteen years of age when she went to sleep, Susie grew to a full sized woman. Her head was crowned with a mass of coal black hair which grew rapidly, but strange to say, her finger nails and toe nails never grew a particle after she went to sleep, and were not trimmed in the twenty-four years.

Miss Godsey was quite bright and intelligent, and when awake enjoyed conversing upon any subject with which she was familiar.

During the twenty-four years of her sleep she was subject to disease the same as others, and had several spells of sickness, one of which was scarlet fever, which she caught from a negro boy who came to the door, no other member of the family contracting it.

It was the opinion of many physicians that if she could outlive the effects of the medicines Wasson gave her she would regain her normal condition, and this theory is borne out by the fact that for several days prior to her death she could be aroused from her slumber, such being impossible before. This would indicate that the effects of the drugs were wearing out, but her poor, tired body had also worn out, and she passed away, apparently of no disease but that produced by Wasson's remedies.

She departed this life October 27, 1873, and was laid to rest beside her father and mother in Antioch cemetery, not far from her home. Watchers guarded her grave several nights for fear her body would be disinterred and offered as a sacrifice upon the altar of medical science.

JONAS JUTTON

WOODLAND MILLS COMMUNITY

Woodland Mills was located in 1868 on the Hickman & Obion R. R., afterwards the N. C. St. L. Railroad. The first improvement was a steam saw and grist mill, operated by W. G. McFetridge & Co. A grocery store soon after was opened by Daniel Burrus and a dry goods store by John Taylor. In the summer of 1886 Davis, Bramham & Co. erected the largest flouring mill in the country. Other business men were Hefley & Odom, general merchandise, Briggs & Son and Joseph Williams, grocers, and H. Briggs, wagon and blacksmith shop.

Among the original settlers at Woodland, locating in Obion County in 1886, was James Hefley, father of Judge J. A. Hefley. Another was Calvin Rogers, who owned hundreds of acres of land in the vicinity of Woodland Mills.

Among the settlers who afterwards became identified as citizens with the history of Woodland Mills and its community of affairs, the following were well known: Cato Davis and family, Dr. G. B. Burrus and family, John Flack and family, William Alexander and family, I. N. Bramham and family, William Sanders and family, Dick Prather and family, L. T. Holliday and wife, Milton Ferguson, George Threlkeld, Dr. Wes Alexander, John Isbell, Will Flack, Robert, Frank and James Pruett, Dick Alexander, John Iler.

Thos H. C. Lownsbrough, native of New York State, settled at Woodland Mills after the Civil War and served as postmaster, railroad and express agent until his death in 1883.

The community, including a section of country in Civil Districts Numbers Two and Ten, consisted of people primarily interested in farming, but taking a general interest in schools, churches and public affairs, among whom were the Whitakers, Whipples, Hamiltons, Latimers, and so on.

At one time a considerable tobacco belt, farm products included corn, cotton, grain, hay and livestock, the latter increasing greatly. For many years Woodland interests were absorbed in grain and flour mills, but that industry has been superseded by cotton cultivation and ginning.

The Growers Gin Company is operated by T. N. Simpson, and business interests include the Ferguson & Jones store, Farmers Bank, Blackburn Service Station, Buck's Service Station.

The Woodland schools are conducted by R. R. Thompson, principal, and teachers as follows: J. M. DeBow, E. L. Clark, Mrs. E. L. Clark, David Clark, Mary Ellen Clark, Miss Allie George Collier, Ronelle Caldwell, Mrs. Pauline F. Thompson, Janie Brown.

OBION COUNTY HISTORY

High school principals since 1921-22 include: C. M. Witherington, W. B. Forrester, J. L. Cortner, T. H. Kennedy, R. G. Wilson, L. W. Jamerson, H. W. Moss, F. S. Stokes, C. A. Palmer, R. R. Thompson.

The Farmers Bank at Woodland Mills is one of the permanent and reliable institutions of that vicinity. The cashier, J. V. Hefley, and his directors, Edgar Bramham, L. T. Holliday, and J. A. Hefley, have been accredited with the operation of one of the soundest and best banks in the county.

WOODLAND BAPTIST CHURCH

In the year 1869, 70 years ago, from the Poplar Grove Baptist Church, near State Line, Ky., there came a band of thirty (30) members and established the first Baptist church in Woodland Mills, Tennessee.

These loyal pioneers realized their growing need of such a step. Not only this, but that others living in and around the little town might have the opportunity to worship God, no other church being at that time established here.

Swannie Burrus, grandfather of J. D. Jones and great-grandfather of A. L. Burrus, had the privilege of giving the land, which was part of his farm, to this great cause.

I give you names of a few charter members: Swannie Burrus, J. D. Jones, Sr., Mrs. Sallie D. Jones, Dan Burrus, Jim Threlkeld (grandfather of Mrs. J. D. Jones), W. D. Alexander (grandfather of the late J. D. Alexander), Mrs. J. D. Jones and Mrs. Nannie Roberts, Dick Alexander, Mrs. Fannie Rice (mother of Alex and Chas. Rice) and Mrs. Susan Hefley (mother of Judge Hefley and Mrs. Rena Pruett.)

This first building was one small room with columns in the center. The Beulah Association was entertained here in 1888.

In 1896, while G. L. Ellis was pastor, this building was sold to Dan Rice. He used the building material in the construction of a home, which is a part of the house in which Alex Rice resides. You'll find one of the seats from this first church in the Farmers' Bank.

The same year a larger and more modern church was erected on the same ground. In 1917 the Beulah Association met in this church building.

In 1925 the Church members took advantage of a county drive for more modern consolidated schools, and sold the property to the county and the building material was used for the negro school.

The present site, which was the old school property, was purchased from the county, and in the spring of 1926, while Rev. H. C. Cox was pastor, the church was remodeled and remains the

WOODLAND MILLS COMMUNITY

same with the exception of redecoration of the inside and the same year, 1937, the association was entertained here.

During the history of the church there have only been four church clerks: J. D. Jones, Sr., Dr. J. W. Alexander, J. D. Alexander and C. F. Fowler.

The first Sunday schools were conducted only through the summer months, later continuing throughout each year. The names of the superintendents are: I. N. Bramham, J. D. Alexander, H. L. Curlin, R. A. Honeycutt, L. B. Isbell, Jno C. Pruett, Oden Fowler and Paul Isbell.

Twenty-seven years ago a ladies aid society of the church was organized, with Mrs. W. H. Sanders, president. This, a short time later, was known as a Woman's Missionary Society, which sponsored the junior organizations. Mrs. Rose Alexander was president.

The Church also had a Baptist Training Union, with Mrs. E. L. Clark, director. Prayer meetings and teachers' meetings were held on Wednesday nights.

Since the organization of this church there have been twenty pastors, as follows:

Rev. McGomere was the first. Others are: Silas Jones, Rev. Burton, Silas Jones again served, Rev. Beauchamp, Rev. Hughes, Rev. Rodman, Rev. Ellis, Rev. H. Stigler, Dr. Savage, B. T. Huey, who served 10 years, Walton Stigler, Nolan Stigler, Dr. Mantey, H. C. Cox, Lum Hall, Ferrel, Dr. E. L. Carr, Rev. Cutlip and Rev. Joe Clapp, Jr.

During the pastorate of Rev. Huey, the church went from one preaching Sunday per month to two Sundays per month, and continued until 1938, during Rev. Clapp's pastorate, from two Sundays to full time. The Sunday school adopted the six-point record system, with 10 teachers, and Paul Isbell, superintendent.

Serving in 1940 the church deacons were: J. D. Jones, A. L. Burrus, C. F. Fowler, Jno. Isbell, H. M. Ferguson and T. M. Flack, and the pastor, Rev. Joe Clapp, Jr. The church treasurer, T. M. Flack.

In 1940 total members enrolled, 264.

SOUTH FULTON COMMUNITY

South Fulton, first known as Jacksonville under an act of incorporation provided by general legislation, was incorporated by an act of the General Assembly of Tennessee, passed April 4, 1895, with the following boundaries: Beginning with J. W. Gholson's northwest corner, west with State Line to Dick J. Bard's northeast corner, south to N. N. & M. V. R. R., southeast side, east to Harris Fork Creek and north to Gholson's.

An act to repeal the charter of South Fulton was passed in February, 1903, followed by a separate act in March, 1903, to incorporate with the following officers: Robt. Milner, mayor; W. W. Morris, Dr. R. N. Whitehead, W. S. Cavendar, W. N. Robinson, J. R. Wilson, Alex Roberts, aldermen; Ed Bradshaw, marshal; S. A. McDade, treasurer.

Petition was again made for repeal under act passed April 6, 1905, by a committee of citizens, led by Walter W. Morris, whose object was to take advantage of the Tennessee Four-mile Law, prohibiting the operation of saloons within four miles of an incorporated school.

Four years from that time a bill was offered by Representative G. R. McDade to again incorporate the City of South Fulton, which was passed in April, 1909, an act naming the following officers of the council: S. A. McDade, mayor; J. P. Swann, W. C. Harwell, W. D. Swiggart, W. W. Morris, W. S. Boulton, R. N. Whitehead, aldermen; W. R. Albritton, recorder; Joe Hemphill, marshal; Jas. Lowe, treasurer.

There were seven saloons in South Fulton in 1905 when the fight was made for prohibition, and among the petitioners with Mr. Morris to repeal the charter were a large number of citizens connected with business interests, schools and churches.

Some of the men who have served as South Fulton officers were: J. S. Crockett, deputy sheriff under T. J. Easterwood, May, 1912, to 1918, six years; Jesse Walker, marshal of South Fulton a number of years; S. A. McDade, corporation magistrate; Will Robey and Heywood Jonakin, magistrates of District No. 16 and members of Obion County Court.

Among the older citizens of South Fulton we were informed of the following: Dr. Nat Morris, Peter Mott, Joe Wade, Robt. S. Morris, J. M. McDowell, Marion Thomas, Dr. S. G. Patterson, Sol Love, Mrs. Jas. Norman, Mrs. H. T. Smith, Dr. G. W. Paschall. Joe Wade operated a furniture and undertaking business and Dr. Patterson a general store.

Esq. S. A. McDade has the right and title to call his home and office in South Fulton the Gretna Green of Obion County, for

SOUTH FULTON

here he has the record of performing to October 22, 1940, the marriage rites which united in matrimony 7258 couples, beginning with Beckham Enoch and Ella Mullins on September 8, 1918.

Speaking of men who have been well known as citizens of South Fulton and the various interests of the community of Civil District No. 16, we begin with Walter W. Morris, farmer, banker, business man who served the City National Bank as president for thirty years (retiring in 1937), an institution whose stockholders and directors reside and do business both in Kentucky and Tennessee. Mr. Morris has large acreage of farming lands lying south and west of 45-W highway in No. 16. There is also the Browder Milling Company constantly keeping pace with the march of progress for the space of thirty years or more, with Joe Browder at the helm and his nephew, Leon Browder, taking hold where the Browder brothers have relinquished. The Browder investments are about equally divided in Kentucky and Tennessee. There is also the Jesse Whitesell estate. Mr. Whitesell was the father of our fellow-citizen, R. P. Whitesell, banker of Union City for many years. A grandson, Hunter Whitesell, has charge of the Whitesell farms in Kentucky and Tennessee.

SOUTH FULTON SCHOOLS

Following are a number of the principals who have heretofore been connected with the Fulton High School: H. L. Jones, H. W. Moss, H. J. Priestly, J. B. Cox. Following is the school faculty of South Fulton for 1940-41: W. H. Cravens, principal; Elsie Bruer, Mrs. W. H. Cravens, J. C. Good, J. W. Haynes, Blanche Howard, Mary B. Jones, Clara N. Kirkland, Nina C. Lowery, Orvin Moore, Sarah Pickle, Mary K. Reed, Martha Roach, Naomi R. Smith, Lena Stokes, Mrs. J. E. Thomason, Allie D. Williams.

DIRECTORY SOUTH FULTON

Mayor, D. A. Rogers; clerk, R. A. Foulks; aldermen: Abe Jolley, Shelby Valentine, R. L. Ferguson, Lon Pickle, Virgil Davis, E. N. Houston; marshal, Parker McClure; water plant manager, Stanley Jones; fire department chief, D. C. Henderson; street superintendent, Barkley James; corporation magistrate, S. A. McDade; constable, No. 16, John Smith.

Census enumeration of South Fulton, population in 1940, 2050.

PIERCE COMMUNITY

Tracing the origin of the Pierce community, it was found to be settled principally before the Civil War, with the Pierce family predominating. Rice B. and Thomas M. Pierce were merchants at Old Jacksonville and some time afterwards moved to the locality which took the name of Pierce. Here Thomas Pierce became active in business. He was appointed postmaster and railroad agent, kept a general store and operated a double-rig saw mill and grist mill.

According to L. H. Blackburn, a native of Trenton locating at Pierce in 1865 (90 years of age and living at Pierce in 1940) work on the Memphis, Paducah & Northern R. R. was begun after the Civil War, but abandoned until 1869 when grading was resumed and the road completed, and in 1872, under a charter granted to operate in Tennessee by the General Assembly, rolling stock was provided and operation of train service was begun.

Thomas M. Pierce was a native of Virginia. His father, Rice B., was captain in the War of 1812 and a man of considerable importance in his home—Southampton County, Va. His son, Thomas M., when a young man located at Halifax N. C., and was married in 1834 to Margaret J. Blacknall, of Lewisburg, N. C. In 1842 Thomas M. Pierce and family moved to Dresden in Weakley County, Tenn. A few years later they settled at Old Jacksonville in Obion County. There were seven children, viz: Harriet E., who became the wife of Wm. B. Gibbs, T. Deveraux, H. Herman, Rice A. (born at Dresden), George Jarvis, Wm. B., and Lawrence.

And here begins the life of Hon. Rice A. Pierce, who was raised on a farm with limited school opportunities In 1862 he joined the Eighth Tennessee Cavalry, Confederate States Army, and 1864 was captured at Bolivar, Tenn., and held as a prisoner of war for nine months. After his return home he entered school at London, Canada, remaining until he became a law student at Halifax, N. C. Licensed to practice in 1868, Mr. Pierce located in Union City, beginning practice, and a short time afterwards was elected attorney-general of his judicial circuit, serving an eight-year term. He was then elected to Congress, serving one term, returning to his practice, while his opponent in the election succeeded him, but for one term only and Mr. Pierce was then returned to Congress, succeeding himself for a twelve-year period. Then again Mr. Pierce resumed the practice of law in Union City and made a brilliant record as a criminal lawyer. Mr. Pierce was married to Miss Mollie Hunter, of Scott County, Mo., and a son, Thos. M., locating in St. Louis, became chief counsel of the St. Louis Terminal Association. Before his death in 1936 Mr.

PIERCE COMMUNITY

Pierce had been honored as a Confederate veteran—as commanding officer of the Forrest Division, U. C. V., for distinguished service. The latter years of his law practice in Union City were in partnership with Hon. J. L. Fry, also a lawyer and citizen connected with important legal practice in West Tennessee and affiliation with the religious and civic life of his home city.

George J. Pierce, younger son of Thomas M. Pierce, became an extensive land owner and operator at Pierce. He was married in Mississippi to Miss Mary L. Gibbs, daughter of Judge Q. D. Gibbs, a well known citizen in his home county.

Among others connected with the community life of Pierce, there were J. M. Armstrong, operating a general store and cotton gin, Bob Davis, Dr. Underwood, Martin Chambers, Dave Rankin, Jack Roberson, Bob Cathey, Tobe Lowe, Ross Hughlett, Wm. Bowers, J. F. Hickman, J. W. Smith.

Among the agents following Mr. Pierce at the railroad station were J. T. Futrell and Dewitt Mathews. Tom Mathews operated a store in 1898, another store being operated by J. T. Futrell. R. J. Lowe was in the mercantile business at Pierce for 41 years. He was succeeded by his son, C. E. Lowe, with Mrs. C. E. Lowe as postmaster.

Chapel Hill was the nearest house of worship after the burning of Hebron Church, both Methodist congregations.

HARRIS COMMUNITY

This place was once called "Mink", afterwards Harris Station, named for the first merchant, John F. Harris. When the Memphis & Paducah Railroad was located at Harris one of the first depot agents was W. H. Powers. Powers & Fry opened a general store, which was sold to J. D. Fry & Co. Afterwards Will D. Fry became sole owner, his father moving to Fulton. Mr. Fry operated the store successfully for many years, and while in business Walter McClanahan became a clerk, remaining in the store for a number of years. Mr. McClanahan was depot agent at Harris for a period of thirty years. He entered the service when the line was known as the Chesapeake, Ohio & Southwestern R. R., and remained after the system was transferred under the name of the Newport News & Mississippi Valley R. R. before it became the I. C. System.

Some of the remaining pioneer business at old Jacksonville was moved to Harris. A house belonging to Dr. Boaz was mounted on wheels and moved to Harris. Dr. Nat Morris of South Fulton was married at Harris to Miss Sue DeBow.

Among old-time citizens were: Geo. R. Holmon, C. G. (Bud) Thomas, L. A. Allen, the Jonakin and Foulks families.

H. D. Lennox operates a store and serves as postmaster at Harris. Floyd Dedmon has a store and filling station.

Another very interesting community is Gibbs, formerly Paducah Junction when the crossing of the N. C. & St. L. Ry. and Illinois Central System was made. Agent serving this station is W. T. Sullivan.

Community was made up of citizens of the family names of Woodfin, Matthews, Cheatham, Ward, Hardy, and later years of Emery, Eddington, Easley, Ray, Brewer, King, Goulder, Pruett, Evanson.

Over in the Bethlehem community in Civil District Number One, one of the early settlers was Milus F. Thomas, son of Jas. Thomas of North Carolina, a veteran of the War of 1812. M. F. Thomas moved to Obion County in 1843 and was married in 1845 to Elizabeth E. Ward. Of the sons there were Geo. D., Littleton H. and Rev. J. H. Thomas, the latter a Cumberland Presbyterian minister. There were two daughters, Mrs. Henderson White and Mary Etta.

OBION COMMUNITY

In arriving at the name of Obion, and finding a parallel with any particular community, we might naturally associate it with the town of Obion in Obion County on the Obion River, since Obion, of Indian origin, means a river of many prongs or branches.

Obion was pictured by her tribe of peaceable red men as a maiden of wondrous beauty and charm. She was the only daughter of a Cherokee chief, and her native graces drew many lovers. Of her suitors, two were shown special favors. They became madly jealous of each other, and one day as Obion wandered hand in hand with the man of her choice his rival crept up behind and assassinated him. Her lover died at her feet. The victor claimed Obion, but she scorned his love and denounced his cowardly act. Overcome with grief that broke her heart, Obion ran straight to the river whose name she bore. Choosing a deep pool she flung herself headlong into the dark waters, and the spirit of beautiful Obion started in its search through the realms of the future for the soul of her lost lover.

W. M. Wilson ("Uncle Billy"), son of Col. William M. and Rebecca Wilson, a man of great vision and indomitable energy, was founder of the town of Obion. Like his father, he became an extensive land owner, residing for some years at Troy. In the home of the senior Wilson, who came to Obion County in 1820, and settled on a tract of land two miles southwest of what was afterwards the township of Troy, the county of Obion was organized on January 19, 1824.

"Uncle Billy", like his father, had the Spartan courage of a conqueror, and set about to tame the forests and establish a new civilization. He therefore with his engineer, Mr. Mansford, started for the banks of Obion River, laid out and platted a site selected as what he then designated as Crescent City.

This was in 1872. The Memphis & Paducah railroad was then in progress of construction and Mr. Wilson found a townsite on the north bank of the river. The land was a primeval forest and the railroad right-of-way was the only sign of human endeavor. But on either side of the railroad track 1200 lots were measured and staked, separated by streets 80 feet wide, and further divided into alleys 16 feet wide. Thoroughfares extended a mile east and west and half a mile north and south. About 320 acres thus embraced were donated to the new city. A steam saw mill, storehouse and depot building were immediately erected notwithstanding the fact that the railroad company had selected a station point a mile and a half farther up the track on Mill creek.

However Uncle Billy's perseverance finally prevailed and Judge Trimble, president of the railroad, conceded the logic of Mr. Wilson's claims and improvements. The depot was erected by Mr. Wilson at a cost of $900 and donated to the company to be used for railroad purposes.

Forests were felled and sawed into lumber. The first church house and the first schoolhouse were built by Mr. Wilson. Business blocks, dwelling houses, and factories took the place of tree stumps, and arrangements were made for sanitary improvements. The lands being cleared, it was soon made manifest that the city of Obion was located in the heart of a rich and fertile valley section of West Tennessee. The new city flourished. Cotton gins, flour mills, cooperage and stave mills, spoke and handle factories, a printing office, brick yards and other industries appeared and Obion assumed importance in trade and shipping.

The city soon had electric lights and improved sidewalks, churches, schools, stores, homes and a population exceeding 1000 people, all the work of prophetic insight and an optimism backed with good judgment and great courage.

These are a few of the instances in the life of a man whose lexicon had no such word as fail. Mr. Wilson was importuned time and again to accept nomination to the General Assembly, but refused political position and particularly the Brownlow administration. His first vote was cast for Millard Filmore, and in 1860 cast his lot with the Federal Union and voted for John Bell. He declined political preference, but espoused uplift and moral movements. He was benevolent and liberal.

As stated, Obion was located on Obion River, six miles southwest of Troy, in 1872. At the same time a station was located there on the Paducah & Memphis railroad. In time, this road by other railroad interests was absorbed and finally became the Illinois Central system. Also in time, the name of Crescent City was changed to Obion, it is presumed with the charter of incorporation. Navigation of Obion River was finally dismissed as impractical by the department of federal engineering and the project abandoned. But in a very short time Obion became a great shipping point for lumber manufacturers in an immediate belt of fine timber. Business sprang up with rapid growth for a number of years and Obion assumed importance like other towns in the fine timber regions of Obion County.

The first business men and leaders of lumber industries during the period came from important manufacturing centers. L. V. Boyle & Company operated a saw mill, cutting about 5,000,000

OBION COMMUNITY

feet of lumber yearly, and a planing mill also at this place, which they made a shipping point. Lyon, Murray & Peck also operated saw and planing mill. Blair, Ashly & Company and Humphrey & Company operated stave factories. The first business men were A. H. Patton, Daniel Shoffner and "Buck" Crittendon. Other business men following in the wake of expansion were Farris & Wylie and D. P. Tucker, general merchants; R. S. Morris, Humphrey & Sanford and A. Wilson, grocers; John R. Walker & Co., undertaking and livery; Bright & Lancaster, drugs; Henry Wilson and Geo. Stine, hotels.

The Forcum-James Lumber Company was organized in 1914 to engage in the retail lumber business and the manufacture of cooperage stock at Obion. First officers of the company were H. Forcum, president; C. A. James, vice-president; V. Forcum, secretary and treasurer. In 1928 the company increased its capital stock from $50,000 to $250,000. The company had four retail lumber yards, one at Obion, one at Trimble, and two at Dyersburg. The company, still operating at the various points, furnish all kinds of building materials. They make contracts for all kinds of bridge and levee work, paving and drainage.

Among some of the contracts and building projects completed by the company are: First Baptist Church of Union City; Fayette County (Tenn.) Courthouse; Somerville Courthouse; Obion High School; First Baptist Church at Dyersburg. Paving and levee work for Dyer County and paving and grading for the State of Tennessee have been undertaken and accomplished with success and approval, by the Forcum-James Lumber Co.

The heavy timber was finally exhausted and the mills vacated, but Obion was still surrounded by a rich farming country, now systematically drained and yielding fine returns in produce. Therefore only Federal and State highways and motor traffic could affect the flow of trade and shipping away from local points, as it did in many of the smaller towns.

Anyway it seems proper and appropriate to speak of a pioneer of well known courage and indomitable energy like Mr. Wilson. Evidently he was much like his famous ancestor, who settled in the lower end of the county near the point afterwards selected as the site of the town of Troy, and in whose home the county was organized.

It is a matter of congratulation and coincidence that Mayor A. Wilson, son of W. M. Wilson ("Uncle Billy"), has a record of continuous service for years as Mayor of Obion and as a member of the Obion County Court. The Wilson Hotel, whose host was Mayor Wilson, enjoyed for many years county-wide reputation for the excellence of its fare and entertainment.

Then there are others who have been closely associated with

the business and public interests, well known citizens of fine character and influence, namely: Fox, Forcum, Morris, Moffat, Nichols, Chiles, King, Buchanan, Beaird, Brown. Among other well known citizens of the vicinity of Obion were P. H. Hurt, John Bright, John Board, Polk McDonald, Calvin Brown, Josh Pryor.

Particularly do we remember the newspapers. It was our fortune to assist in the launching of the first newspaper at Obion, the Independent published by Enfield & Hensley. Other publications followed in succession, viz: Editor James; Arch Johnson, now publisher of the Standard, Benton, Ill.; G. B. and N. B. Baird, publishers of the Enterprise; D. L. Hoover and H. P. Riddick; Harold Henry, publishing the Herald, and the Obion Gazette by C. M. Hughes.

Obion is now a city of paved streets, the work of a WPA project and local aid, a system which covers the entire corporate limits, connecting with paved highways leading north and south, east and west thru the lower end of the county.

BOARD OF MAYOR AND ALDERMEN

Mayor, A. Wilson; aldermen: W. P. Beaird, H. T. King, R. H. Beaird, Frank Board, W. O. Walker, V. Morris; recorder and marshal, H. M. Blevins.

1940 Census Enumeration: Population of Obion, 1151.

OBION SCHOOLS

Obion is the seat of one of the principal county high schools. A new gymnasium and substantial school buildings are conveniently located.

Principals serving Obion schools in the past are C. D. Hilliard and M. E. Whitson. John Richardson, the last elected, enters his school year as principal, with the following faculty of teachers:

High School: Carlos Irwin, Varon Shanklin, Miss Elizabeth Canada, Miss Carolyn Botts, Mrs. John Richardson.

Grammar School: David M. Guy, Mrs. M. Rollins, Miss Dorothy Fox, Miss Genola Cunningham, Mary K. Tice, Mrs. Robert Davidson, Miss Eunice Williams.

COMMERCIAL BANK

The Commercial Bank at Obion was organized in 1903, with Dr. J. J. Wells as president and Clinton Richardson as cashier. Since that time the cashiers serving the bank are as follows: G. W. Reed, L. M. Blackley, C. E. Dean and E. A. Watson. President serving the bank in 1940 was W. P. Beaird.

MERCANTILE SERVICE

Along with the history of merchandising in the county and the service rendered in the old days to the farming community,

OBION COMMUNITY

the names of T. B. Moffat at Rives and Obion and those of J. S. Moffatt & Sons at Troy are particularly important. Moffat & Bonner and T. B. Moffat & Son, Rives and Obion, have been in business continuously for a period of 75 years, the anniversary taking place in July, 1940.

T. B. Moffat opened at Rives, known as Troy Station, seventy-five years ago. T. J. Bonner afterwards became a partner of Mr. Moffat. Years later a branch store was opened by T. B. Moffat & Son at Obion, now in operation and known as the store which succeeded the original T. B. Moffat store at Rives. The store at Obion is still operated under the name of T. B. Moffat & Son, with Thomas B. Moffat in charge.

An example of the system of merchandising—the difference between the old and the new—we take a case in point, either J. S. Moffatt at Troy or T. B. Moffat at Rives. What these merchants and others before and after the Civil War were to the people of the community in which they conducted business—how they stood by the farmers in carrying open accounts until cotton, corn and tobacco came to market—and then again in case of crop failure how these farmers were granted extension for another year, and still others, with no extra charge excepting when the account was converted into a note with small interest—often none at all—all this constitutes a story full of interest as it is compared with present conditions, with Federal mail-order merchandising and subsidized farming—farms mortgaged and fortunes dissolved.

It is indeed a commentary without words, a matter of historical significance traced to sources that have probably forgotten assurance of life, liberty and pursuit of happiness.

OBION CLUBS

Self Culture Club: Organized 18 years ago in 1922. The officers now are: Mrs. L. G. Moffat, president; Mrs. C. P. Higgs, vice-president; Mrs. Woody Cunningham, secretary-treasurer.

Philomathean Club: Mrs. Colpy Upton, president; Mrs. Wade Moore, vice-president; Mrs. Frank Board, secretary-treasurer.

Beta Gamma Book Club: Mrs. Dale Glover, president; Mrs. T. B. Moffat, vice-president; Mrs. Eunice Williams, secretary-treasurer.

Wednesday Club (Literary): Mrs. J. O. Horner, president; Mrs. Eugene Blevins, vice-president; Mrs. John Williams, secretary-treasurer.

Parent-Teachers Association: Mrs. Lawrence Fox, president; Mrs. C. D. Hilliard, vice-president; Carlos Erwin, treasurer; Anita DeSambourg McDaniel, secretary.

OBION COUNTY HISTORY

OBION BUSINESS DIRECTORY

Business and professional directory of Obion for 1941:

Merchandise: T. B. Moffat & Son, H. T. King Company, Lehman Company, Nichols Variety Store, Obion Hardware & Furniture Co. Groceries: King's Grocery, Harry H. Moultrie, Horner & Co., Paul Townsend, Fox Red and White Grocery, Fox Feed Store, Fox Grain Co., Parks Grain Co.

Hotels: Wilson House, Maloney Hotel.

Restaurants: City Cafe, Tom and Jerry, Robt. Davidson, Frank's Lunch Room, Blackley Market.

Filling Stations: Penny Saver Service, E. Bransford, Pan-Am Service Station, Morris & White Service Station, City Service, Phillips 66, Obion Garage Co., Frank Board.

Nancy Freed Beauty Shop, Ford Beauty Shop.
Rawdon Barber Shop, Strand Theatre.
City Dry Cleaners, R. V. Green Shoe Shop.
Insurance: W. O. Walker Agency, Tidroe Agency.
Obion Real Estate. Obion Coal & Ice Co.
Turney Drug Store.
Fox-Watson Lumber Co.
Forcum-James Lumber Co., Obion, Dyersburg, Memphis.
Livestock Dealer, Virgil Morris, Fisher Poultry.
Everett Mule Barn.
Agent I. C. R. R. Co., J. E. Bivens.
Physician, Dr. J. C. Walker.
Dentist, Dr. R. M. Morehead.
King Funeral Home.
Postmaster at Obion, H. B. Fox.
Attorney at law, E. A. Morris.

OBION METHODIST CHURCH

The first religious services in Obion, 52 years ago in 1888, were held in an old lumber shed standing on the present site of the stock pens alongside of the I. C. Railroad tracks. Attendance was not confined to any single denomination. The first minister was Rev. Mason, of Covington.

Only a few years after this the Methodist Church was organized in a little schoolhouse, which was located on the lot now occupied by the Baptist Church. Members of the original organization included the family of W. M. (Uncle Billy) Wilson and about fourteen other families.

The Methodist Church building, erected soon after the congregation was organized, stands as located on the property or grounds donated by W. M. Wilson. At first, limited to a small auditorium facing east, extensions were made afterwards, con-

OBION COMMUNITY

sisting of Sunday School rooms and a south wing, and remodeling the building the entrance was changed to face the south.

One of the first pastors to serve the congregation was Rev. Medling, occupying the pulpit in 1894-97. Rev. Love was the next pastor in 1898. The appointment of Rev. G. W. Evans followed.

Rev. Walker came in 1900, then in rotation Revs. Cook, Norman and Drake. Rev. Stewart, another minister, was not only the pastor, but took special interest in the children, on each Sunday afternoon of his appointments teaching a children's Bible class.

Rev. Whitnell came next, and afterwards Rev. C. D. Hilliard, whose wife died at Obion.

Rev. Hart was next in charge, administering the marriage rites which united Dr. and Mrs. C. E. Upchurch.

Next pastor was Rev. Joyner. Rev. J. T. Bagby served the congregation for the first time in 1911, Rev. W. C. Waters, presiding elder. Next came Revs. J. C. Cason, Bagby, Newsom, and Rev. U. S. McCaslin followed, while Rev. W. W. Armstrong served as presiding elder. At this time the pastor's daughter, Miss Hauty, was united in marriage to Horace Yates.

Rev. Bass was the next pastor, followed by the Rev. C. W. Ehrhart. At this time the Tabernacle was built as assembly place for the Men's Bible Class, as well as for other general church work.

Probably the largest crowds ever to attend religious worship in the town of Obion assembled at a tent meeting during the revival campaign held at Obion by the Rev. Burke Culpepper. Another very interesting revival two years later was conducted by Rev. Geo. Tucker.

Rev. Ehrhart was followed by Rev. J. W. Waters as pastor and Rev. R. L. Norman as presiding elder. At this time a new parsonage was built to take the place of the old one moved away.

Rev. I. M. King was the next pastor in 1928-31. Rev. J. T. Bagby received appointment to return to Obion in November, 1931, remaining till 1934, with Rev. F. B. Jones as presiding elder.

In November, 1934, Rev. Dr. C. A. Warterfield was appointed pastor of the Obion church, with Rev. J. Mack Jenkins as presiding elder. People of Obion enjoy recalling both the minister and his lovely wife, a very rare and beautiful Christian character. They remained with the church in 1935.

Ministers appointed as pastors for Obion Church—1936 to 1940—are as follows: Revs. C. M. Hughes, J. M. Boykin, C. M. Robbins.

Present membership of the Board of Stewards include the following: H. T. King, C. D. Hilliard, Virgil Morris, H. D. Yates,

OBION COUNTY HISTORY

J. O. Horner, E. A. Watson, John F. Williams, Fred Cunningham, Geo. Tubbs.

Sunday School Superintendents serving for a period of years are Geo. W. Tubbs and J. O. Horner.

(This work is indebted to Mrs. Bettie Chiles, a former member at Obion, and Mrs. Virgil Morris for this very interesting paper, somewhat reduced from the original, read at special meeting of the church in 1936.

OBION CHURCH OF CHRIST

The Church of Christ at Obion was organized the second Sunday in May, 1895, with Elder Elihu Scott as minister, who was succeeded in charge of the work by Elder A. G. Freed, with charter members including H. M. Wilson, L. A. Ward, A. M. Albright, Robert Fox, C. C. Brown, A. M. Moultrie, Dr. J. F. Darnell, B. F. Craig and Kirk Wells.

Ministers serving the church following organization are: Elders John Taylor, F. O. Howell, L. K. Harding, T. H. Woodruff and Elder Lambert.

Elder H. H. Royster is the minister now in charge.

UNION CITY

PAST AND PRESENT

TOWN AND PEOPLE

Outline Pioneer Days, First Settlement
Schools and Churches
Local Industry

Primitive Environment — Streets in Mud or Deep in Dust — Water From Shallow Wells — Days of Furniture Manufacture — Staves and Chairs — Woolen Mill — Lumber Market — Cholera — Outbreak of Lawlessness — Growth of Merchandising — Schools — Churches — Farm Interests — Newspapers — County Fair — Confederate Reunions — Centennial Celebration — Baseball.

New Era: Civic Improvements — High School and Grammar School — New Churches — Brown Shoe Company Manufacture of Women's and Children's Shoes — Work Shirt Manufacture — Waterproof Garments — Meat Products Packing Plant — Dolls and Toy Making — Live Stock Shipping — Kitty League Baseball — Turner Ball Park — Chamber of Commerce — Kiwanis — Jaycee — Rotary — Garden — Music — Review — Women's Clubs.

M. G. GIBBS

Native of Union City, locating in Washington City in 1898, Dr. M. G. Gibbs is a grandson of General George W. Gibbs, who became owner of the land in 1829, upon which he located the town of Union City.

Dr. Gibbs is sole owner of the Peoples Drug Stores Inc., an organization beginning with the first store in Washington City in 1905. From that beginning to 1941 Peoples Drug Stores Inc. have become a corporation of nearly two hundred drug stores, embracing a group of stores in Washington City, branch stores in Virginia, Maryland, Ohio, West Virginia, Pennsylvania, New Jersey, Delaware, District of Columbia and Tennessee.

In these stores and executive departments are engaged more than fifty native Obion County people, employed by Dr. Gibbs for the various branches of the business, while many other Tennesseans are also in the service, as a result of psychology and executive foresight in handling such an undertaking.

At a meeting of the Board of Directors in 1939 Dr. Gibbs was elected chairman of the Board, with John G. Bell, Executive Vice President; Geo. B. Burrus, Vice President; Robert H. Driskill, Attorney and Secretary.

OUTLINE OF UNION CITY

This work might appropriately begin with the settlement of Old Jacksonville and the first settler, Elisha Parker, who located in Obion County a few miles northeast of what was afterwards the town of Union City. Parker settled in 1819 and Totten in 1824. Benjamin Totten (great-great grandfather of W. H. Swiggart, Jr.) designated his point of settlement as Totten's Wells. He opened the first store in the county and was appointed postmaster; also operated a cotton gin. Goodspeed's History mentions, among the first merchants in Union City prior to the Civil War, A. H. Patton, Rice and Thomas M. Pierce, James Wilson, Thomas Ray, Felix McGaugh, Isaac Foster, Bynum Bros., Robert and William Seay; also Drs. Samuel Cutter, Robert McMullen and Gus Batte.

Now it is evident from reliable authority that most of these settlers located at Old Jacksonville and afterwards moved to other localities—some to Union City, others to Pierce. Some of the stores and homes, it is said, were moved from Old Jacksonville to Harris when that railroad station was located. One home was moved intact on wheels. Totten's Wells and Old Jacksonville, it is agreed, were practically in the same location.

In the year 1829 the county records show a transfer of 5000 acres of land in Obion County made to Gen. Geo. W. Gibbs, of Nashville. The original deed was made as payment of fees due General Gibbs as attorney for the owners, Martin Armstrong and others, of North Carolina. This tract of land was bound in part by Houser Creek on the west and Grove Creek on the east. On a section of this land General Gibbs located the town of Union City.

Among the pioneers forming a settlement here were John White, Wilson Cage, William Scott, Ezekiel Harelson, Major Ury, Richard Baynes, Major Chambers, Doctors Williams, Chittim and Thompson. It is said that the first grocery store was opened by Sanders Carman, and that Ki Wade opened another store on Third Street not far from the corner of Florida Avenue, and deciding that he was too much out of the way moved, rolling the house on logs to some point probably near the corner of First Street and Washington Avenue. Mr. Wade was the father of B. J. (Bob) Wade. A pioneer home was settled by the family in the vicinity of Pleasant Hill.

Another house was built on the street, afterwards a business center, and opened by Dabney Glass in 1855 as the first general store in Union City. The first hotels in the order of time were conducted by Collins, Pulliam and Wm. Pettus. A business house on Church Street was opened by Isaac Foster, formerly of Old

Jacksonville, as a dry goods store. Cooper Curlin ran a wagon and blacksmith shop. About this time Garrett & Jenkins started a grocery store on the Pink Bennett lot.

Chas. N. Gibbs, whose portrait appears elsewhere, in partnership with Wm. B. Gibbs, opened a general store in which the postoffice was located, the first in Union City. Mr. Gibbs was interested in a number of enterprises. Among others he started a saw mill in 1856, which was sold to James Vincent and afterwards combined with a grist mill. Jacob Palmer and family from North Carolina located in Union City in 1839 and settled upon the site which afterwards became school property. He obtained an option on 200 acres of land and built a log house, hewed from native timbers and chinked with clay, with two rooms 18 feet square and a passage between them, a stick and clay chimney at each end with immense fire places—the type of homes common with pioneers.

Chas. N. Gibbs, son of Gen. Geo. W. Gibbs, donated grounds for the public school buildings, where the Central School, later the grammar school, was located. C. N. Gibbs afterwards became Secretary of State of Tennessee.

Besides the name of Gibbs, other names were used to mark the streets of Union City, such as Ury, Cheatham, Matthews, Todd, etc., in extensions and additions.

Ten acres of ground in Union City, located on Church Street between Depot Street and the express office at the railroad, was deeded for railroad purposes to the Nashville & Northwestern R. R. as a donation made by Gen. Geo. W. Gibbs, deed recorded April 5, 1867. This property was used for many years as a railroad and municipal park and a jockey ground for horse traders. Lower part of the grounds are now utilized for parking cars. General Gibbs also donated a number of lots in Union City for church buildings. The park was finally sold and transferred to the Corporation of Union City.

RAILROAD CROSSING

The Mobile & Ohio R. R., Mobile to Cairo, Ill., was chartered in 1848 by the General Assembly to operate in Tennessee, and completed in 1859, but was badly wrecked during the Civil War. Reconstruction after the war and liquidation of indebtedness in 1870 was followed by regular passenger and freight service from that time.

Col. Lysander Adams, of Troy, and party made original survey of the route from Obion River to Columbus, Ky. H. P. Farns-

UNION CITY

worth was construction superintendent. The northern terminus was then at Columbus, Ky.

For many years also the "Green Line" freight service was operated from the N. C. & St. L. Railroad over the Mobile & Ohio R. R. by way of Union City to Columbus.

Consolidation of the Mobile & Ohio R. R. and the Gulf, Mobile & Northern R. R., under the name of Gulf, Mobile & Ohio R. R., was consummated and reorganization took place August 16, 1940, with I. B. Tigrett, of Jackson, Tenn., as president. "The Rebel" stream-lined passenger trains between Mobile and St. Louis were added on the night runs in a regular schedule of through service.

The Nashville & Northwestern R. R., Nashville to "unnamed terminus" in northwest Tennessee, was chartered in 1852 to operate in Tennessee, but for lack of subscriptions work did not begin for several years. When the Civil War opened only that portion of the road to Kingston Springs was in operation. During the War the Federal Government took charge of the road for military purposes and completed construction to the Tennessee River at Johnsonville. After the War the road was reimbursed for losses to the Government and the road was completed through to Union City.

In the meantime charter was granted to the Hickman & Obion R. R., projected by Gen. Geo. W. Gibbs, and the two roads were combined and completed for operation in 1868 under the name of the Nashville, Chattanooga & St. Louis R. R.

Union City having been designated as a railroad crossing, brought about by the junction formed by the N. C. & St. L. Ry. crossing the M. & O. R. R., the natural result was a union station at this place.

General Gibbs employed James M. Daniel, a civil engineer of Richmond, Va., to survey and locate the Hickman & Obion Railroad. Mr. Daniel returned to the crossing point after the survey had been made, placed his instrument near a large white oak tree about three feet in diameter, blazed the bark off so that it could be marked with red chalk, and wrote the name Union City. General Gibbs, who founded the town, was also author of the name with which Union City was christened.

On January 29, 1858, the Tennessee Legislature authorized the Mississippi River Railroad to be constructed from Memphis to the Kentucky State line in the direction of Cairo. The work of grading was not commenced until 1869, and then soon suspended. In 1871 it was consolidated with the Paducah & Gulf Railroad, a Kentucky corporation under the name of the Memphis & Paducah. The whole line was afterward sold under mortgage, and reorganized as the Memphis, Paducah & Northern. It was later known as the Chesapeake, Ohio & Southwestern, extending from

OBION COUNTY HISTORY

Cecelia, Ky., to Memphis, again succeeded by the Newport News & Mississippi Valley R. R. and finally by the Illinois Central System, with general operations after 1872. Stations in Obion County are South Fulton, Pierce, Harris, Gibbs, Rives, Polk, Obion. The road in 1872 was not much more than completed from Paducah to Obion, and the other end from Memphis to Newbern, leaving a gap across the Obion River bottoms which was not constructed for several years. Through operation and regular train service therefore was begun toward the late seventies.

The first depot was built at the crossing where the present one stands, excepting that the old depot was by court decree made to clear the street lines. The first depot was burned by General Forrest in 1862. Jacob M. Palmer, civil engineer, was the first station agent.

In 1855 Union City was surveyed and a plat of surface lines was made by F. R. Helner, chief engineer of the Nashville & Northwestern R. R. Some months after lots were offered for sale at public auction.

The first lot was sold for $300, location of the Moss Drug Store on Church Street, south side (burned and rebuilt), for some years occupied by radio and electric shops.

Then began the saloon period which flourished with a total of thirteen or more saloons at one time, from 1855, with a number of changes but no less in number until they were closed in 1903.

Elder H. D. Bantau, in 1857, built the first church house in Union City, the Church of Christ, with the aid of the community, and all denominations were invited to use the house for worship.

At the breaking out of the Civil War Union City, on account of its excellent railroad facilities, was made camp of instruction by the Confederate authorities, and at times was occupied by five to twenty thousand men. Afterwards it was captured by a regiment of Illinois cavalry, twice surprised and retaken by Forrest with a small number of Confederate soldiers, but at the close of the war it was in the hands of the Federal troops.

It is said that the first brick business house erected in Union City stood on the lot now occupied by the A. & P. Food Store, up to recently the Wehman Hardware Store, excepting that the building was on the center of the lot facing north on Washington avenue between First and Depot (or Beal) street. The building was the property of C. N. and W. B. Gibbs, used for office and business purposes. The next as far as can be learned, was the corner drug store building on Church and First, now occupied by the LaFonte Drug Store, and with it the Mullins building, in which the John T. Walker Insurance Agency and the dress shop are located. Then came numbers of store buildings constructed in the eighties and nineties.

The old brick and frame houses, ranging along the M. & O. R. R. tracks, included the Haydon & Barry and the Wm. Hamilton grain, hay and feed store. The Brackin Hotel and the Miller House were in the block below. Capt. Wm. Askins had a store on the corner opposite the Miller House facing the railroad, the property of Hugh Smith, razed and rebuilt.

The new Coco-Cola Bottling warehouse built by Mr. Smith on the corner of Bank and Exchange street, extends west on Exchange on the lot occupied by the old express office when R. F. Nailling (Uncle Bob) was express agent.

Along First street, between Church street and Washington avenue, near the center on the east side, was the Murphy store, the principal general merchandising establishment in Union City at that time, and almost exactly opposite on the other side of the street was the Wilkins Hatch grocery store. The old house on the west side where The Commercial newspaper was published (afterwards rebuilt and with the Kaufman, or McGowen & Jones store, converted into the Black & White Store) was built by Captain Cary in 1870.

Then came a period of business house construction, including the Central Benefit Association insurance building, in which the Mayes Drug Store is located, known as "the tallest three-story building in the United States," the Dietzel Hardware Store, Max Layne and R. I. Mann store buildings, Morgan building, destroyed by fire and rebuilt and occupied by Morgan-Verhine Inc., Nailling buildings, Driskill and Bransford buildings, bank buildings, etc.

CHOLERA EPIDEMIC

Soon after the Civil War the town of Union City, recovering from the war and recouping its fortunes, had reached a population of one thousand people when a general attack of Asiatic cholera took place, breaking out in 1873, when the homes were without plumbing and the inhabitants were supplied from shallow wells, hardly suitable for drinking purposes, but the only source of water supply. It may not seem strange that under these conditions, half the population fled as refugees to other places. Of the remainder about one hundred died of the disease, with recovery of perhaps that number. Many of the good women turned to nursing the sick. Among the physicians of the time were Drs. Evans, Warterfield and Harrison, who remained and administered to the patients. The whole community was in sickness and mourning. One particular instance of immolation and sacrifice was that of the late Harvey Caldwell, one of the popular conductors on the N. C. & St. L. Ry., who left his work and gave his entire time to the people of Union City in providing for and rendering all the assistance possible to the sick. For the fine things accomplished and the valuable assistance rendered, the railroad company recognized his services with generous reward and with his choice as conductor of any passenger run on the road.

OLD FURNITURE FACTORIES

The first industrial enterprise in Union City was a saw mill and planing mill, located by Dan P. Shoffner on West Main street, on the lot now occupied by the N. C. & St. L. Ry. freight depot. A pioneer in the movement, Mr. Shoffner afterwards added a planing mill and machinery for making furniture. In a short time he was associated with Moffett and Beck, operating for three years under the name of Shoffner, Moffett & Beck. Mr. Shoffner's interest was then sold to Ben Bransford, the former moving to the country to operate a saw mill. The firm then operating for four years was Moffett, Beck & Bransford, shortly changed to Beck & Bransford, and so continued until January, 1885, when consolidation was made with the Ekdahl Furniture Co., which had been organized in 1882, with Wm. Askins as president. The firm then became the Beck-Bransford & Ekdahl Furniture Co., with J. E. Beck as president and R. Garth, secretary and treasurer.

Mr. Shoffner returned to Union City and operated an independent factory, but due to an epidemic of cholera and depression of business he was forced to make an assignment in 1883 for the benefit of his creditors, and the business until 1886 was conducted by a joint stock company, known as the Union City Furniture Co., with John H. McDowell as president. At this time the Tennessee Furniture and Chair Co. was organized with W. G. Moss as president and general manager; W. A. Posey, vice-president; W. H. Gardner, secretary, and J. H. Whipple, treasurer. This company purchased and absorbed the interests both of the Union City Furniture Co. and the Union City Chair Co.

For a number of years the Beck-Bransford & Ekdahl Furniture Co. operated in the buildings on the corner of Washington avenue and First street, on the southeast corner lot now occupied by the A. & P. Food Store, formerly the Wehman Hardware Store. The finishing room was in the building across the street, now the Nailling Hospital, reached by inclosed bridge overhead passage way. Factory operations were managed by John Elam, with J. H. Lynn, of this city, as foreman of the machine shops. Mr. Lynn, after his connection with the company, was engaged for a number of years in the furniture business at Jackson and Memphis,

UNION CITY

D. P. SHOFFNER

Pioneer founder of Union City industries, a man of great energy and vision, who established the first furniture factory in Union City—the first of any kind of manufacturing industry at this point. Mr. Shoffner was the father of Mrs. Florence Harris and Mrs. Dr. W. M. Turner. Born in Carroll County, Tenn., January 25, 1839. Died in Memphis, Tenn., December 23, 1895.

also for a few years in Hickman. He now conducts his own cabinet shop in Union City near the Red Star Drug Store.

The Tennessee Furniture and Chair Company mentioned above was located in a large brick building between North First street and the G. M. & O. R. R. one block north of the stock pens.

North of the original location of the Beck & Bransford factory on West Main street, J. H. W. Jones operated a large planing mill, afterwards by purchase becoming the property of Moore & Rogers. One of the partners, James Moore, was the father of the present Mrs. J. C. Burdick, Jr., serving as Mayor of Union City during the perilous days of the robber bands in 1885.

Another mill and furniture factory, operated for a time by McIntosh & Noe, was located on the old Askins & Dircks mill site, west of the N. C. & St. L. Ry. tracks, where the county agriculture fair and cattle pens were afterwards located.

Trautwein & Semones operated a stave mill in Union City, yards located on the lot between the G. M. & O. R. R. and Depot street, afterwards used as the jockey yard.

R. E. Gardner operated a stave yard in Union City on the lot on First Street afterwards occupied by the Capitol Theatre and the Grissom buildings. Mr. Gardner did a considerable shipping business, later moving to St. Louis, where, as president and general manager, he operated the Banner Buggy Co., which in turn, with the advent of motor cars, became the Chevrolet Motor Co.

Woolen mills were operated in Union City on East Church street, occupying lots somewhere near the Horner Cash Grocery. J. N. Woodfin first owned and operated the mills. Afterwards J. F. (Fulton) Howard bought the plant and operated in the weaving of blankets and wool thread.

There was one man in Union City during the boom days of furniture manufacture and saw milling in the county, native of Sligo, Ireland, a genius in many respects and a man of fine accomplishments. This was Henry Little, father of the Henry Little later connected with the Alamo Service Station. The elder Little, in his line of business, lumber and furniture manufacture, was skilled in every branch of the work, affable, keen-witted, and his professional ability and personality brought him in contact, in a general way, with all the leaders and operators of that day seeking technical aid and advice, and thus he became better known probably than any other man of that busy time in Union City and contiguous lumber markets.

At the apex of the furniture making period Union City had reached a population of approximately 3500 people, with no street improvements, no electric power and lighting system, shallow

UNION CITY

wells, and muddy streets. It was in 1891 before electric lights and waterworks were installed, and then only enough generation for limited lighting for business and home use at night.

DECLINE OF FURNITURE MAKING

Altogether at one time in Union City there were in operation three large furniture factories and one small one, together with the manufacture of chairs, spokes and staves, and a general spirit of activity not unmixed with the usual sports and diversions.

In 1879 Trautwein & Semones established in Union City a wagon and machine shop. This was operated successfully for many years and sold to C. E. Bushart, who in turn sold to R. H. Rust, converting the plant into a general Ford Agency and Supply House, machine shop and sales depot. Operating for considerable time with general success, Mr. Rust sold to the Union City Motor Co., J. P. Farrell, manager. Beginning in 1879 another machine shop was operated for a few years by Ownby & Sons.

The first flouring mill in Union City was established by F. M. Brown in 1868, and the industry passed on thru the years to the plant of the Monroe Milling Co. The Dahnke-Walker Milling Co. for many years operated a corn and corn products mill, together with a flour mill. The Monroe mill building was destroyed by fire in 1935. The Dahnke-Walker Co. mills were sold in 1921 to the Motlow Milling Co. who operated in corn and flour products for a few years when the plant was dismantled by fire in 1925.

The Mayers Chair Co. was one of the independent manufacturing concerns established by Henry Mayers in the latter period of the nineties, located on the lot now occupied as a whole by the Brown Shoe Co. Mr. Mayers was for a long time engaged in the insurance business, then operated this factory for some years, organizing a stock company, with Hunter Elam as secretary during the latter part of the time in operation. As was the case with other Union City factories before that the chair business also succumbed to failing market conditions.

A farm drain tile factory was instituted by Whipple & Hatcher, in the beginning of the century a very important adjunct to the low swamp sections of this and other sections. This plant was enlarged for concrete work, operated for a time by Beck & Miles, and is still an active enterprise in Union City.

BRICK AND CONCRETE YARDS

T. L. Bransford Son (now operated by Ben Bransford) succeeding an institution which pioneered in brick making and building in Union City, operated by Lee Bransford, one of the original leaders of the building industry. Mr. Bransford was the contractor in the construction of the old Union City courthouse and many of the business houses in Union City. Mr. Bransford also as contractor superintended the construction of the present Methodist Church building in Union City. Mr. Ben Bransford remains the sole owner and operator of the yards north of town, handling brick and cement and building materials.

CHILD SPECIALTY HOUSE

For a number of years the Childs Specialty House manufacturing women's and children's dresses, was a busy industry employing hundreds of operatives. Mrs. Wilma Scates-Bixler was the founder and inspiration of the business in Union City. Beginning single-handed the business grew in volume to the proportions of a corporation with Mrs. Bixler as president, C. E. Beck vice-president and general manager and E. K. Beck sales manager. The company after a few years bought and occupied the building on Washington Avenue known as the Childs Specialty House. With decline of business the making of dresses suffered from over production and the markets discouraged further production.

RAILROAD FOR $10,000

It was sometime in the early years beginning with lumber sawing and shipping in Obion County—about 1870— and Union City was already a lumber market when this city was offered the opportunity of a new railroad. Promoters of the Memphis & Paducah Railroad came to Union City to solicit subscriptions and cooperation in the building of a railroad from Paducah to Memphis, to be routed by way of Union City. This route was advised as the most direct and logical of any of the surveys in the preliminary plans, and on the grounds of mutual interest between the promoters of the enterprise and the citizens of Union City, a Mr. Morris, representing the interests of the road, met with a body of the leading citizens and laid the plans before them, which of course included right of way and stock subscriptions. Amount asked was $10,000. What occurred at that meeting and who were present, we are not prepared to say. It is really not important. But the misfortune that followed that fatal step has for many years on number disturbed our mental processes and come to us in fitful dreams, and the only probable reaction that might come in the way of salvage was that we might realize what the mistake had cost and set about to atone and make restitution for the loss sustained to Union City and community.

The reply made to Mr. Morris was a flat refusal—that in order to get through the Obion River bottoms with a minimum expense and with the least trouble it was necessary that the road be surveyed by Union City. When the representative of the pro-

UNION CITY

posed road left town on the outgoing train, it is related that he told a former citizen of Union City, Mr. George Isbell, on the same train, about the meeting and his ultimatum that there were two places, "Hell and Union City," where the road would never be built.

So the Memphis & Paducah Railroad, as time passed, changed to the Chesapeake & Ohio R. R., then the Chesapeake, Ohio & Southwestern, next the Newport News & Mississippi Valley Railroad, and finally the Illinois Central R. R. System, the greatest in the South, building an empire of towns and cities on the lines from Chicago and St. Louis to the principal cities of the South.

But, if Mr. Morris were living today he would discover that, through the magic of paved highways and motor transfer service, Union City for all practical purposes is actually on the I. C. Railroad, if only Union City desires to do business with the road.

REIGN OF TERROR

An organized band of desperadoes, thugs, thieves and gangsters, operating from Cairo, Ill., to Jackson, Tenn., with leaders, headquarters and hideouts on West Main street in Union City, spread terror with all the savage fury of uncontrolled lawlessness and plunder in Union City and immediate vicinity for a period of fifteen months, beginning with Christmas eve, 1884, and all through the year of 1885, until the following spring of the next year—1886.

The first outbreak was in the home of Tom Montgomery in the vicinity of Mount Zion, near Jordan north of Union City, in the early morning hours just before Christmas eve, 1884. Mr. Montgomery was awakened by a noise on his window. He reached for his gun and fired at a figure thru the window, saying to his wife that he had shot a negro. Then he opened the front door and started out, the outlaws from the west end of the porch shooting him down. His wife ran out and over his body, and across the road thru snow and ice, to her brother's home, and while she was gone the burglars plundered the house. When Mrs. Montgomery and Mr. McMurry returned the burglars had escaped, but the children were left uninjured.

From that time citizens were thoroughly aroused but the officers, few in number, were practically helpless. In the meantime for months, particularly throughout the summer, hardly a night passed without housebreaking and burglary. Money, watches, jewelry, clothing and dry goods, with other articles of merchandise were stolen. No morning came without the report of plunder in one or more homes and business houses. People barred their windows down in the heat of summer and were afraid to sleep.

OBION COUNTY HISTORY

King Henderson, a negro living in the Montgomery neighborhood, suspected as an accomplice in the Montgomery murder, was arrested and held in custody by Chas. McClanahan, but in some way got loose and fled and never again was heard of. McClanahan moved away, returning only for a hasty visit.

Some time after the Montgomery murder Murphy Alexander, residing at his home near Union City, the McRee farm west of Union City, was aroused from bed and found that his house was about to be attacked by burglars. Mr. Alexander was formerly sheriff of Lake County, and from his front door started a gun fight with the burglars, finally dispersing them without injury to himself.

Another case was that of Geo. Gibbs, Sr., former clerk and master of the Chancery Court, who was notified to redeem a stolen watch with a sum of money to be left at a given point in exchange for the watch. The watch was there But Mr. Gibbs did not leave the money until the second notice, written in the nature of a threat.

Early in the operations of the gangsters Officer Bratton followed a party of suspects one night to a rendezvous on East Main street. It was in an old building adjacent to Kroger's Grocery Store. Bratton saw the men enter and quietly stole around toward the back of the house, ducked under the floor, which was high enough to crawl under, and hide. There he heard almost distinctly the burglars plotting to enter a number of places, together with the names of many well known citizens in and around Union City.

Following that another attempt at housebreaking was made at the home of A. J. Corum on North Home street near Cobb's Grocery Store. The suspects were Ward and Farris, followed by Officer Sam Bratton and Tom Ownby. Bratton fired a shotgun as the men entered the yard, but the burglars escaped on the other side of the house before the officers could catch them.

Incensed beyond endurance, leading citizens assembled in a body, men of discretion and forethought, determined upon aggressive measures, seeking Divine help and guidance in a struggle to overtake and wipe out the evils and menace of crime in Union City and community, held a meeting and organized a vigilance committee, comprised of church-going, law-abiding people, a number of whom were Civil-War Veterans, all joined together in sober, solemn, compact to assume the reins of law and to restore peace and tranquility among the people of Union City.

Nevertheless the war of crime continued, conditions being particularly savage and fearful during the summer months. Notwithstanding the vigilantes pursued their work orderly and con-

UNION CITY

sistently, and tho at the time thirteen or more saloons were operated in Union City, none of these men touched liquor.

There was little cessation until the early part of the year 1886, shortly after Christmas. Then one evening Officers Bud Adams and Tom Ownby, assisted by a negro detective, discovered some men in the act of unloading a box car at the crossing of the N. C. & St. L. Railroad tracks on Second street. When the officers saw them they were rolling out a barrel of flour. Discovered in the act the robbers fled to a nearby negro cabin. The officers followed and caught three negroes, Frank Freeman, Ambrose Young and Charles Latham. They were arrested and taken to the City Hall and found to be connected with the band of robbers and criminals. The building used as a City Hall was originally the first Methodist Church in Union City. It was located on the same lot and almost exactly, or slightly, east of the present City Hall. A new Methodist Church was built on East Main street and the old building was taken over by the city for municipal purposes. Here the three prisoners captured found themselves taken from the custody of the officers by the vigilance committee, hooded with masks and wearing numbered badges on their sleeves. The officers were forced to retire and the three captives escorted and marched to the old fair grounds in the southwestern limits of the city, and with the quiet and solemn performance of summary justice hanged to a tall elm tree. The vigilantes completed the work.

Very soon after this another negro named Oscar Smith fled to Hickman and was caught entering the home of "Cotton Ed" Jones, Mr. Jones holding the negro at bay with a small pistol, while Mrs. Jones ran into the house and returned with a shotgun, leveled at the negro. The negro fled and escaped to Arkansas, but was overtaken by a negro officer and killed resisting arrest.

Henry English, another one of the gang of negro burglars, was arrested by Marshal McClanahan, but escaped and fled to Pine Bluff, Ark., followed by T. R. Nolen, deputy sheriff, and special officer, Pad Nolen, who caused his arrest by police officer Fonso Ward. English was held at Pine Bluff pending requisition from the Governor of Tennessee, but again escaped from the officers and fled to parts unknown.

About this time word had reached the hideout of the gang that discovery had been made of headquarters on West Main street and the men giving orders, and one man, under suspicion and surveillance, fled during the hours of midnight with no hope of return nor trace of flight.

Thus for a short time quiet was restored, but ere long plunder and looting began again on a large scale. Some very disreputable characters were still at large with menace foreboding trouble.

About this time a squad of officers, led by Fletcher Nailling and James Ownby, went to Rives and caught Lum Ward and Tobe Holland in the river bottoms north of Rives. Ward was arrested as one of the band of robbers. Holland was arrested and held for breaking in a store at Rives. There being no evidence against Ward he was released. But it was not long until he became involved in an attack on Gentry Palmer, a well known farmer in the vicinity of Pleasant Valley, which resulted in the killing of Ward.

It was not long after the arrest of the negroes at Rives until Freeman Ward, gang leader, was trailed and discovered entering Dick Garrett's saloon, north of the Brackin Hotel and immediately east of the M. & O. R. R. tracks. In the row of buildings facing the railroad, first on the south end was the Brackin Hotel, next the Louie Kistner saloon, next Garrett's, and on the corner farther north the Miller House. As stated, Ward was seen entering Garrett's saloon and the officers were notified immediately. Officers Sam Bratton and Tom Ownby were first to enter following Ward, and knowing the negro as a powerful man and a dangerous character, officers approached quietly until Ward was surrounded. Ownby's gun was leveled at Ward and he was ordered to surrender. Officer Bratton with a club was also ready for action, and when Ward whipped out an oath, Bratton swung, and striking him behind the ear, knocked him to the floor stunned. Ward was soon handcuffed and led away.

Officer Bratton had already arrested Bud Farris, a white man from Illinois known as gang leader and a stool pigeon. Farris and Ward were taken to the City Hall. Farris was found in the vicinity of Black Bottom or near Ury Street.

At the City Hall, Ward, still unterrified, took his arrest coolly and unconcerned, and in a bantering way undertook to joke Farris. Shaken with fear Farris was advised to eat his food, as there would be no supper, also to take a last look at "Old Hannah," the sun shining thru the window—that he would see it for the last time. Whereupon the vigilantes appeared and took charge, marching the captives to the fair grounds, as before, and liquidating in summary fashion the guilty men on the tall elm tree where the other three were hung. This tree for many years was pointed out as a landmark of peace and quiet in Union City.

The Mayor of Union City in 1885 was James Moore, the Marshal, Wm. McClanahan, with police and special officers including Fletcher Nailling, Bud Adams, Jas. and Tom Ownby, S.

UNION CITY

R. Bratton, Billy Nailling, Pad Nolen, Forker Mays and others. During the long siege of terror Sam Bratton rang the curfew bell at 9 o'clock every evening from the Methodist Church steeple.

ANOTHER LYNCHING

Only a few more years had elapsed until a young negro named Wins. Wade was hung with a rope suspended from the joist of the old Law Court Room, second story corner Church and Bank streets, now an office for dress making, reached by iron stairway.

The culprit, attacking a young woman in Union City, was arraigned before Esquire Sacra, and before he could be tried friends and neighbors of the girl's family rushed in and whisked the negro up by the rope, where he was found dead.

NIGHT OFFICER MURDERED

Years ago in Union City, on the night of December 4, 1922, Night Police Officer Dave Yates was murdered by a couple of drunken negroes, Babe Williams and Joe Bailey. The case was tried at the January term of Obion Circuit Court, 1923, and defendants convicted of murder in the first degree. They were sentenced to be electrocuted.

The officer was on his beat and stopped to ask the negroes about some shots he heard in Black Bottom. With no other cause the negroes turned upon Yates and shot him to death.

Excitement ran high, and probably the negroes escaped lynching by making immediate escape from the county.

MURDER OF AGED CITIZEN

It was for some years that Union City citizens rested quietly and peacefully in their homes without fear of lawless elements, particularly secure at night from sneak thieves and disreputable characters. But on the night of March 18, 1913, a horrible deed was committeed. It was on North Division street in the home of S. H. McClure, a Confederate veteran, alone with his wife and two daughters. A drunken negro, John Grinston, had entered the house, a two-story frame, by the back porch to the pantry, and was helping himself to food, making considerable noise and finally roused Mr. McClure, who got up, asking what was wanted. The reply in part was "not you." Mr. McClure then entreated the negro to leave without effect. With the only weapon in the house, an army pistol Mr. McClure had kept from Confederate service, he threatened to fire if the negro didn't leave, and did fire after a short time through the door.

While this was going on the elder daughter, sleeping upstairs, came down and ran out through the front door to the neighbors for help. D. A. Luten was phoned to and hastened over to the McClure's. Reaching the corner next to the house Mr. Luten heard shooting. It seems after Mr. McClure fired at the door the negro opened it and returned the fire from a gun he had on him, shooting Mr. McClure through the mouth, the bullet plowing through and tearing away part of the jaw. At this point Officer T. P. Noah arrived and hearing him the negro fled, tearing through the window sash at the back of the house. Several shots were fired at the fleeing negro as he jumped the fence going west towards the M. & O. R. R. The negro eluded the officer and got away. Mr. Luten and Officer Noah found Mr. McClure in a critical condition. The officer picked up Grinston's gun which had been dropped and found it plugged with a lodged bullet, which must have been the cause of his sudden flight.

Immediate search of the negro began, but it was not until early morning that he was found. He was caught hid in the loft at the home of his people in Baptistville.. He was arrested and on the way to town the officers were forced to retire. Then came the nemesis of retributive justice.

It was again many years before another negro, a young fiend, was caught attempting assault and pursued with the enforcement of lynch law.

JESSE JAMES AT THE FAIR

An incident associated with the old county fair in the eighties was related about a dispute between Jesse James and John Johnson, the latter an old-time citizen of Union City who owned a stable of fine race horses and traveled the circuits of the north and east. The James boys—Frank and Jesse— were at that time located in Humphreys County, Tenn., living under assumed names, and Jesse had a race horse, Red Fox, entered here at the Union City Fair. Red Fox raced against one of Johnson's horses and a dispute over the race resulted between Johnson and Jesse. The affair however was settled amicably as friends of both men intervened. The point is that Johnson did not know that he was contending with one of the James boys, a noted bandit. Therefore when he was taken aside and informed that he had disputed with the real Jesse James he was indeed surprised and pleased that the affair had gone no further.

On another occasion Jesse James was sitting in a party who were discussing the James boys, still under assumed names, some criticizing and Ben Bransford among others defending. When the party dispersed Jesse James presented Mr. Bransford with an acorn watch charm as an appreciation for his kindness.

UNION CITY

NEW INDUSTRIES

With the passing of the Dahnke-Walker Milling Co. and the Monroe Flour Milling Co., this particular field of industry has been amply covered with other large operators. One of the more important is the—

NAILLING MILL & FEED COMPANY

Instituted by Dr. W. A. Nailling, one of the well known citizens of Union City, whose hospital and general practice as a physician and surgeon are known throughout a wide section of territory and whose varied interests include a number of fine farms in Obion County, devoted to agriculture and livestock, the Nailling Mill & Feed Company, operating for a number of years, constitutes one of the busy industries of Union City. Under the management of Will Austin Nailling and the secretary, Mary Arden Nailling, a block of yards and buildings along the Gulf, Mobile & Ohio R. R. tracks embrace a wide variety of trade and building commodities, including corn, wheat and feed products, lumber and building materials, farm implements, tractors, wagons, building concrete and box tile, brick, lime, cement, fertilizer, etc.

As a modern improvement, new show rooms have been added, a section of the main building devoted to the arrangement and display of the various building and finishing materials, including a full line of products made by Johns-Mannville Co., including roofing, ceiling, wall boards, paints and accessories used for interior decoration, a very interesting department equipped and supplied for public inspection.

CORN AND WHEAT MARKETS

J. W. Jefferson is well known in Union City as manager of the Missouri Grain Company. With its mammoth elevator and storage facilities in the locality of the Union City Water and Light Plant, many inducements and advantages are offered to buyers and shippers. Corn and wheat are bought under the most favorable conditions and sold in the most desirable markets. Facilities for storage, corn shelling and cleaning and other accommodations are extended to the trade.

Succeeding the late W. M. Warterfield, the Warterfield Grain Company in Union City, with office and warehouses on West Main street does an extensive business in buying and handling corn, wheat and other products for general shipment to domestic and export trade. Provision is made for shelling and cleaning and a fleet of trucks is employed in local and general transport.

OBION COUNTY HISTORY

WORK SHIRT MANUFACTURE

Salant & Salant Inc. is one of eight Tennessee branch units, with headquarters in Union City, manufacturing a line of well known work shirts, including various styles and numbers. The Union City factory is located and occupies floor space in the second and third stories of the building formerly known as the Childs Specialty House on Washington Avenue, also floor space in the adjoining new building extending south and facing South First street, with offices on First street in the extreme south end of the building.

With a maximum force of 500 operatives and office assistants, the Union City branch is under the management of J. M. Stone, superintendent. The factory produces 1000 dozen all-grade work shirts every day in a five-day week, and anticipating increased production, new floor space and machine units are being installed. The shirts made in the Union City factory are shipped direct to the trade all over the United States, Cuba and Canada, insular countries and other markets.

This industry was located in Union City in 1934, and its growth, gradual for some time, is developing with a popular demand for its products. Under the management of Mr. Jeffrey Stone, the business increases with forecasts of greater demand for this character and type of merchandise. In any event Union City recognizes this as one of its most important industries.

LUMBER YARDS

The Home Lumber Company on Harrison street is one of the thriving new industries in Union City, with Robert McAnulty in charge of yard operations and building projects and David McAnulty of office work, estimates plans and specifications. The yard is complete with lumber supplies and building material.

The Moss Lumber Company succeeds the well known lumberman, the late C. T. Moss, Sr., under the yard management of Jas. Moss. Lumber and building materials are supplied from well stocked yards. C. T. Moss began many years ago with Askins & Dircks Lumber Co., as yard manager, and entering business he succeeded the Sherill Lumber Co., on North First street more than forty years ago.

BROWN SHOE COMPANY — UNION CITY FACTORY

As stated in a special newspaper edition of Union City in 1930 the Brown Shoe Company, of St. Louis, in 1922, entered into an agreement with the people of Union City to locate one of its branch factories at this place in consideration of a building fund of $100,000 and other mutual conditions and arrangements, all

UNION CITY

of which was consummated and the buildings erected and completed, ready for occupation.

The inauguration of this institution was celebrated June 5, 1923, in a generous outpouring of friendly visitors with appropriate ceremonies, accompanied with felicitations and congratulations, by such great orators as Governor Austin Peay, Congressman Finis Garrett and others, responded to by President John A. Bush and others of the officers of the Brown Shoe Company.

The story of the building and success of the manufacture of Brownbilt Shoes in Union City over a period of nearly twenty years is replete with the fruition of great achievement and fine promise. Management and labor have worked in complete harmony and singleness of purpose, with results accruing both to the pleasure and profit of employee and success of production.

The daily factory output has increased to a maximum production of 5400 pairs of women's and children's shoes every work day, with indicated further enlargements and extensions, employing a total of 625 operators and skilled workmen, who are enjoying continued larger average in full-time employment. As heretofore conforming to the policy of the management, as far as practically possible, all available native home people are employed.

The company's special numbers in production are the famous Buster Brown Shoes. Mr. H. B. Sitton, manager of the Union City factory unit, takes pleasure in announcing special numbers in the newest lines, including Women's Sport-welt Shoes, in all the various models and materials known to modern shoe production.

The office division is under the management of E. Russell, the factory units conducted by a maximum of twelve foremen.

In 1940 a building extension was erected to serve the purposes of the company in providing more space for operating units and in a general way for the expansion and increase of operation and storage room.

REYNOLDS PACKING COMPANY

The Reynolds Packing Company, a corporation organized in Union City many years ago and operated under the management and leadership of the late W. G. Reynolds, was instituted by Mr. Reynolds as an individual enterprise, beginning with the grocery and poultry business in Union City and then, with slaughtering pens and abattoir located on the present site of the packing house, finally consolidating his interests exclusively with construction and establishment of a wholesale meat products packing plant, one of the leading industries of its kind in West Tennessee.

The organization operates with a capital stock of $100,000, with the following officers: A. F. Tittsworth, active vice-president;

OBION COUNTY HISTORY

Lowell Beauchamp, secretary-treasurer. Directors: Walker Tanner, C. E. Beck, Polk Beaird, J. C. McRee, Dave Shatz.

With a trade territory extending thru the Mississippi Valley in Kentucky and Tennessee, south into Mississippi and to Ohio north, from the Tennessee River on the east to the Mississippi on the west, the volume of sales for 1939 totaled $1,000,000. The products are made from livestock bought principally in Tennessee, with a small percentage in Kentucky and Mississippi.

Feature products of the company are the Reelfoot brands, with a popular trade also in the Houser Valley products. From 80 to 100 people are employed in the plant.

Twelve trucks are employed regularly in the delivery of the packing house products, with the following salesmen waiting n the trade: E. K. White, Doc Garrison, Dee Etheridge, Merritt Moss, Robt. Wade, J. C. Lowe, J. W. Dunn, J. C. Perkins, J. R. Goodrum, C. W. Woodard, Bernie Tedford, Henry Little.

Provision is made for the gradual expansion of business with plant extensions of power and refrigeration capacity.

The company products are constantly improved in quality and variety, in keeping with the latest and best methods, conducive to popular taste and demand.

Since the death of Mr. Reynolds, who devoted the better part of his life to the management of the packing house in Union City, the stockholders held a meeting to consider the sale of the plant, resulting finally in a reconsideration to continue business, with election of officers as follows: A. F. Tittsworth, president; Dave Shatz, active vice-president. Directors: A. F. Tittsworth, Dave Shatz, J. C. McRee, T. F. Heathcock, Walker Tanner, C. E. Beck, Polk Beaird.

In pursuance of the will of the stockholders to continue business, T. J. (Jeff) Yarbrough, with an experience of 25 years in the meat packing industry, connected for ten years as department manager of the Neuhoff Packing Co., Nashville, Tenn., was employed as general manager of the Reynolds Packing Co., proceeding to take over the management of the plant under executive control.

Buyer for the plant in the livestock market, Chas. Everett, keeps supplies on hand.

FARMING AND LIVESTOCK

No doubt there are three very distinct and important periods affecting the vital interests and progress of the town of Union City and surrounding community. First was the operation of saw mills and the manufacture of furniture, which continued until the timber was practically exhausted and the factories found no other ready source of supply.

UNION CITY

Next was the opening of the Houser Valley and the low farming country around Union City, abounding in soil fertility, which followed the clearing of timber and the conversion of these lands, with a system of soil-tile drainage, into great fields of corn, wheat and tobacco. This was largely a wheat country, and the crop yield and quality of grain proved exceedingly profitable until, by constant use of land for single-crop wheat culture, soil elements were depleted or exhausted and the harvest yield a failure, while other crops were more or less affected by the same cause.

Even with expensive fertilizing experiments there were no immediate prospects of reclaiming the soil, so farmers sought new sources of income in the livestock industry, followed in a short time by a new period of prosperity in Obion County. This industry engaged the attention of farmers who were not willing to depend exclusively on grain, hay and tobacco crops.

LIVESTOCK DEALERS

Dealers who have been very active in the Union City market, shipping principally over the railroads and for a short time in trucks include numbers who have been operating for years, some for fifty years or more.

B. J. (Bob) Wade, feeding and shipping from his farms near Rives, was at one time known in the St. Louis market as the largest shipper in Tennessee. Mr. Wade says he has been in the livestock business all his life, beginning when he grew up on the farm. In a single shipment after the first World War, when market prices were strong, Mr. Wade shipped from Rives 22 cars of hogs, coupled to one train to the St. Louis market, which netted a return of $72,000. Mr. Wade is a large landowner and farmer, whose investments comprise thousands of acres, some of which is in Mississippi. In 1939-40 Mr. Wade shipped both hogs and cattle from the prison farm at Angora, Louisiana.

Dealers who have been very active from the early days as buyers and shippers of cattle and hogs, calves and lambs, include W. Y. Pickard, W. L. Bryan, W. P. Nash, J. T. Owen, J. C. McRee, E. M. Stone, Dr. Nailling, Jess Rogers, Wiley Brothers, Glover & Youngblood, and late years of Logan & Houser, Thompson & Caldwell, including also buyers Ed Green, John Saunders, Ollie Nichols

Walker Pickard and W. L. Bryan, with a business connection, began forty years ago buying, feeding and shipping livestock to the packers. At the peak of business for several years shipments were made by this firm from the stockyards in Union City, averaging one hundred thousand dollars per month. At one time record sales were made of 32 cars of cattle in thirty days.

OBION COUNTY HISTORY

One of the most active men in the market for a long period of years was W. L. Bryan. He and Claude Botts were in partnership for ten years until Mr. Bryan passed away. These men for the same length of time were probably the most active dealers from the Union City yards. Since that time Botts Livestock Company have taken the forefront as buyers and shippers from Union City, particularly strong and active in recent years.

McRee & Elam are feeders and shippers to the markets from the Crockett farms, and J. C. McRee is an active operator in the livestock market, buying, feeding and shipping from Union City.

John T. Owen feeds out and ships both hogs and steers from the yards at Union City and Fulton. He also ships in stock cattle for sale to local farmers.

Wade and Leslie Wiley have been very heavy feeders and shippers from the Union City market.

For some time G. R. Bufford was in the market as buyer for Reynolds Packing Company. Later Charley Everett has taken over the business of keeping the Reynolds Packing Co. supplied with cattle and hogs for the meat market.

LIVESTOCK SHIPMENTS

A busy year for the shipment of livestock from the Union City market over the railroads to St. Louis, Chicago and packing houses at other places was 1938. The records show a total number of cars shipped from the railroad yards in Union City for that year to be 1309, including hogs, cattle, sheep and calves. In 1939 the total shipments over the railroads from this point were 1050 cars. But that did not include the truck shipments, which might have increased the total over the previous year.

In 1940 there was a greater division of shipments between railroad and truck transportation. Records from the railroad stations at Union City show a total number of cars of hogs, cattle, sheep and calves shipped out of the county to be 739. Records of shipments from Union City by truck are not altogether complete, but by careful estimate, based on the number of head per car, the truck shipments from the pens at the N. C. & St. L. station were equal to 492 cars and from the pens at the G. M. & O. station equal to 1176 cars, making a total altogether of 2407 cars shipped out of Union City to the various markets. This does not include shipments from South Fulton, the spur at Moffatt, Obion and Kenton, but it does give an approximate total of livestock shipped from the Union City yards out of the county in 1940.

COCA-COLA BOTTLING INDUSTRY

The Hugh Smith Coca-Cola plant, established in Union City, like other industries having a small beginning, was located years ago in the quarters known as the "Concrete Block" on Bank

UNION CITY

street, between Church and Exchange.

The institution in new buildings of brick and stone, provided with modern machinery and covering an area which has been enlarged a number of times, is a monument to its founder, Mr. Smith, now at rest after an active and useful life.

Leaving constituted authority to carry on, the local manager, P. M. Pitzer, became general manager of the Hugh Smith Coca-Cola enterprises, as heretofore operated in Union City, Dyersburg, Fulton, Martin and Hickman.

The Union City plant is one of the principal Union City industries, housed in modern sanitary buildings and equipped for the bottling of all its products, employing about twenty operatives and operating a fleet of trucks in Obion and Lake Counties.

UNION CITY DAIRY COMPANY

As a branch of the Dairy Corporation of America the Union Dairy Company, on Harrison street, is one of the substantial enterprises of Union City, with Ray Smith as manager. The officers are: Mrs. A. E. Paulson, president; Ray Treon, vice-president; G. B. Scott, secretary; Sue Brown Moss, cashier and accountant. About fifteen or twenty people are employed here. The average pick up from the farms is about 5000 or 6000 pounds of milk daily. The milk is sent to Murray, Ky., in a glass-lined tank truck to be converted into powdered milk by the Murray dairy plant. Sour cream is bought and taken up at Gleason, McKenzie, Rutherford, Dyer, Yorkville and Fulton. Bottle milk is delivered at Martin, McKenzie, Gleason, Hickman and Tiptonville.

CANVAS DECOY COMPANY

This is one of Union City's permanent industries. Instituted many years ago by H. A. Beck, it was some years later enlarged for the manufacture of waterproof garments. Originally its products were confined to the manufacture of decoy ducks, sold all over the country and in the islands and Canada.

For the manufacture of waterproof clothing the company was reorganized, adopting Seth Curlin's patent process, known as the Moon brand, utilized in the making of raincoats and other products.

But for some years due to the changing of markets and decline of demand, the duck business continued only as a feature of the business.

The officers are: C. H. Cobb, president; Emerson Parks, vice-president; J. L. Godown, acting secretary.

SUNDRY INDUSTRIES

Mose Cunningham, Auto Repairs; Isbell Battery Shop; H. L. Houser Welding Shop; Modern Recapping; J. H. Lynn Cabinet

Shop; Hyman Shapiro, Scrap Iron; Chas Quillin, Upholstering; Sam Byrn, Clock and Gun Shop; Union City Bakery; Wonder Bread Depot; Cloys Serum Co., Clint Adams; Dyer Produce Co.; Midwest Dairy; J. B. Akin, Fruit Stand; Union City Hatchery; Mack White; Youngblood & Harrison, Poultry.

Coal Yards: McAdoo Coal Co., Bramham Coal Co., Citizens Coal Co.

C. H. Jenks, Civil Engineering, Power and Light and Paving Contractor in West Tennessee and Southern States.

UNION CITY CANNING CO.

Mr. Edgar Craddock, a pioneer in southern canning and for twenty years operating factories in West Tennessee, is conducting three canning industries with plants in Union City, Newbern and Halls.

Offices and headquarters of the company are in Union City, with local plant in the vicinity north of the N. C. & St. L. railroad freight depot. Plant foreman is A. J. Hayes; field foreman, Ira Nethery.

Products of the Union City plant include tomatoes, string beans, spinach, turnips, mustard salad, sweet potatoes, black-eyed and Crowder peas, Lima and red kidney beans, pork and beans. Capacity of the Union City plant is from 150,000 to 200,000 cases, two dozen each, a year. Three hundred operatives have peak employment for five or six months in the year. Remainder of the time smaller numbers are employed.

Mr. Craddock farms a considerable tomato acreage of his own, but buys his canning supplies from the various sections of this and nearby counties.

HOME ICE COMPANY

The Home Ice Company is an organization of the interests of W. H. McAdoo and L. H. McAdoo, of this city, Wilson Fly and Chas. Goodrich, of Memphis, exclusive owners controlling the plants, one located on Main street, opposite the McAdoo Coal Co. yards, another with new building completed for use in 1940 on Main street opposite the Greyhound Bus Station, and a plant at Kenton.

Officers of the company are: J. M. Sedberry, vice president and secretary, W. H. McAdoo, vice president and treasurer. Yard managers are Robert Alexander and Preston Warren.

The new building constructed on the site of the old Dahnke plant opposite the bus station is a substantial brick house of ample housing room for extensive operations, 80 by 60 feet. The two plants in Union City have a combined capacity of 50 tons daily.

UNION CITY

LAUNDRY AND DRY CLEANERS

The Blue Bell Laundry and Cleaners establishment in Union City is conducted by the owner, P. J. Wiley, Jr., in plant buildings and quarters immediately east and north of the railroad crossing. The units of operation comprise the various processes of laundry work and dry cleaning, which include an extra department for handling rugs of all sizes and for dyeing. Laundry is done in fluff dry and finished work. Men's hats are included in the modern processes of restoring life and color to old hats of various grades.

The Blue Bell plant operates a delivery service of white cars in the city and country points, including Hornbeak, Tiptonville, Obion, Troy and other places.

The Blue Bell company employs an operating service of thirty people.

SCOTTIE CLEANERS

W. L. Scott, for many years well known in Union City as an operator of laundry and dry cleaning, is now conducting an exclusive dry cleaning and hat department, at the old stand on East Church street, making a specialty of dry cleaning work in men's and ladies' garments of all kinds. A delivery service is one of the Scottie advantages.

The Sunshine Cleaners on Second street is another modern enterprise in Union City, which offers distinct advantages to discriminating customers in all kinds of men's and ladies' garments, with special cash and carry prices.

Seven motor trucks are employed in the delivery service in Obion County. Eighteen men are employed in the Union City plants.

DOLLY DEAR TOYS

Beginning like any other normal child with a natural desire for dolls, Mrs. Kirkland found that she was not satisfied with making dresses and keeping the little starry-eyed creature all dressed up and staring. She desired something more, an adventure into the mysteries of the doll world, the origin of the species and creation of the doll race. So she began to investigate by taking the doll to pieces and examining the anatomy. This done she then undertook the problem of reassembling the little plaything, which had been dismantled.

Years passed, but interest in dolls became a passion. She longed for a doll house, a big house with all sorts of little dolls, then the toymaker appeared. That was a suggestion—her ideas of making little doll things and filling up the house with dolls and tiny toys— a dream about to come true. She would create a new market—she would find a sale for dolls and toys.

OBION COUNTY HISTORY

This was more than ten years ago, and today Mrs. Kirkland still loves her dolls and toys. She has made and sold the products of her doll house to a world-wide market, with the satisfaction of knowing that she has not only discovered the secret of doll making but of all the little toys and trinkets, things that fill a playhouse so dear to children.

Many ingenious and beautiful articles have been designed by Mrs. Kirkland, who always finds a ready market, as well as mutual cooperation with other producers in a combination sale of companion pieces.

To describe the things made by Mrs. Kirkland and her assisting operatives would take pages, but most attractive are the little furniture suites, the draperies, the doll beds, the dining table and dishes, the breakfast, luncheon and dinner service, tea sets and above all the almost real plates—entrees, relishes and sweetmeats. It is all so fine that one never tires of looking on.

Mrs. Kirkland in the market is known as R. T. Kirkland and the Dolly Dear Toys and doll house accessories her stock in trade. She sells to manufacturers but principally to department stores and novelty shops all the year round, with rush of business from September until the middle of December. In the busy season 15 to 25 people are employed, a smaller number at other times. Orders come from all over the United States and Canada, peace time orders from Europe.

CHERRY-MOSS GRAIN COMPANY

This company has been established and long known for its general business and trade connections in this section in the wholesale and retail markets handling wheat, corn, oats, barley, all kinds of field seeds and commercial feed. Corn tankage is also one of the commodities. All of these products are handled by a fleet of truck lines reaching thru Kentucky, Tennessee and entering the States of Illinois and Mississippi.

Mr. Henry Moss, one of the pioneers of the rich country south of Union City, and Cecil Moss, the junior partner of the firm, are well known and esteemed in business and in private affairs.

Pioneer grain dealers in Union City were Haydon & Barry and Wm. Hamilton. Former lumber yards: Askins-Dircks Lumber Co., Sherrill Bros., Union City Lumber Co.; brick and concrete: McAdoo-Kelly, T. L. Bransford & Sons; contractors: Kelly, Conn, Conradi, Taylor, Garrett, McCullough, Friel, Burnett.

UNION CITY COTTON GIN

The Union City and Fulton cotton gins are controlled by the same organization. The manager for the company is Joe Davis. Carl Smith attends the office work in Union City, with the assistance of W. T. Garrigan at the plant.

UNION CITY

The gin here is equipped with three stands of eighties, with a capacity of 30 bales a day. The output in 1939 was 800 bales.

Union City Produce Co., Staff-o-Life products.

ELECTRIC AND RADIO SHOPS

Tittsworth Electric and Radio Shop, E. E. Clymer, manager; Baxter & Treadway, Electric Utilities; Dungan Radio and Electric Co.; J. V. Averitt, Electric Contacts and Supplies.

BEAUTY SHOPS

Birdie Shop, Anderson Shop, Lorraine Shop, Modern Shop, Peebles' Shop, Shipp Shop, Morgan-Verhine Shop.

Schleifer's Home-made Candies.

MERCANTILE BUSINESS

The first dry goods merchant in Union City after the Civil War was John Morgan, located on East Main street on lots, now the home of Mayor Miles. The store was an old two-story frame building slightly above the street and on the east edge of the lot. Opposite on Main on the other side of the street was E. B. Sidebottom. Other merchants were Tyler & Murphy, Cary & Patton, Hatch Bros., Curlin & Bynum, some of them west of the railroad on First street.

Then again with the furniture factories came a busy time with the merchants, including Stanbrough, Folz, Plaut, Lowenheim, Siesel, Davis, Friedman, Frankland, Levy, Mann, and continuing from that period were Morgan, Curlin, Verhine, Layne, Coble, Clagett, Walker, Hardy, Sherrill, Haguewood, Malone, Jones, Fish, Robinson, Bransford, Gibbs, Davis, Corum, Jackson, Kirby, Kaufman, Brody, Weille, Pryor, Mitchell, Owen, Arnn, Flanary, Jackson, Eber & Brandes, Crawford-Gatlin, McGowen, Jones, Miller-Jones, Home Supply.

New stores now in operation offering special trade inducements: Morgan-Verhine Inc., Jackson Inc., Shatz Bros., Black & White Store, New York Store, Alfred's, Shatz & Byer, Jerry Malone Clothier, Grand Leader, Draper & Darwin, A. E. Kirkland Clothier, Burnett Brown-bilt Shoes, Bennett Clothing, Harper and Muse Shoes, Potter Shoe Store, McElroy Five-Ten, Caldwell Five-One Dollar, Ben Franklin Store, Freid Five-Ten, Floy Shoppe, Ethel Greer Hat Shop, Dotty Dress Shop, Vogue Shop, Mary Lee Shop, Haynes Hat Shop, Ted Prather Clothing.

GROCERY STORES

Names of grocers heretofore operating in Union City are as follows: Kroger, Crittendon, Woosley, Hale, Evans, Huffman, Killough, Whitley, Cummings, White Bros., Roper, King, Walters, Dietzel, Escue, Vinson, Red & White, Sevier.

OBION COUNTY HISTORY

Grocery dealers now serving Union City and community trade: E. P. Grissom, Herman Scates, M. B. Youree, Cecil Yates, Elva Caldwell, Dee Stanley, S. C. Vaden, Spivey Gro., Dewey Thornton, Thomas Grocery, Horner, John's, E. B. Woodfin, Seth Dunlap, Paul Cloys, Vinson & Roper, E. L. King, Vernon White, Henry Wood, Burkett Grocery, Gantlett Store, Taylor Grocery, Sam Bassett, Ford.

Cash grocers: Kroger's, A. & P., U-Tote-Em, Piggly-Wiggly, Liberty Cash.

Fish and sea food, ice cream, cold drinks, J. C. Burdick and Jack Burdick, Jr.

FURNITURE STORES

Former furniture dealers: Harpole, Walker, Greer, Bell, Dietzel, White Bros. Rhodes-Burford, Hunt Bros.

New stores serving the trade: Jones & Sons, Timm's, Pardue & Verhine, Star Furniture Co.

NOTABLE EXAMPLES IN MERCHANDISING

Among the veterans in mercantile business in Union City were R. T. Curlin, J. P. Verhine and T. J. Malone. The latter, Jerry Malone, is a native of Woodland Mills community, in his school days a pupil of Capt. T. B. Underwood at Mount Olive. Reared on a farm, his ambition to be engaged in merchandising found him as salesman with Smith-Ellison & Co., at Hickman, Ky., then in Union City with Hardy Bros., and progressively advancing he became a merchant in Union City as one of the organization in the Hardy, Malone & Jones Company. Afterwards as salesman for the Mayfield Woolen Mills, Mr. Malone traveled for a time and then opened a men's furnishings store in Union City, and this as cumulative experience began more than sixty years from his first work in Hickman.

The merchants mentioned were never in any sense novices, but practically speaking apprenticed to their work. What they accomplished, no doubt, was due to this early training in the fundamentals of merchandising.

It is said that R. T. Curlin was often requested by lady shoppers to make selections and to judge for them suitable materials, style and color combinations, and often the entire wardrobe they were to buy. In the same manner many of Jerry Malone's customers rely upon his judgment and ability to make their selections in clothing and haberdashery. J. P. Verhine's success was due largely to financial management as well as a practical knowledge of values in buying goods.

Merchandising with these men became a science and a profession. It was due to them, no doubt, that Union City sustained general reputation as a shopping center. There are others since

UNION CITY

then who are carrying on under modern conditions, who will no doubt be worthy of the old regime to keep Union City a banner trading point.

A man of considerable distinction in general management and publicity of the American system of retail merchandising is Charles G. Tomerlin, native of Union City and a son-in-law of the late H. T. Robinson.

Mr. Tomerlin left Union City when a young man, having only a limited experience in a local newspaper office, but with a personality framed in a tall lank figure, shoulders broad and slightly stooping, eyes speculating and the general appearance of friendly approach.

Turning from newspaper surroundings, but impressed with its possibilities, Mr. Tomerlin entered the imposing mercantile establishment of Scruggs-Vandervoort & Barney, St. Louis, Mo. There he remained for a number of years, but useless recounting a well known story. From St. Louis, with the experience he had stored and impounded, he was called to other large cities by merchants whose houses needed reorganization and reanimation, including Detroit, Indianapolis, Cleveland, Scranton, New York City, Utica. After a term of years he finished an important connection with Parker Stores, Utica, N. Y., and was returning to Detroit when overtaken by a motor accident on the highway, which resulted in fracture and disability. Mr. Tomerlin was answering a call to report to an important assignment at Detroit, but was forced to enter a hospital, where he remained for a time and then for a period of rest at home with his people in Union City.

This is a brief sketch, but a notable instance of the application of native ability and an honorable ambition to pursue and achieve a life of usefulness among his fellow business men and friends.

One of the most important merchants in the county for a period of many years was Herman Dietzel, Sr. Mr. Dietzel began business in the early eighties as a hardware merchant, dealer also in farming implements and wagons. His business increased and he built the three-story hardware store on First street in 1889, still one of the best buildings in Union City, occupied later by the Nailling-Keiser Hardware Co. To illustrate the extent of Mr. Dietzel's business, the publisher of the local paper just entering business approached him for an advertisement. In his usual understanding manner, Mr. Dietzel answered: "Vell, but my business is known furder den de paper." This was unanswerable, but the paper got the ad and the merchant and publisher both proceeded to make history in the progress of business in Obion County.

MERCHANT TAILORING

A very interesting business institution in Union City when furniture manufacturing had reached its greatest stride was the Harry T. Robinson tailor shop. Mr. Robinson, having qualified himself as a coatmaker in his father's merchant tailoring house at Paducah, Ky., entered in New York City the Mitchell school of training as a cutter, and then as tailor took a turn touring the cities. He stopped first at Albany, N. Y., then in St. Louis, tarrying for a considerable time. From there to Columbus, Ky., where he was married, Mr. Robinson located in Union City in 1883. Here he opened a shop, and from the beginning the growth of his tailoring business became phenomenal. It was only a short time until he had erected a new building (now the Pittsburg Paint & Glass store on First street) devoted exclusively to the business—the back shop upstairs, the cutting and fitting and salesroom downstairs. There were at one time in the backshop upstairs as high as sixteen coat and pantaloon makers, and patronage of the institution increased until the trade reached from Cairo, Ill., to Jackson, Tenn., and all the inland towns in the county and nearby points were served.

On account of the personality and popularity of Harry Robinson this house became one of the foundation units of a growing mercantile center. Mr. Robinson and his family became identified with all the better social and religious life of the community, and here for a half a century the tailor lived, enjoying the blessings ensuing to a useful life and good citizenship, finally closing after a retirement season from exclusive merchandising with the last chapter in the book of life.

One man in Union City remains from this fine institution, and one of the best coatmakers in the service, barring none, even the Welchman, Dickson. This is Sherman Sutherland, whose patrons, a few, yet remain to have their suits tailored and fitted under the old hand-made system of perfect tailoring.

Like the horse and buggy, the days of merchant tailoring are now confined to the most exclusive sections of the large cities.

DRUG STORES

Former Druggists: Polk, White, Hall, Godwin & Son, Moss, Scates, Kimzey, Whitsett, Cobb, Woods, Niles.

Stores now in operation: Red Star Drug Store, Oliver Drug Co., Mayes Drug Store, Evans Drug Co., LaFonte Drug Co.

HARDWARE

Former Dealers: Latta & Dietzel, Duval & Crittendon, Dietzel, Wehman, Stores now in operation: Nailling-Keiser Hardware Co., Wm. B. Keiser, manager; M. & W. Auto Supply & Hardware Co., W. T. Wirt, manager.

UNION CITY

JEWELRY

Former Dealers: Jaccard, Lukens, Porter & Radebaugh, Bransford & Andrews, Dietzel. Now in operation: Thad Lee, J. M. Andrews. Optometrist, Dr. W. B. Dunlap. V. M. Olive, watch repairs.

WHOLESALE MERCHANTS

Lovelace-Farmer Grocery Co., Shatz Bros., dry goods; Rite Mercantile Corporation; V. E. White, candies.

FARM MACHINERY—AUTO SUPPLIES

Paul Nailling Implement Co.; Oliver Farm Implement Co., J. P. Pegues, manager; Western Auto Co., Legal C. Thorn, manager; Goodyear Service Store, T. E. Baker, manager; Mills-Morris Co., Auto Supplies; Reb Forrester, Farm Machinery.

Other stores and shops: Pittsburgh Paint & Glass Co., Roper's Floral Shop, Sherman Sutherland Tailor Shop.

Former stores and shops: H. T. Robinson, Tailor. Shoe Shops: Walden, Ogles, Morris. Book Stores: Richards and Caldwell.

Heating and Plumbing: Merryman & Wilson, Quint McFadden, A. S. Currey, R. L. Cloys.

Barber Shops: White Way, Tommy Griffin; City Shop, Porter Owens; O. K. Shop, Odie Carmichael; Lannom Shop; Willhauck, Main street. Colored: Morgan Wells, Alfred DeBow, Dewey Dennie.

Western Union Telegraph Co., Mrs. Louella Clark, Mgr.

Tennessee Gas Co., Elizabeth Olive, manager.

Commercial Appeal Agency and News Stand, S. S. Caruthers and W. J. Wright, agents.

News-Scimitar Agency, J. Vern Dailey, manager.

Real Estate, Mitchell & Tittsworth.

Sign Writing, W. D. Tune.

Transfer Service: Easterwood freight trucks, M. L. Pitzer.

American Railway Express: E. B. Council, agent.

Contracting and Building: E. H. Harrison, Geo. Carmen, G. L. Hurt, J. J. Underwood, Clarence Davis.

Public Auctioneer: Capt. W. R. Manley.

UNION CITY BANKS

The Third National Bank is the legitimate successor of the old Bank of Union City, the first bank organized in Union City. This was in 1879, and the bank continued until its liquidation in the early nineties, its resources being absorbed by the Commercial Bank, which was organized with a capital stock of $50,000. The Commercial Bank continued do do business under that name until

1908, when it was reorganized with a capital stock of $60,000 and charter renewed under the name of the Third National Bank. This bank proceeded with a very satisfactory record of growth, and in 1918, with new subscriptions, increased the number of its stockholders and the capital stock to $84,000.

John T. Walker, one of the well known Union City bankers and financiers, president for many years of the Third National Bank, with a number of citizens organized the Farmers and Merchants National Bank, which was operated in Union City until its liquidation in 1894.

The president of the Third National Bank, Hunter Elam who succeeded to the head of the bank after Mr. Walker's death, entered the Commercial Bank in 1902 as bookkeeper. His promotion came in due time, first to the post of assistant cashier, then to the position of cashier, and finally to the presidency, to which he was elected in 1929.

Officers of the Third National Bank in 1940: Hunter Elam, president; Dixon Williams, cashier; Walton Crenshaw, assistant cashier; Mattie Mae Benthal, assistant cashier.

The Farmers Exchange Bank in Union City was organized in 1909 by Harris Parks, with W. C. Farris as president and Mr. Parks as cashier. This popular institution, with new business connections, had a record of fine business and due expansion. In time Mr. Parks became president and C. W. Miles, Jr., cashier, continuing until the death of Mr. Parks. Then Mr. Miles succeeded to the position of president, with T. Edwards Parks as cashier, continuing until a change of officers, resulting in the election of T. Edwards Parks as executive vice-president and Bertram C. Cox as cashier.

The election of officers of Farmers Exchange Bank includes, besides Mr. Miles, Mr. Parks and Mr. Cox, Mary Lou Maxwell, assistant cashier; Mrs. Dee Etheridge, assistant cashier.

The Old National Bank in Union City began with the organization of the First National Bank in 1888, with Dr. T. J. Edwards as president and R. P. Whitesell as cashier. Mr. Whitesell in a short time vacated in favor of Frank O. Watts, whose rise in banking became phenomenal. Mr. Watts is now chairman of the Board of the First National of St. Louis, passing in rapid succession from responsible banking connections in Nashville to St. Louis—at one time serving the American Bankers Association as president. With the reorganization of the First National Bank in 1910, in which the effects of the Union City Bank & Trust Company, resulting from liquidation, were absorbed, a new charter was issued with reorganization under the name of the Old National Bank, and the capital stock increased to $75,000. For some years A. L. Garth served the bank, first entering as bookkeeper, and at the

UNION CITY

FRANK O. WATTS

Native of Paducah, Ky. Educated and trained
    in the operation of banking in Union City
National figure in banking, first advancing to
    presidency of the First and then the First and
    Fourth National Bank of Nashville.
Later in St. Louis to the presidency of the
    First National Bank, consolidation of the Third
    National, St. Louis Union and Mechanics American
    National Banks
Served as president of the American Bankers Association
    and with local organizations of St. Louis bankers
In 1928 elected Chairman of the Board of
    First National Bank of St. Louis
Married in Helena, Ark., to Miss Helen Moore
    Two sons, Lawson and Frank

time of his death in 1930 was serving as president. He was succeeded by J. Walker Kerr as president, re-elected in the annual election in 1941, with C. E. Dean as vice-president and cashier, R. D. Kerr, Miss Birdie Caruthers and A. L. Garth, Jr. as assistant cashiers; Jesse Harris, bookkeeper.

Officers of the First Federal Savings and Loan Association of Union City are as follows: C. E. Beck, president; J. V. Verhine, vice-president; Dave M. Shatz, vice-president; Walker Tanner, vice-president and secretary; T. H. Cowden, treasurer; Catherine Sue Thompson, assistant secretary.

The original organization of the Savings and Loan Association of Union City was chartered under the laws of the State of Tennessee in 1922. In 1934 a reorganization took place under the Federal system, and charter was issued to the First Federal Savings and Loan Association of Union City, Tenn.

Since its organization the association has been instrumental in the financing of extensive home building and various other enterprises helpful to individuals and the community in a general way. Very few cities are without their savings and loan associations.

NYA FEDERAL BUILDING

A new Federal service department in Union City, with the completion of building on the lots south of State highway 22, between the G. M. & O. R. R. and Home street, will be the National Youth Administration training quarters, supplied with equipment for wood and metal work, in which an opportunity is offered to youths either on relief or out of work to learn a trade at the expense of the Federal Government. Youths from 16 to 25 years of age are admitted.

The plant will be equipped with machinery for wood and metal work, to be operated principally in the making of school and office furniture. Number of youths who desire training will be limited to 125 for the first few months with as many as 250 for the year altogether.

The plant and equipment are to be under Federal supervision, erected and installed at an expense of approximately $25,000, not more than twenty per cent of which is to be paid by the taxpayers of Obion County.

Practically speaking this will afford Union City and Obion County an institute of technical training at a nominal expense, provided for the purpose of giving employment to youths on relief or out of work and relieving, to some extent, the unemployment problem.

UNION CITY

SOUTHERN BELL TELEPHONE CO.

Soon after the local office of the Southern Bell Telephone Company was established in Union City, with switch board and equipment, J. W. Temple was assigned to the agency, one of the first in the service in Union City, in which he became very useful and efficient in the extension of the system, establishing mutual understanding and friendly cooperation with subscribers. Serving for a long number of years, Mr. Temple was succeeded to the Union City agency by J. T. Berry, who was also capable, fortunate and successful in popularizing and perfecting the local system and service.

It was during Mr. Berry's administration that the automatic call service was installed and the number of subscribers to the exchange, including residence and business connections, increased to more than one thousand wall and desk sets. Now the installation of hand sets has become general in business houses and offices with increased use in private homes.

Altogether Mr. Berry was in the service of the company for forty years, twenty-three years as manager of the station in Union City, and his organization of operatives, linemen and others, has been satisfactory and successful in all the branches of the work.

Mr. Berry, who has earned retirement, has been succeeded to the Union City Station by J. T. Green, of Nashville, who is entering upon a very important assignment and otherwise associating himself with current local enterprise and social affairs. Mr. Green is assisted in desk and office work by Miss Tennye Reed, who has been for many years faithful and efficient in the discharge of duty. Chief operator is Miss Ruth Penniston, in charge of a corps of very fine and efficiently trained operatives.

The company's rural connections include Rives, Kenton, Obion, Troy, also with independent local lines.

FUNERAL HOMES

The White & Ranson Funeral Home is one of Union City's well established and permanent institutions. The Mutual Burial Association is a cooperative branch of the service, which is essentially equivalent to insurance protection, an organization growing in numbers and in the mutually helpful benefits derived from its service. Members of the company are G. B. White, Sr., G. B. White, Jr., and J. L. Ranson.

CORPORATION OF UNION CITY

Union City received her first charter of incorporation in 1861. The first mayor was Thomas Ray; aldermen, Jesse Garrett, William Askins, Felix McGaugh, Eli Bynum, Green Bynum. In the later sixties, during reconstruction after the Civil War, a new charter was granted by the General Assembly, entitled "An Act to Incorporate Union City in the County of Obion, and for other purposes." This Act was passed December 17, 1867. During the troublous days of 1885 James M. Moore was mayor, Wm. M. McClanahan, marshal. Mayor Moore was succeeded by Seid Waddell, who became mayor in the late eighties, with the following aldermen: W. H. Gardner, H. Dietzel, B. H. Bransford, S. T. Evans, P. Cloys and Taylor Hayden, S. R. Bratton succeeded W. H. McClanahan as marshal.

This form of city government continued until 1925, when by a special act of the General Assembly of Tennessee it was changed to a commission form of three members, now in force with the following organization: Mayor Commissioner, W. M. Miles; Finance Commissioner, D. A. Box; Street Commissioner, L. H. McAdoo; clerk, D. W. Harris; chief of police, D. C. Roberts; day officers, with Mr. Roberts, W. A. Hudson, Foster Frazier; night officers, Arch Hale, Paul Woods, Eddie Lorance, O. B. Manley. Office of desk sergeant and inspector in the City Hall, equipped with police radio. City attorney, J. T. Gwaltney.

Former citizens who have been elected and served Union City as mayor are as near as possible enumerated as follows: Following Mayor Ray were: Dr. J. B. Harrison, Rice A. Pierce, F. W. Moore, J. M. Moore, Seid Waddell, W. H. Gardner, John T. Walker, J. A. Coble, F. L. Pittman, T. R. Reynolds, G. B. White, J. W. Woosley, Dr. W. M. Turner.

W. M. Miles, Mayor Commissioner, was a native of western Kentucky, graduate of Union City Training School, Princeton University and Cumberland University law school. Practiced law in Union City from 1902, including general practice in all the courts of the Western District of Tennessee; member of Tennessee Bar Association and chairman of committee on constitutional amendments. Elected Mayor of Union City in 1935, re-elected in 1939. Record of administration embracing sound finance and civic improvements— amplification and extension of power and light system, co-operation with Federal grant in erection of grammar school, auditorium and gymnasium building, and general street paving contract on Main and First streets, including also opening street to park extensions on the jockey yard south of the City Park.

Mayor Miles is the son of Dr. C. W. Miles, Sr., also a citizen first located in the vicinity of Jordan, Ky., man of learning and skill in medical science and surgery, with practice in Kentucky and Tennessee, associated actively and potentially with schools, churches, public life and community interests generally. Mayor

UNION CITY

W. M. MILES

W. M. Miles, Mayor of Union City
Graduate Princeton University
Cumberland University in Law
Attorney and Counsellor Practicing in
    Circuit, Chancery and Federal Courts
Son of Dr. C. W. Miles,, West Kentucky-Tennessee
    Physician and Surgeon Emeritus
    Scholar, Philosopher, Farmer-Citizen
Brother of C. W. Miles, Jr., Union City
    Banker, U. S. ▆▆▆▆ Marshal, Western
    District of Tennessee
Father of C. W. Miles, III.

Miles is a brother of C. W. Miles, Jr., president of Farmers Exchange Bank of Union City and ~~~~~ U. S. Marshal, Western District of Tennessee.

WATER AND LIGHT DEPARTMENT

The Corporation of Union City Water and Light Department, with other public utilities and local industries, continues with the march of progress.

Plant was established in 1891 with small equipment pumping water from shallow wells and operating electric lighting system only at night, with no power service either night or day.

Latest new equipment consists of steam turbine power and alternating current generators—three turbines having a total capacity of 3500 kilowatts. This includes a new unit installed in 1938 with a capacity of 2000 kilowatts.

Water is pumped from two wells 550 feet deep, with compressed air to mains with direct pressure. Water is of pure rock-bed origin, slightly mineral, but used without chemical treatment.

A number of improvements, including 550 horse-power boiler, with necessary equipment, have been provided. A new smokestack, 180 feet high, takes the place of the former stack 120 feet in height. An addition to the water-spray cooling system, which has been in operation for some time, is a cooling tower on another adjacent property extension. This is a cooling process in which the water circulating through the condenser is carried steaming hot up to the top, where it shoots from pipes and breaks into spray, dropping back down again on a system of breakwater cups and blocks, resulting in the proper reduction of temperature to be returned again to the condenser for use as before and as often as necessary, thus economizing in the water supply and preventing the possibility of flooding the city sanitary or storm sewers. New boiler additions, with the old ones, give the plant a boiler capacity of 1150 horsepower, capable of developing 2000 horsepower.

The plant for years has been noted for its successful operation, practically free from any political influence. C. B. Allen has served for a period of years, from 1899, as engineer and general superintendent of plant operations, beginning when the total capacity of electric generation was 60 kilowatts, enough only to furnish one-third of the current necessary to supply light for the TMF baseball park in Union City.

Whereas in the beginning when new units became necessary and licensed engineers were employed to take charge, as was the case in 1902 when the plant was enlarged and improved, Mr. Allen, in time, became by training and experience, competent to supervise installation of such units, under his personal direction,

UNION CITY

and continued to make use of increased efficiency and economy in plant extension and operation.

Assisting in day and night operation service are men of experience and ability, including Arch Vaught, with E. L. Hurt in charge at night in the work required of engineers. Three firemen and other helpers are employed, including Earl Summers, Claude Cole, T. K. Kelly, and J. Kersey.

Electricians and wiremen include: Joe Moss, superintendent; Red Young, Wallace Adams, Red Doxey.

The fire department is equipped with two modern American La France fire trucks, capacity, 500 and 750, a total of 1250 gallons of water per minute, and extension ladders and hose reaching the tops of the highest buildings.

Richard Semones, chief, and his company of fire fighters, all seasoned men well trained, including drivers, are Geo. Neely, W. T. Russell, Dave Threlkeld, Milton Andrews, Wm. B. Keiser, Maurice Noshey, Harold Semones, Red Young, Wallace Adams, Chas. Quillin.

A very fine tribute to these men is the record of service resulting in a total of minimum losses by fire in Union City.

HIGHWAY AND STREET PAVING

The State Highway Department, in conjunction with the Corporation of Union City, completed in 1940 a general paving contract on the streets of Union City, including curb and gutters and sidewalk construction, complete with water mains, drainage, etc., beginning on Main Street from the end of highway 45w out of Fulton entering on Main Street and crossing the G. M. & O. R. R. tracks to First Street, thence south crossing the N. C. & St. L. Ry. tracks, proceeding south on First Street, crossing Church Street, then Washington Avenue, passing through the main business thoroughfare, continuing to Harrison Street, thence connecting with pavement on First Street heretofore constructed to Highway No. 22, which intersects with Highway 45w and 51 beginning with the southwestern city limits.

This construction was planned to complete Federal and State highway improvement on 45w and 51, a part of the Jeff Davis Highway, leading through the city north to south, making complete and continuous paving of the highway through Union City.

Statement of Condition
CORPORATION OF UNION CITY, TENN.
As of January 20, 1941

ASSETS

GENERAL FUND—			
Cash on hand and in banks		$ 43,921.06	
Taxes receivable			
Current	48,411.56		
Delinquent	23,943.75		
		72,355.31	
Notes and accounts receivable less reserve for doubtful		1,902.30	
Returned checks		145.43	
Material—street department		1,602.83	
Gasoline on hand		759.96	
			120,686.89
WATER AND LIGHT FUND—			
Consumers' account receivable		17,891.41	
Inventory of materials and supplies		10,927.09	
Insurance prepaid		1,163.26	
Fixed properties	654,937.95		
Less: reserve for depreciation	215,125.02		
		439,812.93	
			469,794.69
FIXED ASSETS AND LIABILITIES—			
General City Properties—			
Balance at January 21, 1940		867,631.13	
Addition for the fiscal year ended January 20, 1941		11,572.54	
			879,203.67
TOTAL ASSETS			1,469,685.25

LIABILITIES

GENERAL FUND—		
Notes payable	61,500.00	
Accounts payable	735.32	
Accrued salaries payable	5,007.83	
Accrued interest payable	4,492.98	
Unappropriated surplus—general fund	48,950.76	
		120,686.89
WATER AND LIGHT FUND—		
Meter Deposits	4,504.27	
City's equity in water and light plant	465,290.42	
		469,794.69
FIXED ASSETS AND LIABILITIES—		
Bonded indebtedness	329,500.00	
Surplus invested in fixed assets	549,703.67	
		879,203.67
TOTAL LIABILITIES AND SURPLUS		1,469,685.25

UNION CITY

DR. THOMAS J. EDWARDS

Born in Obion County 1833
Parents of Scotch descent
Dr. Edwards left home at 17
    years of age to attend
    school at Clarksville, Tenn.
Attended St. Louis Medical School
    and University of Nashville
Went to California and practiced
    surgery in San Francisco
In 1863 visited Europe and studied
    at Opthalmic Hospitals in
    London, Paris, Berlin, Vienna
Returning received special degrees
    from New York, Philadelphia and
    New Orleans medical schools
Locating in Union City Dr. Edwards'
    practice as an oculist became general
    in the South and in many other State
Married Miss Clara Bird of Missouri

OBION COUNTY HISTORY

PHYSICIANS, SURGEONS

During the Civil War and since then many fine physicians and surgeons have lived and practiced in Union City. Herewith we undertake to include the names of those well known to the people of Union City and community, some of whom have been removed to the land of the Great Physician:

Included are A. P. Warterfield, John Morton, A. M. McConnell, S. T. Evans, R. R. Winston, D. M. Pearce, C. W. Miles, Sr., J. B. Harrison, F. W. Watson, T. H. Turner, Maney Bell, J. H. Rippy, H. W. Qualls, R. A. Napier, H. S. Sherrill, J. B. Hibbitts, H. T. Butler, M. A. Blanton, W. A. Nailling, B. F. Loring, Ira Park, R. G. Latimer, Mark Butler, Frank Kimzey, M. T. Tipton, R. M. Darnall, M. A. Blanton, Jr.

Oculist: J. D. Carlton.

Osteopaths: C. J. Rhoads, H. T. Bowers.

Opticians: J. F. McMichael, S. E. Allmond, C. L. Andrews, C. R. Herman. Optometrist: W. B. Dunlap.

Dentists: F. M. Trevathan, R. W. Powell, Dr. Bostick, C. B. Rowland, W. W. Slater, W. M. Turner, Jake Park, H. S. Hughes, Dr. Boswell, E. M. Long, C. E. Upchurch, P. A. Hufstedler, W. J. Jones, C. E. Mathis, D. A. Gardner, Homer E. Gibbs.

Chiropractors: C. B. Phebus, N. E. Wentworth.

Former oculists: T. J. Edwards, T. D. Edwards.

HOSPITALS AND CLINICS

New hospital buildings and facilities in Union City for the benefit of the public needing such accommodations have been provided, keeping pace with the advance of surgery and medical science.

During the year 1938 the Union City Clinic was enlarged to more than double its former size and capacity. The offices of Drs. M. A. Blanton, Sr., M. A. Blanton, Jr., F. B. Kimzey, R. G. Latimer and Mrs. Latimer are included. The new building on West Church street, combined with the original unit, and provision for new equipment, have greatly improved this well known institution. In the office of Drs. Blanton and Kimzey, Jane Adams is engaged as assistant.

A separate and entirely new clinic on Exchange street, with new equipment and facilities, has recently been built and established by Dr. M. T. Tipton. Dr. Tipton was formerly in the Old National Bank building.

The oldest hospital in Union City is the large establishment of Dr. W. A. Nailling, whose practice in Union City and community extends over a long period of years. Rooms and surgery

UNION CITY

are located on the second floor of the Nailling Building on the corner of First street and Washington avenue.

Dr. Neely's animal clinic is a new institution in Union City, with buildings and equipment on West Main street. Dr. Neely has achieved considerable distinction in his line of work, which is the care and treatment of horses and all kinds of domestic animals.

LIFE AND FIRE INSURANCE

Union City Insurance Co., Walker Tanner, manager; Mary Clive Lannom, secretary, John T. Walker Insurance Co., B. F. Howard, manager, Sadie Williams, secretary; Fidelity Insurance Agency, W. R. Howell, manager, Marjorie Howell, secretary; R. E. White Insurance Agency, Jack Hubbs, manager; J. C. Burdick and J. C. Jr. Insurance Agency; H. A. Bransford Insurance Agency, Catherine Capps, secretary; C. D. Haskins, Life Insurance; R. H. Bond Insurance Agency, Mrs. Young, secretary; Metropolitan Life Insurance.

RESTAURANTS AND LUNCH STANDS

Bungalow Cafe, Mrs. Petty; The Grill, Hamilton Cafe, Davy Crockett Coffee Shop, Pardue Lunch Car, Main Street Lunch, Little Castle, Top Hat Cafe, Ritzy Lunch, Earl's Restaurant, Red Top Inn, Pete Posey; Uncle Eck's Place, Omer G. Lunch, Twin Gables Lunch, Price Lunch, Hazelrigg Lunch and Fruit Stand, Toasted Sandwich Shop, Dixie Coffee Shop.

RAILROAD AND BUS LINES

Gulf, Mobile & Northern R. R., A. W. Fowler, Agent; W. M. Bransford, Cashier.

N. C. & St. L. Ry., W. W. Lovelace, Agent; C. S. Whitley, cashier.

Train Distpatchers: Lee Verhine, M. E. Clark.

Dixie Greyhound Bus Lines: Ernest Wuench, Agent.

Tri-State Bus Lines: Joe White, Agent.

Six-Forty-Nine Bus Line: Herman Newsom, Manager.

AUTOMOBILE AND TRUCK AGENCIES

Obion County Motor Co., J. L. Rippy, manager.
Andrews Chevrolet Co., C. V. Andrews, owner-operator.
Citizens Auto Co., John and Richard Semones, own.-op.
Berry Bros. Motor Co., owners and operators.
Stubblefield Motor Co., Ralph Stubblefield, own.-op.
Service Motor Co., Joe White, owner-operator.
Adams Motor Co., W. A. Adams, owner-operator.
First Street Garage, Walter Kennon, owner-operator.
Paul Nailling Implement Co., owner and operator.

OBION COUNTY HISTORY

USED CARS AND TRUCKS
Used Car Exchange, Marvin McCord, W. F. Thweatt, op.
Sudden Service Station, Jiggs Latimer, owner-op.

WHOLESALE DISTRIBUTORS PETROLEUM PRODUCTS
Pan-Am Petroleum Corp., Pan-Am, Reynolds Bros.
Tennessee Oil Co., Shell, David Threlkeld.
The Texas Co., Texaco, P. H. Morson.
Phillips Petroleum Co., Phillips, A. A. Thompson.
Cities Service Oil Co., Cities Service, Joe Pittman.
Mid-South Oil Co., Pure Oil, Mike Simmons.
Gulf Refining Co., Gulf, E. A. Pearson.
Sinclair Refining Co., Sinclair, Mosley.
Standard Oil Co., Standard, L. A. Meacham.

USED AUTO PARTS
Brownlow Used Parts Co., Davidson Used Parts Co.

SERVICE STATIONS
Cities Service Station, E. W. Talley, owner
Terrell's Esso Station, J. H. Terrell, owner.
Bond Service Station, Leonard Bond, owner.
700 Service Station, Lewis Griffin, manager.
Berry Bros. Service Station, Berry Bros., owners.
Horner's Service Station, Rob Horner, owner.
Alamo Service Staton, Willie Nelms, owner.
First Street Garage SS, Herman Howard, Sr., owner.
Sinclair Service Staton, Sam Palmer, owner.
Four Point Service Station, Tommy Lewis, owner.
Gateway Service Station, Chester Johnson, owner.
Sam Davis Garage and SS, Sam Davis, owner.
Esso Service Station, Dodson and McCullough, owners.
Brownlow Service Station, owner.
Bluebird SS and Sandwich Shop, Ferrell Tittsworth, owner.
Obion County Motor Co. SS, Bill McNeill, manager.
Cruce's Service Station, W. J. Cruce, owner.
Jiggs Latimer Service Station, owner.
Parkview Motor Co., SS, Frizzell & Passmore, owners
Service Motor Co., SS, Joe White, owner.
Reelfoot Service Station, Irvin Bransford, owner
Twin Gables Service Station, Bob Moore, owner
Park Service Station, H. Crowder, owner.
Pure Oil Station, H. Carter & Farris Starnes, owners

UNION CITY HOUSING AUTHORITY
Following a general understanding that application might be made by local municipalities for Federal housing projects, a

UNION CITY

movement was instituted in Union City in the early part of 1941 by Mayor Miles and others for Federal allotment for slum clearance and low-cost home building in the sum of $400,000, application to be made in proper form to the Federal Housing Authority.

Accordingly a public meeting was held in Union City on the first day of April, 1941, and the Union City Housing Authority was organized with the following officers: B. C. Cox, chairman; C. P. Merryman, vice-chairman; J. M. Andrews, secretary.

Appointment of committee was made to file application in due form for articles of incorporation, and to proceed in the matter of appearing before the Federal Housing Authority seeking allotment for the purposes herein set forth.

UNION CITY POSTMASTERS

Appointment of Chas. N. Gibbs, first postmaster in Union City, beginning February 27, 1857, following is a list, with dates appointed, of postmasters serving the Union City office since that time:

Thomas H. Ray, Jan. 12, 1860.
George W. Patton, April 30, 1861.
Daniel Hughes, May 27, 1865.
William D. Scates, December 26, 1865.
Solomon McMurray, October 11, 1866.
Daniel White, January 3, 1867.
Issac H. Foster, November 7, 1867.
Benjamin F. Scates, March 22, 1869.
William P. Richards, May 18, 1883.
William R. Andrews, August 3, 1885.
Carlos B. Rowland, August 17, 1889.
George A. Gibbs, December 21, 1893.
George Thomas Taylor, October 16, 1897.
Allen D. Keller, January 24, 1912.
George W. Phebus, Jr., February 12, 1915.
William E. Hudgins (acting), April 15, 1923.
William E. Hudgins, Jan. 15, 1924.
Clarence G. Guill, August 1, 1936.
Evelyn A. Guill, February 18, 1938.

POSTAL REVENUES

In 1910 the Union City postoffice had three regular clerks, producing revenue amounting to $3000 each. In 1940 there were five regular clerks, producing an annual revenue of $36,000. City delivery was established in Union City March 15, 1907, with three carriers. Four carriers in 1940 handled more than twice the amount of mail delivered in the city in 1907. Rural delivery service

OBION COUNTY HISTORY

was established April 1, 1900, with five carriers carrying 100 miles of rural routes from the Union City office. In 1940 five carriers served 210 miles and handled six times as much mail as the total of 1900.

The first mail delivered in the county was by stage routed overland by Totten's Wells. In 1858 contract was made with the M. & O. R. R. to handle U. S. Mail service in Obion County.

U. S. CENSUS ENUMERATION

Obion Co. Pop.	Year	Union City
2,099	1830	
4,814	1840	
7,633	1850	
12,817	1860	
15,584	1870	
22,912	1880	1,879
27,273	1890	3,441
28,286	1900	3,407
29,946	1910	4,389
28,393	1920	4,412
29,086	1930	5,865
30,978	1940	7,256

The Federal Enumeration of towns and cities in the United States gives the population of Union City as follows:

Eighteen eighty, 1879; Eighteen ninety, 3441; Nineteen hundred, 3407; Nineteen ten, 4389;—enumerators, W. C. Watts, Henry Moffett. Nineteen twenty, 4412—enumerators, Mary Swiggart, Ruth Crenshaw. Nineteen thirty, 5865—enumerators, Mrs. E. E. Clymer, Mrs. Marvin Owen, Mrs. G. H. Niles. Nineteen forty, 7256—enumerators, Miss Marie Caldwell, Mrs. J. A. Howard, Miss Addie May Clark, Mrs. Frances Roper Major, W. L. Baulch.

COUNTY OFFICES

A courthouse directory and the duties of county officials, for convenience, appear herewith in that part of the county history devoted to the county seat at Union City, as follows:

County Judge, J. A. Hefley; secretary and Budget Director, Evelyn Howse; County Court Clerk, J. F. Semones; deputy clerk, Alwyn Brevard; assistant deputy, Ruby Oliver.

The County Judge is the chief financial officer of the county. He presides over the County Court, calls special sessions of the court, borrows money, signs all warrants on the county general fund, signs all county bonds issued for county funds. He serves as judge of the juvenile court, in which he has authority to place delinquent children in institutions or to take children from immoral homes and place them in private homes. As juvenile judge

UNION CITY

WILLIAM H. SWIGGART

Native of Union City, son of Judge W. H. Swiggart, Sr.
Alumnus Vanderbilt University—law at Cumberland University
Entered law practice with father in Union City
Appointed Assistant Attorney General in 1914
Named in 1926 to succeed Judge Hall (deceased)
    State Supreme Court. Elected in 1934 for
    second term. Resigned to become General
    Counsel N. C. & St. L. Ry. in January, 1935
Married Miss Katherine Mayes, Union City, 1914
Four children born of the union

he also has non-support cases brought before him and makes assessments that are to be paid to children of separated parents.

The County Judge approves all bonds of county officers, guardians, administrators, and signs all commitments to the Western State Hospital at Bolivar. He collects and takes bonds for payment of workhouse fines. He is ex-officio member of the budget committee. He is also authorized to grant temporary injunctions.

The County Court is formed with the organization of magistrates or justices of the peace as follows: Two from each civil district in the county, one from each incorporated town, and one from the county seat, making a total in 1940 of 40 magistrates. They are elected for a period of six years. They meet in quarterly session on the first Monday in January, April, July and October. They elect the county superintendent of schools, county surveyor, ranger, coroner, budget commission, agriculture committee, auditor, and appoint constables in case of death or resignation. They elect to fill unexpired vacancies of the office of sheriff, register, county judge, county court clerk, trustee and tax assessor.

The County Court also elects the county health physician, sets the tax rate, appropriates money to operate the various departments of county government. They fix the county levy, the privilege tax and elect county board of equalizers. They elect notaries public, county school board and county road commission.

The County Court Clerk is commissioned to sell all license authorized to be issued by the county, including automobile license, hunting, fishing, marriage, drivers, privilege, and collect advalorem tax from the merchants. He as clerk of the County Court, is commissioned to make settlement of estates, also with administrators and guardians. He sells lands ordered by the court for public sale, probates wills, keeps the records of the county in minute books. He countersigns all warrants issued on the county general fund, and countersigns all bonds issued to provide funds for the county. He prepares the county tax books, signs all papers providing admission of patients to the Western State Hospital at Bolivar. He issues letters of administration for estates, officiates for non compos mentis, collects State transfer, and mortgage tax.

The budget commission is composed of five members of the County Court. It has control of the general fund of the county, but cannot pay out any money without authority of the court. It makes recommendations to the court as to the tax rate, approves and disapproves all bills payable from the general fund. It acts as purchasing agent for the county, meeting once a month.

Circuit Judge, Robert A. Elkins; Clerk, Robert Ashton Everett; assistant, Mary Lou Gates. State's attorney, John M. Drane.

UNION CITY

Circuit Court of Obion County is organized with Robert A. Elkins as judge and John M. Drane as attorney general. The court tries all violations of State laws, except cases tried in magistrates' court. Civil cases are also tried in Circuit Court, appealed cases from magistrates' court, damage suits, and divorce trials. Election contests are tried in Circuit Court.

The Fourteenth Judicial Circuit is composed of Benton, Weakley, Obion, Lake and Dyer counties. Court is held in Union City on the first Monday in January, May and September; in Dresden on the first Monday in April, August and December; in Camden the fourth Monday in January, May and September; in Tiptonville the third Monday in March, July and November; in Dyersburg the second Monday in February, June and October.

The clerk keeps minutes of the court, files all suits in Circuit Court, makes out cost bills in all cases, and disburses all funds in Circuit Court.

County Sheriff, J. S. Burcham; chief deputy, C. L. Harris.

The Sheriff is the highest peace officer in the county. He has custody of the jail and is responsible for the safe-keeping of all prisoners in jail. He opens court, serves orders for Circuit, Chancery, County and Magistrates' courts. He is authorized to appoint a required number of deputies to keep the peace in the county. He serves papers issued on the county from the court of other counties or States. Constables are allowed to serve papers only from magistrates' court.

The Attorney General represents the State in all criminal matters. In quasi criminal matters he abates nuisances, such as road houses, immoral houses and places where whiskey is sold.

Chancellor, W. W. Herron; Clerk and Master, C. M. Montgomery; deputy clerk, Sue Henderson.

W. W. Herron is presiding judge of the Ninth Chancery Division, composed of Lake, Obion, Weakley, Dyer, Gibson, Lauderdale, Tipton, Haywood and Fayette counties. Chancery Court grants divorces, partitions land through the process of public sale, custodian of minors' funds, and renders judgment to sell land for back taxes. The Clerk and Master conducts land sales, administers on insolvent estates, is empowered to remove minority and hear equity cases. Much of the work of Chancery Court has been simplified by hearings held in chambers on Mondays of each week at Trenton. The Chancellor is authorized to appoint Clerk and Master of his court in each of the counties embraced in his division, who serve for six years.

The Clerk and Master collects back taxes for municipalities, special school districts, county and State. He takes depositions, files all suits in Chancery Court, and keeps the minute books and records of the court.

OBION COUNTY HISTORY

County Trustee, S. W. Easterwood; deputy trustee, J. H. Shore.

The County Trustee serves as the county's banker. He collects all State and county taxes, with the exception of license, which is collected by the County Court Clerk. The collections are apportioned to the various funds, such as the county highway commission, etc. He collects all drainage tax, pays all warrants issued by the County Judge, the County Court Clerk, County Highway Commission, school board and workhouse commission. Back-tax attorney is appointed by the Trustee with approval of the County Judge. Attorney files suit for the collection of back taxes.

County Register, W. A. Jackson; deputy registers, Dathan Smith and Allie V. Naylor.

The Register transcribes on permanent record books, filed in steel cabinet cases, all deeds, trust deeds, mortgages, liens, leases, power of attorney, soldiers' discharge, and contracts. He also records releases on mortgages, trust deeds, liens and leases.

Tax Assessor, Clint A. Adams.

The Tax Assessor, elected for a term of four years, assesses all taxes, both real and personal, starting on the first of January and completing his books on or before the first Monday in June, when the board of equalization meets to review the assessments. He assesses real estate biennially and personal property every year.

Public utilities are assessed by the State Utilities Commission at Nashville.

County Superintendent of Schools, Milton Hamilton; assistant superintendent, Oral Pace.

County Budget Committee: Jesse Finch, chairman; N. L. Williams, J. P. Cloar, Luke Latimer, W. F. Tate.

County Board of Equalization: C. G. Moore, C. C. Vaughn, Dr. J. H. Dorgan, Rice Wilson, J. V. Verhine.

County Farm Commissioners: R. J. Latimer, J. Willis Williams, Walter Philips.

U. T. Farm Extension Service: County Agent, Tom B. Garth; Home Agent, Erin Tice; secretary, Miss Catherine Marshall.

Justice of the Peace (county seat), T. R. Meadow.

County Auditor, G. F. Schleifer.

American Red Cross: Mrs. Lorene Thweatt, executive secretary.

Public Health Department (Headquarters, public health building, West Church street): Violet Crook, principal public health nurse; Margaret Mahoney, senior public health nurse; Mildred Howard, clerk-typist; Dr. E. W. Barkdull, county health officer; Dr. J. A. Caraway, sanitary officer; Ruth Pruett, clerk.

UNION CITY

W. P. A. DEPARTMENT

County Farm Bureau (1941): Woody Cunningham, president; Dr. C. C. Maddox, vice-president; T. F. Heathcock, secretary-treasurer; Miss Bobbie Wright, office secretary.

Farm-to-Market-Road Project: Ralph G. Hornbeak, administrator; L. M. Maxwell, time keeper; Margaret Morton, clerk.

Social Security: Ralph Hughes, Unit Supervisor State Department Public Welfare; Anita Midyett, secretary.

Hot Lunch Gardening and Canning: Mrs. Effie Head.

Recreation and Child Welfare: LaNelle Marshall.

UNION CITY SCHOOLS

It is said that one of the first schools in Union City was taught in a private dwelling by Miss Ebby Whipple, from Montpelier, Vermont. James Fuzzell in 1856 opened a school in the law office of C. N. Gibbs. In the winter of 1860 a house was erected at the cost of $1600 and a school opened. It continued until the beginning of the Civil War, when it was taken by the Federals as a hospital. During the period in Union City following the Civil War private schools flourished and provided the youth of the town with schooling facilities.

One of the earliest of these schools was the Union City "Athenaeum." This school was conducted by Prof. J. W. Hatcher, who taught the higher classes. The curricula included a wide variety of subjects, including Greek, Latin, astronomy, philosophy, and higher mathematics. Teacher of the primary classes was Miss Fannie Foster, long a beloved figure in the Union City schools. This was located on South Home street on an elevation slightly east of the street, immediately south of the N. C. & St. L. Ry. The school was thought to have been opened on or before 1869. Among the first to attend this school were Koss Kimberlin, Jim and Amos Mathis, R. T. Curlin, Eliza and Laura Curlin, Bill Swiggart (father of Judge Will H. Swiggart), Lonzo Cutler, E. Kimberlin, Molly Baynes (daughter of Dr. Baynes). Students of high school branches numbered about thirty or forty and paid a stated tuition of four or five dollars a month. Professor Roseman followed Mr. Hatcher in charge of this school.

Before a general system of graded schools in Tennessee had been adopted there were graded schools in Nashville in 1855 and in Memphis in 1858. The George Peabody Fund of three and one-half million dollars, donated to the Southern States in 1867-69 for public education, was no doubt the cause of a general revival of interest in the public school system of Tennessee.

The origin of the present school system in Union City dates from 1871, when the board of directors included Green Kimberlin, W. R. Neblett, and A. J. Wyatt, who decided to organize a graded school. The first graded school in Union City was therefore opened in the old "John Morgan Hall," once a famous meeting place for the Masons and Odd Fellows. The building was located on what later became the Dr. C. W. Miles, Sr., property, adjoining the home of H. M. Oliver. This was the Lile-Curlin school, organized upon a much larger scale than any of the schools heretofore taught in Union City. It was therefore necessary to find more room for the students, hence, the lease of the old E. B. Sidebottom store house, directly south on the opposite side of Main street, which was divided into class rooms. In addition to Professor Lile, who was also a Cumberland Presbyterian minister, and Prof. J. V. Curlin, who had charge of the school, the faculty included also Prof. A. J. Stanfield (father of Miss Tabbie Stanfield, this city), Dr. W. W. Hall, Miss Womble and Miss Fannie Foster. There was also an art teacher, Mr. Penfield, and Mrs. Cox, a music teacher. The school grades were divided, with Miss Fannie Foster teaching the first and second grades, Miss Womble the third and fourth grades, Professors Hall and Stanfield the fifth and sixth grades. Professors Lile and Curlin divided the work in the higher grades. In Latin and Greek Professor Lile was highly qualified, while Professor Curlin, a college graduate, was well versed in philosophy, astronomy and mathematics.

Interest in this school is thought to have been greatly increased by a general attendance of young men emerging from a period of rehabilitation following the Civil War. Many of these students attending the Lile-Curlin school were grown but eager to employ extra time and effort in order to regain the losses of education sustained in military service. Among the class of Civil War veterans were Eli Bynum and brother, Ben Lancaster, Andrew Harpole (father of Whitesell Harpole, this city), Baylor and Sam Mathis, Bob Goldsby, Will Woodfin. The girls were Tennie and Betty Jenkins (daughters of Methodist ministers), Nannie Curlin, Molly Curlin and Laura Curlin. Tennie (Jenkins) Cloys was the mother of Fred Cloys.

During the last year of this school there was no tuition charge for the pupils up to the fifth grade. Prior to that four dollars per month for the higher classes and three dollars for the lower were the tuition rates. It is said that notwithstanding the necessity of keeping the rates in force the school continued to grow. The school, however, was discontinued when Professor Curlin left Union City to accept the presidency of a school in Missouri, and Professor Lile retired from active teaching duties.

On account of the unsettled conditions after the Civil War private schools still prevailed. Reverend Norton, a Baptist minister, about the year 1877 or later built a one-room schoolhouse

UNION CITY

on North Home street, north of the Scates grocery store. In connection with his church duties the pastor taught during the week all the higher grades in school. It is estimated that at times there were as many as fifteen girls and forty boys attending classes. Students received instruction in algebra, higher mathematics, Latin, and Greek, as well as the ordinary subjects. Cost of tuition was three dollars per month. Among the pupils attending were John Hinemon (later superintendent of Union City public schools), Will Barry, Dena Morgan, Mona Neblett, Nannie Curlin, Ben Bransford.

During the years between 1870 and 1880 there were a number of private schools in Union City. A. J. Wyatt (father of Mrs. Sue Moore, widow of the late Judge F. W. Moore) taught school first on North Home street and then on Florida Avenue in the southwest section of town. Another in that vicinity was taught by Mrs. Etta (Moore) Barry. Professor Bradshaw had a school on South Third Street. Mrs. Neblett taught a private school in southeast Union City, and Mrs. Edwards (mother of W. J. Edwards) taught school on Exchange street.

Schools thus continued until 1879-80, at which time contract was made by the school directors of Union City with the trustees of a private institution known as the Union City College to teach all the pupils between the ages of six and twenty-one years free of charge, stipulating the common school branches, for a compensation of $250 per month. This arrangement continued until 1881, when the trustees of the college agreed to transfer the school building to the school directors upon the latter assuming an indebtedness of $3500 upon the school building. Public school funds were then for two years withheld and applied to the payment of this indebtedness and school was taught by private subscription. It was said that this school was taught by Professor Cravens, with Miss Fannie Foster and Miss Daisy Castleman as assistants, and of the students attending were Laura Dobbins, Sally and Molly Chambers, Alice Priest, Lillie and Lila Stanbrough, Mollie George, John Hinemon, Will Barry, Sam D. Woosley, Nannie Barney. This was a two-room school located on the Westover school grounds on Florida Avenue.

Another private school in Union City was taught by Prof. Charles Wright, for many years a teacher at Troy and other points in the county. This was in the late eighties and school was held in the Captain Cary residence on South First street. Mr. Wright was a native of London, England, a man of very active mind and literary accomplishments, devoting much time to the teaching of business courses.

Rev. John G. Garth writes from Charlotte, N. C., that he and his sister and two of his brothers were pupils of the Wyatt school on North Home street. He adds that Prof. R. E. Crockett began his school teaching in Union City in the "Kitchen," a residence at crossing of the N. C. & St. L. Ry. on Home street. Later Mr. Crockett took a leading part in the work of establishing the Union City Training School. In the opening of the school he was joined by Prof. Thad Thomas, a very fine scholar, who was formerly principal of the Woman's College at Baltimore. This was the last of the important private schools in Union City. It was instituted for the purpose of accommodating patrons outside of the city limits and incorporated as the Union City High School. The building was a brick structure on North First street. As a preparatory school high rank was achieved, having as principals some of the noted teachers in this section of the State, Professors Crockett and Thomas, Duncan Williams, Calvin Brown, W. R. (B.) Moore, F. C. Aydelott. The school was closed in the twenties and the lots transferred as private property.

The Union City public school system proper was instituted in 1879. It was in 1878 that a new brick building was erected on school property donated to Union City by Charles N. Gibbs, which became generally known as "Central," located on East College street. The contractor and builder was T. L. (Lee) Bransford.

It was therefore under the administration of Silas Perkins as superintendent of the City Schools that Central was opened in 1879. Two ladies, Mrs. Eugie Reynolds and Miss Mary Weatherford, well known in Union City for many years, were among the students of the school.

Central school building was first remodeled under the administration of Supt. A. E. Darrah, with a tower and town clock installed.

Another building for the colored schools, known under the name of the Miles Junior High School, was built in the northeastern section of Union City.

By the year 1916 increase of school enrollment and attendance had created a demand for more room, which resulted in the erection of a high school building immediately south of Central across College street, a brick and stone building, three stories high and very large and commodious. The building committee included the names of H. Parks, chairman; J. A. Coble, mayor, and Dr. C. W. Miles, Sr., president of the Board of Education. Architect, R. A. Heavner; time—1917. Improvements and extensions were also made in Westover school building on Florida Avenue, and later an additional wing was built as an annex to Central on College street.

It remained, however, for the most substantial and complete school building in Union City to be constructed in 1936-37 as a Federal WPA project on College street, replacing the entire group

UNION CITY

of old buildings on the Gibbs lot north of the high school building. This project, completed at a cost of $105,000, comprises the east and west main halls of the Union City grammar schools, the auditorium and gymnasium at the rear, entered from the center through a facade of mounted marble columns, inclosing an open area which forms a generally convenient entrance and exit for all the buildings. Names of building committee inscribed on a panel include the City Commissioners: W. M. Miles, mayor; C. G. Guill, L. H. McAdoo; Board of Education: C. W. Miles, Jr., chairman, A. F. Tittsworth, F. W. Watson, W. J. Jones, G. H. Niles, T. E. Parks, G. B. Baird; D. A. Box, secretary and the Superintendent, J. T. Webb.

School enrollment in Union City has grown to a total of 1400 pupils. Superintendents from the beginning serving the Union City schools are as near as possible herewith enumerated: Silas Perkins, T. C. Karns, (1882-85), Carleton Mitchell, J. H. Hinemon, Price Thomas, R. E. McDonald, A. E. Darrah, A. C. Nute, O. E. McGee, F. E. Ranck, C. K. Wilkerson, C. V. Compton, M. J. Clark, J. T. Webb, T. D. Ozment.

The present superintendent, Mr. Ozment, has been connected with the school since 1927, ten years as principal of the high school.

One of the first superintendents, Professor Karns, was afterwards active in school work in other sections of the State, teacher for a number of years in the University of Tennessee. Another superintendent, Mr. Nute, was for some years principal of the Snowden school in Memphis. W. E. Miller, principal of the Union City High School while Mr. Nute was superintendent, after leaving Union City, became Superintendent of the Knox County Schools and followed Mr. Nute (removed by death) as principal of the Snowden school in Memphis.

OFFICERS AND TEACHERS, 1940-41

T. D. Ozment, superintendent; C. W. Thomasson, principal senior high school; T. F. Wallace, principal junior high school; R. G. Wilson, athletic director; Dorothy Barton, home economics; Nelle Bond, French and English; Allen Cash, band and music; Melda Crosthwaite, Latin; Martha Ellen Futrell, junior high history; Christine Johnson, commercial; Pearl Milam, junior high English; T. D. Ozment, Bible; Vera Ray, mathematics; Sarah Spradlin, history; C. W. Thomasson, English; Mrs. C. W. Thomasson, Science and English; Katie Lee Thompson, librarian; T. F. Wallace, mathematics, science, football and basketball coach; O. W. White, junior high mathematics; R. G. Wilson, geography, civics, girls basketball coach; Virginia Hickman, secretary to superintendent.

OBION COUNTY HISTORY

Central Elementary: Mrs. H. F. Bower, first grade; Johne Hornbeak, first grade; Mrs. L. M. Maxwell, second grade; Pearl Floyd, second grade; Mrs. W. C. Kelly, third grade; Virginia Cunningham, third grade; Sarah Chapel, fourth grade; Minnie Lee Beeler, fourth grade; Elizabeth Watson, fifth grade; Mrs. J. G. Palmer, fifth grade; Marene Allen, fifth grade; Iris McCorkle, sixth grade; Mrs. Raymond Mitchell, sixth grade; Mrs. Beth Sutherland, sixth grade principal; Corinne Morton, librarian.

Westover: Callie Howell, first grade; Mrs. Mike Meadow, second grade, Ninnie Barksdale, third; Martha Temple, fourth grade, principal. Substitute: Mrs. R. G. Wilson.

Miles High School, (colored): N. T. Gilbert, principal, mathematics, English; Hattie Lindsey, English, history, civics, music; Davada Roper, first grade; Pearl Jennings, third and fifth grades; Uma Washington, fourth and sixth grades; Vira Clements, second grade, home economics; Ezra Lee Taylor, seventh and eighth grades.

BOARD OF EDUCATION

C. W. Miles, Jr., chairman; A. F. Tittsworth, vice-chairman; D. W. Harris, secretary; C. L. Dismukes, Dr. G. H. Niles, T. E. Parks, Dr. W. J. Jones, Dr. F. W. Watson.

FIELD OF OPPORTUNITY

Early training in Obion County schools found numbers succeeding in various lines of endeavor.

Beginning many years back, T. R. Garth was a student in the Union City schools, then a teacher, and finally finished his education in Columbia University as PhD. He was some years afterwards elected to fill the position of professor of psychology in the University of Denver.

Chas. J. Crockett, student of the schools at Troy, became by training and experience a merchant, manager and counsellor of the various branches of merchandise, advancing to the position of general sales counsellor with headquarters in New York City.

Frederick S. Tisdale, of the Union City schools, advancing as a newspaper reporter, became versatile as a writer in free-lance work and as a contributor to leading American magazines.

W. M. Penick, UCHS, trained in local and general transportation, with years of experience became associated with the United Fruit Dispatch Company, directing from general offices in New York the operation of a fleet of ships plying between New York and the tropics.

Erwin Scates, UCHS, became a teacher of history in the State Teachers College of West Tennessee at Memphis. Mr. Scates is the son of Mrs. Victoria Tams Scates.

UNION CITY

Melvin Tisdale, UCHS, advanced as an architect, became identified with the profession and established offices in Nashville in partnership with Mr. Pinson. The firm submitting plans and specifications was awarded contract for the building of the Grammar School and gymnasium in Union City.

R. M. Garth, UCHS-University of Tennessee, with training received appointment and promotion in the public works division of the U. S. Navy Department, located eight years at the Pearl Harbor Naval Station, advancing to supervision of construction and operation of the power system. Transfer of operations in new construction to Jacksonville, Florida, in connection with naval air bases was made in November, 1940.

Curtis S. Ruddle, UCHS, with a career beginning as accountant in Nashville, advancing to general superintendent of printing plant in St. Augustine, Fla., finally became sales manager for the Cuneo Printing Company in Eastern States and Canada.

Mary Dahnke, UCHS, Kraft Cheese specialist and demonstrator, was appointed to position from University of Tennessee.

Henry M. Oliver, Jr., UCHS-Southwestern and MA degree from Duke University, student in political economy, accepted appointment as faculty instructor at Yale University, resigning to enter Federal service with the National Resources Planning Board as Associate Economist, connected with the Executive Department.

W. C. Pressly, Troy High School, Erskine College, South Carolina, Fontaine Bleu University, France. Began with Peace College, Raleigh, North Carolina, as teacher in 1921; elected and served as president for a period of twelve years, a season of distinct success in college work.

George Carmack, Troy High School-University of Tennessee, began newspaper work in Memphis on the Press-Scimitar. After some time resigned to become editor of the Knoxville News-Sentinel, and making favorable progress, was voted by the Knoxville Junior Chamber of Commerce as "Outstanding Young Man of 1940." Mr. Carmack is the son of Mr. and Mrs. D. M. Carmack at Troy. He is the grandson of G. W. Carmack, a stalwart of the Southern Confederacy attached to the "Obion Avalanche."

Juna Reynolds, UCHS, BA Washington University of Missouri and MA Columbia University of New York. Taught for term of years, later engaged as English Supervisor at State Junior College, Macomb, Ill. Miss Reynolds is a daughter of Mrs. R. C. Reynolds, Union City.

Mark Butler, UCHS, BA and MD degrees in Vanderbilt University, located in New York City and then at Syracuse, N. Y., with Aetna Insurance Company, assigned to rehabilitation department as technical head of the clinic of medicine and surgery.

Charles Edward Keiser, UCHS-Washington University of Missouri, electrical engineering. Filling technical position in the office of the Chicago Surface Lines.

Richard Cabot Nailling, UCHS, BA and MD degrees in Vanderbilt University. Entered Geisinger Memorial Hospital, Danville, Pennsylvania, as interne to complete practical work in medicine and surgery, with fine prospects. Richard is a son of Dr. and Mrs. W. A. Nailling, Union City.

Earl A. Kimzey, UCHS-University of Tennessee, many years sales manager for the Parke-Davis Drug Company began in 1912 with the New Orleans branch, with successful operation and promotion after a period of years to the Chicago division—second largest of the company's interests in the United States— which continued to increase in volume and business prestige.

Rex M. Naylor, UCHS, with university degrees, became faculty member of the New York City University, with classes in history. Mr. Naylor is the son of Mrs. Lucie Naylor.

UCHS ALUMNI ASSOCIATION

Officers elected by the association for 1941:

Dixon Williams, president; Miss Bess Beck, vice president; Campbell Garth, treasurer; Catherine Sue Thompson, recording secretary; Oral Pace, corresponding secretary; Mrs. Beth Sutherland, historian; G. B. White, Jr., poet; Chas. W. Miles, III, orator. Directors: Robert Ashton Everett, Mrs. J. C. Burdick, Paul Hudgins.

DREWRY'S BUSINESS COLLEGE

This institution was established in Union City, now pursuing the seventh year of its work in this city, having a maximum enrollment of 100 students, entering from local and various other communities. The president, R. E. Drewry, is a native West Tennessean, a man of ripe scholarly attainments, assisted in class work in the college by Mrs. Patterson and Mr. Frey Drewry.

The courses of study are secretarial, stenographic, bookkeeping, business administration, civil service and those of a special nature, comprising a combination of one or more of the regular subjects.

The rooms occupied by Drewry's Business College embrace the entire suite over the corner building on First street and Washington avenue, reached by front stairway.

It may be noted that in recalling a number of commercial or business schools organized in Union City, Drewry's Business College is the first exclusive and independent commercial school to become a permanent institution in Union City, with graduate

UNION CITY

students filling important secretarial and office assignments in various business centers.

The enrollment has gradually increased every year until the total number of students has reached one hundred altogether.

TENNESSEE STATE EMPLOYMENT SERVICE

Office located on West Main Street, the Tennessee State Employment Service is affiliated with the Social Security Board, with Jas. D. Swearengen, head of the local office. Junior Interviewer, Mrs. Warren Robeson; secretary, Mary Alice Evans.

FIRST BAPTIST CHURCH
(By SHERMAN SUTHERLAND)

The First Baptist Church was organized in 1867 by the Rev. R. E. McGowan. On October 10, 1870, Alexander W. Campbell and Annie Dixon Campbell, his wife, deeded to Richard C. Jackson, James Sutherlin and John Morgan two lots, in trust for the use of the Baptist Church. Then began erection of a church building under the leadership of Rev. J. H. Milburn, who gave liberally of his time and means. After many hardships and much prayer and supplication, the one-story brick building was finished.

In this brief sketch we cannot give a complete outline of all that has been accomplished. We can only mention the pastors as they came, wrought righteousness, and moved on to other fields. They were as follows: Revs. R. W. Norton, I. N. Strother, J. S. Corpening, Hargrove, W. M. Bruton, J. W. Gillon, Mathis, A. S. Hall, E. L. Watson, J. H. Wright, S. W. Kendick, D. S. Brinkley, H. H. Drake, A. R. McGehee, H. A. Todd, D. F. Marlin, J. W. Jenkins, J. G. Hughes, M. J. White, and E. L. Carnett. These all wrought well, played the part the Lord assigned them, and moved on to bigger and better fields of service.

When Rev. McGehee was pastor we began to talk expansion in a material way. Succeeding him was Rev. Todd, who preached mightily and urged enlargement. But it was not until Rev. Jenkins came that results began to show. After several starts and stops we finally got under way and purchased the lot where the present building now stands. About $25,000 was raised and spent. We were on the "pay as you go" plan and money was not easy, so we decided to lay the first floor and roof it, and use the basement until sufficient funds could be raised to complete the structure, or at least to get the roof on.

On a Sunday morning later, we met in the old building on Division street and marched in a body to the basement of the new home on Church and Ury streets—a very happy family.

Some time after this, Rev. Jenkins resigned and moved to California, and Rev. J. G. Hughes was called, and accepted. At the first deacons' meeting after he came we decided to recommend borrowing money and completing the building. Several plans were discussed and we finally decided to issue bonds. The contract was let, the bonds sold and the building finished at a total cost (including the equipment) of $95,000. Then came the big day—Open House. Were we happy?

Dr. O. E. Bryan, then Executive Secretary of the Tennessee Baptist Convention, preached in the morning. That evening Dr. John D. Freeman, then Editor of the Baptist and Reflector, brought the message, challenging and soul-stirring.

Recently we refinanced our loan at a lower rate of interest and have our budget in reasonable reach.

Our present pastor, Dr. C. E. Autrey, does not appear above, but he is here, a fine preacher, great minister and a faithful servant of God.

The music of the church for many years has been under the leadership of Dr. and Mrs. J. D. Carlton, with wonderful success in song and chorus service.

FIRST METHODIST CHURCH

The Methodist Episcopal Church South was organized in the home of J. C. Foster in 1856. Their first house of worship was a small frame building on the west side of town.

We find the records only from 1868 and from then the first pastor, Rev. W. H. Frost, filled the pulpit for the first two years. The charter members are listed as follows:

W. H. Frost, Martin Shackle, Rev. Hutchinson, Rev. Flack, Mrs. J. B. Harrison, Thos. Curlin and wife, Robt. Curlin, Eliza Curlin, Rev. Foster and wife, Miss Fannie Foster, G. Kimberlin and wife, Eli Bynum.

Ministers of the church from the beginning as they served the church are listed from 1868 to 1898. We presume the church building, frame construction, was erected about the time Rev. Frost's appointment was made by the Conference. The building was located almost exactly where the City Hall on Church street now stands.

Pastors of the M. E. Church South in Union City, in the order of their consecutive ministry here, were as follows: W. H. Frost, 1868-69; J. E. Beck, 1870-71; T. L. Beard, 1872; Rev. Rogers, 1873; W. H. Leigh, 1874; W. T. Bolling, 1875; J. D. Bush, 1876; N. Futrell, 1877-78; J. H. Roberts, 1879-81; G. T. Sullivan, 1882-84.

Conference met in Union City in 1883, and the pastors serving the church from that time were: R. W. Irwin, 1885-86; J. G. Clark, 1887-88; J. C. Hooks, 1889-91; E. B. Ramsey, 1892; W. G. Hefley, 1893-94; G. H. Martin, 1895-98.

It is stated the organization of the Sunday School included

UNION CITY

attendance not only of members of the Methodist Church in Union City but of other denominations here having no church house of worship; still others where the Sunday School had not been organized. Therefore the Sunday School at the Methodist Church was exceptionally large.

The first superintendent was D. D. Bryant; assistant, R. T. Curlin. Teachers in the record appeared as follows: W. B. Giddins, Lee Bransford, B. H. Bransford, Miss Fannie Foster, Mrs. G. Kimberlin, J. T. Walton, W. W. Hall, Green Kimberlin, Thos. Jenkins, H. M. Mullins, Mrs. Lukens, Mrs. Parrott, Mrs. Barfield, R. N. Payne.

The enrollment included three hundred names, some of whom may recall the families best known at the time: Sam McClure, J. H. Lynn, J. E. Lynn, Henry Stanfield, John Beck, W. P. Vance, Dr. Massengill, Jas. Roberts, Thos. Nash, Geo. Hall, W. L. Parrott, Kirk Hall, H. P. Hawkins, A. L. Spradlin, Robt. Roberts, Dr. Neblett, J. A. McMurry, W. H. Swiggart, Wm. Massengill, E. C. Curlin, Wm. Gibbs, Dan Beckham, Fletcher Nailling, Jas. Morgan, Misses Bettie Jenkins, Bettie Hamilton, Sallie Beckham, Jennie Bryant, Lila Stanbrough, Alice Bragg, Clara Bransford, Nora Williams, Annie Cathey, Florence Shoffner, Evy Moss, Winnie Mae Moffett, Nettie Beck, Lilly Stanbrough, Hattie Layne, Mary Killough, Nannie Curlin, Dena Morgan, Ada Morgan, Anna B. Nailling, Ida Harrison, Maggie Walker, Delia Brackin, Laura Curlin, Isa Askins.

Taking up the list of pastors appointed to the Union City Station from the preceding page, the following are named:

J. H. Roberts, 1898-1900; R. H. Mahon, 1900-02; W. J. Mecoy, 1902-05; J. G. Wilson, 1905-06; H. B. Johnston, 1906-07; W. C. Sellars, 1907-11; W. W. Adams, 1911-13; W. W. Armstrong, 1913-14; J. J. Thomas, 1914-16; A. C. Bell, 1916-17; G. J. Evans, 1917-18; R. M. Walker, 1918-19; J. D. Freeman, 1919-20; E. M. Mathis, 1921-24; W. P. Duckworth, 1924-25; W. P. Hamilton, 1925-27; W. F. Maxedon, 1927-30; C. E. Norman, 1930-32; A. N. Goforth, 1932-35; O. C. Wrather, 1935-39; O. A. Marrs, 1939.

Superintendents of the Sunday School, beginning with the close of the last century, were W. L. White, H. T. Robinson, Chas. Dietzel, each serving for a number of years with great interest and fine leadership.

The church organists, with Miss Beulah Allen, who served for many years, an instrumentalist of remarkable ability, included Miss Anita Midyett, Miss Rose Sullivan and others leading and directing the musical service.

The Lawson-Wesley Bible class of men has been one of the interesting branches of Sunday School work. Organized under the name of Judge A. J. Lawson, whose inspirational work in lesson review resulted in the growth of the class, it was continued for many more years after the passing of Judge Lawson, and is today, under the able leadership of Hon. Joe L. Fry, an important and interesting part of the Sunday School work.

Board of Stewards now serving as officials of the church are as follows: W. D. Burdine, C. B. Dement, C. D. Haskins, R. D. Kerr, Lee Norrid, Roy Wehman, M. D. Youree; Alwyn Brevard, M. L. Stroud, Cecil Yates, David Knox, Whitesell Harpole, Fred Nailling, Leon Burkett, Lonnie Curtis, J. T. Green, Joe Rogers, W. P. Burnett, Laudell Harris, E. B. Council, W. F. Thweatt, Tom Pyle, Leslie Boone.

Board of Trustees: R. D. Kerr, Fred Nailling, M. A. Blanton, Ben Bransford, J. L. Fry, F. W. Watson.

The brick building, with its Sunday School departments, erected in 1914, was the work of Contractor Lee Bransford, of Union City, and Architect Heavner. The old building replaced was built in 1884, also by Mr. Bransford.

CHURCH OF CHRIST

The Church of Christ in Union City was established in 1857 with about twelve or fifteen members. H. D. Bantau, minister in charge, had the distinction of organizing the first church in Union City, and as a consequence invited other denominations to join in the services.

Some time after Jacob Creath conducted a meeting, and during this meeting about forty members were added to the church. The growth continued until the Civil War. A number of members were killed and others died, and the church building was destroyed by Federal troops.

A year after the war, by faith and courage, another building was erected, but at this time some of the members ceased to be satisfied with the form of worship requiring instrumental music. About fifty withdrew from the congregation and were given permission to worship in the courthouse. This continued until 1892 when a lot was purchased and a building was erected for $1500.

The first to preach in the new church was Rev. David Lipscomb the first Sunday in February, 1893. Rev. F. W. Smith held the first protracted meeting. The first to labor with the congregation was J. R. Hill, of Murray, Ky. After him came C. E. W. Dorris, followed by Oscar Rodgers. As the years passed many others labored here, including J. E. B. Redgeley, E. Dallas Smith, Holliday Trice, Joe Ratcliff, John R. Williams, L. L. Briggance, A. G. Freed, W. S. Long, A. S. M. Dabney, E. A. Elom, E. P. Smith, Claude Hall, Coleman Owrby, T. B. Lovemore, N. B. Hardeman, Charlie Taylor, H. A. Brown, W. A. Foster, Rev. Lowry, R. L. and Paul Colley.

UNION CITY

In 1928 the building in use was found to be inadequate. Two rooms and a concrete front were erected at a cost of $1400. At this time a building fund to be used for the erection of a new church house was begun, attended with the usual lack of full cooperation until the spring of 1938, when definite plans were formulated and the fund increased to $6000. A lot on First street was purchased for $2750 and sold for $2850. The new building on Exchange street cost about $11,500 The first service at the new church was held November 19, 1938, conducted by Minister N. B. Hardeman. The minister employed to take charge was C. J. Garner.

PRESBYTERIAN CHURCH

By an order of the Western District Presbytery, the Union City Presbyterian Church, South, was organized November 28, 1868, by the Rev. M. M. Marshall, D. D., with the following members: Mrs. Mary Coffin, Mrs. U. J. Bradshaw, E. N. Bradshaw, Mrs. Jane M. McCampbell, Mrs. Rebecca Vooheis, Mrs. L. E. Massengill, Mrs. Harriet Lewis, Miss Jane Coffin, Mrs. Jane C. Wilson, Miss Sue Coffin, P. E. Lewis, W. L. Davis, C. H. Campbell, W. P. Massengill, W. C. McCampbell, Miss M. E. Caldwell, and E. N. Bradshaw. Rev. M. M. Marshall, D.D. was the first pastor, in the progress of the church followed by the Revs. W. Beale, J. B. Carne, C. M. Shepperson, J. D. Latimer, J. T. Rothrock, S. L. Grigsby, S. J. Martin, H. C. Kegley, J. D. Wilson, F. L. Twing, J. B. Zernow, E. P. Lindsay, J. M. Stafford.

The organization of this church took place in a room in Bradshaw's schoolhouse, and here, too, services were held for a time, but during the pastorate of Dr. Marshall and through his instrumentality a house of worship was erected. This was dedicated the first Sabbath in May, 1874. This building, however, was later remodeled and rededicated in 1898 during the pastorate of Rev. H. C. Kegley.

The First Presbyterian Church, located on North First street, has the distinction of being the oldest Presbyterian Church in Obion County, having been organized in 1868. The Rev. Isaac Caldwell moved from East Tennessee, with his family, in 1866 and settled in Union City. They were among the first Presbyterians to live here. Early in 1867 Rev. Caldwell began preaching here, and the same year the Rev. M. M. Marshall of Fayetteville, Tenn., came to Union City on an "evangelizing tour" and preached for several days. The following year his services were obtained for regular preaching on fifth Sundays, in connection with the pastorate he accepted at Trenton. Other Presbyterians having moved to Union City, the church was organized in 1868, with a charter membership of sixteen.

The erection of a building was begun in 1872, which was completed and furnished within a period of one and one-half years, with a congregation of 22 members, at a cost of $4000. The church lot was purchased for the nominal price of $10. On November 28, 1938, the church celebrated its anniversary by breaking ground for a Sunday School building annex attached to the east wall of the church, providing class rooms ample to accommodate the Sunday School and its needs.

Since its organization twenty ministers have served the church as stated supply and regular pastors. Two sons of the church have entered the Gospel ministry, the Rev. Wm. Thorne and Rev. John G. Garth.

The Rev. Geo. F. Johnson came to the church in 1939 and serves a growing congregation in full-time Sunday services, besides taking an active interest in Sunday School, young people's work and giving also attention to Boy Scout Troop work.

Rev. R. J. Hunter, pastor of the Union City church for a number of years, now located in Kentucky, was married in Union City.

FIRST CHRISTIAN CHURCH

The First Christian Church of Union City has completed more than eighty years of service to this community. The church was first organized in 1848 at Old Republican Meeting-house, four miles west of the city. The records show the first meeting was held October 29, 1848. There were thirteen charter members.

General Gibbs, who owned much land embracing Union City, donated to the congregation a lot in the Gibbs addition, corner Second and Lee streets. The first house of worship was erected on this site in 1857, but was destroyed by Federal troops in 1862. The church now has in its possession a letter, from the United States Quartermaster Department, which was accompanied by a check for $1800 to cover damages on the old building.

When the war was over the little band of disciples, nearly all of them stricken by the war, set to work to build another house of worship. This second house, a brick structure, was completed in 1868. About this time a great increase in members is shown by the old records. The consecrated Jacob Creath, of Kentucky, held a revival which was generally effective in the work of the church and its spiritual growth.

The congregation has ever been found in the forefront of every movement which looked to the upbuilding of moral and religious life among its people. The church has been favored with noted ministers in its pulpit. Among the number of the early days are recalled the names of Thomas Osborne and J. H. Roulhac. A list of others include Rev. J. E. Stuart, in the pulpit in 1912

UNION CITY

when the latest splendid building was erected, also Revs. W. H. Sheffer, J. Randall Farris, J. J. Castleberry, E. D. Fritz, C. W. Lipsey. The latter was a native of Georgia and minister for the congregation at Savannah for some time.

Constant growth of the church created the necessity of larger building for Sunday school work. For this purpose Miss Ella Whipple, well-beloved member of the congregation, willed $500 to be used in the construction of an educational building. Miss Whipple's dream, as well as that of many other members, was realized. On May 22, 1938, the "Educational Building" was actually under construction and by September 1st was practically completed.

The new addition, erected at a cost of $10,000 is 65 feet long and 45 feet wide. The first floor has an auditorium with seating capacity of 250, and includes kitchen, serving quarters and stage. On the second floor are nine spacious rooms for Bible school classes, which can be used to accommodate 500 people.

Dedication sermon was delivered by Rev. W. P. Harman, State Secretary and Director of Religious Education for Christian churches in Tennessee.

On Sunday, April 5, 1941, Rev. G. Albert Lollis, succeeding Rev. Lipsey, delivered his first sermon at the First Christian Church in Union City. Rev. Lollis came to Union City from the Clay Street Christian Church in Nashville.

CUMBERLAND PRESBYTERIAN CHURCH

The Union City Cumberland Presbyterian Church was organized in 1858 by Rev. Jo McLeskey and C. W. McBride, with E. B. Lovelace, J. T. Brown and J. S. Whitsett as ruling elders. Disbanded on account of the Civil War, the church was reorganized in 1866. Ruling elders at this time were E. B. Lovelace, J. T. Brown, J. S. Whitsett and F. W. Matthews. During the next fifty years after its organization the church was served by twenty pastors, namely: Revs. C. W. McBride, J. W. Morrow, J. H. W. Jones, M. Lile, D. Brighton, Wm. Robinson, R. A. Cody, F. M. McWherter, S. H. Braley, W. H. Bunton, A. W. McDowell, Silas Perkins, J. A. McDonald, B. T. Watson, E. E. Hendrix, W. R. Atkinson, T. J. Tyler, J. L. Hudgins, J. H. Zwingle, C. M. Zwingle.

The present pastor, W. B. Cunningham, began his pastorate in April, 1916, and has served the congregation for 25 years. four years.

Of the twenty pastors the following only are living at the present time: B. T. Watson, E. E. Hendrix and C. M. Zwingle.

The first church house was a plain frame building, located on the lot where the present manse now stands. In 1892 a very beautiful brick structure was erected on the southwest corner of Church and Home streets, replacing the old frame building, and the church manse was built on the lot vacated by the old church.

The architect for the construction of the new church was J. J. Dugan, the contractor: John Carter. Both of these men died before the building was finished, and one of the elders, T. J. Harvey, took over responsibility of finishing it. Rev. J. A. McDonald was pastor at the time and the church was built at a cost of $12,000, compared to the present building costs, a very small amount of money.

In 1896, when Rev. B. T. Watson was pastor, the church membership numbered 245, only twenty-six of whom are still members. The elders at that time were: J. W. Burney, clerk of the session, J. J. Cherry, A. Fowler, T. J. Harvey, J. F. Howard, T. J. Latimer, F. M. McRee, W. N. Stone, N. K. Moore, C. J. Rogers, H. N. Sherrill. The deacons were: W. J. Edwards, treasurer, and chairman, W. W. Lovelace, secretary, H. C. Philpot, collector, John R. George, A. H. Latimer, W. S. Moore, R. H. Harper, W. McClanahan, Algie Sherrill and T. J. Shoffner. T. J. Harvey was leader and manager of the choir; Mrs C. H. Sherrill, organist and Miss Pearl Pettus, assistant organist. The total amount contributed to all purposes was $1336.61, with an indebtedness of $397.71 at the end of the year.

The second church was destroyed by fire on March 23, 1927, and replaced in 1928 by the beautiful buff brick building erected on the foundation of the old church. The present building was completed at a cost of about $65,000. Rev. W. B. Cunningham, now pastor, was pastor when the new church was built. The architects were Tisdale, Stone and Pinson, of Nashville. The contractors were Hill and Merryman, of Fulton, Ky.

In 1916, when Rev. W. B. Cunningham, the present pastor, took charge of the church, the following were ruling elders: J. F. Howard, F. M. McRee, J. A. Reeves, W. J. Davidson, J. W. Burney, I. S. Kirby, W. E. Hudgins, W. W. Lovelace, J. A. Prieto, G. W. Tucker. Only three of these men are still living: Mr. Tucker, of Colorado, W. W. Lovelace, and W. E. Hudgins, of this city. The board of deacons at that time was as follows: J. A. Baird, H. M. Harper, E. P. Grissom and Wallace Moffett.

Some of those who have served the church as choir directors during its existence are: T. J. Harvey, Mrs. J. F. Howard, Mrs. R. A. Napier, Miss Pearl Pettus, Miss Oral Pace, Mrs. W. B. Cunningham. Of the number who have served the church as organists for the same time: Mrs. Florence Shoffner Harris, Mrs. Allie V. Sherrill, Mrs. Winnie Mae Moffett Napier, Mrs. Levisa Walker Howard, Mrs. Emma Walker Harris, Mrs. Bess Curlin, Miss Keller, Miss

UNION CITY

Marcella Davidson, Mrs. Nannie Coldwell Teas, Mrs. Ada Coldwell Howard, Mrs. Louise Adams Heathcock and Mrs. Margaret Cox.

Some notable facts and statistics during the first forty years of its progress (1856-1896) the church membership grew in number to 245. Of that number 27 are still members. Fourteen pastors had served the congregation, eight years of church organization being interrupted. Rev. B. T. Watson was then pastor. In the year 1916 the membership had been increased to 261, a net increase of only sixteen members in twenty years. Eight pastors had served during that period.

Since 1916 the membership has increased to 464. Of that number 261 were members in 1916, showing a net increase since 1916 of 203 members. The board of ruling elders now in active service are as follows: Wilton J. Berry, F. B. Caldwell, H. P. Conrad, W. I. Garrett, David A. Guy, C. W. Hall, Harry M. Harper, Chas. S. Howard, W. E. Hudgins, W. W. Lovelace, J. S. Lovelace, E. T. Mitchell, R. E. McGowan, J. C. McRee, W. D. McAnulty, W. E. Shropshire, John Walker. Members recently ordained: Mose Cunningham, Seth Dunlap, Joe O. Harmon, Paul G. Hudgins, Fred Muse, Edwin Stone, Carl A. Lowrance, Robt. A. Everett.

Observing the twenty-fifth anniversary of Rev. W. B. Cunningham's connection as pastor of the Cumberland Presbyterian Church in Union City, April 5, 1941, special services were held. The Rev. Geo. W. Burroughs, of Nashville, a classmate in college, delivered an appropriate address on the subject of God's shepherd, in the presence of an overflowing audience.

ST. JAMES EPISCOPAL CHURCH

When Gen. Geo. W. Gibbs laid out the town of Union City, he set aside lots for the Baptist, Methodist, Christian and Presbyterian churches, as there were adherents of those denominations living in the vicinity. The Cumberland Presbyterian Church already had a building lot, so he made no provision for that denomination.

The Episcopal and Catholic churches had not been given lots, so Mrs. Alexander Campbell, of Jackson, a granddaughter of General Gibbs, gave a block on First street large enough for a church and parish house, surrounded by trees and gardens, to the Episcopal church. Years went by and nothing was done about building on this lot. It was suggested to Mrs. Campbell that she ask Bishop Thomas F. Gailor, at the time Bishop of Tennessee, to return the property to her for the purpose of disposing of it for her own benefit, but she would not consider the suggestion. In 1893 or four a minister by the name of Trout asked and received permission from the Waddell family to hold services in the little wooden building which was built and dedicated to the use of the Swedenborgian Church. About that time the Bishop sold the Episcopal property for $1000, which of course, was enough only to build a small church. But there was no lot for a building. So with the spirit of understanding and liberality, in view of the conditions, Dr. W. M. Turner, of Union City, became a genuine benefactor in donating and deeding to the church the lot on which St. James Church was built, which was completed and the corner stone laid in 1905. The church is located on Church street about a block from the N. C. & St. L. Ry. station—and G. M. & O.

According to the Diocesan Journals, the following named ministers have served the church: Rev. Robert W. Rhames, 1905-07; Rev. Emile S. Harper, 1908; Arch Deacon McCabe, 1910-17; Arch Deacon Root, 1925-29; Rev. Geo. W. Whitmeyer, 1929.

In the year 1930 Rector Geo. W. Goodson took charge of the Union City Mission and also that of Dyersburg.

There were in 1939 about 75 baptized and confirmed members of St. James Church and a church school of fifty-nine members.

SWEDENBORGIAN

A Swedenborgian church was organized in Union City in a building on North First street. This was probably in the eighties. Membership was confined mostly to the families of Lawyer Seid Waddell and Judge Joel Waddell. Afterwards a church house was built on East Church street, near St. James Church. For many years Rev. L. G. Landenberger, of St. Louis, was minister.

IMMACULATE CONCEPTION
(Catholic Church)

The Immaculate Conception Catholic Church of Union City was built in 1891 by Father York, who was in charge of the parish at that time. The church building is located on the corner of Church and Fifth streets in Union City.

When the church was built there were enough Catholic families in Union City to make up a substantial congregation. However, due to changing conditions and moving of members for half a century the number was reduced to not more than eighteen families.

For the past twelve years this church has been cared for with priests from Louisville and Owensboro Diocese. During the year, 1938, Bishop William L. Adrain, of Nashville, realizing the need of a resident pastor in Union City, took it back into the Nashville Diocese to be taken care of by Tennessee priests.

In August, 1939, Father Edward Dolan was sent to take charge of the Union City church and the one at Paris. A new modern two-story brick veneer rectory has been built for occupancy.

UNION CITY

Father Dolan comes to Union City from the Sacred Heart Church in Memphis, where he has been stationed for five years past. While there he was associated with several organizations doing young people's work.

By having a resident pastor the members of the Union City church are able to attend mass daily at 7 a. m. as well as each Sunday.

UNION CITY NEWSPAPERS

It is said that the first newspaper in Union City was established by W. C. Lawhorn before the Civil War. Another venture some time after the war was the newspaper established by Chas. N. and Wm. B. Gibbs, sons of Gen. Geo. W. Gibbs, pioneer and founder of the town of Union City. In any event the name of Gibbs has been inseparably linked with local history, beginning with the division of land and lots for railroads and schools, for public uses and private homes. Chas. N. Gibbs was a former Secretary of State of Tennessee (1873-81) and practiced law in Union City. Other members of the family were lawyers, merchants and pioneers in all the local town and county affairs. A descendant of this pioneer family, M. G. Gibbs, now a multi-millionaire druggist, is the founder and managing executive of the People's Drug Stores, Inc., a corporation with headquarters in Washington City.

The publication of the Union City Herald began in 1867, operated by David and Daniel Chambers. The latter in exclusive ownership and control of the Herald, sustained a reputation for some years in the publication of a paper of not a little notoriety, filled with somewhat remarkable and original local racy quips and brevities. The Courier, another local paper, was established by W. R. Hamby. The Reveille, still another, was operated by N. B. Morton, shortly after moving to Texas, and returning started the Anchor, succeeded by W. R. Andrews in 1882. W. W. McDowell, publishing the Anchor for a short time, located in Chicago, and there he met and formed an acquaintance with Marcus Daley, a Montana silver king. Mr. McDowell became Mr. Daley's confidential associate, finally acquiring mining interests in his own name. Some years followed and Wallace McDowell, entering Montana politics, became Lieutenant Governor of Montana, followed some years later by his appointment as Minister to Erin, under President Roosevelt. In Ireland death intervened.

Later in the eighties L. D. Cardwell, native of Dresden, engaged in the newspaper business in Union City. He opened with the Chronicle, which was changed to the Solid South and then Our Country, the latter being consolidated with printing inter-

OBION COUNTY HISTORY

ests of J. J. Cartan. N. B. Morton, who had sold the Anchor, followed Mr. Cardwell and Mr. Cartan took over the job printing outfit.

At this period J. H. McDowell, father of the publisher, instituted a farm paper, supporting the Populist party. Mr. McDowell, Sr., was a leader of the Prohibition movement, first a member of the legislature as direct representative, then the State Senate. He was author of the Tennessee Anti-Gambling Act.

In 1886 W. C. Tatom and W. H. Griffin established the Obion Democrat, soon developing into a leading Tennessee weekly newspaper. The editors and publishers took a general interest in State politics and local affairs. The partnership was finally dissolved, Mr. Tatom going to Nashville to join the editorial staff of the American. The editor then became attached to the American Expeditionary forces with appointment as colonel, and was in command of the contingent in Obion County during the night riding outbreak at Reelfoot Lake. Mr. Griffin assumed publication of the Democrat for some years until his demise in 1899. Mrs. F. W. Preston, sister of L. D. Cardwell, and her husband succeeded to the publication of the Obion Democrat. They continued for some years and then J. M . Brice, publisher of the News-Banner at Troy, took over the plant which was consolidated with the News-Banner. At the time Mr. Brice had located in Union City and published his paper here for a number of years.

E. P. Waddell, assisted by E. R. Kersh, succeeded Mr. Brice and published the News-Banner for a short time. The Waddell interests were then absorbed by John Waddell and G. B. Baird and consolidated with the Commercial, and under the name of The Commercial G. B. Baird continued for some time, with the exception of one year in which E. H. Marshall was again interested. Mr. Baird received appointment in the Browning administration at Nashville and The Commercial interests were acquired by R. A. Harry. Then in 1938 Mr. Harry moved to Virginia to take over a newspaper at Suffolk and Frank W. Smith, from Chicago locating in Union City acquired the newspaper plant of the (Obion County) Commercial, taking over under the name mentioned in 1939. Mr. Smith, assuming publication, had in view the project of improving his plant with offset equipment to modernize the work of publication with tabloid features and enlarging job work facilities.

Returning to the period prior to the twentieth century, a weekly paper known as the Commercial-Courier was instituted by Miles & Wise. W. R. Andrews succeeded in acquiring the plant and publishing for a short time, sold his paper to Pearson & Moore. The latter publishers operated for a few years and relinquished again to W. R. Andrews.

UNION CITY

Mr. Andrews closed in 1901 and the newspaper plant and effects were absorbed by E. H. Marshall and J. A. Baird. On April 29, 1901, Marshall & Baird took control and changed the name of the paper to The Commercial. Then followed a newspaper partnership continuing for twenty-three and one-half years, surviving competition and leading in newspaper achievements. Marshall & Baird's newspaper interests were terminated with the sale of the paper and plant to John Waddell and G. B. Baird in 1924.

G. D. Capps and W. S. Godwin in 1926 began publication of a newspaper in Union City called The Messenger. Paul Bushart afterwards became interested and soon after the press and paper were sold to C. B. Dement, of Rutherford County, Tenn. As announced in the anniversary number of 1937, an edition promoted by the office staff and employees,, The Union City Daily Messenger, attended with the usual struggle, became an established institution in Union City. A new home was built on South First street, with suitable offices, accommodations, modern newspaper equipment, job office, etc., all the elements of successful newspaper production in Union City.

On September 2, 1940, the Union City Daily Messenger newspaper and job equipment, including building on South First street, all complete, was offered for sale and sold to Ed S. Critchlow of Kokomo, Indiana, and mutual negotiations followed, with transfer in full to Mr. Dement's successor, taking charge immediately.

Mr. Critchlow's announcement, as editor, was assurance to the subscription patrons and friends of paper that continued effort for the dissemination of local and general news, would be not only the purpose of the paper, but that newspaper service would be extended and augmented to meet the demands of both readers and advertising patrons. As a Democrat, Mr. Critchlow announced also that the policy of the paper would be in line with the party and the Administration of President Roosevelt.

The editor came to Union City with training and experience as a reporter in Elkhart, Ind., where he was located for several years before moving to Union City.

UNION CITY HOTELS

One of the first hotels in Union City was the Pulliam House on East Main street, on one of the lots now occupied by the Verhine buildings, a little west of the First Methodist Church.

Another hotel was located immediately south of the railroad crossing where the Palace Hotel now stands. It was a frame building known as the Southern Hotel, operated for a time by R. A. Blackman, later used to accommodate overflow guests from the

Brackin Hotel. The floor level of the building was considerably lower than the railroad track. The office faced north with a lobby opening out toward the N. C. & St. L. railroad.

The Fowlkes House, operated in the eighties and nineties by Dick (R. W.) Fowlkes, was located on the postoffice lot, corner Washington and Second streets.

Another hotel was the Miller House on the corner north of the Brackin, now the Blue Bell Laundry and Dry Cleaners.

Before the Brackin Hotel was built Capt. Wm. Askins operated the Metropolitan Hotel, a frame house on the same site, two story with front balcony facing the M. & O. railroad. This building was removed to be replaced by a two-tory brick by J. A. Brackin, who operated the new hotel for many years. The old frame building was rolled back to the lot now occupied by the Coca-Cola Bottling plant, owned and operated by Hugh Smith. Part of the Brackin front wall with office door and windows are still standing as a part of the front of the Blue Bell. With the passing of Mr. Brackin the hotel was operated by a number of managers, Geo. LeFils, Rafe Chitwood, Dave Bryant, S. D. Woosley. The building was finally dismantled by fire in 1912.

The Palace Hotel, east and south of the railroad crossing, was built by J. C. Reynolds, for many years a railroad conductor on the M. & O. R. R., beginning with the Green Line on the N .C. & St. L. Ry. The building was erected in 1896 and operated by J. C. Reynolds, with W. M. Dismukes and Dave Bryant as clerks.

Following the death of Mr. Reynolds the property was sold to J. C. McRee and A. F. Tittsworth, who operated less than a year and sold to Mrs. W. W. Heathcock. This was in July, 1920. From that time to the present Mrs. Heathcock has been proprietor and manager, making extensions on the building, with rooms, baths and equipment amounting to double the amount of first investment.

The Mayflower Hotel on Second street is a popular house, with accommodations and liberal patronage.

The Davy Crockett is the largest hotel in Union City, located on the corner of First and Lee streets. The building is constructed with pressed brick and stone, with lobby and coffee shop on First street. It is six stories high, with one hundred rooms, modern fixtures and furniture, baths, telephones and electric fans. Hotel was built by E. K. Beck, deceased, now under the management of Mrs. Beck and Mr. Ralph Morton.

THEATRES AND MOVIES

The first theatre in Union City was the Union City Opera House, located on the same lot now occupied by the City Hall.

UNION CITY

It was built as a church house by the Methodist congregation in Union City, sometime after the organization of the church in 1856, probably in the early seventies.

In 1883 when the new brick church on the corner of East Main street and Ury street was built, the old building was vacated and converted into a theatre. D. I. Verhine, for many years a salesman with Morgan-Verhine, Inc., remodeled the house, installing stage, seats, scenery and otherwise providing suitable accommodations for theatrical entertainment in Union City. For a period of years Mr. Verhine operated the house as manager, and during that time some well known traveling companies appeared, filling engagements with current theatrical attractions, including the Huntleys in "Rip Van Winkle," the play "Blue Jeans" and others that had big-time billing. The New York Mirror, well known theatrical magazine, from its Union City correspondent, Dave Levy, quoted Mr. Verhine as the youngest operator-manager of his time.

Acquiring some lots on East Main street, H. P. Hawkins built an opera house, as it was called, probably in 1889 or maybe a little before that. Part of the old building remains as the front of the Farmer-Lovelace Wholesale Grocery Co. business house. Mr. Hawkins operated a theatre here for a number of years. In 1898 the property was sold to John T. Walker and became the Walker Opera House, with J. W. Woosley as manager. Mr. Woosley was succeeded by A. L. Cox (now manager of the Capitol Theatre), succeeding Mr. Woosley some five years. Here once the famous singer, Clara Louise Kellogg, filled a star engagement, with other less noted but popular attractions following.

In 1904, with J. C. Reynolds leading the movement, stock subscriptions were taken for a new theatre building in Union City, locating on South First street, to be called Reynolds Theatre, now remodeled and converted into the Liberty Cash Grocery store. A. L. Cox became manager of the Reynolds Theatre, continuing for a period of twenty-two years. Into this theatre came many traveling companies, some of them noted on the stage, including Harry Beresford, Hortense Nielsen, the Isle of Spice (thirty-five people), the Lyman Twins and others. There was one company which made regular annual visits here, and at one time the Dudleys (Frank and wife) brought Miss Aubrey to play Camille, a really interesting dramatic event.

Mr. Cox remained when the theatre was turned into a motion-picture house until the opening of the Capitol.

Probably the first picture show here was introduced to the public by Mr. Clark, who opened the Lyric in the building on First street now occupied by the Freid Five and Ten Cent Store. Here came some of the original two and three-reelers—the "flickers." Following came another opened by W. C. Morris, the Francis Airdome on Washington Avenue. There we saw Francis X. Bushman and Beverly Bayne. Soon afterwards when the Morrises moved and opened the Gem on First street, afterwards the Kaufman store, we saw Mary Pickford, "America's Sweetheart," and others. Fire destroyed the Gem. Other picture shows were here known as Jimmy's, etc.

In 1927 the Capitol was opened on North First street, one of Tony Sudekum's moving picture show houses in the Crescent group of southern picture theatres. Here is where Union City and community really became familiar with the stars and great Hollywood features, here the fade out of the silent screen king, Charley Chaplin, here "flickers" disappeared into currents of smooth flowing cinema—the talkies with the Clark Gables, and Warner Baxters, the Shearers and the Loys, where Dame Nature in technicolor clothed the "Wizard of Oz" and painted Maeterlink's "Bluebird" in rainbow hues. And greatest of all here is where we saw Dionysian genius crowned in the art of the Mitchell epic, "Gone With The Wind".

Mr. Cox, manager of the Capitol, assisted by J. C. Cox, is still the suave and popular gentleman, and the Capitol Theatre is now a modern playhouse, with its redecorated interior, its metal frame plush seats and its Neon front, a blaze of colored lights, a modern theatre in Union City.

CIVIC AFFAIRS

Union City has her Main street but First street is her "Broadway," extending four blocks north and south almost solid with stores and shops, with lateral business streets, including Church street, Washington avenue, Second street and Main from the Fulton highway—west across town to the Turner field ball park.

Our business and shopping sections keep pace with the age. For years Union City has been a popular shopping center, second to none anywhere outside of big cities. Here are some of the department stores, popular price stores, five and ten and five to one dollar, dress shops, numbers of them all over the city, and accommodating and accomplished business sales people to wait on the trade.

Here we have the modern cash grocery stores and the individual service stores, with motor delivery and suitable accommodations.

REDPATH CHAUTAUQUA

The Redpath Chautauqua, under the Harrison management from Chicago, was a regular annual ten-day season of entertain-

UNION CITY

ment in Union City from 1912 to 1929, presenting a varied program under a large tent, usually in the midsummer.

The first season brought Bohumir Kryl and his Chicago Band, Frank Dixon, Opie Read, Judge Blair, Governor Hock, Agnes Doyle and Judge Kavanaugh. The 1913 season brought Hon. Joseph W. Folk, Missouri; the Ben Greet Players and Adam Bede. In 1914 Kryl and his band returned, with Strickland Gillilan, Kellogg Light Opera Co., Dr. Amherst Ott. The 1915 season brought us the Metropolitan Grand Opera star, Alice Nielsen, the tenor, Bartalotti, and the Savranoffs, Russian players. In 1916 came another grand opera star, Julia Claussen, with the White Hussar Band and Genola Maclaren, reader. In 1917 Creatore's Band, Congresswoman, Jeannete Rankin and the Mikado players appeared. In 1918 the platform orator was Sir John Foster Fraser, English war newspaper correspondent, with very little to say of the famous Thirtieth Division in France. In 1919 Kryl came back and with him Ada Ward, the English entertainer in France, more generous to the American soldier. In 1920 Dr. Carolyn Geisel, noted British authority on medical science, spoke and the light opera "Pinafore," was featured. In 1921 Dr. Frederick Monsen spoke on Mexico and Franco Villa, and the play was "The Man From Home." In 1922 Hon. Chas. Brough, of Arkansas, took the platform and the two plays were "Turn to the Right" and "Friendly Enemies." In 1923 John Temple Graves, noted Georgia journalist and orator, was presented, and the play "Meanest Man in the World." In 1924 Hon. Rainey Bennett was the orator, John Ratto the mimic, and the play, "Give and Take." In 1925 the famous light opera, "Robin Hood," and the play "Adam and Eva," were the features. In 1926 Tamaki Muira, vocalist appeared in a concert version of "Madam Butterfly," with the plays, "So This is London" and "Applesauce." In 1927 Ruth Bryan Owen, daughter of Wm. Jennings Bryan, was the principal speaker, with the play, "The Goose Hangs High." In 1929 Hon. Nellie Tayloe Ross, former Governor of Wyoming, Lorna Doone Jackson, singer, and the play "Sun Up," were among the closing numbers of the Redpath Circuit in Union City.

BUSINESS HOUSES IMPROVED—NEW BUILDINGS

The residence sections of Union City have been wonderfully changed in the past thirty years, but many of the buildings in the business center remain with few exceptions much the same in appearance. A cluster of business houses on South First street, including the Davy Crockett Hotel, Obion County Motor Co. (Ford plant), Union City Daily Messenger office, Salant-Salant Shirt Factory and the shops below, Liberty Cash Grocery Co., the Grill, filling stations and restaurants, Roper's Floral Shop, complete a practically new business section in Union City. Buildings in the middle section on First street comparatively new and remodeled are Morgan-Verhine, Inc., Ritz Theatre, McElroy's, Nailling's corner, Shatz & Byer, on the other side the Third National Bank, Andrews Jewelry Store, Black & White Store, Alfred's Piggly-Wiggly, Jones Furniture, Caldwell's Five to One Dollar, Draper & Darwin. First street north of Church are the Capitol Theatre, Pittsburgh Paint Store, Grissom buildings, on the other side the Old National Bank, Hamilton Cafe, Gibbs buildings.

Improvements have been made on First street also on the Shatz Bros., New York and Jackson stores, the Farmers Exchange Bank and the former Wehman Hardware Store remodeled almost completely for the A. & P. Food Store.

Improvements on the Grissom buildings include a Sears branch in Union City, mail-order office and showroom.

A year ago the Paul Nailling Implement Building on Second street, north of Church, a very large salesroom and warehouse, fifty by 100 feet, was built completely new of brick and concrete. Mr. Nailling has one of the most important business establishments in Union City, representing International motors and machinery, and one that is making Union City an important headquarters both of general distribution and sales. Lately Mr. Nailling closed with the County Judge of Obion County for sale and delivery 17 school buses, built by the International Company, to be put into service of the county school system.

On North First street, cornering on Main at the railroad crossing, is the new Esso Station, built and leased to the Standard Oil Co. It is of glazed white brick and red tile, a very fine model of modern service station construction.

On East Main at the M. & O. R. R. crossing J. C. Burdick, Sr., and Jack Burdick have one of the new enterprises, a building remodeled with insurance offices, fish and sea food salesroom and a dispensing department of ices and cold drinks.

The Home Ice Co. completed recently a large brick ice plant on the lot formerly occupied by the Union City Ice & Coal. The building on Main street north of the McAdoo Coal office is also operated by the Home Ice Co.

The building of a new Obion County Courthouse in Union City was a WPA construction project, completed in 1940 at a cost of $200,000. Building is 75 by 100 feet, two main floors, basement, an additional story at the top, reduced in size, for the county jail. Materials used in general construction are, for frame work, concrete and steel, outside walls of stone, doors and window frames of steel. Entire building, interior walls, floors and ceiling, are of standard fireproof materials. Description of departments and offices is found elsewhere in this work.

UNION CITY

The new Central School buildings and gymnasium, Ury and College streets, constructed in 1936-37, is also a WPA construction project, built at a cost of $105,000.

Another WPA project is the County Health Department building in Union City on West Church street, very complete in appointments for the use of the County Physician, Health Nurse and assistants, a $10,000 job.

The City Hall, a comparatively new building on Church at the corner of Third street, complete with general office departments on the main floor, assembly hall above fire department and equipment in the annex on the north side and facing west, is a W. C. Kelly contract completed in 1930.

There are in Union City entire streets of new homes including High street, Sterling Court, South Home street, many new homes in the vicinity of the Brown Shoe Factory buildings, new homes on Todd street and intersections, and new homes filling up vacant lots all over the city.

Mayor Miles' new residence on East Main street and its sloping lawns comprise one of the show places of Union City.

The Armory building, provided for by Federal, State, county and municipal aid, located on West Main street, completed in early part of 1941. This building is 65 by 150 feet feet, with an auditorium 65 by 95 feet, to be used for public assembly on occasions.

BUSINESS BUILDINGS BURNED

In the last century on Church street, north side, between the Dietzel corner on the west to the telephone exchange inclusive on the east, practically all the buildings, most of them two-story, were destroyed by fire. This section was rebuilt with one-story houses up to the Dietzel corner.

Another destructive fire in 1905 swept the Moss Drug Store on Church street, south side, and with it heavy damage was done to the house and the stock of merchandise in the Robinson-Bransford & Co. place of business on First street.

Another fire in the building occupied by Hardy Ligon Furniture Store on the corner of First and Church streets, now the Old National Bank corner, was a total loss to the store and heavy damage to the building. This was probably 1908 or ten, and then a new building was constructed by John T. Walker, who bought the property of Dr. Nailling, and the Harpole-Walker Furniture Store was opened. The Old National Bank now owns and occupies the building which has been extensively improved.

The Old Brackin Hotel, now the Blue Bell Laundry and Cleaners plant, or part of it, was wrecked by fire in 1912. Only a portion of the front, which opened to the office and billiard rooms, now stands as a part of the laundry section.

In 1915 the Gem Theatre building, now part of the Black & White Store, was swept by fire. The picture show and equipment was completely destroyed and the building was burned from the floor to the roof through the center. The improved building, occupied by McGowen & Jones in 1932, burned again, and losses to both stock and buildings ran into thousands of dollars.

Two disastrous fires reduced almost to total loss, first the Nailling and Carter buildings on the corner of First street and Washington avenue July 22, 1909, next on March 23, 1912, the Morgan and Swiggart buildings, about one hundred feet front on east side of First street, between Church street and Washington avenue. The latter were occupied by the merchants, Morgan-Verhine Co. and Beckham-Jones-Murphey.

The large four-story brick building, occupied by the Dahnke-Walker Milling Co., for many years, one of the leading industries in Union City, with its corn and wheat products, was destroyed by fire in 1925.

OLD COUNTY FAIR TO TURNER MEMORIAL FIELD

From the old county fair in the eighties, with the horse races, buggy and riding horses, ball games, farm and field and annual exhibitions, neighborhood associations, romance and rivalry, we arrive after fifty years to the motorized age with new sports and modern diversions.

There are a few probably who remember the first old fair grounds, the amphitheatre and second-story parade circle, the ring below, Dock Thomasson as manager and Billy Massengill as ringmaster. Then the second fair association, with Wilford Farris as president and Walden Woosley as secretary, a week's exhibition of the heavyweight, John L. Sullivan, and another week of Benoit's airplane, which played ante-over the rain shed after several tiresome efforts.

There are those who also remember the ball games, the local matches, and finally the big event between the Jackson and the Union City ball teams, the rivalry which continued for years.

At the time the local ball fans and high priests of popular diversions included such names as Max Layne, Geo. LeFils, Harry Robinson, Soule Warterfield, Will Barry, Will Crittendon, Jack Verhine, George Hardy, Walden Woosley, George Dahnke, John George, Wilford Farris, Will Griffin, Billy and Willis Nailling, Jas. R. Morgan, Jim Mott, George Bell, Charley Gibbs, Will Davis, Will Flack, Will Moore, John Killough, Will White, Wallace McDowell, Sam Carey, Henry Stanfield, Andy Harpole, Dave Caldwell, Robt. Whitesell, Will Scates, Sam Bratton, Dr. T. J. Ed-

UNION CITY

wards, Will Edwards, Tom Greer, Forney Arnn, Gus White, Dave Lowenheim, Jake Levy.

And then later when Frank Watts, president of the Union City Athletic Association, organized his famous baseball team, the sports fans and choice spirits were J. C. Reynolds, Tom Pierce, Dick Edwards, Dave Bryant, W. M. Dismukes, Claude Andrews, Cully McRee, Hunter Elam, Ben Bramham, Dr. W. M. Turner, Joe Prieto, Embrey Beck, Harvey Alexander, Algie Sherrill, Jas. Haguewood, Jerry Malone, Clifford Jones, Ed Grissom, Morris Miles, Jake Gibbs, Joe Rogers, Charley Tomerlin, Tom Lovelace, Will Lovelace.

There is no effort here to recall the young women who reigned in social circles and romantic affairs, just those of the men who found it a duty as well as a pleasure to mingle and keep alive the mutual and friendly relations of homefolks and visiting friends.

Then we turn the pages to the present and find a new age, another generation and the magic of modern invention and advance in all the functions of life. Now we see the motion picture theatre, hear the radio from every quarter of the world, know what other people are doing and hear them speak and sing, as if they were all under one roof. It's a small world. There are no strangers, rubes, or Sally Anns, no city slickers, and lion guards roar only when a virgin passes.

We have marched with the spirit of the age, and the transition brings its compensation. Instead of the county fair, the shining buggy and the prancing beauty, Union City has a glorious ball park, the Turner Memorial Field, and the great national sport of kings and commoners, with mammoth grandstand framed with steel, diamond and grounds flanked with concrete walls, illuminated for evening games with electric floodlights from towering standards.

Union City with its baseball organization is a member of the Kitty League, including Paducah, Owensboro, Mayfield, Fulton, Jackson, Union City, Bowling Green and Hopkinsville.

Elected and serving for two years (1939-40), B. F. Howard, president, of the Kitty League, retired with an administration of record attendance and financial success. Mr. Howard was accorded general approval by the league. A citizen of Union City, Mr. Howard is manager of the John T. Walker Insurance Company.

The local organization, members of the Kitty League in Union City, in the annual election of 1941, honored Cecil Moss with re-election as president for the fourth consecutive year, with Gerald Woosley as secretary succeeding David Walker Harris. Mr. Moss and Mr. Harris were accorded credit in liberal measure for the success and permanency of the great national sport in Union City and the popularity of Union City as a baseball center.

Then again the Turner Memorial Field is an amphitheatre for the annual horse show, another popular and important institution for the promotion of training and preserving the blood lines of the great American stud, sponsored in Union City by the Jaycee, G. B. White, Jr., and a coterie of equine sportsmen.

The shows for the years 1939-40 were distinctly successful, bringing to Union City some of the finest stables—blood, training and talent—aristocrats of the show ring, versatile, tractable and beautiful.

Rare occasions, these, attended with throngs of fans and fine feathers sincerely devoted to fine horses and horsemanship..

SPORTS AND BALL GAMES

It was in the nineties that F. O. Watts, now chairman of the Board of Directors of the First National Bank of St. Louis, was president and manager of the Union City Athletic Association. There was much rivalry then in amateur baseball. All the small towns had home teams. As far back as 1887 there was a game, with Watts as manager of a junior team, and Max Layne, both pitchers, manager of the seniors. The Laynes were champions, but Watts challenged with his boys and defeated the old nine.

A few years later Watts organized a picked team, including Ed Schrader, John Inman, Fitz Smith, Gene Beck, Sam Woosley, Herbert Hunt, John Gault, Charley Warterfield, Frank Watts. They scored many victories. The hardest team to fight were the Tiptonville sluggers, all well proportioned athletes. But the greatest rivalry existing then was between Jackson and Union City. Even at the first old county fair, in the early eighties, Jackson and Union City contested for local championship. So with increased interest there was a conference of sports and fans to consider signing professional players.

In 1893 rivalry reached a climax. Union City and Jackson were matched for a series of games. Jackson had a full team of Southern League players. Union City had semi-pros from St. Louis local teams with only two men, Gault and Wrady, from Union City. The first two games at Jackson tied. The third or last game was played on the athletic park at Union City. It was Greek meet Greek. Union City had employed Pink Hawley, Von der Ahe's strong-arm pitcher. Through a telegraph message, ingeniously designed for the occasion, Hawley was notified to return immediately to St. Louis and left on the outbound train. Game was called and bets posted, and in walked Hawley to the plate. The game was on.

UNION CITY

It was a fight to the finish, and the score was two and two until the tenth frame. Union City was up and fanned and Jackson came in for the last half. The air was tense, Hawley signaled to the little Irish catcher. O'Hearn, to look out for hot ones. They didn't jazz, but they whizzed and Jackson struck groggy for three men down. Union City came up for the eleventh half, and in a din of shouts Sulze and Flynn both hit for bases. Then big Jerry drove to the right and the battle was over.

Just thirty years later in 1923 Jackson came back to Union City for another match of baseball skill and strength. Ben Bramham this time leading the ball forces was manager, and Jackson returned home with another defeat.

So today we have the Turner Memorial Field and the Kitty League to give us professional ball, with rivalry in larger territory but just as keen.

THE FOURTH—UNION CITY IN 1905

The first great Fourth of July celebration in Union City since the Civil War, perhaps, was promoted in honor of the Confederate veterans of the Volunteer State. Managing the enterprise were J. C. Burdick, chairman, Dr. F. M. McRee, marshal of the day, Dr. W. M. Turner, Chas. Dietzel and J. K. Murphy assisting. Quoting from The Commercial, Union City, in 1905, "Pretty girls in white dresses and men with white hair swarmed the streets of Union City and made notable the celebration of the Fourth."

Capt. John W. Morton came from Nashville with two companies of ex-Confederate soldiers. Visitors were Gen. Harvey Hannah, Major Dabney of Mississippi, G. D. Raine and W. A. Collier of Memphis, Col. W. C. Tatum, Asst.-Adjt. H. C. Alexander of Nashville, Dr. J. B. Cowan of Tullahoma, Capt. Richard Beard, Capt. Colyer and others.

Morning salute was followed by band music and street events. Miss Mary Lawson conducted a company of young ladies in an exhibition drill on the public square.

Orator of the day was General Hannah, introduced by Senator Waddell. Henry Head, in make-up impersonating "Teddy Roosevelt," was a picturesque character.

The parade consisted of the Concert Band, Confederate veterans, "Our Bob," the cannon, business floats, Robinson's band and Daughters of the Confederacy.

Two divisions of Confederate forces met at the fair grounds in Sham Battle, one side commanded by Capt. John W. Morton, with the following staff: Major Dabney, W. A. Collier, J. B. Cowan, F. M. McRee, B. L. Ridgeley, R. Beard and W. H. Coley.

Gen. Harvey Hannah commanded the other side, with Col. W. C. Tatum, Col. Alexander, and Maj. John Bell as aides. Major Dabney commanded the artillery.

On the south side of the grounds the Warren McDona'd Camp, U.C.V., and other Confederates were in a fort commanded by Adjt.-Gen. Hannah, while almost a quarter of a mile away were the attacking forces led by Capt. Morton. The fort was protected by "Our Bob."

Gen. Morton made the advance from a position just south of the grand stand. The skirmish lines brought on the attack. Advance was made upon the fort located on the opposite side of the track. Gen. Hannah and his men were concealed behind the fort. Gen. Morton moved with his left flank upon Gen. Hannah's right. The latter was captured, and Gen. Morton's entire force then advanced and swung around to the rear, attacking and overpowering the enemy and capturing the fort. There were about 300 men in action. The spectacle was one long to be remembered.

W. P. Cloys' fine horse, Morning Glory, won track events.

The Memphis Press-Scimitar, by Mr. Fry, reporter, devoted an entire page, with illustrations, in unreserved eulogy over the occasion, and confirmed our claims to a gathering of 20,000 people.

U. C. V. AND INDEPENDENCE DAY

The next great day in Union City of local and State importance was the celebration of the Fourth of July in 1906, under the management of Col. J. H. McDowell, Dr. F. M. McRee, Dr. W. M. Turner, W. C. Farris, George Dahnke and others.

A sham battle with ex-Confederate soldiers on one side, Tennessee veterans, participating in an engagement with the National Guard of Tennessee opposing, was the principal feature. Col. McDowell, on account of his connection with public affairs at the time, was commissioned to extend a general invitation to the veterans, the State Guard, the families and friends all to be present and participate in the entertainment and exercises.

There were various other features of entertainment, opening with the early morning salute of guns, band concerts, grand parade, orations, barbecue dinner, fireworks and evening social activities.

The streets, following arrival of trains, were crowded, bands playing, and distinguished guests entering the city from all parts of the State.

First order of the day was the parade, under the direction of the grand marshal, Dr. F. M. McRee. The Second Tennessee Regiment Band leaders was followed by uniformed military organizations, including three Nashville companies, Chattanooga and Jackson companies, Jackson Drum Corps, Next, in decorated vehicles, were Ex-Gov. and Mrs. Robert L. Taylor, Mr. and Mrs. S. H. Stout, of Memphis, Miss Kate Taylor of Nashville, Miss Mary

UNION CITY

Huey of Springfield, Miss Susie Gentry of Franklin and others.

The Union City Concert Band commanding next position, was followed by various parade numbers, including the U. D. C., the W. C. T. U., the "New York Belles," made up of high school girls, the Elks, the Hay riders in a harvest wagon drawn by mules, and the industrial and floral sections.

At the fair grounds Ex-Gov. Taylor and Adjutant-General Hannah were heard from the stand in patriotic orations.

After dinner came the sham battle, called the "Battle of Franklin," to commemorate that event in the Civil War. The veterans were led by Gen. George W. Gordon, Capt. Hagar commanding the cavalry, Col. John W. Morton the artillery. Gen. Hannah commanded the National Guard, composed of Capt. Levine's Nashville Grays, Capt. Dodson's Humboldt Company and Capt. Collin's Jackson Company.

Attack made by the State Guard was twice repulsed, and on the third charge Capt. Hagar of the veterans came up on the left flank with two companies, Capt. McDowell on the right, driving the enemy to the center. Here General Hannah hoisted the white flag and surrendered.

In a racing event Sir Walter defeated Whirlpool, and in the ball game McKenzie won from Martin.

After supper George Dahnke gave an exhibition of his famous fireworks display, and the band concert followed with ball and reception at the Elks Club.

CONFEDERATE MONUMENT

Through the efforts of the Leonidas Polk Chapter, United Daughters of the Confederacy, a monument was erected in Union City in the year 1909, a shaft of stone fifty feet high, and dedicated to the memory of the soldiers of Obion County who fought for the South, suffered of deprivation and hunger, languished in prison, and emerged from the strife, those who fell and the survivors of a lost cause, with escutcheons of honor untarnished and unsullied.

This monument was dedicated with suitable and appropriate exercises in the presence of the U.D.C. and a great crowd of friends, attended with a number of veterans who were recorded as follows: E. N. Moore, H. P. McMurray, Hugh McDonald, T. R. Inman, Dr. P. Matlock, W. H. Sanders, W. B. Sowell, John Cavenaugh, J. T. Lasley, J. E. Cloar, A. L. Brevard, R. W. Powell, J. B. Caudle, John Barnes, J. R. Hughes, C. G. Thomas, F. M. McRee, J. H. McDowell, Rice Ross, W. W. Casey, W. Z. Massengill, T. R. Inman.

A leader in the movement for raising funds and for erecting a suitable memorial to the Confederate soldiers was Mrs. A. L.

Brevard, whose husband was a private in Company K, Fifth Regiment, Cheatham's Division of Johnston's Army, surrendered at Greensboro, N. C. Mr. Brevard was long a fine citizen of a fine family, including C. W. Brevard and Richard Brevard, the latter at Hickman, Ky.

Following the war the UCV was organized to perpetuate the records of honor of the Confederate service and continued until the last remnant had passed away. One of the best of them was the Warren McDonald Camp, the last to serve.

COL. HUME R. FIELD

Following is a sketch from Goodspeed's History of the First Tennessee (Confederate) Regiment, raised in Middle Tennessee in April, 1861, with George Maney as colonel. After the fall of Fort Donelson the First was ordered to the command of Gen. A. S. Johnston. The left wing of the regiment, with Johnston, participated in the battle of Shiloh on the second day. The right wing was detained at Knoxville, but after Shiloh the wings were reunited, and late in April the First was reorganized, H. R. Field becoming colonel, vice Maney promoted, the First taking its place in Maney's brigade of Cheatham's division. On July 11, 1862, it left Tupelo by way of Chattanooga and moved into Kentucky, reaching Harrodsburg October 6. It fought on the extreme right at Perryville, doing gallant service and losing over one-half its men killed and wounded. It captured four twelve-pound guns and had fifty men killed. It retreated south with Bragg, and in December was consolidated with the Twenty-seventh Tennessee, and later was engaged in the battle of Murfreesboro, with heavy losses. It moved south and in September participated in the battle of Chickamauga with conspicuous daring. Late in November it was engaged in the battle of Missionary Ridge, and then retreated with the Confederate Army. From Dalton to Atlanta the regiment was constantly engaged in all the memorable movements of that campaign, fighting desperately at "Dead Angle." In front of the First were found 385 Federal dead. The First lost 27 killed and wounded. It fought on the 20th and 22nd of July, and at Jonesboro August 19 and 20. It moved north with Hood, fighting at Spring Hill, Franklin and Nashville, and then retreated, moving to North Carolina, where it participated at Bentonville, and finally surrendered April 26, 1865.

After the war Colonel Field lived a citizen of Obion County, near Pleasant Hill, until the passing of his wife, and then for a few years in Union City, quietly until called to rest.

COUNTY FAIR AND HOME COMING

The Obion County Fair Association at the meeting in 1913 made a special feature of Home-Coming Week, with Thursday,

UNION CITY

September 13, as a day set apart for the special entertainment of visitors returning after an absence of years to Union City. Everyone whose address could be obtained was personally invited back home again and enjoy the entertainment provided for them. Also a general invitation was broadcast thru the papers, and Union City homes generally kept open house for all those desiring to return for the occasion.

Responding to the invitation hundreds of former citizens were in the city, and for the evening entertainment a record-breaking crowd lined the streets. Following report in The Commercial the parade was formed starting at the courthouse. The marshal, Dr. W. M. Turner, and his aids, Sheriff Finch, A. L. White, S. R. Bratton, John Adams, J. L. Glover, Ike Carmack, and H. C. Robinson, led on mounts, followed by Robinson's band of musicians specially engaged for the occasion, under the management of W. F. Tate.

After the band came a big log wagon drawn by four bix oxen. On the wagon were President Farris, of the Fair Association, Secretary Walden Woosley and Mrs. Woosley, Mayor Coble and a number of others with banners and bunting, then Mr. Spradlin with the ladies of the Woman's Building in his fine car, the chairman of the parade committee, Mr. Clem Burdick, and Miss Winnie Davis Moore, the Board of Mayor and Aldermen in another car with appropriate banners, J. P. Verhine's car carrying the Business Men's Club advisory committee and a car with the directors of the Fair Association.

There were twenty or thirty trade floats and decorated vehicles, with Sheesley's Italian Band between and in the rear came Swain's Band, engaged for the fair. All three bands were enlarged for the occasion, the White Way ablaze with lights, First Street jammed, banners and bunting waving, all combined into the greatest evening spectable ever seen in Union City. And as a very significant comment upon the scene, the advance agent for the Hundred-and-one Ranch Circus and Shows, arriving stopped in the office to say: "My hat's off to Union City. I've been all along the Pacific coast and have never seen anything like this."

STATE REUNION U. C. V.

The year following the Home-Coming, on October 7, 8 and 9, 1914, State Reunion of Confederate Veterans was held in Union City, with general reception and entertainment. Some six hundred veterans were present and the occasion was memorable. All arrangements moved perfectly with the exception of rain interfering with exercises at the fair grounds and the parade. The barbecue dinner was transferred to one of the business houses up town.

With Commander Gen. Bennett Young presiding election of officers was held, resulting in the re-election of the following: Gen. John P. Hickman, general commander of the division; Brig.-Generals P. C. Crouch, East Tennessee; Evander Shepard, of Middle Tennessee; W. O. Garden, West Tennessee.

At Reynolds Theatre, Dr. F. M. McRee presiding, addresses were made by Dr. C. W. Miles and J. C. Reynolds, with cordial greetings and distinct eulogy to the men of Volunteer fame. Response was made by Gen. Bennett Young of Louisville on behalf of the veterans.

CHAMBER OF COMMERCE

A record of any kind answering the purpose of a civic organization for the period of furniture manufacture in Union City, and attending optimism, does not seem to have been considered necessary, at least it must have been of no particular importance.

The period of the greatest boom, perhaps ever known in Union City, was between 1875 and 1890. It really began after the epidemic of cholera in 1873. To the people of Union City all other towns hereabout seemed atrophied—stupidly dull. Therefore a business men's civic club was hardly significant.

But with the decline of furniture making the population of Union City from 1890 to 1900 fell for a loss of 34 people, and keeping business revived was a proposition. Therefore George Dahnke and some of the live wires in the early part of the new century awoke to the fact that business in Union City had reached a stalemate.

It was, of course, at the time when farming, by reason of clearing and artificial drainage, had greatly increased production in the low-land sections, particularly in Houser Valley surrounding Union City, Obion River bottoms and the Jordan country. The result was so marked that Obion County in agriculture soon ranked third from the highest in the State.

Still Union City needed new life after the fall of furniture. And then a business men's commercial club was organized. Geo. Carter, a booster, was one of the first secretaries. One or two big banquets were held. Local patriotism was stirred. But nothing remarkable turned up more than truck growing and canning, both timidly undertaken. Then there was a mop handle factory which ran for a while.

Without seeming knowledge of the fact, a psychological moment had come for Union City, or Obion County, when Sam Lancaster appeared here in 1906 and made an address to the County Court. Mr. Lancaster had supervised the construction of some thirty miles of hard roads in Madison County, and he came prepared to make a proposition for road building in Obion County. He was here at the invitation of Judge Lawson, and with the use of native

UNION CITY

gravel he offered to supervise construction of 100 or 200 miles of highways—hard roads—including cost of labor and materials (less bridges) for $2400 a mile. The County Court, it seems, had not emerged from primitive ideas. It was really benighted, and Mr. Lancaster was ignored. Ten years after that Mr. Lancaster supervised the construction of some of the super highways on the Pacific coast, with a story of his work in the American Magazine. Fifteen years after that the County Court ordered the building of highways in the county, at the expense of the State and county, at a cost of $40,000 a mile (bridges not included).

While the years rolled along the local papers insisted that Union City, since it was not a station on the I. C. R. R., should take advantage of measures to overcome that trouble, and this was possible with the construction of a paved highway three miles to Gibbs. The editors continued weekly to bring our people face to face with the fact that Union City could be connected to the I. C. R. R. as one of its passenger and shipping points—that the old muddy lane, in the winter half way under water, was one of the burdens of life that a salesman approached with fear and trembling, and that at least in winter kept our kinsfolk and friends at home and the farmers from coming to town. All this could be made simple with a public highway—a hard surfaced road to Gibbs.

So the Union City Commercial Club took it up, and with leaders like Dr. Henry M. Oliver the project was undertaken. A working fund of several thousand dollars was raised, and by general consent Dr. Oliver marshaled his forces for action. Concessions for a 60-foot highway right of way, some freely and others easily convinced, were obtained. Survey was made to follow the old road with variations to make it conform to a perfectly straight line, then came the cuts and fills, grading and finally the gravel surface. With the coming of State highways Union City in time had a paved highway to Gibbs.

The next project, through the aid of the Commercial Club, was undertaken by Mayor F. L. Pittman, the improvement of the public highway from Union City by the way of Pleasant Valley to Stanley bridge in Obion County to the Weakley County line. Realigning, grading, extension, etc., were embraced in general improvement plans to make this a first-class highway.

In the meantime a new enterprise had appeared—practically overnight. This was discovered when it was found that Mrs. Wilma Scates was operating a dress-making factory on Harrison street. She had fifteen or twenty machines humming before it became a local news item. Then the plant was moved to the White Furniture Co. building on South First street, and there was talk of moving the plant to Paducah. Quietly Paducah interests had offered building lots and favorable concessions, and due consideration was being taken. The newspaper again became active and warned our people of impending danger. Club boosters got busy and waited on the officers of the Childs Specialty House, as it was afterwards known. A loan was floated and a building erected (afterwards the Salant & Salant Shirt factory). The Childs Specialty House settled in Union City and became one of the most important industries, moving forward to a volume of business requiring practically four hundred operatives, and the company flourished until the depression disturbed financial conditions and the demand for textiles.

The next step in the way of civic organization was a move to replace the Commercial Club with a chartered institution to be known as the Chamber of Commerce for specific reason. A campaign was to be made which needed the services of a legally constituted body of citizens to treat with the Brown Shoe Company of St. Louis in a proposition involving a consideration of $100,000, to be invested in grounds and factory buildings, for which the Brown Shoe Company had agreed to the location of one of its shoe manufacturing units in Union City, and to proceed, under the joint agreement, with the erection of buildings, installation of power plant and machinery for the manufacture of shoes in Union City.

The enterprising citizen, R. H. (Bob) Rust, by unanimous choice, was to become in fact captain-general of the campaign organization—the spearhead of the movement—and he proceeded promptly to form a civic body after the manner of army departments, including officers, subordinates, rank and file, in the proper formation. This organization was commanded under orders to proceed in a general attack upon the citizens of Union City to raise $100,000 as the sum agreed upon for the consummation of the agreement.

What happened was probably unprecedented. In actually two weeks the total amount required was subscribed, and payments made in the prescribed manner, so that in a few months, awaiting completion of buildings, the obligation was discharged.

Building completed and machinery installed, opening of the factory was celebrated June 5, 1923, attended by hosts of people, the president of the Brown Shoe Company, the Governor of Tennessee and Congressman Garrett—a gala day in Union City history.

Time moved on and the Union City Civic Club took the place of the Chamber of Commerce. Then Sunday School baseball was organized in Union City, the inspiration of a movement to establish a park in Union City for the various athletics and outdoor assemblies.

UNION CITY

Then Mayor Turner, assisted by Commissioner McAdoo, in charge of construction, and the Civic Club, opened an active campaign to acquire grounds and buildings of ample and suitable proportions for an athletic and amusement park. Application was made for PWA aid in 1934, and when everything was ready the grandstand on West Main street, an iron frame structure, was erected, together with bleachers, electric light towers, all inclosed with a cement wall in front and arched entrances, full standard fencing all the way around. Union City then became a member of the Kitty League, organized in West Kentucky and West Tennessee, and continued with some of the most important games and independent engagements for the entire period, in its seventh year in 1941.

Called together on a suitable occasion, Mayor Turner, the baseball organization and hosts of friends met to publicly acknowledge the everlasting obligation of the people of Union City to Mayor Turner for the development of this enterprise. As a token for the good offices and services to Union City rendered by Mayor Turner, the park was in a formal and impressive ceremony named in honor of its founder, the Turner Memorial Field, and a tablet of metal inscribed to Mayor W. M. Turner—a shrine to the memory of a well-beloved citizen.

Here also at the Turner Memorial Field, under Jaycee leadership, with G. B. White, Jr., former president, some of the most wonderful horse shows have been held. Here equine beauty and training from the finest stables have been seen by hosts of distinguished judges, disciples and lovers of the horse and his service and devotion to mankind.

For a number of years Dr. Turner was president of the Lions Club, always without opposition elected by acclamation. This body of representative citizens took a great deal of interest in every good measure affecting the growth and welfare of the people of Union City and Obion County.

The next public project was a WPA job, the Union City grammar school building, which occupies the Central school premises with the old buildings removed. This was completed in 1937 at a cost of $105,000. The City Commissioners and the Board of Education took the lead in this work, with C. W. Miles, Jr., president of the board, representing the interests of the city in the project. The building was constructed from plans submitted by Architect Tisdale, modeled in twin sections, including rooms and halls, cloak rooms, plumbing, heating, etc., with a large area between for convenient entrance and exit, entered through tall stone-capped columns. The gymnasium and assembly hall in the rear become on occasion practically useful as an auditorium.

The last great project after the Chamber of Commerce was

OBION COUNTY HISTORY

reorganized was the campaign in Union City and Obion County, seeking WPA allotment for a county courthouse, which has been generally described, as erected, in another section of this book. The Union City Chamber of Commerce became very active in this movement, cooperating with the courthouse committee appointed by the County Court. It was a campaign of very hard work, continuing over a period of two years, requiring finesse and generalship, handled with patience and perseverance—with confidence in the final result and without surrender to the many obstinate drawbacks. This was a time when the secretary, Harry Harper, had a real job. Selling shoes and collecting tithes was comparatively a small matter, so we gather from the expression "Believe it or not."

The Union City Armory was the latest project, also a WPA building, Union City headquarters for the National Guard of Tennessee, Company K, 117th Infantry under the command of the Adjutant General of Tennessee. Building is ample for use, when necessary for large public gatherings, furnished with portable seats, and is for all practical purposes an auditorium. Cost was about $35,000.

Officers of the Chamber of Commerce recently elected are: B. C. Cox, president; H. M. Harper, secretary; Catherine Capps, recording secretary. Board of directors: J. Walker Kerr, B. F. Howard, H. B. Sitton, Cecil Moss, Ed S. Critchlow.

Junior Chamber of Commerce (Jaycee) officers elected for 1941 were as follows: Cecil Grigsby, president; Dr. M. A. Blanton, Jr., vice-president; R. A. Everett, secretary; Mike Simmons, treasurer.

UNION CITY KIWANIS CLUB

The Kiwanis is an organization for the promotion of good fellowship and mutual community interest, rural cooperation and the application of helpful assistance in individual and local aid measures.

The Kiwanis Club in Union City was organized on Reelfoot Lake at a meeting in Boyett's dining room on the evening of November 14, 1939, under the sponsorship of the Dyersburg Kiwanis Club, with representatives from other clubs, including Paducah, Caruthersville, Memphis, Blytheville, Corinth, Tupelo and Clarksville, all gathered as banquet guests of Union City.

Organization was effected and officers elected with a membership of 30, with a program of entertainment including addresses by visiting Kiwanis, welcome by Mayor Miles and music by popular singers and rythm makers. Officers named to take charge of the new organization were: Milton Hamilton, president; Robert A. Everett, vice-president; H. P. Moss, Jr., secretary; Clint Adams,

UNION CITY

treasurer. Directors: Elwood Hagan, Herman B. Wood, Jack Moffatt, H. C. Johnson, W. T. Latimer, Paul E. Potter, R. B. Andrews.

Since that time many interesting meetings have been held, in which visiting orators have been entertained, including Milburn Cooper, of Dyersburg; Blanchard Tual, of Memphis; Dr. Barkdull, Miss Crook, Obion County Health Department; Chancellor W. W. Herron; Rabbi A. P. Feinsilver, of Paducah; Evan Carroll, of Memphis; F. C. Pogue, Murray State College; D. T. Cooper, Paducah Scout leader; Z. D. Atkins, NYA, Milan; Judge Thomas Johnson, Corinth; Bishop Edmond Dandridge, Nashville; H. B. Sitton, Brown Shoe Company; Ed K'enke, FFA; T. F. Elam, attorney; W. E. Hudgins, attorney, and Union City ministers.

At a recent meeting a review of the Kiwanis in Union City and the achievements accomplished were enumerated as follows:

Grocers school sponsored.

Furnished milk for four undernourished school children.

Twenty-five dollars donated to city charities.

Donated to tuberculosis cabin.

Total of 14,000 baby chicks with feed donated to 280 4-H Clubs and Future Farmer members. Prizes of $35 also given.

Car load of pure-bred cockerels shipped to New York City, netting a return profit to chicken growers clubbing in the shipment.

Sponsored weekly prayers for peace services.

Published 10,000 scenic folders, sold to local concerns, and 10,000 additional ordered.

Donated fund for operation on underprivileged girl.

Sponsored "Big Brother" project.

Annual election of officers for 1941 resulted as follows: Alfred Finkelstein, president; H. C. Johnson, vice-president; Fred Latimer, treasurer; Jack Moffatt, secretary. Board of directors: Milton Hamilton, R. A. Everett, R. B. Andrews, Jas. Terrell, Herman Wood, Jas. McClure, Ralph Morton.

ROTARY CLUB

The Rotary Club of Union City was organized in 1936 with the election of G. B. White, Jr., as president and Carl Timm as secretary.

This club has made steady progress, selecting its membership so that one from each line of business is represented.

The objects of the Rotary are to encourage and foster the ideal of service as a basis of worthy enterprise and, in particular, encourage and foster:

1. The development of acquaintance as an opportunity for service.

2. High ethical standards in business and professions; the

recognition of the worthiness of all useful occupations; and the dignifying by each Rotarian of his occupation as an opportunity to serve society.

3. The application of the ideal of service by every Rotarian to his personal, business, and community life.

4. The advancement of international understanding, good will, and peace through a world fellowship of business and professional men united in ideal service.

Annual election of officers for the Rotary Club in Union City, held in April, 1941, resulted as follows:

J. L. Rippy, president; Dr. M. T. Tipton, vice-president; Walker Martin, secretary; W. P. Burnett, treasurer; Robt. McAnulty and Fenner Heathcock, members of the board succeeding J. C. McRee and H. P. Sitton.

UNION CITY GARDEN CLUB

The Union City Garden Club was organized in May, 1931, at the City Hall. Mrs. W. W. Heathcock organized the club, and was its first president. The charter members were: Mrs. Claude Allen, Mrs. W. P. Nash, Mrs. Guy Miles, Mrs. Hunt Roper, Mrs. Robert White, Mrs. Edward Parks, Mrs. Spencer Millard, Mrs. Walker Martin, Mrs. Hugh Harris, Mrs. C. W. Wakefield, Mrs. J. D. Swearengen, and Mrs. Jas. Brice.

A meeting is held monthly and prizes are given for the most attractive general arrangement of flowers, and special prizes are given for the best specimens of iris and roses. There are two luncheons during the year: one in the spring and another in the fall.

There has always been interest in civic improvements, and some planting has been done in the city park and on the parkway on Florida avenue. They had a part in planting and beautifying the grounds at Turner Memorial Field. Another project was the planting of several hundred Lombardy poplars on the Fulton Highway in 1939.

Every year the gardens in Union City are lovelier, and interest in them is growing all the time. We are very proud of the fact that a picture of Mrs. W. A. Nailling's garden appeared in the Tennessee Garden Club Year Book in 1936.

The club strives to live up to the principle that beauty is not a luxury, but a real need and endeavors to stimulate the knowledge and love of gardening. Gardening not only creates beautiful homes, but true and worthwhile friends.

The Union City club joined the Federation of Garden Clubs May, 1934, and has fifty members.

REVIEW CLUB

On November 22, 1897, a group of women, interested in things of a cultural nature, met together in the home of Mrs. Jno. Wells,

UNION CITY

and organized a club for the purpose of "investigation and free discussion of religious, educational, literary, and other topics."

A constitution was drafted and by-laws adopted, and the club named the Review Club.

Mrs. Griffin, mother of Mrs. Ella Howse of this city, was chosen the first president; Mrs. John Wells, vice-president, Mrs. Charles Gibbs, secretary, and Mrs. Lexie Parks, treasurer.

The charter members of the Review Club were: Mrs. Griffin, Mrs. John Wells, Mrs. Lexie Parks, Mrs. Charles Gibbs, Mrs. W. H. Gardner, Mrs. J. B. Hibbitts, Mrs. Ferd Thomasson, Mrs. Russell Porter, Miss Anice Allen, and Miss Carrie Lee Gardner.

By March of the following year, (1898), the following names were added: Mrs. Will Sheffer, Mrs. J. Lukens, Mrs. W. J. Edwards, Mrs. C. K. Ligon, Miss Nelle Hughes, Mrs. W. F. Barry, Mrs. Clarence Sherrill, Miss Nette White, Miss Masie Garth, and Miss Margaret Freeling. This brought the membership to twenty, which is the limit of the club today.

Our constitution and by-laws are very little different from those drafted forty years ago. The membership limit is the same, and we still meet in the homes of the members, once a week, in alphabetical order, and our subject is the same: "The Improvement of The Heart and Mind."

Our programs of study cover a wide and varied range of subjects: Art, Literature, Travel, History, Biography, Book Review, and Current Events.

Officers: Mrs. John Semones, president; Mrs. Edgar Craddock, secretary.

Junior Review officers: Mrs. R. J. Hubbs, president; Mrs. B. C. Cox, vice-president; Mrs. J. B. Maxwell, treasurer; Mrs. Clifford Houser, secretary and reporter; Mrs. M. A. Blanton, Jr., critic.

TWENTIETH CENTURY CLUB

The Twentieth Century Club was organized in the summer of 1925 at the home of Mrs. H. T. Butler, who sponsored its formation. The following officers were elected: President, Miss Sarah Pickard; vice-president, Mrs. R. D. Kerr; secretary, Mrs. Fred Nailling; treasurer, Miss Mary Lee Rodgers. Other members were Miss Vivian Woodrow, Mrs. Roy Wehman, Mrs. Melvin Watson, Mrs. L. B. Ryan, Mrs. George Phebus, Mrs. Marvin Owens, Mrs. Paul Nailling, Mrs. Meeks Meadow, Mrs. Bob McAnulty, Mrs. I. L. Matchette, Mrs. E. H. Campbell, Mrs. Bob Alexander, and Miss Louise Luten.

The Club was formed for cultural advancement to be secured from the interchange of ideas and by the study of various subjects.

Officers: Mrs. C. E. Mathis, president; Mrs. Evelyn Guill, vice-president; Mrs. Ruth Berndt, secretary.

MATINEE MUSIC CLUB

The Matinee Music Club with a membership of 25 active, and one honorary member, has met bi-monthly, except during the summer months, since its organization in March, 1914. Mrs. James Cunningham was the first president, and it was she who called together a band of music lovers at the home of Mrs. Fred Dahnke and organized this club. The first meeting of the club was held at the home of Mrs. J. D. Carlton. Of these charter members, the names of the following ladies in 1939 were active members: Mrs. J. D. Carlton, Mrs. Thad D. Lee, Mrs. James Brice, Mrs. Robt. Whipple, a charter member, gave the name, "Matinee Music Club" to the new organization. The club has been a member of the National and State Federation of Music Clubs for some years. Miss Aletha Bonner, of Rives, and Nashville, who holds an office in both the State and national federation, is an honorary member of the local club.

Officers for the year 1940 were: Mrs. Thad Lee, president; Mrs. Chas. Fritz, secretary.

UNION CITY SCHOOLS

T. D. Ozment, superintendent; Betty Bell, secretary.

In the 1941 spring election held to name teachers for the 1941-42 term of the City Schools, T. F. Wallace, former coach and teacher, was elected principal of the high school, succeeding C. W. Thomasson. New teachers elected to fill vacancies were: Geraldine Hammack, French and English; Daniel Harrison, biology and science. R. G. Wilson was elected principal of the junior high school. Teachers for the Miles schools were elected as follows:

N. T. Gilbert, principal; Hattie Lindsay, history, civics, English, music; Davada Roper, first grade; Pearl Jennings, third and fifth grades; Uma Washington, fourth and sixth grades; Vira Clements, second grade; Ezra Lee Taylor, seventh and eighth grades; Lily C. Wilkins, English, civics, history, economics, science.

FIRST UNKNOWN SOLDIER IN UNION CITY CEMETERY FOR CONFEDERATE DEAD

The Confederate Monument erected in 1869 in the southeastern suburbs of Union City is claimed to be the first monument ever dedicated to an "Unknown Soldier" as well as the first monument to a Confederate soldier in the South.

The "Old Soldiers' Cemetery" lays south across the N. C. & St. L. railroad track, of the City Cemetery.

UNION CITY

The monument to the Unknown Confederate Soldier was recently repaired and is much more attractive now than in its former neglected state. Formerly the bottom cavity of the monument lay agape, where it had been broken open and the articles contained therein removed. These articles were said to have included a Bible, a Confederate rifle, a history of the monument's inception, and a number of other things, which no one seems to be quite certain about.

One thing the rejuvenated monument lacks, that was on the original monument before its defacement, is the date of erection. Ladies of the Leonidas Polk Chapter, United Daughters of the Confederacy, worked for a long time and tirelessly to have some permanent record made of the memorial. It was thru the influence of this group that the Obion County Court appropriated $100 for repairing the monument.

There are only two graves in this cemetery which contain remains of persons identified. One contains a young doctor from Kentucky who was killed in the service of the Old South and was buried in this county. The other contains the only negro in the cemetery, the father-in-law of Dr. E. D. Walker, local physician, according to information available.

The graves are grouped in plats of quarter sections, separ- toward the monument in the center of the cemetery.

The graves are grouped in plants of quarter sections, separated by walks with pathway circling the monument. An arched gate was originally made to open upon the railroad tracks with descending steps.

The cemetery at the time of its dedication, October 21, 1869, is described in the Union City Herald, a weekly publication at that time, as follows: A beautiful high level half-acre, half a mile from the intersection of the Mobile and Ohio, and Nashville and Northwestern railroads, on the south side of the latter, and connected with it by a flight of oaken steps, which led up to the double arched gates enclosing a magnificent monument erected at the hands of patriotism to the memory of those who sleep around its ten-foot base.

"Towering toward Heaven some forty feet, stands spectre-like in its snowy garb, a lone but faithful sentinel over warriors and patriots, who having filled their caplets of Fame, retired from the ill-fated stage of heroic achievement to the quiet bosom of everlasting peace and repose. On its smooth marble front the same simple but significant inscription as may be found upon the plain white arches over the panel gates of the entrance: 'Unknown Confederate Dead'.

"Next to the fence, on every side are ample walks and intersections, with similar ones on each side of the base of the monument, dividing the ground into four burial plats, so arranged that the foot of each grave is directed toward the center. Ample ground has been reserved in each plat for the planting and growing of flowers and shrubbery."

The rather naive and flowery description of the place—written as was the style of newspapers of the time—was kept in clipping form, along with other things related to the cemetery, in a scrapbook of the late Dr. John H. Morton, who was one of the principal workers for the cause of the cemetery.

The description is taken from the story of the dedication of the monument, and this is written as follows, headed "Dedication of Confederate Cemetery":

"At last, after incessant and persevering labor, the noble work of fitting up a cemetery, erecting a monument, and reinterring the remains of those who fell on the field of honor in defense of Southern rights was accomplished, and the morning of October 21, 1869, fixed for the funeral ceremony and final dedication of the holy place. As by special providence, the morning broke in perfect harmony with the solemn occasion, the heavy clouds hung dark and drifting over the face of the sky, the sun itself scarcely visible, seemed to participate in the pervading gloom, and every individual appeared impressed with the dignity and grandeur belonging to the day.

"About 9 o'clock the death-like stillness was broken by the Union City brass band, by previous arrangement, meeting at the courthouse corner, and as if by inspiration, sounded the grave notes of martial music upon the pulseless air deeper, clearer, sweeter, and sadder than ever before. In the meantime, the courthouse was crowded with ladies and gentlemen waiting to join the procession as soon as it was formed. Shortly afterwards the Independent Order of Odd Fellows, who had formed at Morgan's Hall, in their bright and beautiful regalia, came marching up First street, and halted under the music of the band. Then came the Masonic fraternity, from the same direction, with similar tokens to distinguish them from those who had never entered into obligations to devote their lives to the great cause of suffering humanity. Upon these two associations of Benevolence and Charity the procession was formed as follows:

"The band in front, next, ministers of the gospel, ladies, Odd Fellows, Masons, lawyers, physicians—all followed by the vast throng of strangers and citizens in general. Marching to the slow, solemn strains of the band it passed through the city, and on to the hallowed resting place of departed valor—" Here the description of the cemetery comes in, and this news story of a long-gone day continues:

"After ascending the steps from the railroad, and moving

around the outer walks, the procession paused partly by direction of the Chief Marshal, but more by intuition, long enough to pay respect to the honored dead who sleep beneath the sod and whose virtues were then being commemorated and extolled; during which time a breathless silence prevailed, disturbed only now and then by the deep drawn sigh of some over-swollen heart, or by the gentle drop of emblematic cedar upon a grave whose only epitaph was the then expressive word: 'Unknown,' inscribed upon a simple white wooden head board. But few witnessed with tearless eyes the solemn scene as they turned slowly and sadly away and moved on to the C. P. Church.

"After an able and touching prayer by the Rev. Mr. Beck, the Rev. W. T. Harris was introduced by Maj. C. N. Gibbs, Chief Marshal, to deliver the funeral oration. After more than meeting the expectations excited so highly by his exalted reputation, he was successively followed by Capts. J. A. McCall and J. J. Brooks, the former displaying that depth of reflection, that serious thought which never fails to give him a complete mastery of his subject, and always enables him to advocate his cause with the strength and earnestness peculiar only to those of great mind and heart.

All of the orations were of that high and dignified order which, while it pleases the fancy, informs the understanding. Not only were they a tribute of honor and respect to the victims of war but were a pleasure and consolation to the hearts which are still left to beat proudly for the sacred cherished principles of justice, right and liberty, to which the fallen ones sealed their devotion with their lives. The living may well be proud to know such advocates yet remain to battle and contend with inflexible fidelity for sweet liberty while they hand down to posterity in immortal speech, the deeds of those who laid their lives upon the holy altar."

This dedication took place during the Reconstruction days, right after the War, and purses were short, though sentiment still ran high.

The cemetery was planned to accommodate the Confederate dead buried all over the county, and when it was finished, these bodies were disinterred and reburied there. The conception of this plan was evident in an appeal in an earlier issue of the Union City Herald, by Dr. Morton and the U. C. Fire Co., committee, which was then apparently one of the most influential organizations of the town.

The U. D. C. is still working for the proper recognition of the monument and that it is kept in repair. They have suggested also that a driveway be constructed from the highway to the cemetery.

REELFOOT LAKE

There were no doubt very few settlements around Reelfoot Lake in 1825-26 when Davy Crockett first found the huntsman's paradise, otherwise he would have given an account of them in his memoirs of the lake. He did however mention meeting two or three settlers on his bear hunts on the lake during the fall, winter and spring of the same year. One party joined Crockett and his boy and shared in the killing of three or four bears. Another man complained of losing his winter's meat and Crockett accommodated him with a supply of bear meat.

It was therefore no wonder that Crockett called Reelfoot Lake "Red Foot Lake." He made no mistake however in his description of the country in saying that it had been shaken and riven apart in ditches by the earthquakes of 1811-12. His hunting took him from Big Clover Creek around the bluffs bordering the lake and gave him the sport of his life—the fall, winter and spring that he killed 105 bears.

The first mention to be found of Reelfoot Lake shore points embraces Wheeling, afterwards Shaw's Park—Samburg, and Carpenter's, near Walnut Log. An old frame building at Carpenter's, used for a hotel, was caught in a hurricane and blown into scattering fragments all around the place for hundreds of yards. It was in that vicinity that the Rankin tragedy occurred.

It is said that J. C. Burdick, who settled on the lake in the early seventies, arriving there from Cairo, Ill., on a trip of adventure, located and gave Walnut Log its name. Afterwards Mr. Burdick superintended the opening of a ditch from Bayou de Chien to the main body of the lake. Mr. Burdick settled there and became an active operator in the fishing industry. He was also mutually interested with all the fishermen in friendly laws governing Reelfoot Lake fishing. For years Mr. Burdick defended the fishermen in legislation proposed to limit the amount and variety of fish to be caught for the market and the devices used in catching fish. It was this that resulted in the assessment of royalties on the fish caught for market on Reelfoot Lake.

Mr. Burdick lost no occasion to be present when new bills were offered in the State Assembly, with the purpose of limiting or restricting the operations of fishermen on the lake, whether by special interests or disinterested parties. He was not only an operator but a wholesale dealer, and conducted a place of business in Union City, beginning in 1889.

J. C. Burdick, Jr., took up the business after his father's death, but on account of an unfortunate fire a few years ago, damaging his plant, he retired from the wholesale fish business, continuing only in the retail market in the sale of fish and sea foods.

The town of Wheeling was laid off at the foot of the bluffs, near the mouth of Indian Creek, about 1852 by William Henry. Shaw's Park took its place, and afterwards Samburg became the center of business and fishing.

Some years later J. Q. Stanbrough, of Union City bought location for hunting lodge and hotel at Old Idlewild. His son-in-law, Theo Williams, kept a restaurant and bar at that place. In the years 1888-89 W. D. Reeves operated a saw mill at Idlewild, cutting millions of feet of virgin poplar and oak timber.

John Shaw operated a store for years at Shaw's Park, contiguous to the Samburg locality. Hotels, docks and other accommodations were provided for hunting and fishing on the lake.

FISHERMEN

Only a few pioneers of the fishing industry on the lake are now in active service. Inquiry about the old fishermen operating at Wheeling, Idlewild, Carpenter's, Bayou de Chien and all along the east shores of the lake revealed many familiar names, numbers of whom have long since laid away their nets and fishing tackle, some reposing in their last resting places, while others are retired to their homes along the waters of the lake. The list includes Ike Johnson (63 years a lake fisherman), Frank Mitchell, Tom Diehl, Bob Hamilton (not only a fisherman but an officer connected with the State docks and one of the best known citizens at the lake), Bud Lee, Finger Jim Wilson, Frank Wrady, Elbert Nation, Ed Powell, Bud Wade, John Townsley, Luke Gore, Buck Spain, Will Riddle, Chunk Applewhite, Bose Hutchcraft, Charley Parkerson, Dee Shaw, P. C. Ward, Charley Allen, Irve Agnew, Will Burton, Bonie Dyer, Fred Brannon, W. T. Fentress, Jim Kaysacker, Albert Wallace, Will Griffith, Boy Ranson, Otis and Buck Adams, Charley Lee, Bob Wallace, Little Bob Wallace, Irve Burton, Cap Blythe, Sam Applewhite, Ans Shaw, Charley Lassiter, Tip Ranson.

Charles Downing, fisherman, ran a dock for years. John Cochran operated a hotel and for years he was engaged as trapper and hunter on the lake.

At the time of taking this report there were two State docks, one at Samburg and the other at Blue Bank. State Game Wardens are C. C. Summers and Bob Hamilton. Deputies: Mat Huffman, Whit Vance, A. G. Harris, Grover McQueen.

Operators of fish docks and accommodations along the east and south shores of the lake are listed as follows: O. T. Wallaston, Walnut Log Lodge; Harry McQueen, dock, store and cottages;

Hutchcraft dock and lunch stand at Samburg; Elbert Spicer Co., wholesale and retail fish market; Elbert Nation, dock and cabins; Fraley, operating Burdick dock; Bob Murphy fish dock; Bullock, Box Slough dock and cabins; Bennie Montgomery dock; Murdock & McKinney, Spillway dock and cabins; Marvin Hays, Blue Bank dock; Bryant dock at Lakeview.

SAMBURG DIRECTORY

Following are the stores and business places at Samburg: Byrd Denton Store, W. I. Gantlett Variety Store, Herman Cole, Dee Shaw Store, Mrs. Rosa Cole, Mrs. Walter Hayes' Reelfoot Hotel, Jim Hutchcraft, candy shop and recreation hall, F. Jordan Barber Shop, Chas. Creason saw mill.

CAMPS AND CABINS

Kennon's, Smith's, Morris, Lakeview, Esso Station and Dining Room, Mrs. Boyett's, Bryant's, Thomas & Johnson, Morris' Spillway Restaurant, Laster Service Station.

BEACH AND CLUBS

Edgewater and Sunkist Beaches, Thurman McCain, operator. Samburg: Claude Botts and Hugh Smith Clubs. Blue Bank: State Club, Mrs. Cecil Moss Club, Gum Point: Chas. Reynolds, McKenzie and Red Boyett Clubs. Near Gum Point: Lorene Waddell, Armour Ratliff Clubs. Blue Wing: Clarksdale Club. Box Slough: McAnulty Bros. Club. Samburg-Spillway: Wakefield, Roper and Chapel Clubs. Old Idlewild: Gun and Rod Club, Fulton, Dyersburg and Newbern Clubs. Grassy Island: McAlister-Dietzel-White Club. Samburg: Mrs. Jas. Scott (Dyersburg) Club, Dredge Ditch Club House. American Legion Milton Talley Post Lodge.

FEDERAL IMPROVEMENT PROJECT—BLUE BANK PARK

Before the Spillway was constructed there were very few residents and very little activity on the south banks of the lake, but since that time this locality has undergone many changes.

Most important are the park improvements made at Blue Bank, under State and Federal supervision, with Mr. Connelly in charge, operating a CCC Camp of 175 young men, all engaged in the various branches of the work. The project began in 1935 and was completed in 1938. This work included the building of State Docks, an eight-foot wire fence about twelve miles in length, inclosing the State Game Reservation on the south and west borders of the lake, beginning at Champion Pocket on the west and crossing Brewer's Bar on the east, and general improvements in the park, consisting of filling with dirt and gravel, grading, making serpentine walks inclosed with railing, boring

REELFOOT LAKE

artesian well and laying pipes all through the park, with a number of jets at various points, building grand stand, keeper's lodge, etc.

All this required cutting and moving timber for all buildings, some of it from the islands, all used in the construction of State docks, park stand, keeper's lodge, etc. Another part of the general project was the building of camp at Walnut Log, dredging and cleaning Bayou de Chien, road construction from Walnut Log to the State Biological Station, filling and grading main streets at Samburg.

It is of interest to know that the State Game Reservation is now stocked with one hundred or more fine deer, and that provision is made for a keeper to superintend maintenance of park and keeping the deer herd in the proper condition.

(Through the courtesy of T. H. Alexander of the Nashville Tennessean, we are reproducing his story of Reelfoot Lake.)

Reelfoot Lake, known for half a century or more as one of the greatest resorts for hunting and fishing, lies like a sprawling monster crab in the western portion of Obion County with headquarters over the line in Kentucky, its western shore forming the border line between Obion and Lake counties. The story of its formation has been handed down by story and legend.

As is well known, Reelfoot Lake was formed by a series of earthquakes, equal in violence to those which took such a terrific death toll in Japan. The quakes began in December 1811, and continued until February of the following year. The land gradually sank possibly on an average of seven feet deep, though much deeper at some points in the lake, notably at what is known as Blue Basin.

The area of the lake is approximately 30,000 acres. What it must have been in 1812 no one knows. Possibly it was 40,000 to 50,000 acres in extent. Little authentic is known of that, but certain it is that at least 10,000 or 15,000 acres of the lake's area have been lost by the rapid filling in of erosion from the nearby hills.

FOREST SUNK IN QUAKE

The vast inland empire, thus sunk was due in all probability to subterranean explosions, for many observers agreed that quakes were accompanied by horrible rumblings, as of distant thunder, but louder. With the land went down many miles of virgin forests. Windstorms have blown many of them down in the century which has elapsed and decay has done for many others, but thousands of these trees still rear their heads up from the waters, gaunt spectres of the primeval forest that was. The tops of most of them are dead, but the trunks under the water still live. Black walnut, gum, oak, willow and cypress trees and stumps rear above water in some parts of the lake, giving these sections a grim and forbidding appearance. It is an arboreal graveyard.

By no means all of the lake is covered with trees, however. Blue Basin, in the northern portion of the lake, is more than two miles long, 400 yards or more wide, ten feet and more deep and free from trees. Other little inlets free from trees dot the south portion of the lake.

When this land sank it might well be presumed to have belonged to some individual and so it appears. What is known as the Doherty grants, covering a large part of the land which afterwards sank, were made by the State of North Carolina in 1788, several years before the State of Tennessee was formed and before the Reelfoot land became a part of the United States. Court records show four principal grants totaling 12,000 acres.

SHORE LINE OF FIFTY MILES

Reelfoot is owned to low water mark by the State of Tennessee, later increased. It has a shore line of about 50 miles. It is estimated that more than nine-tenths of this shore line was owned by the West Tennessee Land Company. Grassy Island, so called although it is in reality a peninsula, otherwise it would be subject to State ownership, is itself a vast empire of about 400 acres suitable for the breeding of bear, deer, fur bearing animals and small game.

After the decision by the Supreme Court in 1913 the people of Tennessee promptly forgot about Reelfoot Lake until half a dozen years later when the State highway department began the construction of a road from Samburg to Tiptonville around the southern end of the lake. This road was built atop a high levee which dammed up the natural drainage of the lake. An eighty foot spillway was built at the most southern point of the lake to carry off the surplus waters into a drainage ditch to the Obion River and finally to the Father of Waters, the Mississippi.

SPILLWAY IS INADEQUATE

If one believes the stories of high waters told by the riparian owners to the north of the lake near the Kentucky border—and one is forced by occular evidence to credit them—this spillway has proven hopelessly inadequate to carry off the flood waters in the spring and early summer. Contention over the Spillway between owners of land above and below the lake has never been satisfactorily settled.

But through the clouds of litigation and a miasma of violence the fact still remains that Reelfoot is the paradise of sportsmen. It is beyond a doubt the finest fish hatchery in the world. In the blue depths reveals millions of pounds of trout, channel cat, sun perch, brim, goggle eyed perch, white carp, German carp, eel, drum, buffalo, mud cat, striped jack and other varieties of fish. Nature has endowed a vast pisciculture plant, ever to be fashioned by the hand of man.

DUCKS GATHER IN FALL

In the fall it looks as if all the wild ducks of North America gather to feast along its shallow banks. The wintry winds sweep them from the North over the broad breast of the Mississippi. Some fly, with the speed of an aeroplane, to the rice marshes of Louisiana and the delta of Mississippi and Arkansas, but most of them seem to stay at Reelfoot.

Along the banks and in the islands of the lake roam countless small furbearing animals—muskrat, otter, opossum and others. Once roamed the bear and deer in the fatnesses of Reelfoot, and that not so many years ago. With a sufficient reservation they may still be propagated at Reelfoot, for in few spots in the civilized portions of the globe has nature been so kind to wild life.

REELFOOT LAKE LITIGATION

J. C. Harris, of Lake County, undertook to establish title to the North Carolina land grants and began to drain the lake. Complainants representing themselves to be owners of land, hotels and fish docks along the east shore of the lake brought suit in Chancery Court to restrain Mr. Harris from draining the lake on the grounds that the lake is a navigable stream in a technical legal sense and as a matter of fact Chancellor W. H. Swiggart sustained the complainants, but the Supreme Court reversed him a few months later, and it was not until 1913 that the Supreme Court reversed itself and agreed with the view of the noted Union City jurist.

The West Tennessee Land Company began to acquire the lands around the lake and the title to the lake itself in 1902.

REELFOOT LAKE

The leaders in the acquisition of the property by the land company were Judge Harris, previously mentioned as having tried to drain the lake; Col. R. Z. Taylor and J. R. Deason of Gibson County; and Seid Waddell and John Shaw of Obion County.

No sooner had it acquired the Harris properties and others around the lake than the land company established agencies and leased out to various persons the right of controlling sections of the lake for fishing. Fishermen and hunters for profit were excluded, although sportsmen were not molested.

Much bitterness aroses against the company as a result of

this policy. Feeling was particularly intense in the neighborhood of Samburg, on the eastern shore of the lake. Early in 1908 suits were instituted by the land company in the chancery court of Obion County at Union City, and a temporary injunction was issued against several of the Samburg people restraining their claim to an unrestricted right to the use of the waters of the lake.

"NIGHT RIDERS"

At about this time, in 1907 and 1908, a wave of lawlessness swept over Tennessee and Kentucky. An organization known as "Night Riders" began operations in the tobacco sections of the two States, the purpose of the hooded bands being to force tobacco raisers to join an association formed to control the price of the crop. Plant beds had been scraped, threatened letters sent and at one time raid on the city of Clarksville was rumored.

An organization of "Night Riders" came into being at Reelfoot to resist the ownership and control of the lake by the West Tennessee Land Company. Apparently, the "Night Riders" were well organized.

The first serious violence came on the night of April 13, 1908, when a dock belonging to the Reelfoot Fish and Game Co., stockholders of the West Tennessee Land Co., was destroyed by fire. A small storehouse and other buildings were also burned.

THE RANKIN CASE

About the middle of October there was a term of the chancery court at Union City at which the injunction prayed by the land company to restrain fishermen from fishing on the lake property of the land company were made perpetual. Captain Quentin Rankin of Trenton, a popular and able lawyer and a stockholder in the land company, was in Union City representing the company. He remained until Thursday, October 15, when he returned home after making an engagement with a citizen to show him some land on Grassy Island which he desired to lease. An engagement was made for the visit to the lake on Monday, October 19.

Captain Rankin and Col. R. Z. Taylor of Trenton, another stockholder in the land company and a prominent citizen, left their homes at Trenton on Sunday night and went to Union City. On Monday morning they went by train to Hickman, Ky., over the N. C. & St. L. Ry. and thence by vehicle to Ward's Hotel at Walnut Log on the banks of Bayou de Chien, a short distance from where the Bayou empties into the lake. Shortly after noon they were joined by Carpenter, the citizen who wished to lease the company's 3600-acre strip of land known as Grassy Islands. The

REELFOOT LAKE

inspection of the land consumed the afternoon. Rankin and Taylor returning to the hotel that night.

At midnight the "Night Riders" came—armed and masked.

It was the theory of the State in the prosecutions that followed that "Night Riders" had not been able to catch any stockholders in the land company in the vicinity of the lake since the band's organization, and that their vengeance was wreaked on the first who happened to come about.

A mile or so northeast of Ward's Hotel at Walnut Log was the home of Ed Powell. Shortly after 11 p. m. Powell was awakened by the call of the "Night Riders" who demanded that he make a light. The "Night Riders," about 50 in number, then compelled Powell to guide them to the hotel and awaken P. C. Ward, proprietor.

Mr. Ward's hotel was a series of connecting rooms, built in much the fashion of the old time summer resorts of Tennessee and connected by porches. It was but the work of a few seconds, however, to find the room occupied by the Trenton lawyers and capitalists. Taylor, they found, was awake and sitting on the side of the bed. They compelled both to dress and leave the hotel with them.

TAYLOR QUESTIONED

Proceeding to the east, the band came to a bluff where their horses were tied and there they questioned Colonel Taylor. He was asked how much he had to pay the chancellor to decide the injunction cases in favor of the company. Colonel Taylor replied Chancellor Cooper was an honest man and decided the cases according to the law.

Questioned about his titles to the lake property, Col. Taylor said he and his associates had secured the Galloway and Bennett titles from the heirs of Galloway. He was asked why he did not turn the titles over to the people along the shores of the lake instead of giving them to Mr. Harris and the land company, but, before he could answer, a "Night Rider" struck at Taylor and hit him on the chest.

Threatened with death, Col. Taylor replied:

"You can't scare me in that way. You can kill me, but I am not afraid to die. You can't cheat me out of anything much by killing, for I have been here 62 years and haven't got much longer to stay anyway. You're not going to cheat me much, but it is different with Captain Rankin—he is a young man."

The "Night Riders" then left some of their number with the horses and proceeded back on the road to the bayou, and then to a leaning ash tree which forked eight or ten feet above the ground. They placed a rope around Captain Rankin's neck, threw it over the tree branch and lifted him from the ground. Colonel Taylor had been left 10 or 15 feet away, near the bayou, and was guarded by two or three men.

As the "Night Riders" pulled Captain Rankin from the ground, one of their number suggested:

"Let's give him time to pray."

"I have already attended to that matter," replied the intrepid Rankin.

As the rope tightened around his neck, Captain Rankin exclaimed:

"Gentlemen, don't do that, you are killing me," and one of the "Night Riders" said:

"Damn you, that's what we intended to do."

RANKIN DIES GAME

There is a tradition around the lake that "Night Riders" had no idea of killing Captain Rankin, but merely intended to frighten the two men into giving over title to their land or into promising never to return to the lake. In defense of the "Night Riders" it is said that some of them—given courage by potent whiskey—decided to kill Captain Rankin on the spur of the moment.

At any event, some one fired a shot, then came the spit-spit of an automatic revolver firing twice. Captain Rankin uttered a cry and then came a volley of pistol shots piercing the peaceful air of the lake. Captain Rankin, a brave Southern gentleman, was dead.

Just how Colonel Taylor managed to escape may never be publicly known. It is said that he gave a Masonic sign of distress to his small squad of captors, who stood a dozen feet from the scene of the murder of Captain Rankin. According to his story he was allowed to escape by jumping into the bayou.

He waited until apparently all the weapons had been discharged and then he jumped into the slough and waded to the opposite shore in the excitement of the killing of Captain Rankin.

Fifty feet across on the opposite bank he found a log parallel with the stream, and there he hid while a volley of shots was poured into the bayou and across the opposite bank. The "Night Riders" struck matches and searched the bayou with a pole, but did not locate Colonel Taylor.

"He's at the bottom of the lake," grumbled one of their number, and so the search was at length abandoned.

TAYLOR GETS AWAY

After lying in hiding for hours, Colonel Taylor traveled westward from the scene of the murder. Cold and hungry, he walked through Monday night, Tuesday, Tuesday night, and until Wednesday morning. At length, nearly dead, he recognized a location in Lake county, just south of Hickman, Ky., and from there he was taken to Tiptonville, suffering terribly from exposure.

The tragedy at Walnut Log shocked the moral conscience of the nation. Malcolm R. Patterson, of Memphis, was Governor of Tennessee. Governor Patterson was delivering a political speech when the news of the tragedy became known. He at once ordered out the State militia, established a camp for them, called Camp Nemo, at Samburg, and came to the scene of "Night Rider" troubles himself.

All told, 40 or 50 men were arrested charged with being implicated in the crime. The men who were convicted were Garrett Johnson, said to be the "Night Rider's" leader; Sam Applewhite, Arthur Cloar, Roy Ransom, Fred Pinion, Rob Huffman, Tid Burton and Bud Morris.

ALL FOUND GUILTY

The "Night Rider" grand jury returned indictments against the eight men mentioned above on October 8, 1908, at a special session of the Circuit Court of Obion County, which was presided over by the late Joseph E. Jones, of Dresden. The indictments charged murder in the first degree. The defendants pleaded not guilty and went to trial on December 14. The trial continued until January 7, when the jury returned a verdict of guilty of murder in the first degree, with mitigating circumstances against the defendants Johnson, Cloar, Pinion, Burton, Ransom and Applewhite, and of murder in the second degree against Morris and Huffman, fixing the punishment of the last two at imprisonment for 20 years.

After overruling a motion for a new trial, Judge Jones expressed the opinion that there was nothing in the evidence to mitigate the offense of murder in the first degree. He therefore disregarded the finding of the jury as to mitigating circumstances and sentenced the six men to be executed by hanging.

The case went to the Supreme Court of the State at the April term, 1909, at Jackson, and was there reversed and remanded for a new trial on technical grounds. The prosecution thereafter languished and no punishment was meted out to the men accused of murder.

And so, finally, did peace come to Reelfoot at the cost of thousands of dollars in court costs and one human life.

SPORT OF KINGS

There is but one Sport of Kings and it is not horse racing—it is casting for black bass in Reelfoot Lake.

There is no thrill equal to your strike when fishing for the black bass of Reelfoot. It is the thrill that comes once in a lifetime.

The black bass is not the only fish in the lake nor is he the largest. He is, however, the autocrat, the prince of the purple. Besides the bass there are the pike, the channel catfish, goggle-eyed perch, buffalo, white carp, striped jack, German carp, eel, mud cat, white perch, sun perch and the gar, the last the very scum of the piscatorial kingdom.

Only the big mouthed bass is found at Reelfoot. Possibly in times gone by the small mouth bass was found, not in recent years. The big mouth bass weighs from one to nine pounds. A three-pound bass caught on a bob at the end of 50 feet of line attached to a limber pole feels like the whale that swallowed Jonah. The lucky fisherman who lands a nine-pounder might as well call it a day and go home and brag the rest of his life. He ought to be a hero even to his valet.

While some of the varieties of fish have decreased in numbers the black bass had apparently greatly increased at Reelfoot for a number of years. One reason is the strict enforcement of the state game laws. The bass feeds on small fish and the peculiar moss formation growing in the lake.

"GO DEVIL" GETS 'EM

The professional fishermen at Reelfoot have a peculiar way of going about a battle with a bass. They take a short stick, 2 or 3 feet long, and attach a short cord. To the end is attached a "go devil." It is simply a black rubber with feathers on it, or some contrivance crudely made at home. This they idly swish thru the waters like a child playing and dabbling in a rain barrel. But marvelous to tell, the bass strike at this home-made contrivance sometimes when all the high-priced products of the sporting goods shop fail.

The bass brings the fishermen the highest price of all lake fish.

The channel cat is the aristocrat of the cat fish family at Reelfoot. There is, however, a skeleton in his family closet for he is a scavenger and varies his diet with live minnows and crawfish. What must be considered reprehensible conduct even in the lowest circles of fish society is the channel cat's habit of eating the eggs of other fish as he adventures about in the eddy waters. The channel cat grows to 20 pounds in weight and he brings from six to eight cents a pound to the professional fishermen.

AS TO CRAPPIES

Probably the best fish in Reelfoot, from a gastronomic standpoint, is the crappie. He is a member of the perch family in good standing. He has no bad habits. He only dines on minnows, cock roaches and worms. He grows to be about two and one-half pounds in weight and sells at the same price as commanded by the black bass.

Lucullus padded the expense account of the feast by melting pearls in vinegar and drinking it. Unfortunately, Reelfoot had not been formed at that time, nor America discovered, and the poor epicurean died without a taste of the real food of the gods.

The carp is, literally, a "poor fish," although found in abundance at Reelfoot. He is a scavenger and he eats spawn.

Although not in the class with the crappie or the bass, the brim is a little Chesterfield, so far as manners are concerned. Brim travel in schools. When you get one bite from a brim you are liable to have them biting your bate for hours. Your wrist will grow tired pulling them in. Most of them weigh about a half pound or a pound, though they grow to two pounds. They are particularly fond of cock roaches on a hook. So fond indeed that many followers of Izaak Walton have gone to the lake and caught from 100 to 200 brim in a few hours. The fishermen get from three to six cents a pound for the brim.

Although he fights like a bass and has a mouth like a bass the goggle-eyed perch, or rock bass, is not a bass. There are not so many of the goggle-eyed perch in the lake. They used to be found there more plentifully and they were sometimes two pounds in weight.

Almost gone, too, is the spoonbill catfish alias the shovel bill cat.

The shovel bill was formerly very plentiful. He was all shoulders and bill, but a good catch of this variety meant wealth to the fishermen for the eggs brought $1 per pound.

When one thinks of caviar it invariably recalls a scene of Volga boatmen, a weird Russian folk song and the hunt for the giant sturgeon. But, up until recent years, when you ordered Russian caviar in almost any restaurant from Broadway and Forty-second Street in New York to Market Street in San Francisco, or from a Chicago boulevard to Canal Street in New Orleans, you got Reelfoot Lake caviar instead of the roe of the sturgeon and you probably enjoyed the relish just as much.

The spoon bill cat grew to weigh from 125 to 150 pounds. Sometimes as much as 20 or 30 pounds of eggs were found in the female.

Natives around the lake will tell you that the spoon bill cats left Reelfoot when the State Highway Department dug the spillway at the south end of the lake. It afforded them an easy exit from the lake to the Mississippi River and there, they say, the big fish have gone. He could not go to the river from Black Bayou or the other natural drainage outlets of the lake because of the obstruction of trees and stumps in the channels, but at any event the spoon bill cat, so far as Reelfoot is concerned, is almost as extinct as the dodo.

PIKES LESS NUMEROUS

Not so numerous now at Reelfoot is the pike family, that voracious fresh water fish. The pike grows to about 10 pounds and is not so much sought after as a table delicacy.

The buffalo at Reelfoot grows to sometimes 40 pounds in weight. The buffalo is caught mostly by fishermen in trammel nets for market. In Tennessee fishermen may use that trammel net only in Reelfoot, the Cumberland, Mississippi, French Broad, Big Hatchie and Forked Deer rivers. It is questionable among fish and game authorities whether this practice should be permitted at Reelfoot, but the supply of buffalo seems practically inexhaustible.

The white carp resembles the drum and is not very good eating. He, too, is a scavenger.

The villain of the lake is the gar. Gars are found at Reelfoot by the millions, as in other lakes and bayous near the Mississippi River. He destroys the young fish with his long, sharp bill and he is absolutely worthless unless gathered in quantities to be used for fertilizer. The disgusted fisherman who catches a gar throws it on the bank to die. The Reelfoot gars range from six to ten pounds each.

As an edible fish the striped jack, or the skipjack, is also worthless. The skipjack travels in schools. They can skip over the water like a flat stone hurled by a boy. Sometimes they skip and jump on the surface of the water for 50 yards.

EELS ALSO LARGE

The Reelfoot eel weighs as much as six or seven pounds and grows to about three feet long. The eel is often caught on a trot line or in a basket net, or he will bite worms and bugs on a hook. The flesh of the eel, to say the least, is not so bad as the long, slimy creature looks. His skin is slick and he looks like a snake and has no pelvic fins. He is a great Whosis in the fish sideshow and he is certainly a slippery customer to try to hold.

The white perch and the sun perch are found at Reelfoot growing to about two pounds in weight. The bull head cat, or the pollywog, is also found. He is a darkish fish and a scavenger.

Bullfrogs are still found by the thousands at Reelfoot but they are not so plentiful as in years gone by. Some years ago at the fish dock at Samburg a professional fisherman brought in 140 dozen frog legs. One night's catch. They hunt bull frogs with a light on the front end of the boat. The frog is gigged as he sits

REELFOOT LAKE

on the lily bonnets around the shores of the lake.

Water moccasins and cotton mouth moccasins are found in the lake and in the surrounding swamps while a few rattlesnakes are in the hills around the lake and copperheads around the shores. However, as most sportsmen are provided with various distilled remedies for snake bite they do not worry about the snakes. It would be unusual if there were not some few inconveniences in such a paradise for sportsmen, and these are found in the shape of chigres, mosquitoes and black gnats. However, all the club houses and hotels are screened against mosquitoes and the little pests are not more numerous than at other points in the Mississippi Valley.

FINE DUCK HUNTING

Reelfoot is one of the finest haunts left in America for duck shooting. The duck shooting season opens Nov. 1 and from that day on the lake will be crowded with sportsmen. The teal is among the first varieties of duck to come to Reelfoot lake. The teal will be there by the thousands early in October. He leaves, however, about the 10th of November and wings his way southward in search of warmer climes. For the rest of the winter the rice marshes of Louisiana and innumerable islands that dot the Mississippi, the Arkansas and other rivers will be his home.

There are few living creatures as fast as a teal. He cannot be outdistanced by an ordinary aeroplane. The teal is a small brownish duck with wings striped in green. It is fine sport to push your boat into the grass after the teal have come down and shoot as they rise with the speed of lightning.

The black jack, with his black body and his clerical white vest, but his clerical habits belied by his fierce red eyes—can fly almost as fast as the teal.

The beautiful black mallard has gray trimmings on his body and blue wings of a superb shade. The breast is larger than the green head mallard and the bird is wiry and wild.

The graceful pin teal duck is grayish with white breast, wings and tail trimmed in black with a border of dark brown on his wings. The widgeon resembles the pin tail but he is not as large. The widgeon feeds on fish.

One of the greatest ducks at Reelfoot is the green head mallard. His head is green and his wings are trimmed in green with a white border. He has a brownish tan breast. The green head mallard is a large duck, some of them weighing three or four pounds.

AS TO CANVAS BACK

The Son of Cush who is able to dine at Reelfoot on crappies and canvas back duck at the same time is a lucky devil. The canvas back is the best duck on the lake from a gastronomic standpoint. In the summer he feeds in the celery fields of Canada and at the first sign of frost he wings his way to the inviting lakes of the Mississippi Valley. The canvas back, like the mallard, comes to the lake during the last week in October.

The wood duck is at Reelfoot all summer, secure in the knowledge apparently that both State and Federal laws have declared a closed season on him indefinitely. The wood duck is one of the most beautiful of all ducks, his feathers blending all colors of the rainbow. Because of his singular beauty he has been hunted for plumes for Milady's hat until he was almost annihilated by the pot hunters. But he has been protected. The wood duck at Reelfoot has grown almost tame and nests in trees.

Beautiful water fowls wade in the waters of the lake and softly fly through are air. The crane is there and his smaller cousin, the rail, as well as some herons and a few egrets—all protected by State and Federal game laws. The demand for egrets, the long plumes which the egret bears during the breeding season, has long since caused a closing season on this species of the heron family. At Reelfoot also are found in great numbers sea gulls, useless except as scavengers, and several species of eagles.

FEW WILD TURKEYS

There are a few wild turkeys on the islands of the lake, chiefly on Starve Island. There is a closed season at all times on the wild turkeys and the State Game Department is trying to breed them on Starve Island.

The water turkey is found at Reelfoot in profusion, but he is fit for nothing except a scavenger. The drive of a flock of water turkeys on the fish is a superb sight. They advance in military formation, beating the water with their wings as they fly up a little inlet, scaring the fish toward the shallow bank in front. Sometimes hundreds of small fish are caught in a water turkey drive and fish even as large as five pounds have been gashed by their sharp bills.

SINKING OF REELFOOT LAKE
Told by an Eye Witness in the Early Part of the Nineteenth Century

The following letter, written in 1826, to the Rev. Lorenzo Dow, graphically describing the horrible earthquake of 1811 and the consequent sinking of Reelfoot Lake, known the country over for its superiority as a fishing and hunting resort, was recently found among some old letters. As will be seen, in those days it took weeks and oftentimes months to receive a letter after being mailed.

REELFOOT LAKE

"Dear Brother: I have just received your kind letter, written some three or four weeks ago, requesting me to give you a description of the late horrible visitation of Providence, and the sinking of Reelfoot Lake in this section.

"The morning of December 15, 1811, was cloudy and a dense fog prevailed, and towards nightfall the heavens showed signs of distress. On the following morning, the 16th, about five o'clock a. m., we felt the shock of an earthquake, accompanied by a rumbling noise resembling the distant firing of a cannon, which was followed in a few minutes by the complete saturation of the atmosphere with sulphurous vapor. The moon was shining brilliantly, but the sulphurous vapor caused the earth to be wrapped in absolute darkness. The wailing inhabitants, the stampede of fowls and beasts, the noise of falling timber, the roaring of the Mississippi—the current of which was retrograde for a few minutes—formed a scene too appalling to conceive of. Then until daylight a number of lighter shocks occurred, one that was more violent and severe than the first one, and the terror which prevailed after the first shock was now even worse than before. The people fled hither and yon, supposing that there was less danger at a distance from the river, which was boiling, foaming and roaring terrifically. Men, women and children gave up in despair, some praying and others fainting, so great was their fear.

"There were light shocks each day until January 23, 1812, when one as hard as the first occurred, followed by the same phenomena. From this time until February 4 the earth was in continual agitation, visibly waving as a gentle sea. That day a shock, almost as severe as the others, occurred, and on the 8th, about sunrise, a concussion took place, so much more violent than the others that it was called "the hard shock". The earth was transformed into total darkness, the chickens went back to roost, the cows mooed and the frightened horses pitifully neighed. At first the Mississippi River seemed to recede from its banks, and its waters, gathering up like a mountain, leaving for a short period of time many boats which were passing down the river, on the bottom of the river, during which time the crews escaped to land in safety. The river rose ten to fifteen feet perpendicularly, expanding, as it were, at the same time the banks were overflowed with a retrograde current. The river falling immediately, receded within its banks again with such violence that it took with it whole groves of young cottonwood trees and much cattle and stock.

"A great many fish were left on the banks, being unable to keep up with the water, and an old canoe, antique in construction, was washed ashore. The river was a mass of floating wrecks of boats, and it is said that one was wrecked in which there was a lady and six children, all of whom were lost.

"In the hard shocks described, the earth was horribly lacerated—the surface from time to time was covered over of uneven depths by the sand which issued from the fissures, which were made in great numbers all over the country, some of which closed up immediately after they had vomited forth their sand and water. In many places, however, there was a substance resembling coal thrown up with the sand. It is impossible to say what the depth of the fissures or irregular breaks were. The site of New Madrid, Missouri, was settled down at least fifteen feet, and not more than half a mile below that town there does not appear to be any alteration of the river, but back from the river a short distance the numerous large ponds or lakes, which covered a great part of the country, were totally dried up. The beds of some of them bulge above their former banks several feet.

"The most remarkable feature of all the entire disturbances, which was not generally known for some months afterwards, was the discovery of a huge lake on the Tennessee side of the Mississippi River, upwards of 25 miles long and from one-half to eight miles in width. This lake was later called Reelfoot Lake. There are places in it the bottom of which has never been found, though many efforts have been made to ascertain the depth of these places.

"The lake has communication with the Mississippi River at both ends, and it is conjectured that it will not be many years before the principal part, if not the whole, of the Mississippi will pass that way. In the last year or so an herb, resembling moss, has literally covered the surface of the lake, and during the winter months wild fowls, such as ducks, geese, cranes, etc., winter on the lake and eat this moss as food. Deer and other animals seem to enjoy it.

"It is said that where the lake was formed was a vast area of fine timbered lands, and in places only the tops of trees can be seen. The lake runs north and south, and each end has a neck shape, widening out about the center, or nearer the northern terminus than the center. The water in it does not seem to rise or lower to any marked degree, and the lake is distined to become the great hunting and fishing resort of the west.

"It is said that where this lake was formed was formerly the Indians' hunting grounds, and also where they held their annual war dances; but since the terrible visitation of the earthquake it is a rare thing that one ventures in that vicinity. By some method, known only to themselves, they marked a warning on the trees for other Indians to keep away. Most of those who fled from the vicinity during the hard shocks returned, but always greatly alarmed at the slightest trembling of the earth. We have, since their commencement in 1811, and occasionally felt light shocks. Hardly a week passes but we feel one. There were two the past winter, much more severe than we have felt them for several years before. Since then, however, they are lighter than ever, and as the months and years pass the inhabitants are becoming more and more reconciled to the surroundings.

"One circumstance worthy of mention is: This section was once subject to severe thunder, but for a long time previous to the first shocks there was no thunder at all and but very little since.

"Respectfully yours,

"New Madrid, Mo." "E. BRYAN

OLD COURTHOUSE AT TROY—1852-90

"Let not Ambition mock their useful toil,
　　Their homely joys and destinies obscure,
Nor Grandeur hear with a disdainful smile
　　The short and simple annals of the poor."

www.ingramcontent.com/pod-product-compliance
Lightning Source LLC
Chambersburg PA
CBHW020644300426
44112CB00007B/233